Other books published by Lone Eagle Productions, Inc.

SCHEDULE IT RIGHT! *How long will it take to shoot your film?*
By Ralph S. Singleton and Joan E. Vietor

BUDGET IT RIGHT! *How much will it cost?*
By Ralph S. Singleton and Joan E. Vietor

DIRECTORS

A COMPLETE GUIDE

Compiled and Edited by Michael Singer
in association with Flying Armadillo

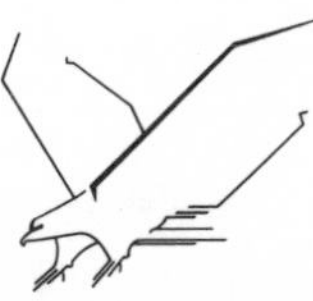

LONE EAGLE PRODUCTIONS, INC.

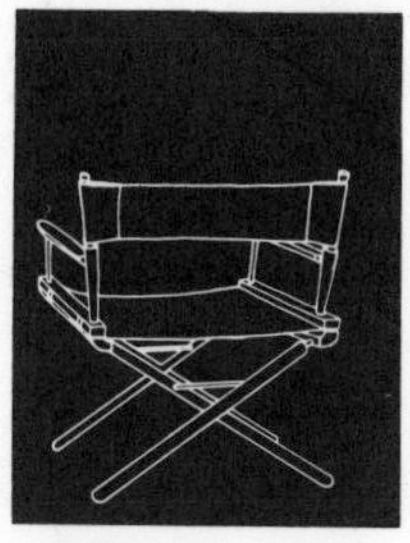

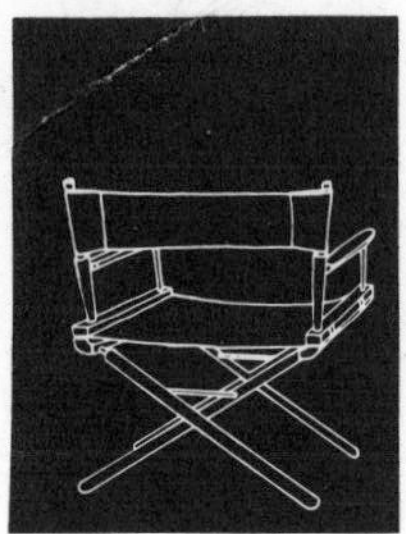

Published by Lone Eagle Productions, Inc.
9903 Santa Monica Boulevard — Suite 204
Beverly Hills, California 90212

Designed and produced by Graphiques Unlimited, Inc.
North Hollywood, California

Cover designed by Liz Vietor

Manufactured in the United States of America

ISSN: 0732-4359

ISBN: 0-943728-00-2

NOTE: We have made every reasonable effort to ensure that the information contained herein is as accurate as possible. However, errors and omissions are sure to occur. We would appreciate your notifying us of any which you find.

ACKNOWLEDGEMENTS

Many thanks for the fine services of the Margaret Herrick Library of the Academy of Motion Pictures Arts and Sciences, as well as the Theatre Arts department of the UCLA Research Library, both in Los Angeles.

We are also indebted to other worthy reference books: James Robert Parish and Michael R. Pitts' Film Directors: A Guide to Their American Films (The Scarecrow Press, 1974), Parish's Film Directors Guide: Western Europe (The Scarecrow Press, 1976), D. Richard Baer's The Film Buff's Checklist of Motion Pictures (1912-1979) (Hollywood Film Archive, 1979), Ephraim Katz's The Film Encyclopedia (Thomas Y. Crowell Publishers, 1979), Alvin H. Marill's Movies Made For Television (Arlington House Publishers, 1980) and last, but certainly not least, the Directors Guild of America, Inc. Directory of Members, 1981 edition.

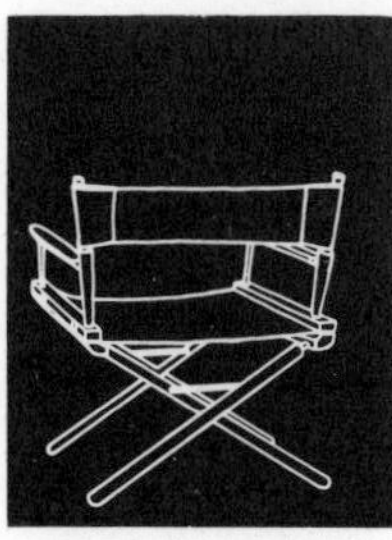

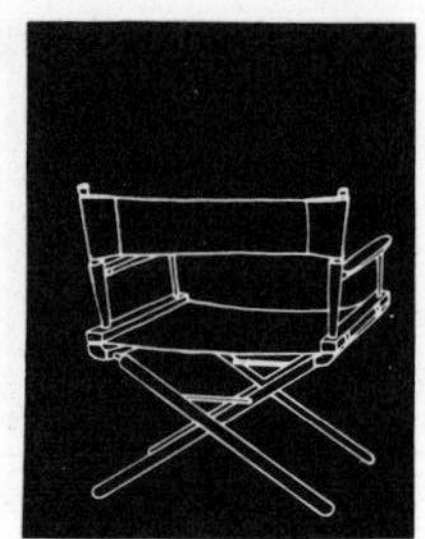

TO

JOAN-CARROL

and

LOUIS & LILLY SINGER

TABLE OF CONTENTS

INTRODUCTION

The intention of this book is simple — to provide an easy, practical and comprehensive guide to active film directors and their work. This is a reference guide for motion picture industry personnel, film students, actors, or anyone interested in examining directors' careers by scanning the titles of their movies. There are more than enough excellent books which analyze filmmakers and their creations in detail, but there's been a need for an impartial, alphabetical listing which a producer can pluck off the shelf when trying to find out who's done what. Hopefully, Directors: A Complete Guide fulfills that need.

A few words about the listings herein:

DIRECTORS — Over one thousand film directors, American and foreign, are listed in this book. The choices were selective by necessity. If every living director who's ever helmed a feature film were included here, this guide would rival the Encyclopedia Britannica in bulk. The foreign directors listed are those whose films have made some impact in this country, although many of their names may be familiar only to those in the "art film" enclaves of major cities or university towns. As a practical guide, the idea was to include only those filmmakers who are still working — although some directors disappear for years, only to return again and direct a major feature or television movie after a long hiatus. A few recognizably retired moviemakers — Frank Capra, for example — are retained out of sheer respect for their place in film history. Birthdates, birthplaces and contacts have been provided whenever possible. It's well known that artists sometimes change their agents almost as frequently as their socks, so it should be kept in mind that several of the agency listings may already be obsolete.

FILMS — Needless to say, we have attempted to make these listings as complete as possible. Some movies, however, become lost or forgotten — network movies never aired, feature films locked away in vaults. All of which is by way of apology for any glaring omissions. The criteria for listed films are simple:
Features: a running time of sixty minutes or longer (exceptions have been made in unusual cases, such as Andy Warhol's films, which have run anywhere from sixty seconds to twenty-four hours).
Telefeatures: motion pictures made for television with an air time of ninety minutes to four-and-a-half hours.

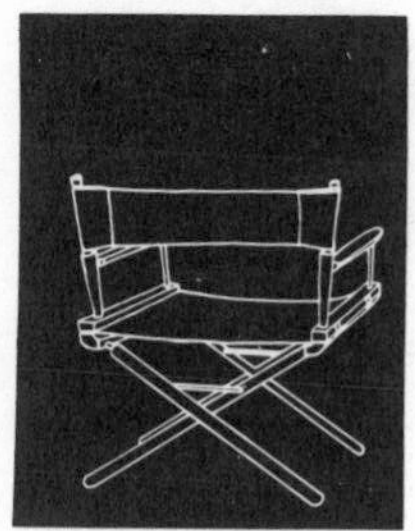

Television Mini-series: motion pictures made for television with an air time of five hours or longer.

Videotaped television dramas of the familiar BBC variety, with very few exceptions, are not included. Alternate titles by which the films may have been known are added in parentheses. And we've also included certain features in production as of press time.

DISTRIBUTORS & PRODUCTION COMPANIES: In most cases, the original American distributors of feature films are listed, although movies often change their distributors throughout the years. Occasionally, an original foreign distributor will be included for a film never released in the United States (if such information were available). For television features and mini-series, the production companies are mentioned rather than the network on which they aired. Production companies are also listed for features which haven't yet found distributors.

YEAR OF RELEASE — A very tricky problem. Usually, a foreign film will be released in the United States a year or two after an initial appearance in its home country. Therefore, the original year of release has been provided as often as possible, rather than the American date. This provides a more realistic overview of the director's progress. Still, there is often difference of opinion as to when certain films, domestic and foreign, first saw the light of a theatre projector. The dates herein may be at variance with other sources.

COUNTRY OF ORIGIN — Another dilemma. How does one explain that a film made in England with an American director, French producer and international cast is actually registered in Panama for tax purposes — and therefore a Panamanian movie? Suffice to say that in these times of complicated film finance, it's often impossible to know whether a film is American, French, West German or Libyan. We've been as accurate as possible.

A NOTE — As we are entirely responsible for the research, compilation and editing of this book, we therefore welcome all corrections, additions, criticism, praise and damnation, so that future volumes may be more complete and informative. Please use the insert cards, which we've included for that very purpose.

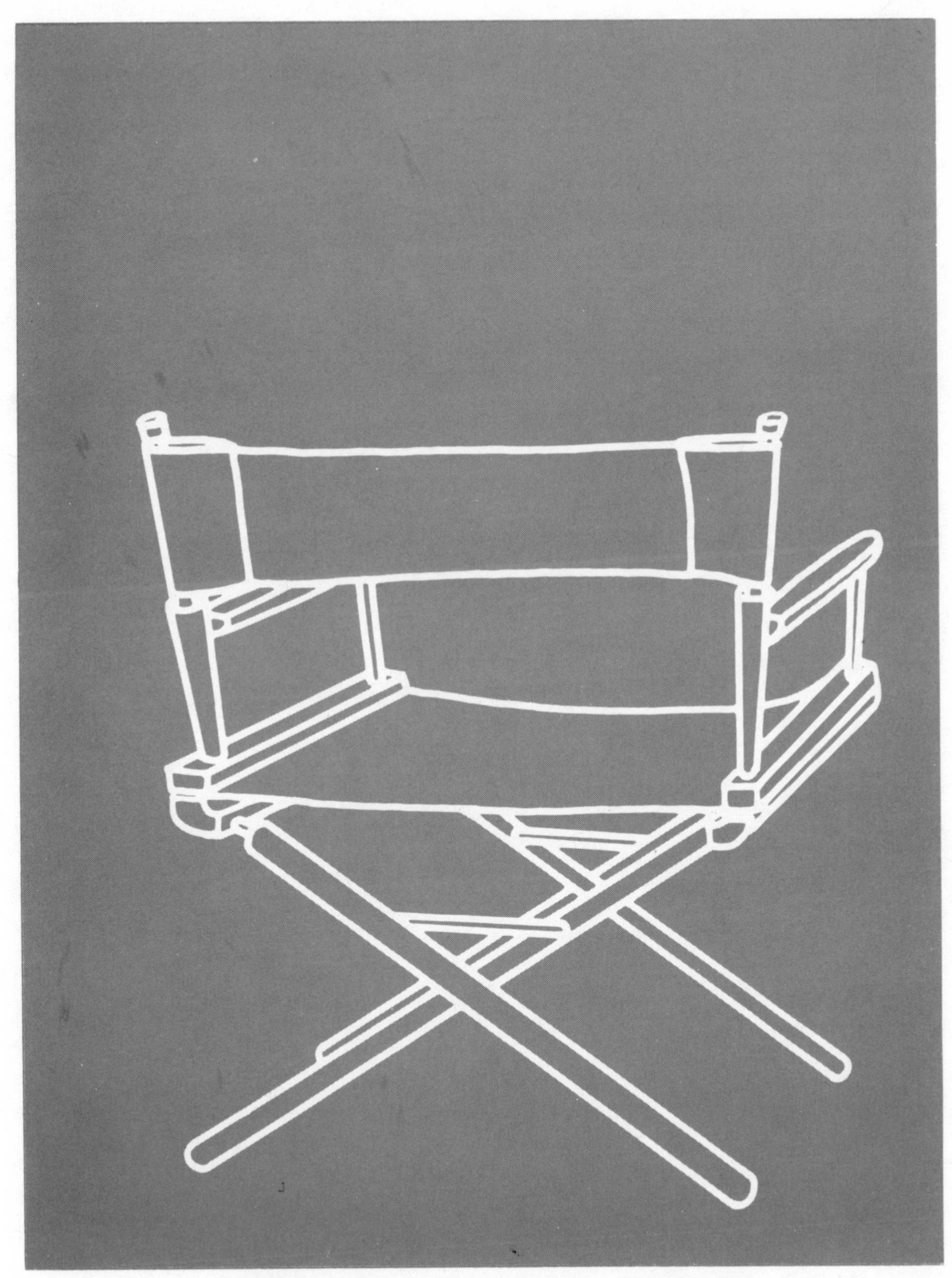

Alphabetical Listing

Aaron, Paul
Business:
Elsboy, Inc.
1604 Courtney Avenue
Los Angeles, CA 90046
(213) 874-6003

A DIFFERENT STORY
Avco Embassy; 1978
A FORCE OF ONE
American Cinema; 1979
THE MIRACLE WORKER
Katz-Gallin Productions/Half-Pint Productions; telefeature; 1979
THIN ICE
CBS Entertainment; telefeature; 1981

Abel, Robert J.
Business:
Robert Abel & Associates
953 Highland Avenue
Hollywood, CA 90038
(213) 462-8100
Attorney:
Norman Garey
(213) 858-7700

ELVIS ON TOUR
co-director with Pierre Adidge; M-G-M; 1972
LET THE GOOD TIMES ROLL
co-director with Sid Levin; Columbia; 1973

Abrahams, Jim
Business:
19746 Pacific Coast Highway
Malibu, CA 90265
(213) 456-8942

AIRPLANE!
co-director with David & Jerry Zucker; Paramount; 1980

Abroms, Edward A.
Business:
EMA Enterprises, Inc.
1866 Marlowe Street
Thousand Oaks, CA 91360
(805) 495-0701
Agent:
Philip Rogers & Associates
(213) 278-2015, 343-5682

THE IMPOSTER
Warner Brothers TV; telefeature; 1975

Adamson, Al
Business:
Independent-International
165 West 46th Street
New York, N.Y. 10036
(212) 869-9333

TWO TICKETS TO TERROR
Victor Adamson; 1964
BLOOD OF DRACULA'S CASTLE
Crow International; 1969
SATAN'S SADISTS
Independent-International; 1970
HELL'S BLOODY DEVILS
Independent-International; 1970
FIVE BLOODY GRAVES
Independent-International; 1971
HORROR OF THE BLOOD MONSTERS
Independent-International; 1971
THE FEMALE BUNCH
Dalia; 1971
LAST OF THE COMANCHEROS
Independent-International; 1971
BLOOD OF GHASTLY HORROR
Independent-International; 1972
THE BRAIN OF BLOOD
Hemisphere; 1972
DRACULA VS. FRANKENSTEIN
Independent-International; 1973
THE DYNAMITE BROTHERS
Cinemation; 1974
GIRLS FOR RENT
Independent-International; 1974
THE NAUGHTY STEWARDESSES
Independent-International; 1975
STUD BROWN
Cinemation; 1975
BLAZING STEWARDESSES
Independent-International; 1975

continued

Adamson, Al
continued

JESSIE'S GIRLS
Manson International; 1976
BLACK HEAT
Independent-International; 1976
CINDERELLA 2000
Independent-International; 1977
BLACK SAMURAI
B.L.L.J. International; 1977
SUNSET COVE
Cal-Am Artists; 1978
DEATH DIMENSION
Movietime; 1978
NURSE SHERRI
Independent-International; 1978

Adidge, Pierre

JOE COCKER/MAD DOGS & ENGLISHMEN
M-G-M; 1971
ELVIS ON TOUR
co-director with Robert J. Abel; M-G-M; 1972

Adler, Lou
Contact:
Directors Guild of America
Los Angeles
(213) 656-1220

UP IN SMOKE
Paramount; 1978
ALL WASHED UP
Paramount; 1981

Akkad, Moustapha

MOHAMMAD, MESSENGER OF GOD
Tarik Films; 1977; Lebanese
LION OF THE DESERT
United Film Distribution; 1981; Libyan

Alda, Alan
b. January 28, 1936
New York City
Agent:
William Morris Agency
Beverly Hills
(213) 274-7451

THE FOUR SEASONS
Universal; 1981

Aldrich, Adell
Business:
The Aldrich Company
606 N. Larchmont Blvd.
Los Angeles, CA 90004
(213) 462-6511
Agent:
Talent Management Int.
(213) 273-4000

DADDY, I DON'T LIKE IT LIKE THIS
CBS Entertainment; telefeature; 1978
THE KID FROM LEFT FIELD
Gary Coleman Productions/Deena Silver-Kramer's Movie Company; telefeature; 1979

Aldrich, Robert
b. August 9, 1918
Cranston, Rhode Island
Business:
The Aldrich Company
606 N. Larchmont Blvd.
Los Angeles, CA 90004
(213) 462-6511
Agent:
William Morris Agency
Beverly Hills
(213) 274-7451

THE BIG LEAGUER
M-G-M; 1953
WORLD FOR RANSOM
Allied Artists; 1954
APACHE
United Artists; 1954
KISS ME DEADLY
United Artists; 1955
THE BIG KNIFE
United Artists; 1955
AUTUMN LEAVES
Columbia; 1956
ATTACK!
United Artists; 1956
TEN SECONDS TO HELL
United Artists; 1959; British

continued

Aldrich, Robert
continued

THE ANGRY HILLS
M-G-M; 1959; British
THE LAST SUNSET
Universal; 1961
WHAT EVER HAPPENED TO BABY JANE?
Warner Brothers; 1962
SODOM AND GOMORRAH
20th Century-Fox; 1963; Italian-French-U.S.
4 FOR TEXAS
Warner Brothers; 1963
HUSH...HUSH, SWEET CHARLOTTE
Warner Brothers; 1964
THE FLIGHT OF THE PHOENIX
20th Century-Fox; 1965
THE DIRTY DOZEN
M-G-M; 1967
THE LEGEND OF LYLAH CLARE
M-G-M; 1968
TOO LATE THE HERO
Cinerama Releasing Corporation; 1970
THE GRISSOM GANG
Cinerama Releasing Corporation; 1971
ULZANA'S RAID
Universal; 1972
EMPEROR OF THE NORTH (Emperor of the North Pole)
20th Century-Fox; 1973
THE LONGEST YARD
Paramount; 1974
HUSTLE
Paramount; 1975
TWILIGHT'S LAST GLEAMING
Allied Artists; 1977; U.S.-West German
THE CHOIRBOYS
Universal; 1977
THE FRISCO KID
Warner Brothers; 1979
...ALL THE MARBLES
M-G-M/United Artists; 1981

Allen, Corey
b. 1934
Cleveland, Ohio
Agent:
Contemporary-Korman Artists
Beverly Hills
(213) 278-8250

PINOCCHIO
EUE: 1971
SEE THE MAN RUN
Universal TV; telefeature; 1971
CRY RAPE!
Leonard Freeman Productions; telefeature; 1973
YESTERDAY'S CHILD
co-director with Bob Rosenbaum; Paramount TV; telefeature; 1977
THUNDER AND LIGHTNING
20th Century-Fox; 1978
AVALANCHE
New World; 1979
STONE
Stephen J. Cannell Productions/Universal TV; telefeature; 1979)
THE MAN IN THE SANTA CLAUS SUIT
Dick Clark Productions; telefeature; 1979
THE RETURN OF FRANK CANNON
QM Productions; telefeature; 1980

Allen, Irwin
b. June 12, 1916
New York City
Business:
Warner Brothers
4000 Warner Blvd.
Burbank, CA 91522
(213) 954-6000
Agent:
I.C.M.
Hollywood
(213) 550-4000

THE SEA AROUND US
RKO Radio; 1951
THE ANIMAL WORLD
Warner Brothers; 1956
THE STORY OF MANKIND
Warner Brothers; 1957
THE LOST WORLD
20th Century-Fox; 1960
VOYAGE TO THE BOTTOM OF THE SEA
20th Century-Fox; 1961
FIVE WEEKS IN A BALLOON
20th Century-Fox; 1962

continued

Allen, Irwin
continued

CITY BENEATH THE SEA
20th Century-Fox TV/Motion Pictures International; telefeature; 1971
THE TOWERING INFERNO
director of action sequences only; 20th Century-Fox; 1974
THE SWARM
Warner Brothers; 1978
BEYOND THE POSEIDON ADVENTURE
Warner Brothers; 1979

Allen, Woody
(Allen Stewart Konigsberg)
b. December 1, 1935
Brooklyn, New York
Personal Manager:
Jack Rollins-Charles Joffe
130 West 57th Street
New York, N.Y.
(212) 582-1940

WHAT'S UP, TIGER LILY?
American International; 1966
TAKE THE MONEY AND RUN
Cinerama Releasing Corporation; 1969
BANANAS
United Artists; 1971
EVERYTHING YOU ALWAYS WANTED TO KNOW ABOUT SEX* (*BUT WERE AFRAID TO ASK)
United Artists; 1972
SLEEPER
United Artists; 1973
LOVE AND DEATH
United Artists; 1975
ANNIE HALL
United Artists; 1977
INTERIORS
United Artists; 1978
MANHATTAN
United Artists; 1979
STARDUST MEMORIES
United Artists; 1980
WOODY ALLEN'S 1981 UNTITLED #1
Orion Pictures/Warner Brothers; 1981
WOODY ALLEN'S 1981 UNTITLED #2
Orion Pictures/Warner Brothers; 1982

Almond, Paul
b. April 26, 1931
Montreal, Quebec, Canada
Business:
Quest Film Productions, Ltd.
1272 Redpath Crescent
Montreal, Quebec, Canada
H3G 2K1
(514) 845-1921
Agent:
Agency for the Performing Arts
Hollywood
(213) 273-0744

ISABEL
Paramount; 1968; Canadian
ACT OF THE HEART
Universal; 1970; Canadian
JOURNEY
EPOH; 1977; Canadian
FINAL ASSIGNMENT
1980; Canadian

Alonzo, John A.
Agent:
I.C.M.
Hollywood
(213) 550-4000

FM
Universal; 1978
CHAMPIONS...A LOVE STORY
Warner Brothers TV; telefeature; 1979
PORTRAIT OF A STRIPPER
Moonlight Productions/Filmways; telefeature; 1979
BELLE STARR
Entheos Unlimited Productions/Hanna-Barbera Productions; telefeature; 1980
BLINDED BY THE LIGHT
Time-Life Films; telefeature; 1980

Alston, Emmett

NEW YEAR'S EVIL
Cannon; 1981

Altman, Robert
b. February 20, 1925
Kansas City, Missouri
Business:
Lion's Gate Films
1861 S. Bundy Drive
Los Angeles, CA 90025
(213) 820-7751

THE DELINQUENTS
United Artists; 1957
THE JAMES DEAN STORY
co-director with George W. George; Warner Brothers; 1957
NIGHTMARE IN CHICAGO
MCA-TV; telefeature; 1964
COUNTDOWN
Warner Brothers; 1968
THAT COLD DAY IN THE PARK
Commonwealth United; 1969; Canadian-U.S.
M*A*S*H
20th Century-Fox; 1970
BREWSTER McCLOUD
M-G-M; 1970
McCABE & MRS. MILLER
Warner Brothers; 1971
IMAGES
Columbia; 1972; Irish
THE LONG GOODBYE
United Artists; 1973
THIEVES LIKE US
United Artists; 1974
CALIFORNIA SPLIT
Columbia; 1974
NASHVILLE
Paramount; 1976
BUFFALO BILL AND THE INDIANS or SITTING BULL'S HISTORY LESSON
United Artists; 1976
3 WOMEN
20th Century-Fox; 1977
A WEDDING
20th Century-Fox; 1978
A PERFECT COUPLE
20th Century-Fox; 1979
QUINTET
20th Century-Fox; 1979
HEALTH
20th Century-Fox; 1980
POPEYE
Paramount; 1980

Amateau, Rod
b. December 20, 1923
New York, N.Y.
Business:
Cottage Films, Inc.
9744 Wilshire Blvd.
Beverly Hills, CA 90212
(213) 275-9480

THE BUSHWHACKERS
Realart; 1951
MONSOON
United Artists; 1952
PUSSYCAT, PUSSYCAT, I LOVE YOU
United Artists; 1970; British
THE STATUE
Cinerama Releasing Corporation; 1971; British
WHERE DOES IT HURT?
American International; 1972; British
DRIVE IN
Columbia; 1976
THE SENIORS
Cinema Shares International; 1978
HITLER'S SON
1978; British

Anderson, Lindsay
b. April 17, 1923
Bangalore, India
Contact:
British Film Institute
127 Charing Cross Road
London W.C. 2, England
01-437-4355

THIS SPORTING LIFE
Continental; 1962; British
IF...
Paramount; 1969; British
O LUCKY MAN!
Warner Brothers; 1973; British
IN CELEBRATION
American Film Theatre; 1975; British-Canadian
BRITTANIA HOSPITAL
Universal/AFD; 1982; British

Anderson, Michael

b. January 30, 1920
London, England
Agent:
Chasin-Park-Citron
Hollywood
(213) 273-7190

PRIVATE ANGELO
co-director with Peter Ustinov; Associated British Picture Corporation; 1949; British
WATERFRONT WOMEN (Waterfront)
Rank; 1950; British
HELL IS SOLD OUT
Eros; 1951; British
NIGHT WAS OUR FRIEND
Monarch; 1951; British
WILL ANY GENTLEMAN?
Associated British Picture Corporation; 1953; British
THE HOUSE OF THE ARROW
Associated British Picture Corporation; 1953; British
THE DAM BUSTERS
Warner Brothers; 1955; British
1984
Columbia; 1956; British
AROUND THE WORLD IN 80 DAYS
United Artists; 1956
BATTLE HELL (Yangtse Incident)
DCA; 1957; British
CHASE A CROOKED SHADOW
Warner Brothers; 1958; British
SHAKE HANDS WITH THE DEVIL
United Artists; 1959; British
THE WRECK OF THE MARY DEARE
M-G-M; 1959
ALL THE FINE YOUNG CANNIBALS
M-G-M; 1960
THE NAKED EDGE
United Artists; 1961
FLIGHT FROM ASHIYA
United Artists; 1964
WILD AND WONDERFUL
Universal; 1964
OPERATION CROSSBOW
M-G-M; 1965; British-Italian
THE QUILLER MEMORANDUM
Paramount; 1966; British
THE SHOES OF THE FISHERMAN
M-G-M; 1968
POPE JOAN
Columbia; 1972; British
DOC SAVAGE, THE MAN OF BRONZE
Warner Brothers; 1975
CONDUCT UNBECOMING
Allied Artists; 1975; British
LOGAN'S RUN
M-G-M/United Artists; 1975
ORCA
Paramount; 1976
DOMINIQUE
1979
THE MARTIAN CHRONICLES
Charles Fries Productions/Stonehenge Productions; telefeature; 1980
BELLS
Robert Cooper Productions; 1981; Canadian

Annakin, Ken

b. August 10, 1914
Beverley, England
Agent:
FCA Agency
Hollywood
(213) 277-8422

HOLIDAY CAMP
Universal; 1947; British
MIRANDA
Eagle-Lion; 1948; British
BROKEN JOURNEY
Eagle-Lion; 1948; British
HERE COME THE HUGGETTS
General Film Distributors; 1948; British
QUARTET
co-director with Ralph Smart, Harold French & Arthur Crabtree; Eagle-Lion; 1948; British
VOTE FOR HUGGETT
General Film Distributors; 1949; British

continued

Annakin, Ken
continued

THE HUGGETTS ABROAD
General Film Distributors; 1949; British
LANDFALL
Associated British Picture Corporation; 1949; British
TRIO
co-director with Harold French; Paramount; 1950; British
HOTEL SAHARA
United Artists; 1951; British
THE STORY OF ROBIN HOOD
co-director with Alex Bryce; RKO Radio; 1952; U.S.-British
OUTPOST IN MALAYA (The Planter's Wife)
United Artists; 1952; British
THE SWORD AND THE ROSE
RKO Radio; 1953; U.S.-British
DOUBLE CONFESSION
Stratford; 1953; British
YOU KNOW WHAT SAILORS ARE
United Artists; 1954; British
LAND OF FURY (The Seekers)
Universal; 1955; British
LOSER TAKES ALL
British Lion; 1956; British
VALUE FOR MONEY
Rank; 1957; British
THREE MEN IN A BOAT
DCA; 1958; British
ACROSS THE BRIDGE
Rank; 1958; British
THIRD MAN ON THE MOUNTAIN
Buena Vista; 1959; U.S.-British
ELEPHANT GUN (Nor the Moon By Night)
Lopert; 1959; British
SWISS FAMILY ROBINSON
Buena Vista; 1960
THE HELLIONS
Columbia; 1962; British
A COMING-OUT PARTY (Very Important Person)
Union; 1962; British
THE FAST LADY
Rank; 1962; British
CROOKS ANONYMOUS
Allied Artists; 1962; British
THE LONGEST DAY
co-director with Andrew Marton & Bernhard Wicki;20th Century-Fox; 1962
THOSE MAGNIFICENT MEN IN THEIR FLYING MACHINES
20th Century-Fox; 1965; British
BATTLE OF THE BULGE
Warner Brothers; 1965
UNDERWORLD INFORMERS (The Informers)
Continental; 1966; British
THE LONG DUEL
Paramount; 1967; British
THE BIGGEST BUNDLE OF THEM ALL
M-G-M; 1968; U.S.-Italian)
THOSE DARING YOUNG MEN IN THEIR JAUNTY JALOPIES
Paramount; 1969; British-Italian-French
CALL OF THE WILD
Constantin; 1975; West German-Spanish
PAPER TIGER
Joseph E. Levine Presents; 1976; British
MURDER AT THE MARDI GRAS
The Jozak Company/Paramount TV; telefeature; 1978
HAROLD ROBBINS' THE PIRATE
Howard W. Koch Productions/Warner Brothers TV; telefeature; 1978
THE 5TH MUSKETEER
Columbia; 1979; Austrian
INSTITUTE FOR REVENGE
Gold-Driskill Productions/Columbia TV; telefeature; 1979
CHEAPER TO KEEP HER
American Cinema; 1980
THE PIRATE MOVIE
20th Century-Fox; 1982; Australian

Annaud, Jean-Jacques
Contact:
French Film Office
745 Fifth Avenue
New York, N.Y. 10151
(212) 832-8860

BLACK AND WHITE IN COLOR
Allied Artists; 1978; French-Ivory Coast-Swiss
COUP DE TETE (Hothead)
1980; French
QUEST FOR FIRE
20th Century-Fox; 1981; Canadian

Anthony, Joseph
b. May 24, 1912
Milwaukee, Wisconsin

THE RAINMAKER
Paramount; 1956
THE MATCHMAKER
Paramount; 1958
CAREER
Paramount; 1959
ALL IN A NIGHT'S WORK
Paramount; 1961
CONQUERED CITY
American International; 1966; Italian
TOMORROW
Filmgroup; 1972

Antonio, Lou
Agent:
Creative Artists Agency
Los Angeles
(213) 277-4545

SOMEONE I TOUCHED
Charles Fries Productions; telefeature; 1975
LANIGAN'S RABBI
Universal TV; telefeature; 1976
THE GIRL IN THE EMPTY GRAVE
NBC-TV; telefeature; 1977
SOMETHING FOR JOEY
MTM Productions; telefeature; 1977
THE CRITICAL LIST
MTM Productions; telefeature; 1978
A REAL AMERICAN HERO
Bing Crosby Productions; telefeature; 1978
BREAKING UP IS HARD TO DO
Green-Epstein Productions/Columbia TV; telefeature; 1979
SILENT VICTORY: THE KITTY O'NEILL STORY
Channing-Debin-Locke Company; telefeature; 1979
THE CONTENDER
co-director with Harry Falk; Universal TV; telefeature; 1980
WE'RE FIGHTING BACK
Highgate Pictures; telefeature; 1981
THE STAR MAKER
Channing-Debin-Locke Productions/Carson Productions; telefeature; 1981

Antonioni, Michelangelo
b. September 29, 1912
Ferrara, Italy
Contact:
Minister of Tourism
Via Della Ferratella
No. 51
00184 Rome, Italy
06-7732

STORY OF A LOVE AFFAIR
New Yorker; 1950; Italian
I VINTI
Film Costellazione; 1953; Italian
LA SIGNORA SENZA CAMELIE
1953; Italian
LE AMICHE
Trion Falcine/Titanus; 1955; Italian
IL GRIDO
Astor; 1957; Italian
L'AVVENTURA
Janus; 1961; Italian
LA NOTTE
Lopert; 1961; Italian-French
L'ECLISSE
Times; 1962; Italian-French
RED DESERT
Rizzoli; 1965; Italian-French
I TRE VOLTI
co-director; 1965; Italian

continued

Antonioni, Michelangelo
continued

BLOW-UP
Premier; 1966; British-Italian
ZABRISKIE POINT
M-G-M; 1970
CHUNG KUO
1972; Italian
THE PASSENGER
M-G-M/United Artists; 1975; Italian-French-Spanish-U.S.
THE MYSTERY OF OBERWALD
1981; Italian
IDENTIFICATION OF A WOMAN
Iter Film; 1981; Italian

Apted, Michael
b. England
Business:
Universal Studios
100 Universal City Plaza
Bungalow 81
Universal City, CA 91608
(213) 508-1803

THE TRIPLE ECHO
Altura; 1973; British
STARDUST
Columbia; 1975; British
STRONGER THAN THE SUN
BBC-TV; telefeature; 1977; British
THE SQUEEZE
Warner Brothers; 1977; British
AGATHA
Warner Brothers; 1979; British
COAL MINER'S DAUGHTER
Universal; 1980
CONTINENTAL DIVIDE
Universal; 1981

Argento, Dario
b. 1943
Italy
Contact:
Minister of Tourism
Via Della Ferratella
No. 51
00184 Rome, Italy
06-7732

THE BIRD WITH THE CRYSTAL PLUMAGE
UMC; 1970; Italian-West German
CAT O'NINE TAILS
National General; 1971; Italian-West German-French
FOUR FLIES ON GREY VELVET
Paramount; 1972; Italian-French
LE CINQUE GIORNATE
1973; Italian
DEEP RED
Howard Mahler Films; 1976; Italian
SUSPIRIA
International Classics; 1977; Italian
INFERNO
20th Century-Fox; 1981; Italian

Arkin, Alan
b. March 26, 1934
New York, N.Y.
Business Manager:
Saul B. Schneider
New York
(212) 489-0990
Agent:
Robinson & Associates
Beverly Hills
(213) 275-6114

LITTLE MURDERS
20th Century-Fox; 1970
FIRE SALE
20th Century-Fox; 1977

Arkush, Allan
Home:
14134 Chandler Blvd.
Van Nuys, CA 91401
(213) 763-7291
Agent:
William Morris Agency
Beverly Hills
(213) 274-7451

HOLLYWOOD BOULEVARD
co-director with Joe Dante; New World; 1976
DEATHSPORT
co-director with Henry Suso; New World; 1978
ROCK 'N' ROLL HIGH SCHOOL
New World; 1979
HEARTBEEPS
Universal; 1981

Armitage, George
Contact:
Directors Guild of America
Los Angeles
(213) 656-1220

PRIVATE DUTY NURSES
New World; 1972
HIT MAN
M-G-M; 1973
VIGILANTE FORCE
United Artists; 1976
HOT ROD
ABC Circle Films; telefeature; 1979

Armstrong, Gillian
Contact:
Australian Film Commission
9229 W. Sunset Blvd.
Los Angeles, CA 90069
(213) 275-7074

MY BRILLIANT CAREER
Analysis; 1980; Australian
STARSTRUCK
Elfick/Brennan; 1981; Australian

Arnold, Jack
b. October 14, 1916
New Haven, Connecticut
Home:
4860 Nomad Drive
Woodland Hills, CA 91364
(213) 346-1413
Agent:
Diamond Artists, Ltd.
Hollywood
(213) 278-8146

GIRLS IN THE NIGHT
Universal; 1953
IT CAME FROM OUTER SPACE
Universal; 1953
THE GLASS WEB
Universal; 1953
THE CREATURE FROM THE BLACK LAGOON
Universal; 1954
REVENGE OF THE CREATURE
Universal; 1955
THE MAN FROM BITTER RIDGE
Universal; 1955
TARANTULA
Universal; 1955
OUTSIDE THE LAW
Universal; 1956
RED SUNDOWN
Universal; 1956
THE INCREDIBLE SHRINKING MAN
Universal; 1957
THE TATTERED DRESS
Universal; 1957
MAN IN THE SHADOW
Universal; 1958
THE LADY TAKES A FLYER
Universal; 1958
THE SPACE CHILDREN
Paramount; 1958
MONSTER ON THE CAMPUS
Universal; 1958
THE MOUSE THAT ROARED
Columbia; 1959; British
NO NAME ON THE BULLET
Universal; 1959
BACHELOR IN PARADISE
M-G-M; 1961
THE LIVELY SET
Universal; 1964
A GLOBAL AFFAIR
M-G-M; 1964
HELLO DOWN THERE
Paramount; 1969
BLACK EYE
Warner Brothers; 1974
THE GAMES GIRLS PLAY
General Films; 1975
BOSS NIGGER
Dimension; 1975
THE SWISS CONSPIRACY
S.J. International; 1977
SEX AND THE MARRIED WOMAN
Universal TV; telefeature; 1977
MARILYN: THE UNTOLD STORY
co-director with John Flynn & Lawrence Schiller; Lawrence Schiller Productions; telefeature; 1980

Arthur, Karen
Agent:
Agency for the Performing Arts
Los Angeles
(213) 273-0744

LEGACY
Kino International; 1976
THE MAFU CAGE
Clouds Productions; 1979
CHARLESTON
Robert Stigwood Productions/RSO, Inc.; telefeature; 1979

Ashby, Hal
b. 1936
Ogden, Utah
Business:
North Star Productions
Los Angeles
(213) 204-6030

THE LANDLORD
United Artists; 1970
HAROLD AND MAUDE
Paramount; 1971
THE LAST DETAIL
Columbia; 1973
SHAMPOO
Columbia; 1975
BOUND FOR GLORY
United Artists; 1976
COMING HOME
United Artists; 1978
BEING THERE
United Artists/Lorimar; 1979
SECOND HAND HEARTS
Paramount/Lorimar; 1981; filmed in 1979
LOOKIN' TO GET OUT
Paramount/Lorimar; 1981

Asher, William
b. 1919
Contact:
Directors Guild of America
Los Angeles
(213) 656-1220

LEATHER GLOVES
co-director with Richard Quine; Columbia; 1948
THE SHADOW ON THE WINDOW
Columbia; 1956
THE 27TH DAY
Columbia; 1956
BEACH PARTY
American International; 1963
JOHNNY COOL
United Artists; 1963
MUSCLE BEACH PARTY
American International; 1963
BIKINI BEACH
American International; 1964
BEACH BLANKET BINGO
American International; 1965
HOW TO STUFF A WILD BIKINI
American International; 1965
FIREBALL 500
American International; 1966
BUTCHER, BAKER, NIGHTMARE MAKER
Royal American; 1981

Astin, John
b. March 30, 1930
Baltimore, Maryland
Home:
Box 385
Beverly Hills, CA 90213
Agency:
Creative Artists Agency
Los Angeles
(213) 277-4545

OPERATION PETTICOAT
Universal TV; telefeature; 1977
ROSSETTI AND RYAN: MEN WHO LOVE WOMEN
Universal TV; telefeature; 1977

Attenborough, Richard
b. August 29, 1923
Cambridge, England
Business:
Beaver Lodge
Richmond Green
Surrey, England
01-940-7234

OH! WHAT A LOVELY WAR
Paramount; 1969; British
YOUNG WINSTON
Columbia; 1972; British
A BRIDGE TOO FAR
United Artists; 1977; British
MAGIC
20th Century-Fox; 1978
GANDHI
Columbia; 1982; British-Indian

Avakian, Aram
Agent:
William Morris Agency
Beverly Hills
(213) 274-7451

LAD: A DOG
co-director with Leslie H. Martinson; Warner Brothers; 1961
END OF THE ROAD
Allied Artists; 1970
COPS AND ROBBERS
United Artists; 1973
11 HARROWHOUSE
20th Century-Fox; 1974; British

Avedis, Howard (Hikmet)

THE STEPMOTHER
Crown International; 1973
THE TEACHER
Crown International; 1974
DR. MINX
Dimension; 1975
THE SPECIALIST
Crown International; 1975
SCORCHY
American International; 1976
TEXAS DETOUR
Cinema Shares International; 1978
THE FIFTH FLOOR
Film Ventures International; 1980
SEPARATE WAYS
Crown International; 1981

Averback, Hy
b. 1925
Agent:
Creative Artists Agency
Los Angeles
(213) 277-4545

CHAMBER OF HORRORS
Warner Brothers; 1966
WHERE WERE YOU WHEN THE LIGHTS WENT OUT?
M-G-M; 1968
I LOVE YOU, ALICE B. TOKLAS
Warner Brothers; 1968
THE GREAT BANK ROBBERY
Warner Brothers; 1969
SUPPOSE THEY GAVE A WAR AND NOBODY CAME?
Cinerama Releasing Corporation; 1970
RICHIE BROCKELMAN: MISSING 24 HOURS
Universal TV; telefeature; 1976
THE LOVE BOAT II
Aaron Spelling Productions; telefeature; 1977
MAGNIFICENT MAGNET OF SANTA MESA
Columbia TV; telefeature; 1977
THE NEW MAVERICK
Cherokee Productions/Warner Brothers TV; telefeature; 1978
A GUIDE FOR THE MARRIED WOMAN
20th Century-Fox TV; telefeature; 1978
PEARL
Silliphant-Konigsberg Productions/Warner Brothers TV; telefeature; 1978
THE NIGHT RIDER
Stephen J. Cannell Productions/Universal TV; telefeature; 1979
SHE'S IN THE ARMY NOW
ABC Circle Films; telefeature; 1981
THE GIRL, THE GOLD WATCH AND DYNAMITE
Fellows-Keegan Company/Paramount TV; telefeature; 1981

Avildsen, John G.
b. 1937
Chicago, Illinois
Home:
45 East 89th Street
New York, N.Y. 10028
Agent:
Marvin Moss
Hollywood
(213) 274-8483

TURN ON TO LOVE
Haven International; 1969
GUESS WHAT WE LEARNED IN SCHOOL TODAY?
Cannon; 1970
JOE
Cannon; 1970
CRY UNCLE!
Cambist; 1971
OKAY BILL
Four Star Excelsior; 1971

continued

Avildsen, John G.
continued

THE STOOLIE
Jama; 1972
SAVE THE TIGER
Paramount; 1973
FORE PLAY
co-director with Bruce Malmuth & Robert McCarty; Cinema National; 1975
W.W. AND THE DIXIE DANCEKINGS
20th Century-Fox; 1975
ROCKY
United Artists; 1976
SLOW DANCING IN THE BIG CITY
United Artists; 1978
THE FORMULA
M-G-M/United Artists; 1980
NEIGHBORS
Columbia; 1981

Axelrod, George
b. June 9, 1922
New York, N.Y.
Agent:
Irving Paul Lazar
Beverly Hills
(213) 275-6153

LORD LOVE A DUCK
United Artists; 1966
THE SECRET LIFE OF AN AMERICAN WIFE
20th Century-Fox; 1968

Badham, John
Agent:
Adams, Ray & Rosenberg
Hollywood
(213) 278-3000

THE IMPATIENT HEART
Universal TV; telefeature; 1971
ISN'T IT SHOCKING?
ABC Circle Films; telefeature; 1973
THE LAW
Universal TV; telefeature; 1974
THE GUN
Universal TV; telefeature; 1974
REFLECTIONS OF MURDER
ABC Circle Films; telefeature; 1974
THE GODCHILD
MGM-TV; telefeature; 1974
THE KEEGANS
Universal TV; telefeature; 1976
THE BINGO LONG TRAVELING ALL STARS AND MOTOR KINGS
Universal; 1976
SATURDAY NIGHT FEVER
Paramount; 1977
DRACULA
Universal; 1979
WHOSE LIFE IS IT ANYWAY?
M-G-M/United Artists; 1981

Badiyi, Reza
Home:
8952 Dicks Street
Los Angeles, CA 90069
(213) 275-0582
Agent:
A.P.A.
Hollywood
(213) 273-0744

DEATH OF A STRANGER
Delta Commerz; 1972
THE EYES OF CHARLES SAND
Warner Brothers TV; telefeature; 1972
TRADER HORN
M-G-M; 1973
THE BIG BLACK PILL
Filmways/NBC Entertainment; telefeature; 1981

Baer, Max, Jr.
b. December 4, 1937
Oakland, California
Business:
Max Baer Productions
10433 Wilshire Blvd.
Los Angeles, CA 90024
(213) 470-2808

THE WILD McCULLOCHS
American International; 1975
ODE TO BILLY JOE
Warner Brothers; 1976
HOMETOWN, U.S.A.
Film Ventures International; 1979

Bail, Chuck
Home:
1421 Morningside Drive
Burbank, CA 91506
Agent:
F.A.M.E.
Hollywood
(213) 656-7590

BLACK SAMSON
Warner Brothers; 1974
CLEOPATRA JONES AND THE CASINO OF GOLD
Warner Brothers; 1975
GUMBALL RALLY
Warner Brothers; 1976

Baker, Graham

THE FINAL CONFLICT
20th Century-Fox; 1981

Baker, Roy Ward
b. 1916
London, England
Contact:
British Film Institute
127 Charing Cross Road
London W.C. 2, England
01-437-4355

THE OCTOBER MAN
Eagle-Lion; 1947; British
THE WEAKER SEX
Eagle-Lion; 1948; British
PAPER ORCHID
1949; British
OPERATION DISASTER (Morning Departure)
Universal; 1950; British
HIGHLY DANGEROUS
Lippert; 1951; British
I'LL NEVER FORGET YOU (The House in the Square)
20th Century-Fox; 1951; British
DON'T BOTHER TO KNOCK
20th Century-Fox; 1952
NIGHT WITHOUT SLEEP
20th Century-Fox; 1952
INFERNO
20th Century-Fox; 1953
PASSAGE HOME
1955; British
JACQUELINE
Rank; 1956; British
TIGER IN SMOKE
1956; British
THE ONE THAT GOT AWAY
Rank; 1958; British
A NIGHT TO REMEMBER
Rank; 1958; British
THE SINGER NOT THE SONG
Warner Brothers; 1962; British
FLAME IN THE STREETS
Atlantic Pictures; 1962; British
THE VALIANT
co-director with Giorgio Capitani; United Artists; 1962; British-Italian
TWO LEFT FEET
1963; British
FIVE MILLION YEARS TO EARTH (Quatermass and the Pit)
20th Century-Fox; 1968; British
THE ANNIVERSARY
20th Century-Fox; 1968; British
THE SPY KILLER
Halsan Productions/ABC-TV; telefeature; 1969
FOREIGN EXCHANGE
Halsan Productions; telefeature; 1970
MOON ZERO TWO
Warner Brothers; 1970; British
THE VAMPIRE LOVERS
American International; 1970; British
THE SCARS OF DRACULA
American Continental; 1971; British
DR. JEKYLL AND SISTER HYDE
American International; 1972; British
ASYLUM
Cinerama Releasing Corporation; 1972; British
THE VAULT OF HORROR
Cinerama Releasing Corporation; 1973; British
AND NOW THE SCREAMING STARTS
Cinerama Releasing Corporation; 1973; British

continued

Baker, Roy Ward
continued

THE 7 BROTHERS MEET DRACULA (The Legend of the Seven Golden Vampires)
Dynamite Entertainment; 1979; British
THE MONSTER CLUB
ITC; 1981; British

Bakshi, Ralph
b. 1939
Brooklyn, N.Y.
Business:
Bakshi Productions, Inc.
8132 Sunland Blvd.
Sun Valley, CA 91352
(213) 768-4000

FRITZ THE CAT
American International; 1972
HEAVY TRAFFIC
American International; 1973
COONSKIN
Bryanston; 1974
HEY GOOD LOOKIN'
Warner Brothers; unreleased
WIZARDS
20th Century-Fox; 1977
THE LORD OF THE RINGS
United Artists; 1978
AMERICAN POP
Columbia; 1981
FIRE AND ICE
Aspen/Bakshi; 1982

Baldwin, Peter
Business:
The Baldwin Co.
5900 Wilshire Blvd.
Los Angeles, CA 90036
(213) 937-5500

THE HARLEM GLOBETROTTERS ON GILLIGAN'S ISLAND
Sherwood Schwartz Productions; telefeature; 1981

Ballard, Carroll
Contact:
Directors Guild of America
Los Angeles
(213) 656-1220

THE BLACK STALLION
United Artists; 1979
NEVER CRY WOLF
Buena Vista; 1981

Bancroft, Anne
Business:
Brooksfilm
Zoetrope Studios
1040 N. Las Palmas Avenue
Los Angeles, CA 90038
(213) 463-7191

FATSO
20th Century-Fox; 1980

Band, Albert
b. May 7, 1924
Paris, France
Agent:
Paul Kohner Agency
Hollywood
(213) 550-1060

THE YOUNG GUNS
Allied Artists; 1956
I BURY THE LIVING
United Artists; 1958
FACE OF FIRE
Allied Artists; 1959
THE AVENGER
Medallion; 1962; Italian-French
GRAND CANYON MASSACRE
1963; Italian
THE TRAMPLERS
Embassy; 1966; Italian
DRACULA'S DOG
Crown International; 1978
SHE CAME TO THE VALLEY
R.G.V. Pictures; 1979

Bare, Richard L.
b. 1909
Turlock, California
Home:
700 Harbor Island Drive
Newport Beach, CA 92660
(714) 675-6269

SMART GIRLS DON'T TALK
Warner Brothers; 1948
FLAXY MARTIN
Warner Brothers; 1949

continued

Bare, Richard L.
continued

THE HOUSE ACROSS THE STREET
Warner Brothers; 1949
THIS SIDE OF THE LAW
Warner Brothers; 1950
RETURN OF THE FRONTIERSMAN
Warner Brothers; 1950
PRISONERS OF THE CASBAH
Columbia; 1953
THE OUTLANDERS
Warner Brothers; 1956
THE STORM RIDERS
Warner Brothers; 1956
BORDER SHOWDOWN
Warner Brothers; 1956
THE TRAVELLERS
Warner Brothers; 1957
SHOOT-OUT AT MEDICINE BEND
Warner Brothers; 1957
GIRL ON THE RUN
Warner Brothers; 1958
THIS REBEL BREED
Warner Brothers; 1960
WICKED, WICKED
M-G-M; 1973

Barris, Chuck
Business:
Chuck Barris Productions
6430 Sunset Blvd.
Hollywood, CA 90028
(213) 469-9080

THE GONG SHOW MOVIE
Universal; 1980

Barron, Arthur

THE WRIGHT BROTHERS
PBS-TV; telefeature; 1971
JEREMY
United Artists; 1973
BROTHERS
Warner Brothers; 1977

Bartel, Paul
Messages:
(213) 650-8878

THE SECRET CINEMA
Aries; 1968
PRIVATE PARTS
M-G-M; 1972
DEATH RACE 2000
New World; 1975
CANNONBALL
New World; 1976
THE BLANDS
Bartel Film; 1982

Bartlett, Hall
b. November 27, 1922
Kansas City, Missouri
Home:
861 Stone Canyon Road
Los Angeles, CA 90024
(213) 476-3916
Business:
Hall Bartlett Films
9200 Sunset Blvd.
Los Angeles, CA 90069
(213) 278-8883

UNCHAINED
Warner Brothers; 1955
DRANGO
co-director with Jules Bricken; United Artists; 1957
ZERO HOUR
Paramount; 1957
ALL THE YOUNG MEN
Columbia; 1960
THE CARETAKERS
United Artists; 1963
CHANGES
(Cinerama Releasing Corporation; 1969)
THE WILD PACK (The Sandpit Generals)
American International; 1972
JONATHAN LIVINGSTON SEAGULL
Paramount; 1973
THE CHILDREN OF SANCHEZ
Lone Star; 1978; U.S.-Mexican

Barzyk, Fred
Home:
(617) 256-4868

BETWEEN TIME & TIMBUKTU
PBS-TV; telefeature; 1974
THE PHANTOM OF THE OPEN HEARTH
co-director with David Loxton; PBS-TV; telefeature; 1976
CHARLIE SMITH AND THE FRITTER TREE
co-director with David Loxton; PBS-TV; telefeature; 1978
THE LATHE OF HEAVEN
co-director with David Loxton; The Television Laboratory/WNET-13/Taurus Film; telefeature; 1980

Bass, Saul
Business:
Saul Bass/Herb Yager & Assoc.
7039 Sunset Blvd.
Los Angeles, CA 90028
(213) 466-9701

PHASE IV
Paramount; 1974

Bat-Adam, Michal
Contact:
The Israel Film Centre
30 Agron Street
P.O. Box 229
Jerusalem, Israel
02-227241

EACH OTHER (Moments)
Franklin Media; 1979; Israeli-French
THE THIN LINE
1980; Israeli

Bean, Robert B.
Business:
(212) 628-0500

MADE FOR EACH OTHER
20th Century-Fox; 1971

Beatty, Warren
b. March 30, 1937
Richmond, Virginia
Contact:
Directors Guild of America
Los Angeles
(213) 656-1220

HEAVEN CAN WAIT
co-director with Buck Henry; Paramount; 1978
REDS
Paramount; 1981

Beaumont, Gabrielle
Home:
(213) 550-6916
Agent:
Contemporary-Korman
Beverly Hills
(213) 278-8250

THE GODSEND
Cannon; 1980; British
THE MAGENTA MOTH
1981

Becker, Harold
Agent:
Adams, Ray & Rosenberg
Hollywood
(213) 278-3000

THE RAGMAN'S DAUGHTER
Penelope Films; 1972; British
THE ONION FIELD
Avco Embassy; 1979
THE BLACK MARBLE
Avco Embassy; 1980
TAPS
20th Century-Fox; 1981

Bellamy, Earl
b. March 11, 1917
Minneapolis, Minnesota
Business Manager:
Fred Barman
Hollywood
(213) 276-6666
Agent:
Herb Tobias & Associates
Century City
(213) 277-6211

SEMINOLE UPRISING
Columbia; 1955
BLACKJACK KETCHUM, DESPERADO
Columbia; 1956
TOUGHEST GUN IN TOMBSTONE
United Artists; 1958
STAGECOACH TO DANCERS' ROCK
Universal; 1962

continued

Bellamy, Earl
continued

FLUFFY
Universal; 1965
INCIDENT AT PHANTOM HILL
Universal; 1966
GUNPOINT
Universal; 1966
MUNSTER, GO HOME
Universal; 1966
THREE GUNS FOR TEXAS
co-director with David Lowell Rich & Paul Stanley; Universal; 1968
BACKTRACK
Universal; 1969
THE PIGEON
Thomas/Spelling Productions; telefeature;1969
DESPERATE MISSION
20th Century-Fox TV; telefeature; 1971
THE TRACKERS
Aaron Spelling Productions; telefeature; 1971
SEVEN ALONE
Doty-Dayton; 1975
SIDECAR RACERS
Universal; 1975; Australian
PART 2 WALKING TALL
American International; 1975
AGAINST A CROOKED SKY
Doty-Dayton; 1975
FLOOD!
Irwin Allen Productions/20th Century-Fox TV; telefeature; 1976
FIRE!
Irwin Allen Productions/20th Century-Fox TV; telefeature; 1977
SIDEWINDER ONE
Avco Embassy; 1977
SPEEDTRAP
First Artists; 1978
DESPERATE WOMEN
Lorimar Productions; telefeature; 1978
THE CASTAWAYS OF GILLIGAN'S ISLAND
Sherwood Schwartz Productions; telefeature; 1979
VALENTINE MAGIC ON LOVE ISLAND
Dick Clark Productions/PKO/Osmond TV; telefeature 1980
MAGNUM THRUST
Shenandoah Films; 1981

Belson, Jerry
Business Manager:
Jess Morgan & Co.
Hollywood
(213) 651-1601

JEKYLL AND HYDE...TOGETHER AGAIN
Paramount; 1981

Benedek, Laslo
b. March 5, 1907
Budapest, Hungary
Agent:
Paul Kohner Agency
Hollywood
(213) 550-1060

THE KISSING BANDIT
M-G-M; 1948
PORT OF NEW YORK
Eagle-Lion; 1949
DEATH OF A SALESMAN
Columbia; 1951
THE WILD ONE
Columbia; 1954
BENGAL BRIGADE
Columbia; 1954
KINDER, MUTTER UND EIN GENERAL
1955; West German
AFFAIR IN HAVANA
Allied Artists; 1957
MALAGA
Warner Brothers; 1959; British
RECOURSE EN GRACE
1960; French

continued

Benedek, Laslo
continued

NAMU, THE KILLER WHALE
United Artists; 1966
DARING GAME
Paramount; 1968
THE NIGHT VISITOR
UMC; 1971
ASSAULT ON AGATHON
Nine Network; 1976

Benedict, Richard
Agent:
Shapiro-Lichtman Agency
Los Angeles
(213) 557-2244

WINTER A GO-GO
Columbia; 1965
IMPASSE
United Artists; 1968

Benner, Richard
Agent:
William Morris Agency
New York City
(212) 586-5100

OUTRAGEOUS!
Cinema 5; 1977; Canadian
HAPPY BIRTHDAY GEMINI
United Artists; 1980; U.S.-Canadian

Bennett, Richard C.
Home:
17136 Index Street
Granada Hills, CA 91344
(213) 363-3381
Agent:
Contemporary-Korman Artists
Los Angeles
(213) 278-8250

HARPER VALLEY PTA
April Fools; 1978
THE ESCAPE OF A ONE-TON PET
Tomorrow Entertainment; telefeature; 1978

Benton, Robert
b. September 29, 1932
Waxahachie, Texas
Agent:
I.C.M.
New York City
(212) 556-6800

BAD COMPANY
Paramount; 1972
THE LATE SHOW
Warner Brothers; 1976
KRAMER VS. KRAMER
Columbia; 1979
STAB
United Artists; 1981

Beresford, Bruce
Contact:
Australian Film Commission
9229 W. Sunset Blvd.
Los Angeles, CA 90069
(213) 275-7074

THE ADVENTURES OF BARRY McKENZIE
Columbia-Warners; 1973; Australian
BARRY McKENZIE HOLDS HIS OWN
EMI; 1974; Australian
SIDE BY SIDE
1976; Australian
DON'S PARTY
1978; Australian
THE MONEY MOVERS
1979; Australian
THE GETTING OF WISDOM
Atlantic; 1980; Australian
BREAKER MORANT
New World/Quartet; 1980; Australian
THE CLUB
South Australia Film Corporation; 1981; Australian
PUBERTY BLUES
Limelight Productions; 1981; Australian
TENDER MERCIES
EMI; 1982

Bergman, Andrew
Contact:
Directors Guild of America
Los Angeles
(213) 656-1220

SO FINE
Warner Brothers; 1981

Bergman, Ingmar
b. July 14, 1918
Uppsala, Sweden
Contact:
Swedish Film Institute
P.O. Box 27126
S-10252 Stockholm
Sweden
08-630510

CRISIS
Svensk Filmindustri; 1945; Swedish
IT RAINS ON OUR LOVE
Sveriges Folkbiografer; 1946; Swedish
THE LAND OF DESIRE
Sveriges Folkbiografer; 1947; Swedish
NIGHT IS MY FUTURE
Terrafilm; 1948; Swedish
PORT OF CALL
Janus; 1948; Swedish
THE DEVIL'S WANTON
Terrafilm; 1949; Swedish
THREE STRANGE LOVES
Janus; 1949; Swedish
TO JOY
Janus; 1950; Swedish
THIS CAN'T HAPPEN HERE
Svensk Filmindustri; 1951; Swedish
ILLICIT INTERLUDE
Janus; 1951; Swedish
SECRETS OF WOMEN
Janus; 1952; Swedish
MONIKA
Janus; 1953; Swedish
SAWDUST AND TINSEL
Janus; 1953; Swedish
A LESSON IN LOVE
Janus; 1954; Swedish
DREAMS
Janus; 1955; Swedish
SMILES OF A SUMMER NIGHT
Janus; 1955; Swedish
THE SEVENTH SEAL
Janus; 1957; Swedish
WILD STRAWBERRIES
Janus; 1957; Swedish
SO CLOSE TO LIFE
Janus; 1958; Swedish
THE MAGICIAN
Janus; 1958; Swedish
THE VIRGIN SPRING
Janus; 1960; Swedish
THE DEVIL'S EYE
Janus; 1960; Swedish
THROUGH A GLASS DARKLY
Janus; 1961; Swedish
WINTER LIGHT
Janus; 1962; Swedish
THE SILENCE
Janus; 1963; Swedish
ALL THESE WOMEN
Janus; 1964; Swedish
PERSONA
United Artists; 1966; Swedish
HOUR OF THE WOLF
United Artists; 1968; Swedish
SHAME
United Artists; 1968; Swedish
THE RITUAL
Janus; 1969; Swedish; made for television
THE PASSION OF ANNA
United Artists; 1969; Swedish
THE TOUCH
Cinerama Releasing Corporation; 1971; Swedish; made for television
CRIES AND WHISPERS
New World; 1972; Swedish
SCENES FROM A MARRIAGE
Cinema 5; 1973; Swedish; made for television
THE MAGIC FLUTE
Surrogate; 1975; Swedish
FACE TO FACE
Paramount; 1976; Swedish
THE SERPENT'S EGG
Paramount; 1978; West German
AUTUMN SONATA
New World; 1978; West German
FROM THE LIFE OF THE MARIONETTES
Universal/AFD; 1980; West German

Berlatsky, David
Contact:
Directors Guild of America
Los Angeles
(213) 656-1220

THE FARMER
Columbia; 1977

Berman, Ted
Business:
Walt Disney Productions
500 S. Buena Vista Street
Burbank, CA 91521
(213) 845-3141

THE FOX AND THE HOUND
co-director with Art Stevens & Richard Rich; Buena Vista; 1981

Bernstein, Walter
b. 1920
Brooklyn, New York
Contact:
Directors Guild of America
New York City
(212) 581-0370

LITTLE MISS MARKER
Universal; 1980

Berri, Claude
(Claude Langmann)
b. July 1, 1934
Paris, France
Business:
Renn Films
Paris, France

LE BAISERS
co-director; 1964; French
LE CHANCE ET L'AMOUR
co-director; 1964; French
THE TWO OF US
Cinema 5; 1968; French
MARRY ME! MARRY ME!
Allied Artists; 1969; French
THE MAN WITH CONNECTIONS
Columbia; 1970; French
LE CINEMA DU PAPA
Columbia; 1971; French
LE SEX SHOP
Peppercorn Wormser; 1973; French
MALE OF THE CENTURY
Joseph Green; 1975; French
THE FIRST TIME
EDP; 1978; French
ONE WILD MOMENT
Quartet/Films Inc.; 1978; French

Berry, John
b. 1917
New York, New York
Attorney:
Alan Schwartz
New York
(212) PL. 8-4010

MISS SUSIE SLAGLE'S
Paramount; 1945
FROM THIS DAY FORWARD
RKO Radio; 1946
CROSS MY HEART
Paramount; 1946
CASBAH
Universal; 1948
TENSION
M-G-M; 1949
HE RAN ALL THE WAY
United Artists; 1951
C'EST ARRIVE A PARIS
1952; French
CA VA BARDER
1954; French
JE SUIS UN SENTIMENTAL
1955; French
PANTALOONS
United Motion Picture Organization; 1956; French-Spanish
OH, QUE MAMBO
1958; French
TAMANGO
Valiant; 1959; French

continued

Berry, John
continued

MAYA
M-G-M; 1966
A TOUT CASSER
1967; French
CLAUDINE
20th Century-Fox; 1974
THIEVES
Paramount; 1977
THE BAD NEWS BEARS GO TO JAPAN
Paramount; 1978
ANGEL ON MY SHOULDER
Mace Neufeld Productions/Barney Rosenzweig Productions/Beowulf Productions; telefeature; 1980

Bertolucci, Bernardo
b. March 16, 1940
Parma, Italy
Contact:
Minister of Tourism
Via Della Ferratella
No. 51
00184 Rome, Italy
06-7732

THE GRIM REAPER
1962; Italian
BEFORE THE REVOLUTION
New Yorker; 1965; Italian
LOVE AND ANGER
co-director; 1967; Italian
PARTNER
New Yorker; 1968; Italian
THE CONFORMIST
Paramount; 1971; Italian-French-West German
THE SPIDER'S STRATAGEM
New Yorker; 1973; Italian
LAST TANGO IN PARIS
United Artists; 1973; Italian-French
1900
Paramount; 1977; Italian
LUNA
20th Century-Fox; 1979; Italian-U.S.
A MAN'S TRAGEDY
The Ladd Company/Warner Brothers; 1981; Italian

Bianchi, Edward
Business:
Bianchi Films
141 Fifth Avenue
New York, N.Y. 10010
(212) 533-3010

THE FAN
Paramount; 1981

Bill, Tony
Business:
Tony Bill Productions
73 Market Street
Venice, CA 90291
(213) 396-5937
Agent:
Bill Robinson & Associates
Beverly Hills
(213) 275-6114

MY BODYGUARD
20th Century-Fox; 1980

Bilson, Bruce
Business:
Downwind Enterprises, Inc.
4444 Radford Avenue
N. Hollywood, CA 91607
(213) 985-5121
Agent:
Shapiro-Lichtman Agency
Century City
(213) 557-2244

THE GIRL WHO CAME GIFT-WRAPPED
Spelling-Goldberg Productions; telefeature; 1974
DEAD MAN ON THE RUN
Sweeney-Finnegan Productions; telefeature; 1975
THE NEW DAUGHTERS OF JOSHUA CABE
Spelling-Goldberg Productions; telefeature; 1976
BJ & THE BEAR
Universal TV; telefeature; 1978
THE NORTH AVENUE IRREGULARS
Buena Vista; 1979
DALLAS COWBOYS CHEERLEADERS
Aubrey-Hamner Productions; telefeature; 1979
PLEASURE COVE
Lou Shaw Productions/David Gerber Company/ Columbia TV; telefeature; 1979
THE GHOSTS OF BUXLEY HALL
Walt Disney Productions; telefeature; 1980

Billington, Kevin
b. 1933
England
Contact:
British Film Institute
127 Charing Cross Road
London W.C. 2, England
01-437-4355

INTERLUDE
Columbia; 1968; British
THE RISE AND RISE OF MICHAEL RIMMER
Warner Brothers; 1970; British
THE LIGHT AT THE EDGE OF THE WORLD
National General; 1971; U.S.-Spanish
VOICES
Hemdale; 1973; British
AND NO ONE COULD SAVE HER
Associated London Films; telefeature; 1973; British
ECHOES OF THE SIXTIES
ALA Productions; television documentary; 1979

Binder, John
Contact:
Directors Guild of America
Los Angeles
(213) 656-1220

UFORIA
20th Century-Fox; 1981

Bing, Mack
Agent:
Eisenbach-Greene-Duchow, Inc.
Hollywood
(213) 659-3420

ALL THE LOVING COUPLES
U-M; 1969
GABRIELLA
1974

Bixby, Bill
b. January 22, 1934
San Francisco, California
Personal Manager:
Paul Brandon
Hollywood
(213) CR. 3-6173

THE BARBARY COAST
Paramount TV; telefeature; 1975
THREE ON A DATE
ABC Circle Films; telefeature; 1978

Black, Noel
b. 1937
Business:
Highway Productions
120 Greenfield Avenue
Los Angeles, CA 90049
(213) 476-4719
Agent:
Chasin-Park-Citron
Hollywood
(213) 273-7190

PRETTY POISON
20th Century-Fox; 1968
COVER ME BABE
20th Century-Fox; 1970
JENNIFER ON MY MIND
United Artists; 1971
MULLIGAN'S STEW
Paramount TV; telefeature; 1977
MIRRORS
First American; 1978
A MAN, A WOMAN AND A BANK
Avco Embassy; 1979; Canadian

Blatty, William Peter
b. 1928
New York
Attorney:
Silverberg, Rosen, Leon & Behr
Century City
(213) 277-4500

THE NINTH CONFIGURATION
Warner Brothers; 1979; re-released under title "Twinkle, Twinkle 'Killer' Kane in 1980 by United Film Distribution

Blier, Bertrand
b. March 14, 1939
Paris, France
Contact:
French Film Office
745 Fifth Avenue
New York, N.Y. 10151
(212) 832-8860

HITLER CONNAIS PAS
1962; French
BREAKDOWN
1967; French
GOING PLACES
Cinema 5; 1974; French
FEMMES FATALES
New Line Cinema; 1977; French
GET OUT YOUR HANDKERCHIEFS
New Line Cinema; 1978; French
COLD CUTS
1979; French
BEAU PERE
New Line Cinema; 1981; French

Bloom, Jeffrey
Agent:
Adams, Ray and Rosenberg
Hollywood
(213) 278-3000

DOGPOUND SHUFFLE
Paramount; 1974; Canadian
THE STICK UP
Trident-Barber; 1978; British
BLOOD BEACH
Jerry Gross Organization; 1981

Bloomfield, George
Agent:
William Morris Agency
Beverly Hills
(213) 274-7451

JENNY
Cinerama Releasing Corporation; 1970
TO KILL A CLOWN
20th Century-Fox; 1972
CHILD UNDER A LEAF
Cinema National; 1975; Canadian
RIEL
CBC; 1979; Canadian
NOTHING PERSONAL
American International; 1980; Canadian
DOUBLE NEGATIVE
Quadrant; 1981; Canadian
GOING FOR BROKE
1981; Canadian

Boetticher, Budd
(Oscar Boetticher, Jr.)
b. July 29, 1916
Chicago, Illinois
Contact:
Directors Guild of America
Los Angeles
(213) 656-1220

ONE MYSTERIOUS NIGHT
Columbia; 1944
THE MISSING JUROR
Columbia; 1944
A GUY, A GAL AND A PAL
Columbia; 1945
ESCAPE IN THE FOG
Columbia; 1945
YOUTH ON TRIAL
Columbia; 1945
THE FLEET THAT CAME TO STAY
Paramount; 1946
ASSIGNED TO DANGER
Eagle-Lion; 1948
BEHIND LOCKED DOORS
Eagle-Lion; 1948
THE WOLF HUNTERS
Monogram; 1949
BLACK MIDNIGHT
Monogram; 1949
KILLER SHARK
Monogram; 1950
THE BULLFIGHTER AND THE LADY
Republic; 1951
THE SWORD OF D'ARTAGNAN
Universal; 1951
THE CIMARRON KID
Universal; 1951
RED BALL EXPRESS
Universal; 1952
BRONCO BUSTER
Universal; 1952
HORIZONS WEST
Universal; 1952
CITY BENEATH THE SEA
Universal; 1953
SEMINOLE
Universal; 1953
THE MAN FROM THE ALAMO
Universal; 1953
EAST OF SUMATRA
Universal; 1953
WINGS OF THE HAWK
Universal; 1953
THE MAGNIFICENT MATADOR
20th Century-Fox; 1955
THE KILLER IS LOOSE
United Artists; 1956
SEVEN MEN FROM NOW
Warner Brothers; 1956

continued

Boetticher, Budd
continued

THE TALL T
Columbia; 1957
DECISION AT SUNDOWN
Columbia; 1957
BUCHANAN RIDES ALONE
Columbia; 1958
RIDE LONESOME
Columbia; 1959
WESTBOUND
Warner Brothers; 1959
COMANCHE STATION
Columbia; 1960
THE RISE AND FALL OF LEGS DIAMOND
Warner Brothers; 1960
A TIME FOR DYING
Etoile; 1971
ARRUZA
Avco Embassy; 1972

Bogart, Paul
b. November 21, 1919
New York, New York
Business:
Tiber Productions
760 N. La Cienega Blvd.
Los Angeles, CA 90069
(213) 652-0222
Agent:
Irv Schechter
Beverly Hills
(213) 278-8070

MARLOWE
M-G-M; 1969
HALLS OF ANGER
United Artists; 1970
SKIN GAME
Warner Brothers; 1971
IN SEARCH OF AMERICA
Four-Star Productions; telefeature; 1971
CLASS OF '44
Warner Brothers; 1973
CANCEL MY RESERVATION
Warner Brothers; 1974
TELL ME WHERE IT HURTS
Tomorrow Entertainment; telefeature; 1974
MR. RICCO
M-G-M; 1975
WINNER TAKE ALL
The Jozak Company; telefeature; 1975
THE THREE SISTERS
NTA; 1977

Bogdanovich, Peter
b. July 30, 1939
Kingston, New York
Agent:
The Ufland Agency
Beverly Hills
(213) 273-9441

TARGETS
Paramount; 1968
DIRECTED BY JOHN FORD
American Film Institute; 1971
THE LAST PICTURE SHOW
Columbia; 1971
WHAT'S UP, DOC?
Warner Brothers; 1972
PAPER MOON
Paramount; 1973
DAISY MILLER
Paramount; 1974
AT LONG LAST LOVE
20th Century-Fox; 1975
NICKELODEON
Columbia; 1976
SAINT JACK
New World; 1979
THEY ALL LAUGHED
Time-Life Productions; 1981

Bolt, Robert
b. August 15, 1924
Sale, England
Contact:
British Film Institute
127 Charing Cross Road
London W.C. 2, England
01-437-4355

LADY CAROLINE LAMB
United Artists; 1973; British

Bondarchuk, Sergei
b. September 25, 1920
Belozersk, Ukraine

FATE OF A MAN
Lopert; 1961; Soviet
WAR AND PEACE
Continental; 1968; Soviet
WATERLOO
Paramount; 1971; Italian-Soviet
THEY FOUGHT FOR THE MOTHERLAND
Mosfilm; 1975; Soviet
THE PEAKS OF ZELENGORE
1976; Yugoslavian
THE STEPPE
Mosfilm; 1978; Soviet

Bonerz, Peter
Personal Manager:
Shapiro-West & Associates
Beverly Hills
(213) 278-8896

NOBODY'S PERFEKT
Columbia; 1981

Boorman, John
b. January 18, 1933
Shepperton, England
Business Manager:
International Business
Management
Century City
(213) 277-4455

HAVING A WILD WEEKEND (Catch Us If You Can)
Warner Brothers; 1965; British
POINT BLANK
M-G-M; 1967
HELL IN THE PACIFIC
Cinerama Releasing Corporation; 1968
LEO THE LAST
United Artists; 1970; British
DELIVERANCE
Warner Brothers; 1972
ZARDOZ
20th Century-Fox; 1974; British
THE HERETIC: EXORCIST II
Warner Brothers; 1977
EXCALIBUR
Orion Pictures/Warner Brothers; 1981; British-Irish

Boulting, John
b. November 21, 1913
Bray, Buckinghamshire,
England
Contact:
British Film Institute
127 Charing Cross Road
London W.C. 2, England
01-437-4355

JOURNEY TOGETHER
RKO Radio; 1945; British
YOUNG SCARFACE (Brighton Rock)
Mayer-Kingsley; 1947; British
SEVEN DAYS TO NOON
Mayer-Kingsley; 1950; British
THE MAGIC BOX
Rank; 1952; British
CREST OF THE WAVE (Seagulls Over Sorrento)
co-director with Roy Boulting; M-G-M; 1954
PRIVATE'S PROGRESS
DCA; 1956; British
LUCKY JIM
Kingsley International; 1957; British
I'M ALL RIGHT, JACK
Columbia; 1960; British
THE RISK (Suspect)
co-director with Roy Boulting; Kingsley International; 1961; British
HEAVEN'S ABOVE!
Janus; 1963; British
ROTTEN TO THE CORE
Cinema 5; 1965; British

Boulting, Roy
b. November 21, 1913
Bray, Buckinghamshire,
England
Agent:
Creative Artists Agency
Hollywood
(213) 277-4545

TRUNK CRIME
Angelo; 1939; British
INQUEST
Grand National; 1939; British
PASTOR HALL
United Artists; 1940; British

continued

Boulting, Roy
continued

THUNDER ROCK
English Films; 1942; British
DESERT VICTORY
Army Film Unit; 1943; British
TUNISIAN VICTORY
co-director with Frank Capra; Army Film Unit; 1943; British
BURMA VICTORY
Army Film Unit; 1945; British
THE OUTSIDER (The Guinea Pig)
Pathe; 1948; British
FAME IS THE SPUR
Two Cities; 1949; British
HIGH TREASON
Rank; 1951; British
SAILOR OF THE KING (Single-Handed)
20th Century-Fox; 1953; British
CREST OF THE WAVE (Seagulls Over Sorrento)
co-director with John Boulting; M-G-M; 1954
JOSEPHINE AND MEN
1955; British
RUN FOR THE SUN
United Artists; 1956
BROTHERS IN LAW
1957; British
HAPPY IS THE BRIDE
Kassler; 1959; British
MAN IN A COCKED HAT (Carlton-Browne of the F.O.)
co-director with Jeffrey Dell; Show Corporation; 1960; British
A FRENCH MISTRESS
Films Around the World; 1960; British
THE RISK (Suspect)
co-director with John Boulting; Kingsley International; 1961; British
THE FAMILY WAY
Warner Brothers; 1967; British
TWISTED NERVE
National General; 1969; British
THERE'S A GIRL IN MY SOUP
Columbia; 1970; British
UNDERCOVERS HERO (Soft Beds and Hard Battles)
United Artists; 1975; British
THE LAST WORD
Variety International; 1979

Bowers, George

THE HEARSE
Crown International; 1980
BODY AND SOUL
Cannon; 1981

Brando, Marlon
b. April 3, 1924
Omaha, Nebraska
Contact:
Directors Guild of America
Los Angeles
(213) 656-1220

ONE-EYED JACKS
Paramount; 1961

Bresson, Robert
b. September 25, 1907
Bromont-Lamothe, France
Contact:
French Film Office
745 Fifth Avenue
New York, N.Y. 10151
(212) 832-8860

LES AFFAIRES PUBLIQUE
Arc Films; 1934; French
LES ANGES DU PECHE
Synops/Roland Tual; 1943; French
THE LADIES OF THE PARK
Brandon; 1945; French
DIARY OF A COUNTRY PRIEST
Brandon; 1950; French
A MAN ESCAPED
Continental; 1956; French

continued

Bresson, Robert
continued

PICKPOCKET
New Yorker; 1959; French
THE TRIAL OF JOAN OF ARC
Pathe Contemporary; 1962; French
AU HASARD, BALTHAZAR
Cinema Ventures; 1966; French
MOUCHETTE
1967; French
UNE FEMME DOUCE
New Yorker; 1969; French
FOUR NIGHTS OF A DREAMER
New Yorker; 1972; French
LANCELOT OF THE LAKE
New Yorker; 1975; French-Italian
THE DEVIL, PROBABLY
1979; French

Brest, Martin
Agent:
The Ufland Agency
Beverly Hills
(213) 273-9441

HOT TOMORROWS
American Film Institute; 1977
GOING IN STYLE
Warner Brothers; 1979

Bridges, Alan
b. September 28, 1927
England
Contact:
British Film Institute
127 Charing Cross Road
London W.C. 2, England
01-437-4355

ACT OF MURDER
Warner-Pathe/Anglo-Amalgamated; 1964; British
INVASION
Warner-Pathe/Anglo-Amalgamated; 1966; British
THE HIRELING
Columbia; 1973; British
BRIEF ENCOUNTER
Carlo Ponti Productions/Cecil Clarke Productions; telefeature; 1974; British
OUT OF SEASON
Athenaeum; 1975; British
AGE OF INNOCENCE
Rank; 1977; British
VERY LIKE A WHALE
Black Lion; 1981; British
RETURN OF A SOLDIER
Barry R. Cooper/Skreba Film Ltd.; 1982; British

Bridges, James
b.
Paris, Arkansas
Agent:
Creative Artists Agency
Hollywood
(213) 277-4545

THE BABY MAKER
National General; 1970
THE PAPER CHASE
20th Century-Fox; 1973
9/30/55 (September 30, 1955)
Universal; 1977
THE CHINA SYNDROME
Columbia; 1979
URBAN COWBOY
Paramount; 1980

Brinckerhoff, Burt
Contact:
Directors Guild of America
Los Angeles
(213) 656-1220

DOGS
R.C. Riddell; 1977
ACAPULCO GOLD
R.C. Riddell; 1978
THE CRACKER FACTORY
Roger Gimbel Productions/EMI TV; telefeature; 1979
CAN YOU HEAR THE LAUGHTER? THE STORY OF FREDDIE PRINZE
Roger Gimbel Productions/EMI TV; telefeature; 1979
MOTHER AND DAUGHTER - THE LOVING WAR
Edgar J. Scherick Associates; telefeature; 1980
BRAVE NEW WORLD
Universal TV; telefeature; 1980
THE DAY THE WOMEN GOT EVEN
Otto Salaman Productions/PKO; telefeature; 1980

Bromfield, Rex
Business:
Bromfilms, Inc.
1237 Howe Street
Vancouver, British Columbia
Canada

LOVE AT FIRST SIGHT
Movietime; 1978; Canadian
TULIPS
Avco Embassy; 1981; Canadian
MELANIE
Avco Embassy; 1982; Canadian

Brook, Peter
b. March 21, 1925
London, England
Contact:
British Film Institute
127 Charing Cross Road
London W.C. 2, England
01-437-4355

THE BEGGAR'S OPERA
Warner Brothers; 1953; British
MODERATO CANTABILE
Royal International; 1963; French-Italian
LORD OF THE FLIES
Continental; 1963; British
THE PERSECUTION AND ASSASSINATION OF JEAN-PAUL MARAT AS PERFORMED BY THE INMATES OF THE ASYLUM OF CHARENTON UNDER THE DIRECTION OF THE MARQUIS DE SADE (Marat/Sade)
United Artists; 1967; British
TELL ME LIES
Continental; 1968; British
KING LEAR
Altura; 1971; British-Danish
MEETINGS WITH REMARKABLE MEN
Libra Films; 1979; British

Brooks, Albert
Business Manager:
Gelfand & Macnow
Los Angeles
(213) 553-1707

REAL LIFE
Paramount; 1979
MODERN ROMANCE
Columbia; 1981

Brooks, Bob
Contact:
Directors Guild of America
Los Angeles
(213) 656-1220

TATTOO
20th Century-Fox; 1981

Brooks, Joseph
Business:
The Light and Sound Co.
41-A East 74th Street
New York, N.Y. 10021
(212) 759-8720

YOU LIGHT UP MY LIFE
Columbia; 1977
IF EVER I SEE YOU AGAIN
Columbia; 1978
HEADIN' FOR BROADWAY
20th Century-Fox; 1980

Brooks, Mel
(Melvin Kaminsky)
b. 1926
New York, New York
Business:
Brooksfilm
Zoetrope Studios
1040 N. Las Palmas Avenue
Los Angeles, CA 90038
(213) 463-7191

THE PRODUCERS
Avco Embassy; 1968
THE TWELVE CHAIRS
UMC; 1970
BLAZING SADDLES
Warner Brothers; 1973
YOUNG FRANKENSTEIN
20th Century-Fox; 1974
SILENT MOVIE
20th Century-Fox; 1976
HIGH ANXIETY
20th Century-Fox; 1977
HISTORY OF THE WORLD, PART I
20th Century-Fox; 1981

Brooks, Richard
b. May 18, 1912
Philadelphia, Pennsylvania
Attorney:
Gerald Lipsky
Beverly Hills
(213) 878-4100

CRISIS
M-G-M; 1950
THE LIGHT TOUCH
M-G-M; 1951
DEADLINE - U.S.A.
M-G-M; 1952
BATTLE CIRCUS
M-G-M; 1953

continued

Brooks, Richard
continued

TAKE THE HIGH GROUND
M-G-M; 1953
FLAME AND THE FLESH
M-G-M; 1954
THE LAST TIME I SAW PARIS
M-G-M; 1954
THE BLACKBOARD JUNGLE
M-G-M; 1955
THE LAST HUNT
M-G-M; 1956
THE CATERED AFFAIR
M-G-M; 1956
SOMETHING OF VALUE
M-G-M; 1957
CAT ON A HOT TIN ROOF
M-G-M; 1958
THE BROTHERS KARAMAZOV
M-G-M; 1958
ELMER GANTRY
United Artists; 1960
SWEET BIRD OF YOUTH
M-G-M; 1962
LORD JIM
Columbia; 1964
THE PROFESSIONALS
Columbia; 1966
IN COLD BLOOD
Columbia; 1967
THE HAPPY ENDING
United Artists; 1969
$ (Dollars)
Columbia; 1971
BITE THE BULLET
Columbia; 1975
LOOKING FOR MR. GOODBAR
Paramount; 1977
WRONG IS RIGHT
Columbia; 1981

Brown, Barry
Home:
770 Amalfi Drive
Pacific Palisades, CA 90272
(213) 459-4455
Agent:
Phil Gersh Agency
Hollywood
(213) 274-6611

THE WAY WE LIVE NOW
United Artists; 1970
CLOUD DANCER
Blossom; 1980

Brown, Georg Stanford
Contact:
Directors Guild of America
Los Angeles
(213) 6560-1220

ROOTS: THE NEXT GENERATIONS
co-director with John Erman, Charles Dubin & Lloyd Richards; Wolper Productions; television mini-series; 1979
GRAMBLING'S WHITE TIGER
Jenner-Wallach Productions/Inter Planetary Productions; telefeature; 1981

Browning, Kirk
Home:
7 Springfarms
487 Chappaqua Road
Briarcliff, N.Y. 10510
(914) 941-0859

BIG BLONDE
PBS-TV; telefeature; 1980

Buchanan, Larry
Home:
4159 Nogales Drive
Tarzana, CA 91356
(213) 344-0976

FREE, WHITE AND 21
American International; 1963
UNDER AGE
Falcon International; 1964

continued

Buchanan, Larry
continued

A BULLET FOR PRETTY BOY
American International; 1970
GOODBYE, NORMA JEAN
Stirling Gold; 1976
HUGHES AND HARLOW: ANGELS IN HELL
Pro International; 1978
THE LOCH NESS HORROR
Omni-Leisure International; 1982

Bunuel, Luis
b. February 22, 1900
Calanda, Spain
Contact:
French Film Office
745 Fifth Avenue
New York, N.Y. 10051
(212) 832-8860

UN CHIEN ANDALOU
co-director with Salvador Dali; 1928; French
L'AGE D'OR
1930; French
LAS HURDES
1932; Spanish
GRAN CASINO
1946; Mexican
EL GRAN CALAVERA
1949; Mexican
LOS OLVIDADOS (The Young and the Damned)
Mayer-Kingsley; 1950; Mexican
SUSANA
1950; Mexican
LA HIJA DEL ENGANO
1951; Mexican
UNA MUJER SIN AMOR
1951; Mexican
SUBIDA AL CIELO
1951; Mexican
EL BRUTO
1952; Mexican
THE ADVENTURES OF ROBINSON CRUSOE
United Artists; 1952; Mexican
EL
1952; Mexican
ABISMOS DE PASION
1953; Mexican
THE ILLUSION TRAVELS BY STREETCAR
Bauer International; 1953; Mexican
THE RIVER AND DEATH
Bauer International; 1954; Mexican
THE CRIMINAL LIFE OF ARCHIBALDO DE LA CRUZ
Talbot; 1955; Mexican
CELA S'APPELLE L'AURORE
1955; French-Italian
DEATH IN THE GARDEN
Bauer International; 1956; French-Mexican
NAZARIN
Altura; 1958; Mexican
LA FIEVRE MONTE A EL PASO
1959; French-Mexican
THE YOUNG ONE
Valiant; 1960; Mexican
VIRIDIANA
Kingsley International; 1961; Spanish-Mexican
THE EXTERMINATING ANGEL
Altura; 1962; Mexican
DIARY OF A CHAMBERMAID
International Classics; 1963; French-Italian
SIMON OF THE DESERT
Altura; 1965; Mexican
BELLE DE JOUR
Allied Artists; 1967; French-Italian
THE MILKY WAY
UM; 1968; French-Italian
TRISTANA
Maron Films Limited; 1970; French-Spanish-Italian
THE DISCREET CHARM OF THE BOURGEOISE
20th Century-Fox; 1972; French
THE PHANTOM OF LIBERTE
20th Century-Fox; 1974; French
THAT OBSCURE OBJECT OF DESIRE
First Artists; 1977; French

Burge, Stuart
b. January 15, 1918
Brentwood, England
Contact:
British Film Institute
127 Charing Cross Road
London W.C. 2, England
01-437-4355

THERE WAS A CROOKED MAN
United Artists; 1962; British
UNCLE VANYA
Arthur Cantor; 1963; British
OTHELLO
Warner Brothers; 1965; British
THE MIKADO
Warner Brothers; 1967; British
JULIUS CAESAR
American International; 1971; British

Burke, Martyn
Business:
113 N. San Vicente Blvd.
Beverly Hills, CA 90211
(213) 655-4115
Agent:
I.C.M.
New York City
(212) 556-5600

THE CLOWN MURDERS
Canadian
POWER PLAY
1978; Canadian
THE LAST CHASE
Crown International; 1981; Canadian

Burrows, Jim
Agent:
Bob Broder
Hollywood
(213) 274-8291

MORE THAN FRIENDS
Reiner-Mishkin Productions/Columbia TV; telefeature; 1978
PARTNERS
Paramount; 1981

Butler, Robert
Agent:
I.C.M.
Hollywood
(213) 550-4273

THE COMPUTER WORE TENNIS SHOES
Buena Vista; 1970
THE BAREFOOT EXECUTIVE
Buena Vista; 1971
SCANDALOUS JOHN
Buena Vista; 1971
DEATH TAKES A HOLIDAY
Universal TV; telefeature; 1971
NOW YOU SEE HIM, NOW YOU DON'T
Buena Vista; 1972
THE BLUE KNIGHT
Lorimar Productions; telefeature; 1973
THE ULTIMATE THRILL
General Cinema; 1974
STRANGE NEW WORLD
Warner Brothers TV; telefeature; 1975
DARK VICTORY
Universal TV; telefeature; 1976
JAMES DEAN
The Jozak Company; telefeature; 1976
MAYDAY AT 40,000 FEET
Andrew J. Fenady Associates/Warner Brothers TV; telefeature; 1976
IN THE GLITTER PALACE
The Writer's Company/Colum-ia TV; telefeature; 1977
HOT LEAD AND COLD FEET
Buena Vista; 1978
A QUESTION OF GUILT
Lorimar Productions; telefeature; 1978
LACY AND THE MISSISSIPPI QUEEN
Lawrence Gordon Productions/Paramount TV; telefeature; 1978
NIGHT OF THE JUGGLER
Columbia; 1980
UNDERGROUND ACES
Filmways; 1981

Byrum, John
Agent:
William Morris Agency
Beverly Hills
(213) 274-7451

INSERTS
United Artists; 1976; British
HEART BEAT
Orion Pictures/Warner Brothers; 1980

Caan, James
b. March 26, 1939
Bronx, New York
Business Manager:
Licker & Pines
Beverly Hills
(213) 858-1276

HIDE IN PLAIN SIGHT
M-G-M/United Artists; 1980

Cacoyannis, Michael
b. June 11, 1922
Cyprus
Contact:
Greek Film Center
Panepistimiou Street
Athens 10, Greece

WINDFALL IN ATHENS
Audio Brandon; 1953; Greek
STELLA
Milas Films; 1955; Greek
THE FINAL LIE
Finos Films; 1958; Greek
OUR LAST SPRING
Cacoyannis; 1959; Greek
A GIRL IN BLACK
Kingsley International; 1959; Greek
THE WASTREL
Lux/Tiberia; 1960; Greek
ELECTRA
Lopert; 1962; Greek
ZORBA THE GREEK
International Classics; 1964; Greek
THE DAY THE FISH CAME OUT
20th Century-Fox; 1967; British-Greek
THE TROJAN WOMEN
Cinerama Releasing Corporation; 1971; U.S.-Greek
THE STORY OF JACOB AND JOSEPH
Screen Gems/Columbia TV; telefeature; 1974
ATTILA '74
1975; Greek
IPHIGENIA
Cinema 5; 1977; Greek

Caffey, Michael
Agent:
Shapiro-Lichtman Agency
Los Angeles
(213) 557-2244

SEVEN IN DARKNESS
Paramount TV; telefeature; 1969
THE SILENT GUN
Paramount TV; telefeature; 1969
THE DEVIL AND MISS SARAH
Universal TV; telefeature; 1971
THE HANGED MAN
Fenady Associates/Bing Crosby Productions; telefeature; 1974

Cammell, Donald
Agent:
William Morris Agency
Beverly Hills
(213) 274-7451

PERFORMANCE
co-director with Nicolas Roeg; Warner Brothers; 1970; British
DEMON SEED
M-G-M/United Artists; 1977

Camp, Joe
b. 1940
Dallas, Texas
Business:
Mulberry Square Productions
10300 N. Central Expressway
Dallas, Texas 75231
(214) 369-2430

BENJI
Mulberry Square; 1974
HAWMPS
Mulberry Square; 1976
FOR THE LOVE OF BENJI
Mulberry Square; 1978
THE DOUBLE McGUFFIN
Mulberry Square; 1979
OH HEAVENLY DOG
20th Century-Fox; 1980

Campbell, Norman
Home:
20 George Henry Blvd.
Willowdale, Ontario
Canada M2J 1E2
(416) 494-8576
Agent:
I.C.M.
Hollywood
(213) 550-4000

THE MAGIC SHOW
Movie Magic Productions; 1981; Canadian

Campus, Michael
Agent:
Paul Kohner Agency
Los Angeles
(213) 55--1060

Z.P.G.
  Paramount; 1972
THE MACK
  Cinerama Releasing Corporation; 1973
THE EDUCATION OF SONNY CARSON
  Paramount; 1974
THE PASSOVER PLOT
  Atlas; 1977; U.S.-Israeli

Capra, Frank
b. May 18, 1897
Palermo, Sicily
Home:
P.O. Box 98
La Quinta, CA 92253

TRAMP TRAMP TRAMP
  co-director with Harry Edwards; First National; 1926
THE STRONG MAN
  First National; 1926
LONG PANTS
  First National; 1927
FOR THE LOVE OF MIKE
  1927
THAT CERTAIN THING
  1928
SO THIS IS LOVE
  1928
THE MATINEE IDOL
  1928
THE WAY OF THE STRONG
  1928
SAY IT WITH SABLES
  1928
SUBMARINE
  1928
THE POWER OF THE PRESS
  1928
THE YOUNGER GENERATION
  1929
THE DONOVAN AFFAIR
  1929
FLIGHT
  Columbia; 1929
LADIES OF LEISURE
  Columbia; 1930
RAIN OR SHINE
  Columbia; 1930
DIRIGIBLE
  Columbia; 1931
THE MIRACLE WOMAN
  Columbia; 1931
PLATINUM BLONDE
  Columbia; 1931
FORBIDDEN
  Columbia; 1932
AMERICAN MADNESS
  Columbia; 1932
THE BITTER TEA OF GENERAL YEN
  Columbia; 1933
LADY FOR A DAY
  Columbia; 1933
IT HAPPENED ONE NIGHT
  Columbia; 1934
BROADWAY BILL
  Columbia; 1934
MR. DEEDS GOES TO TOWN
  Columbia; 1936
LOST HORIZON
  Columbia; 1937
YOU CAN'T TAKE IT WITH YOU
  Columbia; 1938
MR. SMITH GOES TO WASHINGTON
  Columbia; 1939
MEET JOHN DOE
  Warner Brothers; 1941
PRELUDE TO WAR
  1942
THE NAZIS STRIKE
  co-director with Anatole Litvak; 1942

continued

Capra, Frank
continued

DIVIDE AND CONQUER
co-director with Anatole Litvak; 1943
BATTLE OF BRITAIN
co-director; 1943
BATTLE OF CHINA
co-director with Anatole Litvak; 1943
THE NEGRO SOLDIER
1944
TUNISIAN VICTORY
co-director with Roy Boulting; Army Film Unit; 1944; British
ARSENIC AND OLD LACE
Warner Brothers; 1944
KNOW YOUR ENEMY: JAPAN
co-director with Joris Ivens; 1945
TWO DOWN AND ONE TO GO
1945
IT'S A WONDERFUL LIFE
RKO Radio; 1946
STATE OF THE UNION
M-G-M; 1948
RIDING HIGH
Paramount; 1950
HERE COMES THE GROOM
Paramount; 1951
A HOLE IN THE HEAD
United Artists; 1959
POCKETFUL OF MIRACLES
United Artists; 1961

Cardiff, Jack

b. September 18, 1914
Yarmouth, England
Contact:
British Film Institute
127 Charing Cross Road
London W.C. 2, England
01-437-4355

WEB OF EVIDENCE (Beyond This Place)
Allied Artists; 1959; British
INTENT TO KILL
20th Century-Fox; 1959; British
HOLIDAY IN SPAIN
1960; British
SCENE OF MYSTERY
Todd; 1960; British
SONS AND LOVERS
20th Century-Fox; 1960; British
MY GEISHA
Paramount; 1962
THE LION
20th Century-Fox; 1962; British
THE LONG SHIPS
Columbia; 1964; British-Yugoslavian
YOUNG CASSIDY
M-G-M; 1965; British
THE LIQUIDATOR
M-G-M; 1966; British
DARK OF THE SUN (The Mercenaries)
M-G-M; 1968; British
THE GIRL ON A MOTORCYCLE (Naked Under Leather)
Claridge; 1968; British-French
PENNY GOLD
Scotia-Barber; 1973; British
THE MUTATIONS
Columbia; 1974; British

Cardos, John "Bud"

Home:
19116 Enadia Way
Reseda, CA 91335
(213) 434-4077
Agent:
Film Artists Management
Hollywood
(213) 656-7590

SOUL SOLDIER (The Red, White and Black)
Fanfare; 1972
KINGDOM OF THE SPIDERS
Dimension; 1977
THE DARK
Film Ventures International; 1979
THE DAY TIME ENDED
Compass International; 1979

Carlino, Lewis John

Agent:
Creative Artists Agency
Los Angeles
(213) 277-4545

THE SAILOR WHO FELL FROM GRACE WITH THE SEA
Avco Embassy; 1976; British
THE GREAT SANTINI (The Ace)
Orion Pictures/Warner Brothers; 1980

Carpenter, John
Agent:
Phil Gersh Agency
Beverly Hills
(213) 274-6611

DARK STAR
Jack H. Harris Enterprises; 1974
ASSAULT ON PRECINCT 13
Turtle Releasing Corporation; 1976
HALLOWEEN
Compass International; 1978
SOMEONE IS WATCHING ME
Warner Brothers TV; telefeature; 1978
ELVIS
Dick Clark Productions; telefeature; 1979
THE FOG
Avco Embassy; 1980
ESCAPE FROM NEW YORK
Avco Embassy; 1981
THE THING
Universal; 1982

Carradine, David
b. December 8, 1936
Hollywood, California

YOU AND ME
Filmmakers International; 1975
AMERICANA
David Carradine Studios; 1981

Carreras, Michael
b. 1927
London, England
Contact:
British Film Institute
127 Charing Cross Road
London W.C. 2, England
01-437-4355

THE STEEL BAYONET
United Artists; 1958; British
PASSPORT TO CHINA (Visa to Canton)
Columbia; 1961; British
THE SAVAGE GUNS
M-G-M; 1962; Spanish-U.S.
MANIAC
Columbia; 1963; British
WHAT A CRAZY WORLD
Warner-Pathe; 1963; British
THE CURSE OF THE MUMMY'S TOMB
Columbia; 1965; British
PREHISTORIC WOMEN
20th Century-Fox; 1967; British
THE LOST CONTINENT
20th Century-Fox; 1968; British
CALL HIM MR. SHATTER
Avco Embassy; 1975; British-Hong Kong

Carter, Peter
Agent:
Film Artists Management
Los Angeles
(213) 656-7590

THE ROWDYMAN
Crawley; 1973; Canadian
RITUALS
Day & Date International; 1978; Canadian
HIGH-BALLIN'
American International; 1978; Canadian
A MAN CALLED INTREPID
Lorimar Productions/Astral Bellevue Pathe Ltd.; telefeature; 1979; U.S.-Canadian
JACK LONDON'S KLONDIKE FEVER
World Entertainment Corporation; 1980; Canadian
THE INTRUDER WITHIN
Furia-Oringer Productions; telefeature; 1981
HIGHPOINT
1981; Canadian

Carver, Steve
Home:
1010 Pacific Avenue
Venice, CA 90291
(213) 296-9905
Agent:
Charter Management
Hollywood
(213) 278-1690

THE ARENA
New World; 1974
BIG BAD MAMA
New World; 1974
CAPONE
20th Century-Fox; 1975
DRUM
United Artists; 1976

continued

Carver, Steve
continued

FAST CHARLIE...THE MOONBEAM RIDER
Universal; 1979
STEEL (Look Down and Die)
World Northal; 1980
AN EYE FOR AN EYE
Avco Embassy; 1981

Cassavetes, John
b. December 9, 1929
New York, New York
Contact:
Directors Guild of America
Los Angeles
(213) 656-1220

SHADOWS
Lion International; 1961
TOO LATE BLUES
Paramount; 1962
A CHILD IS WAITING
United Artists; 1963
FACES
Continental; 1968
HUSBANDS
Columbia; 1970
MINNIE AND MOSKOWITZ
Universal; 1971
A WOMAN UNDER THE INFLUENCE
Faces International; 1974
THE KILLING OF A CHINESE BOOKIE
Faces International; 1976
OPENING NIGHT
Faces International; 1979
GLORIA
Columbia; 1980

Cates, Gilbert
Business:
The Cates Brothers Co.
9200 Sunset Boulevard
Los Angeles, CA 90069
(213) 273-7773
Agent:
Creative Artists Agency
Los Angeles
(213) 277-4545

RINGS AROUND THE WORLD
Columbia; 1967
I NEVER SANG FOR MY FATHER
Columbia; 1970
TO ALL MY FRIENDS ON SHORE
Jemmin & Jamel Productions; telefeature; 1972
SUMMER WISHES, WINTER DREAMS
Columbia; 1973
THE AFFAIR
Spelling-Goldberg Productions;telefeature; 1973
ONE SUMMER LOVE (Dragonfly)
American International; 1976
JOHNNY, WE HARDLY KNEW YE
Talent Associates/Jamel Productions;
telefeature; 1977
THE PROMISE
Universal; 1979
THE LAST MARRIED COUPLE IN AMERICA
Universal; 1980
OH, GOD! BOOK II
Warner Brothers; 1980

Cates, Joseph
Business:
The Cates Brothers Co.
(See Above)

GIRL OF THE NIGHT
Warner Brothers; 1960
WHO KILLED TEDDY BEAR?
Magna; 1965
FAT SPY
Magna; 1966

Cavani, Liliana
b. January 12, 1936
Capri, Italy
Contact:
Minister of Tourism
Via Della Ferratella
No. 51
00184 Rome, Italy
06-7732

FRANCIS OF ASSISI
1966; telefeature; Italian
GALILEO
1968; Italian-Bulgarian
THE CANNIBALS
1969; Italian
L'OSPITE
1971; Italian
THE NIGHT PORTER
Avco Embassy; 1974; Italian
BEYOND EVIL
1978; Italian
LA PELLE
Gaumont; 1981; Italian-French

Cellan-Jones, James

Home:
19 Cumberland Road
Kew, Surrey
England 13731
01-940-8742
Agent:
William Morris Agency
Beverly Hills
(213) 274-7451

THE NELSON AFFAIR
Universal; 1973; British
CAESAR AND CLEOPATRA
NBC-TV; telefeature; 1976; U.S.-British
THE DAY CHRIST DIED
Martin Manulis Productions/20th Century-Fox TV; telefeature; 1980

Chabrol, Claude

b. June 24, 1930
Paris, France
Contact:
French Film Office
745 Fifth Avenue
New York, N.Y. 10151
(212) 832-8860

LE BEAU SERGE
1958; French
THE COUSINS
Films Around the World; 1959; French
A DOUBLE TOUR
1959; French
LES BONNES FEMMES
1960; French
LES GODELUREAUX
1961; French
SEVEN CAPITAL SINS
co-director; Embassy; 1962; French-Italian
THE THIRD LOVER
1962; French-Italian
OPHELIA
New Line Cinema; 1962; French-Italian
LANDRU
Embassy; 1963; French-Italian
THE BEAUTIFUL SWINDLERS
co-director; 1964; French-Italian-Japanese
THE TIGER LIKES FRESH BLOOD
1964; French-Italian
SIX IN PARIS
co-director; 1964; French
MARIE-CHANTAL CONTRE LE DOCTEUR KAH
1965; French-Italian-Moroccan
AN ORCHID FOR THE TIGER
1965; French-Spanish-Italian
LA LIGNE DE DEMARCATION
1966; French
THE CHAMPAGNE MURDERS
Universal; 1967; French
THE ROAD TO CORINTH
1967; French-Italian-West German
LES BICHES
VGC; 1968; French-Italian
LA FEMME INFIDELE
Allied Artists; 1968; French-Italian
THIS MAN MUST DIE
Allied Artists; 1969; French-Italian
LE BOUCHER
Cinerama Releasing Corporation; 1969; French-Italian
LA RUPTURE
New Line Cinema; 1970; French-Italian-Belgian
JUST BEFORE NIGHTFALL
Libra Films; 1971; French-Italian
TEN DAYS' WONDER
Levitt-Pickman; 1971; French
DOCTEUR POPAUL
1972; French-Italian
WEDDING IN BLOOD
New Line Cinema; 1973; French-Italian
DE GREY - LE BANC DE DESOLATION
telefeature; 1973; French
THE NADA GANG (Nada)
New Line Cinema; 1974; French-Italian
UNE PARTIE DE PLAISIR
Joseph Green Pictures; 1975; French
DIRTY HANDS
New Line Cinema; 1975; French-Italian-West German
THE TWIST
1975; French

continued

Chabrol, Claude
continued

FOLIES BOURGEOISES
1976; French
ALICE OR THE LAST ESCAPADE
Filmel-PHPG; 1977; French
LES LIENS DE SANG
1978; French
VIOLETTE
Gaumont/New Yorker; 1978; French
SPLINTERED
1980; French
HORSE OF PRIDE
Planfilm; 1980; French

Chaffey, Don
b. August 5, 1917
England
Home:
7020 La Presa
Los Angeles, CA 90068
Agent:
Contemporary-Korman Artists
Beverly Hills
(213) 278-8250

THE MYSTERIOUS POACHER
General Film Distributors; 1950; British
THE CASE OF THE MISSING SCENE
General Film Distributors; 1951; British
SKID KIDS
Associated British Film Distributors/Children's Film Foundation; 1953; British
TIME IS MY ENEMY
Independent Film Distributors; 1954; British
THE SECRET TENT
British Lion; 1956; British
THE GIRL IN THE PICTURE
Eros; 1957; British
THE FLESH IS WEAK
DCA; 1957; British
A QUESTION OF ADULTERY
Eros; 1958; British
THE MAN UPSTAIRS
Kingsley International; 1958; British
DANGER WITHIN
British Lion; 1959; British
DENTIST IN THE CHAIR
Ajay; 1960; British
LIES MY FATHER TOLD ME
Eire; 1960; British
NEARLY A NASTY ACCIDENT
Brittania; 1961; British
GREYFRIARS BOBBY
Buena Vista; 1961; U.S.-British
A MATTER OF WHO
Herts Lion; 1962; British
THE PRINCE AND THE PAUPER
Buena Vista; 1962; U.S.-British
THE WEBSTER BOY
RFI; 1963; British
THE HORSE WITHOUT A HEAD
Buena Vista; 1963; British
JASON AND THE ARGONAUTS
Columbia; 1963; British
THEY ALL DIED LAUGHING (A Jolly Bad Fellow)
Continental; 1963; British
THE THREE LIVES OF THOMASINA
Buena Vista; 1963; British-U.S.
THE CROOKED ROAD
7 Arts; 1965; British-Yugoslavian
ONE MILLION YEARS B.C.
20th Century-Fox; 1967; British
THE VIKING QUEEN
American International; 1967; British
A TWIST OF SAND
United Artists; 1968; British
CREATURES THE WORLD FORGOT
Columbia; 1971; British
CLINIC XCLUSIVE
Doverton; 1972; British
CHARLEY-ONE-EYE
Paramount; 1973; British
THE TERROR OF SHEBA (Persecution)
Blueberry Hill; 1974; British
RIDE A WILD PONY
Buena Vista; 1976; U.S.-Australian

continued

Chaffey, Don
continued

PETE'S DRAGON
  Buena Vista; 1977
THE MAGIC OF LASSIE
  International Picture Show; 1978
THE GIFT OF LOVE
  Osmond Productions; telefeature; 1978
C.H.O.M.P.S.
  American International; 1979
CASINO
  Trellis Productions/Aaron Spelling Productions; telefeature; 1980

Chambers, Everett
Agent:
William Morris Agency
Beverly Hills
(213) 274-7451

RUN ACROSS THE RIVER
  Omat Corporation; 1959
THE LOLLIPOP COVER
  Continental; 1964

Chomsky, Marvin J.
Agent:
F.A.M.E.
Hollywood
(213) 656-7590
Business Manager:
Plant Cohen & Co.
Beverly Hills
(213) 278-6171

ASSAULT ON THE WAYNE
  Paramount TV; telefeature; 1971
MONGO'S BACK IN TOWN
  Bob Banner Associates; telefeature; 1971
EVEL KNIEVEL
  Fanfare; 1972
FIREBALL FORWARD
  20th Century-Fox TV; telefeature; 1972
FAMILY FLIGHT
  Universal TV; telefeature; 1972
FEMALE ARTILLERY
  Universal TV; telefeature; 1973
THE MAGICIAN
  Paramount TV; telefeature; 1973
MRS. SUNDANCE
  20th Century-Fox TV; telefeature; 1974
THE FBI STORY: THE FBI VERSUS ALVIN KARPIS, PUBLIC ENEMY NUMBER ONE
  QM Productions/Warner Brothers TV; telefeature; 1974
ATTACK ON TERROR: THE FBI VS. THE KLU KLUX KLAN
  QM Productions; telefeature; 1975
MACKINTOSH AND T.J.
  Penland; 1975
LIVE A LITTLE, STEAL A LOT (Murph the Surf)
  American International; 1975
KATE McSHANE
  Paramount TV; telefeature; 1975
BRINK'S: THE GREAT ROBBERY
  QM Productions/Warner Brothers TV; telefeature; 1976
A MATTER OF WIFE...AND DEATH
  Columbia TV; telefeature; 1976
LAW AND ORDER
  Paramount TV; telefeature; 1976
VICTORY AT ENTEBBE
  Wolper Productions; telefeature; 1976
ROOTS
  co-director with David Greene, John Erman & Gilbert Moses; Wolper Productions; television mini-series; 1977
LITTLE LADIES OF THE NIGHT
  Spelling-Goldberg Productions; telefeature; 1977
DANGER IN PARADISE
  Filmways; telefeature; 1977
HOLOCAUST
  Titus Productions; television mini-series; 1978
GOOD LUCK, MISS WYCKOFF
  Bel Air/Gradison; 1979
HOLLOW IMAGE
  Titus Productions; telefeature; 1979
ATTICA
  ABC Circle Films; telefeature; 1980

continued

Chomsky, Marvin J.
continued

KING CRAB
Titus Productions; telefeature; 1980
EVITA PERON
Hartwest Productions/Zephyr Productions; telefeature; 1981

Chong, Thomas
Contact:
Directors Guild of America
Los Angeles
(213) 656-1220

THE NEXT CHEECH & CHONG MOVIE
Universal; 1980
CHEECH & CHONG'S NICE DREAMS
Columbia; 1981

Chudnow, Byron
Home:
10551 Rochester Avenue
Los Angeles, CA 90024
(213) GR. 4-3856

THE DOBERMAN GANG
Dimension; 1973
THE DARING DOBERMANS
Dimension; 1973
THE AMAZING DOBERMANS
Golden; 1976

Cimber, Matt

SINGLE ROOM FURNISHED
Crown International; 1968
CALLIOPE
Moonstone; 1971
THE BLACK SIX
Cinemation; 1974
THE CANDY TANGERINE MAN
Moonstone; 1975
GEMINI AFFAIR
Moonstone; 1975
LADY COCOA
Dimension; 1975
THE WITCH WHO CAME FROM THE SEA
Moonstone; 1976
SEVEN GRAVES FOR ROGAN
1981
BUTTERFLY
Analysis; 1981
FAKE OUT
Par-Par; 1982

Cimino, Michael
b. 1943
Agent:
William Morris Agency
Beverly Hills
(213) 274-7451
Attorney:
Bruce Ramer
Beverly Hills
(213) 276-8087

THUNDERBOLT AND LIGHTFOOT
United Artists; 1974
THE DEER HUNTER
Universal; 1978
HEAVEN'S GATE
United Artists; 1980

Ciupka, Richard
Home:
71 Cornwall Street
Quebec, Canada
(514) 738-9996

CURTAINS
Simcon; 1981; Canadian

Clark, Bob
Business Manager:
Harold Cohen
New York City
(212) 550-0570

DEATHDREAM
1972
CHILDREN SHOULDN'T PLAY WITH DEAD THINGS
Gemini Film; 1972
DEAD OF NIGHT
Europix International; 1974
BLACK CHRISTMAS
Warner Brothers; 1975; Canadian

continued

Clark, Bob
continued

BREAKING POINT
20th Century-Fox; 1976; Canadian
MURDER BY DECREE
Avco Em-assy; 1979; Canadian-British
TRIBUTE
20th Century-Fox; 1980; U.S.-Canadian
PORKY'S
20th Century-Fox; 1981; U.S.-Canadian

Clark, Bruce

NAKED ANGELS
Favorite; 1969
THE SKI BUM
Avco Embassy; 1971
HAMMER
United Artists; 1972
GALAXY OF TERROR
New World; 1981

Clark, Frank C.

BEYOND THE REEF
Universal; 1981

Clark, Greydon

TOM
Four Star International; 1973
BLACK SHAMPOO
Dimension; 1976
THE BAD BUNCH
Dimension; 1976
SATAN'S CHEERLEADERS
World Amusement; 1977
HI-RIDERS
Dimension; 1978
ANGELS BRIGADE
Arista; 1980
WITHOUT WARNING
Filmways; 1980
THE RETURN
1981
WACKO
World Amusement; 1981

Clark, James B.
Home:
10051-5 Valley Circle Blvd.
Chatsworth, CA 91311
(213) 998-0962
Business Manager:
Larry Nash
Northridge, CA
(213) 993-8522

UNDER FIRE
20th Century-Fox; 1957
SIERRA BARON
20th Century-Fox; 1958
VILLA
20th Century-Fox; 1958
THE SAD HORSE
20th Century-Fox; 1959
A DOG OF FLANDERS
20th Century-Fox; 1960
ONE FOOT IN HELL
20th Century-Fox; 1960
THE BIG SHOW
20th Century-Fox; 1961; U.S.-West German
MISTY
20th Century-Fox; 1961
FLIPPER
M-G-M; 1963
DRUMS OF AFRICA
M-G-M; 1963
ISLAND OF THE BLUE DOLPHINS
20th Century-Fox; 1964
AND NOW MIGUEL
Paramount; 1966
MY SIDE OF THE MOUNTAIN
Paramount; 1969
THE LITTLE ARK
National General; 1972

Clark, Peter

KAVIK: THE WOLF DOG
Pantheon/Stanley Chase/Joan Sloan Productions; telefeature; 1980

Clark, Ron

GAS
Paramount; 1981; Canadian
COMICS
Filmplan; 1981; Canadian

Clark, Shirley

THE CONNECTION
Films Around the World; 1962
THE COOL WORLD
Cinema 5; 1964
PORTRAIT OF JASON
Film-Makers; 1967

Clavell, James
b. October 10, 1924
Sydney, Australia
Agent:
Creative Artists Agency
Los Angeles
(213) 277-4545

FIVE GATES TO HELL
20th Century-Fox; 1959
WALK LIKE A DRAGON
Paramount; 1960
TO SIR, WITH LOVE
Columbia; 1967; British
WHERE'S JACK?
Paramount; 1969; British
THE LAST VALLEY
Cinerama Releasing Corporation; 1971; British

Claxton, William F.
Home:
1065 Napoli Drive
Pacific Palisades, CA 90272
Agent:
Contemporary-Korman Artists
Beverly Hills
(213) 278-8250

HALF PAST MIDNIGHT
20th Century-Fox; 1948
TUCSON
20th Century-Fox; 1949
ALL THAT I HAVE
Family Films; 1951
STAGECOACH TO FURY
20th Century-Fox; 1956
THE QUIET GUN
20th Century-Fox; 1957
YOUNG AND DANGEROUS
20th Century-Fox; 1957
ROCKABILLY BABY
20th Century-Fox; 1957
GOD IS MY PARTNER
20th Century-Fox; 1957
DESIRE IN THE DUST
20th Century-Fox; 1960
YOUNG JESSE JAMES
20th Century-Fox; 1960
LAW OF THE LAWLESS
Paramount; 1963
STAGE TO THUNDER ROCK
Paramount; 1964
NIGHT OF THE LEPUS
M-G-M; 1972

Clayton, Jack
b. 1921
Brighton, England
Home:
Heron's Flight
Highfield Park
Marlow, Bucks
England
Agent:
William Morris Agency
Beverly Hills
(213) 274-7451

ROOM AT THE TOP
Continental; 1959; British
THE INNOCENTS
20th Century-Fox; 1962; British
THE PUMPKIN EATER
Royal International; 1964; British
OUR MOTHER'S HOUSE
M-G-M; 1967; British
THE GREAT GATSBY
Paramount; 1974
SOMETHING WICKED THIS WAY COMES
Buena Vista; 1982

Clegg, Tom
Contact:
British Film Institute
127 Charing Cross Road
London W.C. 2, England
01-437-4355

SWEENEY 2
EMI; 1978; British
McVICAR
Crown International; 1981; British

Clement, Dick
b. September 5, 1937
West Cliff-on-Sea, England
Home:
9700 Yoakum Drive
Beverly Hills, CA 90210
(213) 276-4916

OTLEY
Columbia; 1969; British
A SEVERED HEAD
Columbia; 1971; British
CATCH ME A SPY
1971; British
KEEP YOUR FINGERS CROSSED
1971; British
PORRIDGE
ITC; 1979; British

Clement, Rene
b. March 18, 1913
Bordeaux, France
Contact:
French Film Office
745 Fifth Avenue
New York, N.Y. 10151
(212) 832-8860

BATTLE OF THE RAILS
1946; French
MR. ORCHID
1946; French
THE DAMNED
1947; French
THE WALLS OF MALAPAGA
Films International of America; 1949; Italian-French
LE CHATEAU DE VERRE
1950; French-Italian
FORBIDDEN GAMES
Times Film Corporation; 1952; French
LOVERS, HAPPY LOVERS! (Knave of Hearts)
20th Century-Fox; 1954; French-British
GERVAISE
Continental; 1956; French
THIS ANGRY AGE
Columbia; 1958; Italian-French
PURPLE NOON
Times Film Corporation; 1960; French-Italian
QUELLE JOIE DE VIVRE
1961; French-Italian
THE DAY AND THE HOUR
M-G-M; 1962; French-Italian
JOY HOUSE
M-G-M; 1964; French
IS PARIS BURNING?
Paramount; 1966; French-U.S.
RIDER ON THE RAIN
Avco Embassy; 1970; French-Italian
THE DEADLY TRAP
National General; 1971; French-Italian
...AND HOPE TO DIE
20th Century-Fox; 1972; French
LA BABY-SITTER
1975; Italian-French-German

Clifford, Graeme
Contact:
Directors Guild of America
Los Angeles
(213) 656-1220

FRANCES
AFD/Universal; 1982

Clifton, Peter
Contact:
British Film Institute
127 Charing Cross Road
London W.C. 2, England
01-437-4355

POPCORN
Sherpix; 1969; U.S.-Australian
SUPERSTARS IN FILM CONCERT
National Cinema; 1971; British
THE SONG REMAINS THE SAME
co-director with Joe Massot; Warner Brothers; 1976; British
THE LONDON ROCK & ROLL SHOW
1978; British
ROCK CITY
Columbia; 1981; British; filmed in 1974

Clouse, Robert
Agent:
The Paul Kohner Agency
Hollywood
(213) 550-1060

DARKER THAN AMBER
National General; 1970
DREAMS OF GLASS
Universal; 1970
ENTER THE DRAGON
Warner Brothers; 1973; U.S.-Hong Kong
BLACK BELT JONES
Warner Brothers; 1974
GOLDEN NEEDLES
American International; 1974
THE ULTIMATE WARRIOR
Warner Brothers; 1976
THE AMSTERDAM KILL
Columbia; 1978; U.S.-Hong Kong
THE PACK
Warner Brothers; 1978
GAME OF DEATH
Columbia; 1979; U.S.-Hong Kong
THE OMEGA CONNECTION
NBC-TV; telefeature; 1979
THE KIDS WHO KNEW TOO MUCH
Walt Disney Productions; telefeature; 1980
THE BIG BRAWL
Warner Brothers; 1980
FORCE: FIVE
American Cinema; 1981

Coates, Lewis

STARCRASH
New World; 1979

Coe, Peter

LOCK UP YOUR DAUGHTERS
Columbia; 1969; British

Cohen, Annette
Home:
77 Roxborough Drive
Toronto, Ontario M4W 1X2
Canada
(416) 364-4193/920-3745

LOVE
co-director with Nancy Dowd, Liv Ullmann & Mai Zetterling; Coup Films; 1981; Canadian

Cohen, Larry
Contact:
Directors Guild of America
New York City
(212) 581-0370

BONE
Jack H. Harris Enterprises; 1972
BLACK CAESAR
American International; 1973
HELL UP IN HARLEM
American International; 1973
IT'S ALIVE
Warner Brothers; 1974
DEMON (God Told Me To)
New World; 1977
IT LIVES AGAIN
Warner Brothers; 1978
THE PRIVATE FILES OF J. EDGAR HOOVER
American International; 1978
FULL MOON HIGH
Filmways; 1981
THE SERPENT
Larco; 1982

Cohen, Rob
Home:
1383 Miller Place
Los Angeles, CA 90069
(213) 654-6289
Agent:
I.C.M.
Hollywood
(213) 550-4333

A SMALL CIRCLE OF FRIENDS
United Artists; 1980

Colla, Richard A.

Agent:
William Morris Agency
Beverly Hills
(213) 274-7451

THE WHOLE WORLD IS WATCHING
Universal TV; telefeature; 1969
ZIGZAG
M-G-M; 1970
McCLOUD: WHO KILLED MISS U.S.A.?
Universal TV; telefeature; 1970
THE OTHER MAN
Universal TV; telefeature; 1970
SARGE: THE BADGE OR THE CROSS
Universal TV; telefeature; 1971
THE PRIEST KILLER
Universal TV; telefeature; 1971
FUZZ
United Artists; 1972
TENAFLY
Universal TV; telefeature; 1973
THE QUESTOR TAPES
Universal TV; telefeature; 1974
LIVE AGAIN, DIE AGAIN
Universal TV; telefeature; 1974
THE TRIBE
Universal TV; telefeature; 1974
THE UFO INCIDENT
Universal TV; telefeature; 1975
OLLY OLLY OXEN FREE
Sanrio; 1978
BATTLESTAR GALACTICA
Universal; 1979
DON'T LOOK BACK
TBA Productions/Satie Productions/TRISEME; telefeature; 1981

Collier, James F.

Home:
11345 Brill Drive
Studio City, CA 91604

FOR PETE'S SAKE!
Worldwide; 1966
HIS LAND
Worldwide; 1967
TWO A PENNY
Worldwide; 1970; British
CATCH A PEBBLE
Worldwide; 1971; British
TIME TO RUN
Worldwide; 1972
THE HIDING PLACE
Worldwide; 1975
JONI
Worldwide; 1980

Collins, Robert

Agent:
Phil Gersh Agency
Beverly Hills
(213) 274-6611

SERPICO: THE DEADLY GAME
Dino De Laurentiis Productions/Paramount TV; telefeature; 1976
THE LIFE AND ASSASSINATION OF THE KINGFISH
Tomorrow Entertainment; telefeature; 1977
WALK PROUD
Universal; 1979
GIDEON'S TRUMPET
Gideon Productions; telefeature; 1980
SAVAGE HARVEST
20th Century-Fox; 1981
OUR FAMILY BUSINESS
Lorimar Productions; telefeature; 1981

Compton, Richard

Agent:
Agency for the Performing Arts
Los Angeles
(213) 273-0744
Business Manager:
Fred Altman
Beverly Hills
(213) 278-4201

ANGELS DIE HARD
New World; 1970
WELCOME HOME, SOLDIER BOYS
20th Century-Fox; 1972
MACON COUNTY LINE
American International; 1974
RETURN TO MACON COUNTY
American International; 1975
MANIAC
New World; 1977

continued

Compton, Richard
continued

DEADMAN'S CURVE
Roger Gimbel Productions/EMI TV; telefeature; 1978
RAVAGERS
Columbia; 1979
WILD TIMES
Metromedia Producers Corporation/Rattlesnake Productions; telefeature; 1980

Connor, Kevin
b. 1940
England
Contact:
Directors Guild of America
Los Angeles
(213) 656-1220

FROM BEYOND THE GRAVE
Howard Mahler; 1975; British
THE LAND THAT TIME FORGOT
American International; 1975; British
AT THE EARTH'S CORE
American International; 1976; British
DIRTY KNIGHTS' WORK (A Choice of Weapons)
Gamma III; 1976; British
THE PEOPLE THAT TIME FORGOT
American International; 1977; British
WARLORDS OF ATLANTIS
Columbia; 1978; British
ARABIAN ADVENTURE
AFD; 1979; British
MOTEL HELL
United Artists; 1980

Conrad, William
b. September 27, 1920
Louisville, Kentucky
Agent:
Creative Artists Agency
Los Angeles
(213) 277-4545

THE MAN FROM GALVESTON
Warner Brothers; 1964
TWO ON A GUILLOTINE
Warner Brothers; 1965
MY BLOOD RUNS COLD
Warner Brothers; 1965
BRAINSTORM
Warner Brothers; 1965
SIDE SHOW
Krofft Entertainment; telefeature; 1981

Conway, James L.

IN SEARCH OF NOAH'S ARK
Sunn Classic; 1976
THE LINCOLN CONSPIRACY
Sunn Classic; 1977
THE INCREDIBLE ROCKY MOUNTAIN RACE
Sunn Classic; telefeature; 1977
THE LAST OF THE MOHICANS
Sunn Classic; telefeature; 1977
BEYOND AND BACK
Sunn Classic; 1978
DONNER PASS: THE ROAD TO SURVIVAL
Sunn Classic; telefeature; 1978
GREATEST HEROES OF THE BIBLE
Sunn Classic; television mini-series; 1978
THE FALL OF THE HOUSE OF USHER
Sunn Classic; 1979
HANGAR 18
Sunn Classic; 1980
THE LEGEND OF SLEEPY HOLLOW
Sunn Classic; telefeature; 1980
EARTHBOUND
Taft International; 1981
NASHVILLE GRAB
Taft International; telefeature; 1981

Cook, Fielder
b. March 9, 1923
Atlanta, Georgia
Agent:
The Paul Kohner Agency
Los Angeles
(213) 550-1060

PATTERNS
United Artists; 1956
HOME IS THE HERO
Showcorporation; 1961; Irish
A BIG HAND FOR THE LITTLE LADY
Warner Brothers; 1966

continued

Cook, Fielder
continued

HOW TO SAVE A MARRIAGE AND RUIN YOUR LIFE
Columbia; 1968
PRUDENCE AND THE PILL
20th Century-Fox; 1968; British
SAM HILL: WHO KILLED THE MYSTERIOUS MR. FOSTER?
Universal TV; telefeature; 1971
GOODBYE, RAGGEDY ANN
Metromedia Producers Corporation; telefeature; 1971
THE HOMECOMING
Lorimar Productions; telefeature; 1971
EAGLE IN A CAGE
National General; 1972; British-Yugoslavian
MIRACLE ON 34TH STREET
20th Century-Fox TV; telefeature; 1973
FROM THE MIXED-UP FILES OF MRS. BASIL E. FRANKWEILER Cinema 5; 1973
THAT WAS THE WEST THAT WAS
Universal TV; telefeature; 1974
MILES TO GO BEFORE I SLEEP
Tomorrow Entertainment; telefeature; 1975
THE RIVALRY
NBC-TV; telefeature; 1975
VALLEY FORGE
NBC-TV; telefeature; 1975
BEAUTY AND THE BEAST
Palm Films Ltd.; telefeature; 1976; British
JUDGE HORTON AND THE SCOTTSBORO BOYS
Tomorrow Entertainment; telefeature; 1976
A LOVE AFFAIR: THE ELEANOR AND LOU GEHRIG STORY
Charles Fries Productions/Stonehenge Productions; telefeature; 1977
TOO FAR TO GO
Sea Cliff Productions; telefeature; 1979
I KNOW WHY THE CAGED BIRD SINGS
Tomorrow Entertainment; telefeature; 1979
GAUGUIN THE SAVAGE
Nephi Productions; telefeature; 1980
FAMILY REUNION
Creative Projects Inc./Columbia TV; telefeature; 1981

Cooke, Alan
Agent:
Phil Gersh Agency
Beverly Hills
(213) 274-6611

THE MIND OF MR. SOAMES
Columbia; 1970; British
THE HUNCHBACK OF NOTRE DAME
BBC-TV; telefeature; 1978; British

Cooper, Jackie
b. September 15, 1921
Los Angeles, California
Business:
Jackie Enterprises, Inc.
9621 Royalton Drive
Beverly Hills, CA 90210
Agent:
Creative Artists Agency
Los Angeles
(213) 277-4545

STAND UP AND BE COUNTED
Columbia; 1971
HAVING BABIES III
The Jozak Company/Paramount TV; telefeature; 1978
PERFECT GENTLEMEN
Paramount TV; telefeature; 1978
RAINBOW
Ten-Four Productions; telefeature; 1978
SEX AND THE SINGLE PARENT
Time-Life Productions; telefeature; 1979
MARATHON
Alan Landsburg Productions; telefeature; 1980
WHITE MAMA
Tomorrow Entertainment; telefeature; 1980
RODEO GIRL
Steckler Productions/Marble Arch Productions; telefeature; 1980
LEAVE 'EM LAUGHING
Julian Fowles Productions/Charles Fries Productions; telefeature; 1981

Cooper, Stuart
Contact:
British Film Institute
127 Charing Cross Road
London W.C. 2, England
01-437-4355

LITTLE MALCOLM AND HIS STRUGGLE AGAINST THE EUNUCHS
Multicetera Investments; 1974; British
OVERLORD
1975; British
THE DISAPPEARANCE
Levitt-Pickman; 1977; Canadian

Coppola, Francis Ford
b. April 7, 1939
Detroit, Michigan
Business:
Zoetrope Studios
1040 N. Las Palmas Avenue
Los Angeles, CA 90038
(213) 463-7191

TONIGHT FOR SURE
1961
DEMENTIA 13
American International; 1963
YOU'RE A BIG BOY NOW
7 Arts; 1966
FINIAN'S RAINBOW
Warner Brothers; 1968
THE RAIN PEOPLE
Warner Brothers; 1969
THE GODFATHER
Paramount; 1972
THE CONVERSATION
Paramount; 1974
THE GODFATHER, PART II
Paramount; 1974
APOCALYPSE NOW
United Artists; 1979
ONE FROM THE HEART
Paramount; 1981

Corea, Nicholas
Business:
Mad-Dog Productions
c/o Laura Lizer
3518 Cahuenga West
Hollywood, CA 90068

THE ARCHER: FUGITIVE FROM THE EMPIRE
Mad-Dog Productions/Universal TV; telefeature; 1981

Corman, Roger
b. April 5, 1926
Los Angeles, CA
Business:
New World Pictures
11600 San Vicente Blvd.
Los Angeles, CA 90049
(213) 820-6733

FIVE GUNS WEST
American International; 1955
THE APACHE WOMAN
American International; 1955
THE DAY THE WORLD ENDED
American International; 1956
SWAMP WOMAN
Woolner Brothers; 1956
THE OKLAHOMA WOMAN
American International; 1956
THE GUNSLINGER
ARC; 1956
IT CONQUERED THE WORLD
American International; 1956
NOT OF THIS EARTH
Allied Artists; 1957
THE UNDEAD
American International; 1957
NAKED PARADISE
American International; 1957
ATTACK OF THE CRAB MONSTERS
Allied Artists; 1957
ROCK ALL NIGHT
American International; 1957
TEENAGE DOLL
Allied Artists; 1957
CARNIVAL ROCK
Howco; 1957
SORORITY GIRL
American International; 1957
THE VIKING WOMEN AND THE SEA SERPENT
American International; 1957
WAR OF THE SATELLITES
Allied Artists; 1958

continued

Corman, Roger
continued

THE SHE GODS OF SHARK REEF
American International; 1958
MACHINE GUN KELLY
American International; 1958
TEENAGE CAVEMAN
American International; 1958
I, MOBSTER
20th Century-Fox; 1959
A BUCKET OF BLOOD
American International; 1959
THE WASP WOMAN
American International; 1959
SKI TROOP ATTACK
Filmgroup; 1960
THE HOUSE OF USHER
American International; 1960
THE LITTLE SHOP OF HORRORS
Filmgroup; 1960
THE LAST WOMAN ON EARTH
Filmgroup; 1960
CREATURE FROM THE HAUNTED SEA
Filmgroup; 1961
ATLAS
Filmgroup; 1961
THE PIT AND THE PENDULUM
American International; 1961
THE INTRUDER (I Hate Your Guts)
Pathe American; 1962
THE PREMATURE BURIAL
American International; 1962
TALES OF TERROR
American International; 1962
TOWER OF LONDON
United Artists; 1962
THE RAVEN
American International; 1963
THE TERROR
American International; 1963
"X" - THE MAN WITH THE X-RAY EYES
American International; 1963
THE HAUNTED PALACE
American International; 1963
THE YOUNG RACERS
American International; 1963
THE SECRET INVASION
United Artists; 1964
THE MASQUE OF THE RED DEATH
American International; 1964; British-U.S.
THE TOMB OF LIGEIA
American International; 1965
THE WILD ANGELS
American International; 1966
THE ST. VALENTINE'S DAY MASSACRE
20th Century-Fox; 1967
THE TRIP
American International; 1967
TARGET: HARRY
directed under pseudonym of Harry Neill; ABC Pictures International; 1968
BLOODY MAMA
American International; 1970
GAS-S-S-S!
American International; 1970
VON RICHTOFEN AND BROWN
United Artists; 1971

Cornfield, Hubert
b. February 9, 1929
Istanbul, Turkey

SUDDEN DANGER
United Artists; 1955
LURE OF THE SWAMP
20th Century-Fox; 1957
PLUNDER ROAD
20th Century-Fox; 1957
THE THIRD VOICE
20th Century-Fox; 1959

continued

Cornfield, Hubert
continued

ANGEL BABY
co-director with Paul Wendkos; Allied Artists; 1961
PRESSURE POINT
United Artists; 1962
THE NIGHT OF THE FOLLOWING DAY
Universal; 1969
LES GRANDS MOYENS
1976; French

Coscarelli, Don
Business:
Coscarelli/Pepperman Corp.
15445 Ventura Blvd.
Sherman Oaks, CA 91413
(213) 784-8822

JIM - THE WORLD'S GREATEST
Universal; 1976
KENNY AND COMPANY
20th Century-Fox; 1976
PHANTASM
Avco Embassy; 1979

Cosmatos, George Pan
Agent:
Agency for the Performing Arts
Hollywood
(213) 273-0744

MASSACRE IN ROME
National General; 1973; Italian-French
THE CASSANDRA CROSSING
Avco Embassy; 1977; British-Italian-West German
RESTLESS
Joseph Brenner; 1978
ESCAPE TO ATHENA
AFD; 1979; British

Costa-Gavras
(Konstantinos Gavras)
b. 1933
Athens, Greece

THE SLEEPING CAR MURDERS
7 Arts; 1966; French
SHOCK TROOPS (Un Homme de Trop)
United Artists; 1968; French-Italian
Z
Cinema 5; 1969; French-Algerian
THE CONFESSION
Paramount; 1970; French
STATE OF SIEGE
Cinema 5; 1973; French
SPECIAL SECTION
Universal; 1975; French-Italian-West German
CLAIR DE FEMME
Atlantic; 1979; French
MISSING
Universal; 1982

Couffer, Jack
Agent:
I.C.M.
Hollywood
(213) 550-4000

NIKKI, WILD DOG OF THE NORTH
Buena Vista; 1961; U.S.-Canadian
RING OF BRIGHT WATER
Cinerama Releasing Corporation; 1969; British
LIVING FREE
Columbia; 1972; British
THE DARWIN ADVENTURE
20th Century-Fox; 1972; British
THE LAST GIRAFFE
Westfall Productions; telefeature; 1979

Courtland, Jerome
b. December 27, 1926
Knoxville, Tennessee
Business:
Walt Disney Productions
500 S. Buena Vista St.
Burbank, CA 91521
(213) 845-3141

RUN, COUGAR, RUN
Buena Vista; 1972
DIAMONDS ON WHEELS
Buena Vista; 1972; U.S.-British
THE SKY TRAP
Walt Disney Productions; telefeature; 1979

Coutard, Raoul
b. September 16, 1924
Paris, France

HOA-BINH
Transvue; 1971; French

Crain, William
Business:
Box 744
Beverly Hills, CA 90213
Agent:
Chasin-Park-Citron
Hollywood
(213) 273-7190

BLACULA
American International; 1972
DR. BLACK, MR. HYDE
Dimension; 1976
THE WATTS MONSTER
Dimension; 1979

Crane, Barry
Business Manager:
Brad Marer & Associates
Beverly Hills
(213) 278-6690

THE HOUND OF THE BASKERVILLES
Universal TV; telefeature; 1972

Craven, Wes
Agent:
Marvin Moss
Los Angeles
(213) 274-8483

LAST HOUSE ON THE LEFT
Hallmark; 1973
THE HILLS HAVE EYES
Vanguard; 1977
STRANGER IN OUR HOUSE
Inter Planetary Pictures/Finnegan Associates; telefeature; 1978
DEADLY BLESSING
United Artists; 1981
SWAMP THING
Avco Embassy; 1982

Crenna, Richard
b. November 30, 1926
Los Angeles, California
Agent:
William Morris Agency
Beverly Hills
(213) 274-7451

BETTER LATE THAN NEVER
Ten-Four Productions; telefeature; 1979

Crichton, Michael
b. October 23, 1942
Chicago, Illinois
Business Manager:
Segal and Goldman
Hollywood
(213) 278-9200

PURSUIT
ABC Circle Films; telefeature; 1972
WESTWORLD
M-G-M; 1973
COMA
M-G-M/United Artists; 1978
THE GREAT TRAIN ROBBERY
United Artists; 1979; British
LOOKER
The Ladd Company/Warner Brothers; 1981

Cronenberg, David
Home:
184 Cottingham Street
Toronto, Ontario M4V 7C7
Canada
(416) 961-0482/964-6674

THEY CAME FROM WITHIN
Trans-America; 1976; Canadian
RABID
New World; 1977; Canadian
THE BROOD
New World; 1979; Canadian
FAST COMPANY
Topar; 1979; Canadian
SCANNERS
Avco Embassy; 1981; Canadian
VIDEODROME
Universal; 1982; Canadian

Cukor, George
b. July 7, 1899
New York, New York
Agent:
I.C.M.
Los Angeles
(213) 550-4000

GRUMPY
co-director with Cyril Gardner;Paramount;1930
THE VIRTUOUS SIN
co-director with Louis Gasnier;Paramount;1930
THE ROYAL FAMILY OF BROADWAY
co-director with Cyril Gardner;Paramount;1930

continued

Cukor, George
continued

TARNISHED LADY
  Paramount; 1931
GIRLS ABOUT TOWN
  Paramount; 1931
WHAT PRICE HOLLYWOOD?
  RKO Radio; 1932
A BILL OF DIVORCEMENT
  RKO Radio; 1932
ROCKABYE
  RKO Radio; 1932
OUR BETTERS
  RKO Radio; 1933
DINNER AT EIGHT
  M-G-M; 1933
LITTLE WOMEN
  RKO Radio; 1933
DAVID COPPERFIELD
  M-G-M; 1935
SYLVIA SCARLETT
  RKO Radio; 1935
ROMEO AND JULIET
  M-G-M; 1936
CAMILLE
  M-G-M; 1937
HOLIDAY
  Columbia; 1938
ZAZA
  Paramount; 1939
THE WOMEN
  M-G-M; 1939
THE PHILADELPHIA STORY
  M-G-M; 1940
SUSAN AND GOD
  M-G-M; 1940
A WOMAN'S FACE
  M-G-M; 1941
TWO-FACED WOMAN
  M-G-M; 1941
HER CARDBOARD LOVER
  M-G-M; 1942
KEEPER OF THE FLAME
  M-G-M; 1943
GASLIGHT
  M-G-M; 1944
WINGED VICTORY
  20th Century-Fox; 1944
A DOUBLE LIFE
  Universal; 1947
EDWARD, MY SON
  M-G-M; 1949
ADAM'S RIB
  M-G-M; 1949
A LIFE OF HER OWN
  M-G-M; 1950
BORN YESTERDAY
  Columbia; 1950
THE MODEL AND THE MARRIAGE BROKER
  20th Century-Fox; 1951
THE MARRYING KIND
  Columbia; 1952
PAT AND MIKE
  M-G-M; 1952
THE ACTRESS
  M-G-M; 1953
A STAR IS BORN
  Warner Brothers; 1954
IT SHOULD HAPPEN TO YOU
  Columbia; 1954
BHOWANI JUNCTION
  M-G-M; 1956
LES GIRLS
  M-G-M; 1957
WILD IS THE WIND
  Paramount; 1957
HELLER IN PINK TIGHTS
  Paramount; 1960

continued

Cukor, George
continued

SONG WITHOUT END
co-director with Charles Vidor; Columbia; 1960
LET'S MAKE LOVE
20th Century-Fox; 1960
THE CHAPMAN REPORT
Warner Brothers; 1962
SOMETHING'S GOT TO GIVE
20th Century-Fox; 1962; incomplete
MY FAIR LADY
Warner Brothers; 1964
JUSTINE
20th Century-Fox; 1969
TRAVELS WITH MY AUNT
M-G-M; 1972; British
LOVE AMONG THE RUINS
ABC Circle Films; telefeature; 1975
THE BLUE BIRD
20th Century-Fox; 1976; U.S.-Soviet
THE CORN IS GREEN
Warner Brothers TV; telefeature; 1979
RICH AND FAMOUS
M-G-M/United Artists; 1981

Culp, Robert
b. August 16, 1930
Berkeley, California
Business:
Stone Productions
1880 Century Park East
Los Angeles, CA 90067
(213) 553-1707

HICKEY AND BOGGS
United Artists; 1972

Cunningham, Sean S.
Contact:
Directors Guild of America
New York City
(212) 581-0370

TOGETHER
Hallmark; 1971
THE CASE OF THE SMILING STIFFS
Seaberg; 1974
SEX ON THE GROOVE TUBE
Newport; 1977
HERE COME THE TIGERS
American International; 1978
FRIDAY THE 13TH
Paramount; 1980
A STRANGER IS WATCHING
M-G-M/United Artists; 1981

Curtis, Dan
Business:
Dan Curtis Productions
5451 Marathon Street
Hollywood, CA 90038
(213) 468-5000, ext. 1091

HOUSE OF DARK SHADOWS
M-G-M; 1970
NIGHT OF DARK SHADOWS
M-G-M; 1971
THE NIGHT STRANGLER
ABC Circle Films; telefeature; 1973
THE NORLISS TAPES
Metromedia Producers Corporation; telefeature; 1973
SCREAM OF THE WOLF
Metromedia Producers Corporation; telefeature; 1974
DRACULA
Universal TV/Dan Curtis Productions; telefeature; 1974
MELVIN PURVIS: G-MAN
American International TV; telefeature; 1974
TURN OF THE SCREW
Dan Curtis Productions; telefeature; 1974
THE GREAT ICE RIP-OFF
ABC Circle Films; telefeature; 1974
TRILOGY OF TERROR
ABC Circle Films; telefeature; 1975
THE KANSAS CITY MASSACRE
ABC Circle Films; telefeature; 1975

continued

Curtis, Dan
continued

BURNT OFFERINGS
United Artists; 1976
DEAD OF NIGHT
NBC-TV; telefeature; 1977
CURSE OF THE BLACK WIDOW
Dan Curtis Productions/ABC Circle Films; telefeature; 1977
WHEN EVERY DAY WAS THE FOURTH OF JULY
Dan Curtis Productions; telefeature; 1978
THE LAST RIDE OF THE DALTON GANG
NBC Productions/Dan Curtis Productions; telefeature; 1979
MRS. R'S DAUGHTER
NBC Productions/Dan Curtis Productions; telefeature; 1979
THE LONG DAYS OF SUMMER
Dan Curtis Productions; telefeature; 1980
THE WINDS OF WAR
Paramount TV/Dan Curtis Productions; television mini-series; 1982

Da Costa, Morton
(Morton Tecosky)
b. March 7, 1914
Philadelphia, Pennsylvania
Agent:
Coleman-Rosenberg
New York City
(212) 838-0734

AUNTIE MAME
Warner Brothers; 1958
THE MUSIC MAN
Warner Brothers; 1962
ISLAND OF LOVE
Warner Brothers; 1963

Dalva, Robert
Business:
Zoetrope Studios
1040 N. Las Palmas Avenue
Hollywood, CA 90038
(213) 463-7191

THE BLACK STALLION RETURNS
United Artists; 1982

Damski, Melvin
Home:
10533 Dunleer Drive
Los Angeles, CA 90064
Agent:
Phil Gersh Agency
Beverly Hills
(213) 274-6611

LONG JOURNEY BACK
Lorimar Productions; telefeature; 1978
THE CHILD STEALER
The Production Company/Columbia TV; telefeature; 1979
A PERFECT MATCH
Lorimar Productions; telefeature; 1980
WORD OF HONOR
Georgia Bay Productions; telefeature; 1981
AMERICAN DREAM
Mace Neufeld Productions/Viacom; telefeature; 1981
WALKS FAR WOMAN
Roger Gimbel Productions/EMI TV; telefeature; 1981
FOR LADIES ONLY
The Catalina Production Group/Viacom; telefeature; 1981

Daniels, Marc
Agent:
William Morris Agency
Beverly Hills
(213) 274-7451

PLANET EARTH
Warner Brothers TV; telefeature; 1974
EMILY, EMILY
NBC-TV; telefeature; 1977
THE FATHER KNOWS BEST REUNION
NBC-TV; telefeature; 1977

Danska, Herbert
Personal Manager:
Mickelson Management
Beverly Hills
(213) 858-1097

SWEET LOVE, BITTER (It Won't Rub Off, Baby)
Peppercorn-Wormser; 1967
RIGHT ON!
L-P; 1970

Dante, Joe

HOLLYWOOD BOULEVARD
co-director with Allan Arkush; New World; 1976
PIRANHA
New World; 1978
THE HOWLING
Avco Embassy; 1980

Danton, Ray
Business Manager:
Joel Rosenbaum
Encino
(213) 872-0231

THE DEATHMASTER
American International; 1972
CRYPT OF THE LIVING DEAD
Atlas; 1973
PSYCHIC KILLER
Avco Embassy; 1975

D'Antoni, Philip
Business:
8 East 63rd Street
New York, N.Y. 10021
(212) 688-4205

THE SEVEN UPS
20th Century-Fox; 1973

Darling, Joan
Agent:
William Morris Agency
Beverly Hills
(213) 274-7451

FIRST LOVE
Paramount; 1977
WILLA
co-director with Claudio Guzman; GJL Productions/ Dove Inc.; telefeature; 1979

Dassin, Jules
b. December 18, 1911
Middletown, Connecticut
Home:
25 Anagnostopoulou Street
Athens, Greece
3-629-751
Agent:
I.C.M.
Hollywood
(213) 550-4000

NAZI AGENT
M-G-M; 1942
THE AFFAIRS OF MARTHA
M-G-M; 1942
REUNION IN FRANCE
M-G-M; 1942
YOUNG IDEAS
M-G-M; 1943
THE CANTERVILLE GHOST
M-G-M; 1944
A LETTER FOR EVIE
M-G-M; 1945
TWO SMART PEOPLE
M-G-M; 1946
BRUTE FORCE
Warner Brothers; 1947
THE NAKED CITY
Universal; 1948
THIEVES' HIGHWAY
RKO Radio; 1949
NIGHT AND THE CITY
20th Century-Fox; 1950; British
RIFIFI
Pathe; 1954; French
WHERE THE HOT WIND BLOWS
M-G-M; 1960; Italian-French
NEVER ON SUNDAY
Lopert; 1960; Greek
PHAEDRA
Lopert; 1962; Greek-U.S.-French
TOPKAPI
United Artists; 1964
10:30 P.M. SUMMER
Lopert; 1966; U.S.-Spanish
SURVIVAL '67
United; 1968; U.S.-Israeli
UP TIGHT
Paramount; 1968
PROMISE AT DAWN
Avco Embassy; 1970; French-U.S.
A DREAM OF PASSION
Avco Embassy; 1978; Greek-U.S.
CIRCLE OF TWO
World Northal; 1981; Canadian

Daugherty, Herschel
Business Manager:
Brown & Associates
Beverly Hills
(213) 273-5580

THE LIGHT IN THE FOREST
Buena Vista; 1958
THE RAIDERS
Universal; 1963
WINCHESTER '73
Universal TV; telefeature; 1967
THE VICTIM
Universal TV; telefeature; 1972
SHE CRIED "MURDER!"
Universal TV; telefeature; 1973
TWICE IN A LIFETIME
Martin Rackin Productions; telefeature; 1974

Davidson, Boaz
Business:
Cannon Films
9911 W. Pico Blvd.
Los Angeles, CA 90035
(213) 553-5978

AZIT THE PARATROOPER DOG
Liran Corporation; 1972; Israeli
CHARLIE AND A HALF
Filmonde; 1973; Israeli
LUPO GOES TO NEW YORK
Noah Films; 1977; Israeli
THE TZANANI FAMILY
Noah Films; 1978; Israeli
LEMON POPSICLE
Noah Films; 1981; Israeli
GOING STEADY
Cannon; 1981; Israeli
SEED OF INNOCENCE
Cannon; 1981
X-RAY
Cannon; 1981
HOT BUBBLEGUM (LEMON POPSICLE III)
Cannon; 1981; Israeli
CADETS
Cannon; 1982

Davidson, Gordon
Business:
Mark Taper Forum
135 N. Grand Avenue
Los Angeles, CA 90012
(213) 973-7388
Agent:
William Morris Agency
Beverly Hills
(213) 274-7451

THE TRIAL OF THE CATONSVILLE NINE
Cinema 5; 1972

Davidson, Martin
Home:
1505 Viewsite Terrace
Los Angeles, CA 90069
(213) 659-6178

THE LORDS OF FLATBUSH
co-director with Stephen Verona; Columbia; 1974
ALMOST SUMMER
Universal; 1978
HERO AT LARGE
M-G-M/United Artists; 1980

Davis, Desmond
b. 1928
London, England
Contact:
British Film Institute
127 Charing Cross Road
London W.C. 2, England
01-437-4355

THE GIRL WITH GREEN EYES
United Artists; 1964; British
TIME LOST AND TIME REMEMBERED (I Was Happy Here)
Continental; 1966; British
THE UNCLE
Lennart; 1966; British
SMASHING TIME
Paramount; 1967; British
A NICE GIRL LIKE ME
Avco Embassy; 1969; British
CLASH OF THE TITANS
M-G-M/United Artists; 1981; British

Davis, Ossie
b. December 18, 1917
Cogdell, Georgia

COTTON COMES TO HARLEM
United Artists; 1970

continued

Davis, Ossie
continued

BLACK GIRL
Cinerama Releasing Corporation; 1972
KONGI'S HARVEST
Tan Communications; 1973
GORDON'S WAR
20th Century-Fox; 1973
COUNTDOWN AT KUSINI
Columbia; 1976; U.S.-Nigerian

Davis, Peter

HEARTS AND MINDS
Warner Brothers; 1975

Day, Robert
b. September 11, 1922
Sheen, England
Agent:
Creative Artists Agency
Los Angeles
(213) 277-4545

THE GREEN MAN
DCA; 1957; British
STRANGERS' MEETING
Rank; 1957; British
THE HAUNTED STRANGLER (Grip of the Strangler)
M-G-M; 1958; British
CORRIDORS OF BLOOD
M-G-M; 1958; British
FIRST MAN INTO SPACE
M-G-M; 1959; British
LIFE IN EMERGENCY WARD 10
1959; British
BOBBIKINS
20th Century-Fox; 1960; British
TWO-WAY STRETCH
Showcorporation; 1960; British
TARZAN THE MAGNIFICENT
Paramount; 1960; British
CALL ME GENIUS (The Rebel)
Continental; 1961; British
OPERATION SNATCH
Continental; 1962; British
TARZAN'S THREE CHALLENGES
M-G-M; 1963; British
SHE
M-G-M; 1965; British
TARZAN AND THE VALLEY OF GOLD
American International; 1966; U.S.-Swiss
TARZAN AND THE GREAT RIVER
Paramount; 1967
I THINK WE'RE BEING FOLLOWED
1967; British
THE HOUSE ON GREENAPPLE ROAD
QM Productions; telefeature; 1970
RITUAL OF EVIL
Universal TV; telefeature; 1970
BANYON
Warner Brothers TV; telefeature; 1971
IN BROAD DAYLIGHT
Aaron Spelling Productions; telefeature; 1971
MR. AND MRS. BO JO JONES
20th Century-Fox TV; telefeature; 1971
THE RELUCTANT HEROES
Aaron Spelling Productions; telefeature; 1971
THE GREAT AMERICAN BEAUTY CONTEST
ABC Circle Films; telefeature; 1973
DEATH STALK
Wolper Productions; telefeature; 1975
THE TRIAL OF CHAPLAIN JENSEN
20th Century-Fox TV; telefeature; 1975
SWITCH
Universal TV; telefeature; 1975
A HOME OF OUR OWN
QM Productions; telefeature; 1975
TWIN DETECTIVES
Charles Fries Productions; telefeature; 1976
KINGSTON: THE POWER PLAY
Universal TV; telefeature; 1976
HAVING BABIES
The Jozak Company; telefeature; 1976

continued

Day, Robert
continued

BLACK MARKET BABY
Brut Productions; telefeature; 1977
THE INITIATION OF SARAH
Charles Fries Productions; telefeature; 1978
THE GRASS IS ALWAYS GREENER OVER THE SEPTIC TANK
Joe Hamilton Productions; telefeature; 1978
MURDER BY NATURAL CAUSES
Richard Levinson/William Link Productions; telefeature; 1979
WALKING THROUGH THE FIRE
Time-Life Productions; telefeature; 1979
THE MAN WITH BOGART'S FACE (Sam Marlow, Private Eye) 20th Century-Fox; 1980
PETER AND PAUL
Universal TV; telefeature; 1981
SCRUPLES
Lou-Step Productions/Warner Brothers TV; telefeature; 1981

Dayton, Lyman
Business:
Lyman Dayton Pictures
10850 Riverside Drive
N. Hollywood, CA 91602
(213) 980-7202

BAKER'S HAWK
Doty-Dayton; 1976
RIVALS
World Entertainment; 1979
THE STRANGER AT JEFFERSON HIGH
Lyman Dayton Productions; telefeature; 1981
THE AVENGING
Comworld Productions; 1981

de Antonio, Emile
b. 1920
Scranton, Pennsylvania

POINT OF ORDER
Point; 1963
RUSH TO JUDGMENT
Impact; 1967
AMERICA IS HARD TO SEE
1968
IN THE YEAR OF THE PIG
Pathe Contemporary; 1969
MILLHOUSE: A WHITE COMEDY
New Yorker; 1971
PAINTERS PAINTING
New Yorker; 1973
UNDERGROUND
co-director with Mary Lampson & Haskell Wexler; New Yorker; 1976
IN THE KING OF PRUSSIA
1981

de Bosio, Gianfranco
Contact:
Minister of Tourism
Via Della Ferratella No. 51
00184 Rome, Italy

MOSES THE LAWGIVER
ATV, Ltd./ITC-TV/RAI-TV; television mini-series; 1975; British-Italian
MOSES
Avco Embassy; 1976; British-Italian; feature film version of MOSES THE LAWGIVER

de Broca, Philippe
b. March 15, 1933
Paris, France
Contact:
French Film Office
745 Fifth Avenue
New York, N.Y. 10151

PLAYING AT LOVE
1960; French
THE JOKER
Lopert; 1961; French
THE FIVE DAY LOVER
Kingsley International; 1961; French-Italian
SEVEN CAPITAL SINS
co-director; Embassy; 1962; French-Italian
CARTOUCHE
Embassy; 1962; French-Italian
LES VEINARDS
co-director; 1962; French
THAT MAN FROM RIO
Lopert; 1964; French-Italian
MALE COMPANION
International Classics; 1966; French-Italian

continued

de Broca, Philippe
continued

UP TO HIS EARS
Lopert; 1966; French-Italian
KING OF HEARTS
Lopert; 1967; French-Italian
THE OLDEST PROFESSION
co-director; Goldstone; 1968; French-Italian-West German
THE DEVIL BY THE TAIL
Lopert; 1969; French-Italian
GIVE HER THE MOON
United Artists; 1970; French-Italian
TOUCH AND GO
Libra Films; 1971; French
CHERE LOUISE
1972; French
LE MAGNIFIQUE
Cine III; 1974; French
INCORRIGIBLE
EDP; 1975; French
JULIE POT DE COLLE
1977; French
DEAR DETECTIVE (Dear Inspector)
Cinema 5; 1978; French
PRACTICE MAKES PERFECT
Quartet/Films Inc.; 1980; French
JUPITER'S THIGH
Quartet/Films Inc.; 1981; French

de Felitta, Frank
Agent:
Paul Kohner Agency
Los Angeles
(213) 550-1060

TRAPPED
Universal TV; telefeature; 1973
THE TWO WORLDS OF JENNY LOGAN
Joe Wizan TV Productions/Fries Enterprises; telefeature; 1979
DARK NIGHT OF THE SCARECROW
Joe Wizan TV Productions; telefeature; 1981

DeGuere, Philip
Agent:
Marvin Moss
Hollywood
(213) 274-8483

DR. STRANGE
Universal TV; telefeature; 1978

De Luise, Dom
b. August 1, 1933
Brooklyn, New York
Business Manager:
Executive Business Management
Beverly Hills
(213) 858-2000

HOT STUFF
Columbia; 1979

Demme, Jonathan
Agent:
I.C.M.
Hollywood
(213) 550-4000

CAGED HEAT
New World; 1974
CRAZY MAMA
New World; 1975
FIGHTING MAD
20th Century-Fox; 1976
CITIZENS BAND (Handle With Care)
Paramount; 1977
LAST EMBRACE
United Artists; 1979
MELVIN AND HOWARD
Universal; 1980

Demy, Jacques
b. June 5, 1931
Pont-Chateau, France
Contact:
French Film Office
745 Fifth Avenue
New York, N.Y. 10051
(212) 832-8860

LOLA
Films Around the World; 1961; French
SEVEN CAPITAL SINS
co-director; Embassy; 1962; French-Italian
BAY OF THE ANGELS
Pathe Contemporary; 1964; French
THE UMBRELLAS OF CHERBOURG
Landau; 1964; French-West German

continued

Demy, Jacques
continued

THE YOUNG GIRLS OF ROCHEFORT
Warner Brothers; 1968; French
MODEL SHOP
Columbia; 1969
DONKEY SKIN
Janus; 1971; French
THE PIED PIPER
Paramount; 1972; British-West German
A SLIGHTLY PREGNANT MAN
S.J. International; 1977; French
LADY OSCAR
Toho; 1978; Japanese-French

De Palma, Brian
b. 1941
Philadelphia, Pennsylvania
Business
25 Fifth Avenue
New York, N.Y. 10003

MURDER A LA MOD
Aries; 1968
GREETINGS
Sigma III; 1968
THE WEDDING PARTY
co-director with Wilford Leach & Cynthia Munroe;
Powell Productions Plus/Ondine; 1969
DIONYSUS IN '69
co-director with Robert Fiore & Bruce Rubin;
Sigma III; 1970
HI, MOM!
Sigma III; 1970
GET TO KNOW YOUR RABBIT
Warner Brothers; 1972
SISTERS
American International; 1973
PHANTOM OF THE PARADISE
20th Century-Fox; 1974
OBSESSION
Columbia; 1976
CARRIE
United Artists; 1976
THE FURY
20th Century-Fox; 1978
HOME MOVIES
United Artists Classics; 1980
DRESSED TO KILL
Filmways; 1980
BLOW OUT
Filmways; 1981

Deray, Jacques
(Jacques Deray Desrayaud)
b. February 19, 1929
Lyons, France
Contact:
French Film Office
745 Fifth Avenue
New York, N.Y. 10051
(212) 832-8860

LE GIGOLO
1960; French
RIFIFI IN TOKYO
M-G-M; 1961; French-Italian
SYMPHONY FOR A MASSACRE
7 Arts; 1965; French-Italian
PAR UN BEAU MATIN D'ETE
1964; French
THAT MAN GEORGE! (Our Man in Marrakesh)
Allied Artists; 1966; French-Italian-Spanish
AVEC LA PEAU DES AUTRES
1967; French
THE SWIMMING POOL
Avco Embassy; 1970; French-Italian
BORSALINO
Paramount; 1970; French-Italian
DOUCEMENT LES BASSES
1971; French
THE OUTSIDE MAN
United Artists; 1973; French-U.S.
BORSALINO AND CO.
1974; French-Italian
FLIC STORY
1975; French
LE GANG
1977; French
UN PAPILLON SUR L'EPAULE
1978; French

Derek, John
(Derek Harris)
b. August 12, 1926
Hollywood, California
Contact:
Directors Guild of America
Los Angeles
(213) 656-1220

ONCE BEFORE I DIE
7 Arts; 1967; U.S.-Filipino
A BOY...A GIRL
Jack Hanson; 1968
CHILDISH THINGS
Filmworld; 1969
AND ONCE UPON A TIME
PG Professional Films; 1973
TARZAN, THE APE MAN
M-G-M/United Artists; 1981

Deschanel, Caleb
Business:
Zoetrope Studios
1040 N. Las Palmas Avenue
Los Angeles, CA 90038
(213) 463-7191

THE ESCAPE ARTIST
Orion Pictures/Warner Brothers; 1981

DeSimone, Tom

HELL NIGHT
Compass International; 1981
THE CONCRETE JUNGLE
Ideal Films; 1982

Dexter, John
b. 1935
England
Contact:
British Film Institute
127 Charing Cross Road
London W.C. 2, England
01-437-4355

THE VIRGIN SOLDIERS
Columbia; 1970; British
PIGEONS (Sidelong Glances of a Pigeon Kicker)
M-G-M; 1970
I WANT WHAT I WANT
Cinerama Releasing Corporation; 1972; British

Dexter, Maury
b. 1927
Home:
1384 Camino Magenta
Thousand Oaks, CA 91360
(805) 498-0540

THE HIGH POWERED RIFLE
20th Century-Fox; 1960
WALK TALL
20th Century-Fox; 1960
THE PURPLE HILLS
20th Century-Fox; 1961
WOMAN HUNT
20th Century-Fox; 1961
THE FIREBRAND
20th Century-Fox; 1962
AIR PATROL
20th Century-Fox; 1962
THE DAY MARS INVADED EARTH
20th Century-Fox; 1962
HOUSE OF THE DAMNED
20th Century-Fox; 1962
HARBOR LIGHTS
20th Century-Fox; 1963
THE YOUNG SWINGERS
20th Century-Fox; 1963
POLICE NURSE
20th Century-Fox; 1963
YOUNG GUNS OF TEXAS
20th Century-Fox; 1963
SURF PARTY
20th Century-Fox; 1963
RAIDERS FROM BENEATH THE SEA
20th Century-Fox; 1964
THE NAKED BRIGADE
Universal; 1965
WILD ON THE BEACH
20th Century-Fox; 1965
MARYJANE
American International; 1968
THE MINI-SKIRT MOB
American International; 1968
BORN WILD
American International; 1968
HELL'S BELLES
American International; 1969

Dixon, Ivan
Home:
3432 N. Marengo Avenue
Altadena, CA 91001
(213) 681-1327

TROUBLE MAN
20th Century-Fox; 1972
THE SPOOK WHO SAT BY THE DOOR
United Artists; 1973
LOVE IS NOT ENOUGH
Universal TV; telefeature; 1978

Dmytryk, Edward
b. September 4, 1908
Grand Forks, Canada
Agent:
Richard Heckenkamp
Hollywood
(213) 652-6230

THE HAWK
Herman Wohl; 1935
TELEVISION SPY
Paramount; 1939
EMERGENCY SQUAD
Paramount; 1940
MYSTERY SEA RAIDERS
Paramount; 1940
GOLDEN GLOVES
Paramount; 1940
HER FIRST ROMANCE
Monogram; 1940
THE DEVIL COMMANDS
Columbia; 1941
UNDER AGE
Columbia; 1941
SWEETHEART OF THE CAMPUS
Columbia; 1941
THE BLONDE FROM SINGAPORE
Columbia; 1941
CONFESSIONS OF BOSTON BLACKIE
Columbia; 1941
SECRETS OF THE LONE WOLF
Columbia; 1941
COUNTER ESPIONAGE
Columbia; 1942
SEVEN MILES FROM ALCATRAZ
RKO Radio; 1942
THE FALCON STRIKES BACK
RKO Radio; 1943
HITLER'S CHILDREN
RKO Radio; 1943
CAPTIVE WILD WOMAN
Universal; 1943
BEHIND THE RISING SUN
RKO Radio; 1943
TENDER COMRADE
RKO Radio; 1943
MURDER MY SWEET
RKO Radio; 1945
BACK TO BATAAN
RKO Radio; 1945
TILL THE END OF TIME
RKO Radio; 1945
CROSSFIRE
RKO Radio; 1947
SO WELL REMEMBERED
RKO Radio; 1947
THE HIDDEN ROOM (Obsession)
British Lion; 1949; British
GIVE US THIS DAY (Salt to the Devil)
Eagle Lion; 1949; British
MUTINY
Universal; 1952
THE SNIPER
Columbia; 1952
EIGHT IRON MEN
Columbia; 1952
THE JUGGLER
Columbia; 1953
THE CAINE MUTINY
Columbia; 1954
BROKEN LANCE
20th Century-Fox; 1954
THE END OF THE AFFAIR
Columbia; 1954
SOLDIER OF FORTUNE
20th Century-Fox; 1955

continued

Dmytryk, Edward
continued

THE LEFT HAND OF GOD
20th Century-Fox; 1955
THE MOUNTAIN
Paramount; 1956
RAINTREE COUNTY
M-G-M; 1957
THE YOUNG LIONS
20th Century-Fox; 1958
WARLOCK
20th Century-Fox; 1959
THE BLUE ANGEL
20th Century-Fox; 1959
WALK ON THE WILD SIDE
Columbia; 1962
THE RELUCTANT SAINT
Davis-Royal; 1962; Italian-U.S.
THE CARPETBAGGERS
Paramount; 1963
WHERE LOVE HAS GONE
Paramount; 1964
MIRAGE
Universal; 1965
ALVAREZ KELLY
Columbia; 1966
ANZIO
Columbia; 1968; Italian
SHALAKO!
Cinerama Releasing Corporation; 1968; British
BLUEBEARD
Cinerama Releasing Corporation; 1972; Italian-French-West German
THE HUMAN FACTOR
Bryanston; 1974; British-U.S.
HE IS MY BROTHER
Atlantic; 1976

Doheny, Lawrence
Agent:
Contemporary-Korman Artists
Hollywood
(213) 278-8250

TEEN-AGE MILLIONAIRE
United Artists; 1961
HOUSTON, WE'VE GOT A PROBLEM
Universal TV; telefeature; 1974

Donen, Stanley
b. April 13, 1924
Columbia, South Carolina
Business Manager:
Traubner & Flynn
Los Angeles
(213) 277-3000

ON THE TOWN
co-director with Gene Kelly; M-G-M; 1949
ROYAL WEDDING
M-G-M; 1951
SINGIN' IN THE RAIN
co-director with Gene Kelly; M-G-M; 1952
LOVE IS BETTER THAN EVER
M-G-M; 1952
FEARLESS FAGAN
M-G-M; 1952
GIVE A GIRL A BREAK
M-G-M; 1953
SEVEN BRIDES FOR SEVEN BROTHERS
M-G-M; 1954
DEEP IN MY HEART
M-G-M; 1954
IT'S ALWAYS FAIR WEATHER
co-director with Gene Kelly; M-G-M; 1955
FUNNY FACE
Paramount; 1957
THE PAJAMA GAME
co-director with George Abbott; 1957
KISS THEM FOR ME
20th Century-Fox; 1957
INDISCREET
Warner Brothers; 1958; British
DAMN YANKEES
co-director with George Abbott; Paramount; 1958

continued

Donen, Stanley
continued

ONCE MORE, WITH FEELING
Columbia; 1960
SURPRISE PACKAGE
Columbia; 1960
THE GRASS IS GREENER
Universal; 1961
CHARADE
Universal; 1964
ARABESQUE
Universal; 1966; British-U.S.
TWO FOR THE ROAD
20th Century-Fox; 1967; British-U.S.
BEDAZZLED
20th Century-Fox; 1967; British
STAIRCASE
20th Century-Fox; 1969; British
THE LITTLE PRINCE
Paramount; 1974; British
LUCKY LADY
20th Century-Fox; 1975
MOVIE MOVIE
Warner Brothers; 1978
SATURN 3
AFD; 1980

Doniger, Walter
b. July 1, 1917
New York, New York
Home:
555 Huntley Drive
Los Angeles, CA 90048
(213) 659-2787

DUFFY OF SAN QUENTIN
Warner Brothers; 1953
THE STEEL CAGE
United Artists; 1954
THE STEEL JUNGLE
Warner Brothers; 1955
UNWED MOTHER
Allied Artists; 1958
HOUSE OF WOMEN
Warner Brothers; 1960
SAFE AT HOME!
Columbia; 1962
MAD BULL
co-director with Len Steckler; Steckler Productions/Filmways; telefeature; 1977

Donner, Clive
b. January 21, 1926
London, England
Agent:
William Morris Agency
Beverly Hills
(213) 274-7451

THE SECRET PLACE
Rank; 1957; British
HEART OF A CHILD
Rank; 1958; British
MARRIAGE OF CONVENIENCE
Allied Artists; 1961; British
THE SINISTER MAN
Allied Artists; 1961; British
SOME PEOPLE
American International; 1962; British
THE GUEST (The Caretaker)
Janus; 1963; British
NOTHING BUT THE BEST
Royal Films International; 1964; British
WHAT'S NEW PUSSYCAT?
United Artists; 1965; British
LUV
Columbia; 1967
HERE WE GO ROUND THE MULBERRY BUSH
Lopert; 1968; British
ALFRED THE GREAT
M-G-M; 1969; British
OLD DRACULA (Vampira)
American International; 1975; British
SPECTRE
20th Century-Fox TV; telefeature; 1977
THE THIEF OF BAGHDAD
Palm Films Ltd.; telefeature; 1979; British
THE NUDE BOMB
Universal; 1980
CHARLIE CHAN AND THE CURSE OF THE DRAGON QUEEN
American Cinema; 1980

Donner, Richard
Business Manager:
Gelfand, Breslauer,
Rennert & Feldman
Los Angeles
(213) 553-1707

X-15
United Artists; 1961
SALT AND PEPPER
United Artists; 1968; British
LOLA (Twinky)
American International; 1970; British-Italian
LUCAS TANNER
Universal TV; telefeature; 1974
SENIOR YEAR
Universal TV; telefeature; 1974
A SHADOW IN THE STREETS
Playboy Productions; telefeature; 1975
SARAH T. - PORTRAIT OF A TEENAGER ALCOHOLIC
Universal TV; telefeature; 1975
THE OMEN
20th Century-Fox; 1976
SUPERMAN
Warner Brothers; 1978; U.S.-British
INSIDE MOVES
AFD; 1980

Donohue, Jack
b. November 3, 1908
New York, New York
Home:
13900 Panay Way
R. 204
Marina del Rey, CA 90291

CLOSE-UP
Eagle Lion; 1948
THE YELLOW CAB MAN
M-G-M; 1950
WATCH THE BIRDIE
M-G-M; 1951
LUCKY ME
Warner Brothers; 1954
BABES IN TOYLAND
Buena Vista; 1961
MARRIAGE ON THE ROCKS
Warner Brothers; 1965
ASSAULT ON A QUEEN
Paramount; 1965

Donovan, Tom

TRISTAN AND ISOLT
1981; British

Douglas, Gordon
b. December 5, 1909
New York, New York
Agent:
Phil Gersh Agency
Beverly Hills
(213) 274-6611

GENERAL SPANKY
co-director with Fred Newmayer; M-G-M; 1936
ZENOBIA
United Artists; 1939
SAPS AT SEA
United Artists; 1940
ROAD SHOW
co-director with Hal Roach & Hal Roach, Jr.;
United Artists; 1941
BROADWAY LIMITED
United Artists; 1941
NIAGATA FALLS
United Artists; 1941
THE DEVIL WITH HITLER
RKO Radio; 1942
THE GREAT GILDERSLEEVE
RKO Radio; 1942
GILDERSLEEVE'S BAD DAY
RKO Radio; 1943
GILDERSLEEVE ON BROADWAY
RKO Radio; 1943
A NIGHT OF ADVENTURE
RKO Radio; 1944
GILDERSLEEVE'S GHOST
RKO Radio; 1944
GIRL RUSH
RKO Radio; 1944
THE FALCON IN HOLLYWOOD
RKO Radio; 1944
ZOMBIES ON BROADWAY
RKO Radio; 1945

continued

Douglas, Gordon
continued

FIRST YANK INTO TOKYO
RKO Radio; 1945
DICK TRACY VS. CUEBALL
RKO Radio; 1946
SAN QUENTIN
RKO Radio; 1946
IF YOU KNEW SUSIE
RKO Radio; 1948
THE BLACK ARROW
Columbia; 1948
WALK A CROOKED MILE
Columbia; 1948
MR. SOFT TOUCH
co-director with Henry Levin; Columbia; 1949
THE DOOLINS OF OKLAHOMA
Columbia; 1949
THE NEVADAN
Columbia; 1950
FORTUNES OF CAPTAIN BLOOD
Columbia; 1950
ROGUES OF SHERWOOD FOREST
Columbia; 1950
KISS TOMORROW GOODBYE
United Artists; 1950
BETWEEN MIDNIGHT AND DAWN
Columbia; 1950
THE GREAT MISSOURI RAID
Paramount; 1951
ONLY THE VALIANT
Warner Brothers; 1951
I WAS A COMMUNIST FOR THE FBI
Warner Brothers; 1951
COME FILL THE CUP
Warner Brothers; 1951
MARU MARU
Warner Brothers; 1952
THE IRON MISTRESS
Warner Brothers; 1952
SHE'S BACK ON BROADWAY
Warner Brothers; 1953
THE CHARGE AT FEATHER CREEK
Warner Brothers; 1953
SO THIS IS LOVE
Warner Brothers; 1953
THEM
Warner Brothers; 1954
YOUNG AT HEART
Warner Brothers; 1954
THE McCONNELL STORY
Warner Brothers; 1955
SINCERELY YOURS
Warner Brothers; 1955
SANTIAGO
Warner Brothers; 1956
THE BIG LAND
Warner Brothers; 1957
BOMBERS B-52
Warner Brothers; 1957
FORT DOBBS
Warner Brothers; 1958
THE FIEND WHO WALKED THE WEST
20th Century-Fox; 1958
UP PERISCOPE
Warner Brothers; 1959
YELLOWSTONE KELLY
Warner Brothers; 1959
GOLD OF THE SEVEN SAINTS
Warner Brothers; 1961
THE SINS OF RACHEL CADE
Warner Brothers; 1961
CLAUDELLE INGLISH
Warner Brothers; 1961
FOLLOW THAT DREAM
United Artists; 1962
CALL ME BWANA
United Artists; 1963

continued

Douglas, Gordon
continued

ROBIN AND THE SEVEN HOODS
Warner Brothers; 1964
RIO CONCHOS
20th Century-Fox; 1964
SYLVIA
Paramount; 1965
HARLOW
Paramount; 1965
STAGECOACH
20th Century-Fox; 1966
WAY...WAY OUT!
20th Century-Fox; 1966
IN LIKE FLINT
20th Century-Fox; 1967
CHUKA
Paramount; 1967
TONY ROME
20th Century-Fox; 1967
THE DETECTIVE
20th Century-Fox; 1968
LADY IN CEMENT
20th Century-Fox; 1968
SKULLDUGGERY
Universal; 1970
BARQUERO
United Artists; 1970
THEY CALL ME MISTER TIBBS!
United Artists; 1970
SLAUGHTER'S BIG RIP-OFF
American International; 1973
NEVADA SMITH
Rackin-Hayes Productions/Paramount TV; telefeature; 1975
VIVA KNIEVEL!
Warner Brothers; 1978

Douglas, Kirk
(Issur Danielovitch)
b. December 9, 1916
Amsterdam, New York
Business:
The Bryna Company
141 El Camino Drive
Beverly Hills, CA 90212
(213) 274-5294

SCALAWAG
Paramount; 1973; U.S.-Italian
POSSE
Paramount; 1975

Dowd, Nancy

LOVE
co-director with Annette Cohen, Liv Ullmann & Mai Zetterling; Coup Films; 1981; Canadian

Downey, Robert
b. June, 1936
Business:
8497 Crescent Drive
Hollywood, CA 90046
Attorney:
Franklin, Wienrib, Rudell
New York
(212) 489-0680

BABO 73
1963
CHAFED ELBOWS
Grove Press; 1965
NO MORE EXCUSES
Rogosin; 1968
PUTNEY SWOPE
Cinema 5; 1969
POUND
United Artists; 1970
GREASER'S PALACE
Greaser's Palace; 1972
TWO TONS OF TURQUOISE TO TAOS TONIGHT
1976
JIVE
1979
MAD MAGAZINE PRESENTS UP THE ACADEMY
Warner Brothers; 1980

Dragoti, Stan
Agent:
Creative Artists Agency
Los Angeles
(213) 277-4545
Business:
E.U.E.-Screen Gems
3701 Oak Street
Burbank, CA 91505
(213) 843-3221

DIRTY LITTLE BILLY
Columbia; 1972
LOVE AT FIRST BITE
American International; 1979

Dreifuss, Arthur
b. March 25, 1908
Frankfurt am Main, Germany
Home:
3950 Los Feliz Blvd.
Los Angeles, CA 90027
(213) 662-5262
Agent:
George Michaud Agency
Encino
(213) 981-6680
Business:
1508½ W. Victory Blvd.
Burbank, CA 91506
(213) 841-1459

MYSTERY IN SWING
1940
REG'LAR FELLERS
1941
BABY FACE MORGAN
1942
THE BOSS OF BIG TOWN
1942
THE PAY-OFF
1942
SARONG GIRL
1943
MELODY PARADE
1943
CAMPUS RHYTHM
1943
NEARLY EIGHTEEN
1943
THE SULTAN'S DAUGHTER
1944
EVER SINCE VENUS
1944
EDDIE WAS A LADY
1945
BOSTON BLACKIE BOOKED ON SUSPICION
Columbia; 1945
BOSTON BLACKIE'S RENDEZVOUS
Columbia; 1945
THE GAY SENORITA
Columbia; 1945
PRISON SHIP
Columbia; 1945
JUNIOR PROM
1946
FREDDIE STEPS OUT
1946
HIGH SCHOOL HERO
1946
VACATION DAYS
1947
BETTY CO-ED
1947
LITTLE MISS BROADWAY
Columbia; 1947
TWO BLONDES AND A REDHEAD
1947
SWEET GENEVIEVE
1947
GLAMOUR GIRL
1948
MARY LOU
Columbia; 1948
I SURRENDER DEAR
1948
AN OLD-FASHIONED GIRL
1949
MANHATTAN ANGEL
Columbia; 1948
SHAMROCK HILL
1949
THERE'S A GIRL IN MY HEART
1950
LIFE BEGINS AT 17
Columbia; 1958

continued

Dreifuss, Arthur
continued

THE LAST BLITZKRIEG
Columbia; 1959
JUKE BOX RHYTHM
Columbia; 1959
THE QUARE FELLOW
Astor; 1962; Irish-British
RIOT ON SUNSET STRIP
American International; 1967
THE LOVE-INS
Columbia; 1967
FOR SINGLES ONLY
Columbia; 1968
A TIME TO SING
M-G-M; 1968
THE YOUNG RUNAWAYS
M-G-M; 1968

Dubin, Charles S.
Home:
651 Lorna Lane
Los Angeles, CA 90049
Agent:
Creative Artists Agency
Los Angeles
(213) 277-4545

MISTER ROCK & ROLL
Paramount; 1957
TO DIE IN PARIS
co-director with Allen Reisner; Universal TV; telefeature; 1968
MURDER ONCE REMOVED
Metromedia Productions; telefeature; 1971
MURDOCK'S GANG
Don Fedderson Productions; telefeature; 1973
MOVING VIOLATION
20th Century-Fox; 1976
THE DEADLY TRIANGLE
Columbia TV; telefeature; 1977
TOPPER
Cosmo Productions/Robert A. Papazian Productions; telefeature; 1979
ROOTS: THE NEXT GENERATIONS
co-director with John Erman, Lloyd Richards & Georg Stanford Brown; Wolper Productions; television mini-series; 1979
THE GATHERING, PART II
Hanna-Barbera Productions; telefeature; 1979
THE MANIONS OF AMERICA
co-director with Joseph Sargent; Roger Gimbel Productions/EMI TV/Argonaut Films Ltd.; television mini-series; 1981

Duchowny, Roger
Agent:
Creative Artists Agency
Los Angeles
(213) 277-4545

MURDER CAN HURT YOU!
Aaron Spelling Productions; telefeature; 1970

Duffell, Peter John
Contact:
British Film Institute
127 Charing Cross Road
London W.C. 2, England
01-437-4355

PARTNERS IN CRIME
Allied Artists; 1961; British
THE HOUSE THAT DRIPPED BLOOD
Cinerama Releasing Corporation; 1971; British
ENGLAND MADE ME
Cine Globe; 1973; British
INSIDE OUT
Warner Brothers; 1976; British
CAUGHT ON A TRAIN
BBC-TV; telefeature; 1980; British

Duke, Daryl
Agent:
I.C.M.
Hollywood
(213) 550-4000

THE PSYCHIATRIST: GOD BLESS THE CHILDREN
Universal TV; telefeature; 1970
PAYDAY
Cinerama Releasing Corporation; 1972
HAPPINESS IS A WARM CLUE
Universal TV; telefeature; 1973
THE PRESIDENT'S PLANE IS MISSING
ABC Circle Films; telefeature; 1973

continued

Duke, Daryl
continued

I HEARD THE OWL CALL MY NAME
Tomorrow Entertainment; telefeature; 1973
A CRY FOR HELP
Universal TV; telefeature; 1975
THEY ONLY COME OUT AT NIGHT
M-G-M TV; telefeature; 1975
GRIFFIN AND PHOENIX
ABC Circle Films; telefeature; 1976
THE SILENT PARTNER
EMC Film/Aurora; 1979; Canadian
HARD FEELINGS
Astral Bellevue; 1981; Canadian

Durand, Rudy
Business:
361 N. Canon Drive
Beverly Hills, CA 90210
(213) 654-8882
Business Manager:
Sandy Singer
Beverly Hills
(213) 478-3002

TILT
Warner Brothers; 1979

Dylan, Bob

RENALDO AND CLARA
Circuit; 1978

Eastman, Charles
Business:
(213) 376-0411
(213) 376-0251

THE ALL-AMERICAN BOY
Warner Brothers; 1973

Eastwood, Clint
b. May 31, 1930
San Francisco, California
Business:
The Malpaso Company
1900 Avenue of the Stars
Los Angeles, CA 90067
(213) 277-1900
Agent:
William Morris Agency
Beverly Hills
(213) 274-7451

PLAY MISTY FOR ME
Universal; 1971
HIGH PLAINS DRIFTER
Universal; 1972
BREEZY
Universal; 1973
THE EIGER SANCTION
Universal; 1974
THE OUTLAW - JOSEY WALES
Warner Brothers; 1976
THE GAUNTLET
Warner Brothers; 1977
BRONCO BILLY
Warner Brothers; 1980
FIREFOX
Warner Brothers; 1982

Edwards, Blake
b. July 26, 1922
Tulsa, Oklahoma
Business:
Trellis Enterprises
1888 Century Park East
Los Angeles, CA 90067
(213) 553-6741

BRING YOUR SMILE ALONG
Columbia; 1955
HE LAUGHED LAST
Columbia; 1956
MISTER CORY
M-G-M; 1957
THIS HAPPY FEELING
Universal; 1958
THE PERFECT FURLOUGH
Universal; 1959
OPERATION PETTICOAT
Universal; 1959
HIGH TIME
20th Century-Fox; 1960
BREAKFAST AT TIFFANY'S
Paramount; 1961
EXPERIMENT IN TERROR
Warner Brothers; 1962
THE LAST ADVENTURE
Universal; 1969; Italian-French

continued

Edwards, Blake
continued

DAYS OF WINE AND ROSES
Warner Brothers; 1962
THE PINK PANTHER
United Artists; 1964
A SHOT IN THE DARK
United Artists; 1964
THE GREAT RACE
Warner Brothers; 1965
WHAT DID YOU DO IN THE WAR, DADDY?
United Artists; 1966
GUNN
Warner Brothers; 1967
THE PARTY
United Artists; 1968
DARLING LILI
Paramount; 1970
WILD ROVERS
M-G-M; 1971
THE CAREY TREATMENT
M-G-M; 1972
THE TAMARIND SEED
Avco Embassy; 1974
RETURN OF THE PINK PANTHER
United Artists; 1975; British
THE PINK PANTHER STRIKES AGAIN
United Artists; 1976; British
REVENGE OF THE PINK PANTHER
United Artists; 1978; British
10
Orion Pictures/Warner Brothers; 1979
S.O.B.
Paramount/Lorimar; 1981
VICTOR/VICTORIA
M-G-M/United Artists; 1982

Edwards, Vince
(Vincent Edward Zoimo)
b. July 9, 1928
New York, New York

MANEATER
Universal TV; telefeature; 1973

Elfstrom, Robert

THE NASHVILLE SOUND
co-director with David Hoffman; 1970
JOHNNY CASH! THE MAN, HIS WORLD, HIS MUSIC
Continental; 1970
PETE SEEGER...AND SONG AND A STONE
Theatre Exchange; 1972
THE GOSPEL ROAD
20th Century-Fox; 1973
MYSTERIES OF THE SEA
co-director with Al Giddings; Polygram Pictures/Ocean Films Ltd.; 1980

Elikann, Larry
Business:
The Larry Elikann Company
100 S. Doheny Drive
Los Angeles, CA 90048
(213) 271-4406

THE GREAT WALLENDAS
Daniel Wilson Productions; telefeature; 1978
CHARLIE AND THE GREAT BALLOON CHASE
Daniel Wilson Productions; telefeature; 1981

Elliott, Lang
Business:
TriStar Pictures, Inc.
3390 Peachtree Road, N.E.
Atlanta, Georgia 30326
(404) 231-8726

THE PRIVATE EYES
New World; 1980

Enders, Robert
Agent:
Peter Crouch Associates
59 Frith Street
London W.1., England
01-734-2167

STEVIE
First Artists; 1978; British

Endfield, Cy
(Cyril Raker Endfield)
b. November, 1914
South Africa
Contact:
British Film Institute
127 Charing Cross Road
London W.C. 2, England
01-437-4355

GENTLEMAN JOE PALOOKA
Monogram; 1946
STORK BITES MAN
United Artists; 1947; British
THE ARGYLE SECRETS
Film Classics; 1948; British
JOE PALOOKA IN THE BIG FIGHT
Monogram; 1949
THE UNDERWORLD STORY
United Artists; 1950
THE SOUND OF FURY
United Artists; 1950
TARZAN'S SAVAGE FURY
RKO Radio; 1952
LIMPING MAN
co-director with Charles De Lautour; uncredited; Lippert; 1953; British
COLONEL MARCH INVESTIGATES
Criterion; 1953; British
THE MASTER PLAN
directed under pseudonym of Hugh Raker; Astor; 1954; British
IMPULSE
co-director with Charles De Lautour; uncredited; 1955; British
THE SECRET
Eros; 1955; British
CHILD IN THE HOUSE
co-director with Charles De Lautour; uncredited; Eros; 1956; British
HELL DRIVERS
Rank; 1957; British
SEA FURY
Lopert; 1958; British
JET STORM
United Producers Organization; 1959; British
MYSTERIOUS ISLAND
Columbia; 1961; British
HIDE AND SEEK
Universal; 1964; British
ZULU
Embassy; 1964; British
SANDS OF THE KALAHARI
Paramount; 1965; British
DE SADE
American International; 1969; U.S.-West German
UNIVERSAL SOLDIER
1971; British

Englund, George
b. June 22, 1926
Washington, D.C.
Business:
Englund Productions
4000 Warner Blvd.
Burbank, CA 91522
(213) 954-6000

THE UGLY AMERICAN
Universal; 1963
SIGNPOST TO MURDER
M-G-M; 1965
ZACHARIAH
Cinerama Releasing Corporation; 1970
SNOW JOB
Warner Brothers; 1972
A CHRISTMAS TO REMEMBER
George Englund Enterprises; telefeature; 1978

Enrico, Robert
b. April 13, 1931
Lievin, France
Contact:
French Film Office
745 Fifth Avenue
New York, N.Y. 10151
(212) 832-8860

AU COEUR DE LA VIE
1962; French
LA BELLE VIE
1963; French
THE WISE GUYS
Universal; 1965; French

continued

Enrico, Robert
continued

ZITA
Regional; 1968; French
HO!
1968; French
UN PEU...BEAUCOUP...PASSIONEMENT
1971; French
BOULEVARD DU RHUM
1972; French
LES CAIDS
1972; French
LE COMPAGNON INDESIRABLE
1973; French
LE SECRET
Cinema National; 1974; French
THE OLD GUN
Surrogate; 1976; French
COUP DE FOUDRE
1978; French
UN NEVEU SILENCIEUX
1978; French

Erman, John
Agent:
Creative Artists Agency
Los Angeles
(213) 277-4545

MAKING IT
20th Century-Fox; 1971
ACE ELI AND RODGER OF THE SKIES
directed under pseudonym of Bill Sampson; 20th Century-Fox; 1973
LETTERS FROM THREE LOVERS
Spelling-Goldberg Productions; telefeature;1973
GREEN EYES
ABC-TV; telefeature; 1977
ROOTS
co-director with David Greene, Marvin J. Chomsky & Gilbert Moses; Wolper Productions; television mini-series; 1977
ALEXANDER: THE OTHER SIDE OF DAWN
Douglas Cramer Productions; telefeature; 1977
JUST ME & YOU
Roger Gimbel Productions/EMI TV; telefeature; 1978
ROOTS: THE NEXT GENERATIONS
co-director with Charles S. Dubin, Lloyd Richards & Georg Stanford Brown; Wolper Productions; television mini-series; 1979
MY OLD MAN
Zeitman-McNichol-Halmi Productions; telefeature; 1979
MOVIOLA
Wolper-Margulies Productions/Warner Brothers TV; television mini-series; 1980

Falk, Harry
Agent:
William Morris Agency
Beverly Hills
(213) 274-7451

THREE'S A CROWD
Screen Gems/Columbia TV; telefeature; 1969
THE DEATH SQUAD
Spelling-Goldberg Productions; telefeature; 1974
MEN OF THE DRAGON
Wolper Productions; telefeature; 1974
THE ABDUCTION OF SAINT ANNE
QM Productions; telefeature; 1975
MANDRAKE
Universal TV; telefeature; 1979
CENTENNIAL
co-director with Bernard McEveety & Virgil Vogel; Universal TV; television mini-series; 1979
BEULAH LAND
co-director with Virgil Vogel; David Gerber Company/Columbia TV; television mini-series; 1980
THE NIGHT THE CITY SCREAMED
David Gerber Company; telefeature; 1980
THE CONTENDER
co-director with Lou Antonio; Universal TV; telefeature; 1980
THE SOPHISTICATED GENTS
Daniel Wilson Productions; telefeature; 1981

Fanaka, Jamaa

WELCOME HOME, BROTHER CHARLES
Crown International; 1975
EMMA MAE
Pro-International; 1977
PENITENTIARY
Jerry Gross Organization; 1980
PENITENTIARY II
Ideal Films; 1982

Fargo, James

Contact:
Directors Guild of America
Los Angeles
(213) 656-1220

THE ENFORCER
Warner Brothers; 1976
EVERY WHICH WAY BUT LOOSE
Warner Brothers; 1978
CARAVANS
Universal; 1979; U.S.-Iranian
GAME FOR VULTURES
1979
THE JADE JUNGLE
M-G-M/United Artists; 1982

Fassbinder, Rainer Werner

b. May 31, 1946
Bad Worishofen, Bavaria,
West Germany
Contact:
Bundesverband Deutscher Film
Produzenten
Lagenbeck Street, No. 9
6200 Wiesbaden, West Germany
306 200

LOVE IS COLDER THAN DEATH
New Yorker; 1969; West German
KATZELMACHER
New Yorker; 1969; West German
THE AMERICAN SOLDIER
1970; West German
WHY DOES HERR R. RUN AMOK?
New Yorker; 1970; West German
GODS OF THE PLAGUE
New Yorker; 1970; West German
THE NIKLASHAUSER DRIVE
WDR-TV; telefeature; 1970; West German
BEWARE OF A HOLY WHORE
New Yorker; 1971; West German
RIO DAS MORTES
ARD-TV; telefeature; 1971; West German
PIONEERS IN INGOLSTADT
ZDF-TV; telefeature; 1971; West German
WHITY
1971; West German
THE BITTER TEARS OF PETRA VON KANT
New Yorker; 1972; West German
THE MERCHANT OF FOUR SEASONS
New Yorker; 1972; West German
EIGHT HOURS DON'T MAKE A DAY
WDR-TV; television mini-series;
1972; West German
GAME PASS
SFB-TV; telefeature; 1973; West German
WORLD ON A WIRE
WDR-TV; telefeature; 1973; West German
FEAR EATS THE SOUL - ALI
New Yorker; 1974; West German
MARTHA
WDR-TV; telefeature; 1974; West German
MOTHER KUSTERS GOES TO HEAVEN
New Yorker; 1975; West German
SURVIVAL OF THE FITTEST
1975; West German
FOX AND HIS FRIENDS
New Yorker; 1976; West German
FEAR OF FEAR
1976; West German
CHINESE ROULETTE
New Yorker; 1976; West German
SATAN'S BREW
New Yorker; 1976; West German
IN A YEAR OF 13 MOONS
New Yorker; 1977; West German
JAIL BAIT
New Yorker; 1977; West German
EFFI BRIEST
New Yorker; 1977; West German

continued

Fassbinder, Rainer Werner
continued

DESPAIR
New Line Cinema; 1978; West German
THE MARRIAGE OF MARIA BRAUN
New Yorker; 1979; West German
BERLIN-ALEXANDERPLATZ
television mini-series; 1979; West German
THE THIRD GENERATION
New Yorker; 1979; West German
LILI MARLEEN
United Artists Classics; 1981; West German
LOLA
Rialto Film; 1981; West German

Feldman, Marty
b. 1938
London, England
Business Manager:
Shapiro-West & Associates
Beverly Hills
(213) 278-8896

THE LAST REMAKE OF BEAU GESTE
Universal; 1977
IN GOD WE TRUST
Universal; 1980

Fellini, Federico
b. January 20, 1920
Rimini, Italy
Contact:
Minister of Tourism
Via Della Ferratella
No. 51
00184 Rome, Italy
06-7732

VARIETY LIGHTS
co-director with Alberto Lattuada; Pathe Contemporary; 1950; Italian
THE WHITE SHEIK
Contemporary; 1952; Italian
I VITTELONI
API Productions; 1953; Italian
LOVE IN THE CITY
co-director; Italian Films Export; 1953; Italian
LA STRADA
Trans-Lux; 1954; Italian
IL BIDONE
Astor; 1955; Italian
NIGHTS OF CABIRIA
Lopert; 1957; Italian
LA DOLCE VITA
Astor; 1960; Italian
BOCCACCIO '70
co-director with Luchino Visconti & Vittorio De Sica; Embassy; 1962; Italian
8½
Embassy; 1963; Italian
JULIET OF THE SPIRITS
Rizzoli; 1965; Italian-French-West German
SPIRITS OF THE DEAD
co-director with Roger Vadim & Louis Malle; American International; 1969; French-Italian
FELLINI SATYRICON
United Artists; 1970; Italian-French
THE CLOWNS
Levitt-Pickman; 1971; Italian-French-West German; made for television
FELLINI'S ROMA
United Artists; 1972; Italian-French
AMARCORD
New World; 1974; Italian
CASANOVA
Universal; 1977; Italian
ORCHESTRA REHEARSAL
New Yorker; 1979; Italian; made for television
CITY OF WOMEN
New Yorker; 1981; Italian-French

Fenady, Georg J.
Agent:
Jim Jacobson Agency
Los Angeles
(213) 275-0804

ARNOLD
Cinerama Releasing Corporation; 1974
TERROR IN THE WAX MUSEUM
Cinerama Releasing Corporation; 1974
HANGING BY A THREAD
Irwin Allen Productions/Warner Brothers TV; telefeature; 1979

Ferrer, Jose

(Jose Vincente Ferrer de Otero y Cintron)
b. January 8, 1912
Santurce, Puerto Rico
Business:
2 Penn Plaza
New York, N.Y. 10001
(212) 947-9930

THE SHRIKE
Universal; 1955
THE COCKLESHELL HEROES
Columbia; 1956; British
THE GREAT MAN
Universal; 1956
I ACCUSE!
M-G-M; 1958
THE HIGH COST OF LOVING
M-G-M; 1958
RETURN TO PEYTON PLACE
20th Century-Fox; 1961
STATE FAIR
20th Century-Fox; 1962

Ferrer, Mel

b. August 25, 1917
Elberon, New Jersey

THE GIRL OF THE LIMBERLOST
Columbia; 1945
VENDETTA
RKO Radio; 1950
THE SECRET FURY
RKO Radio; 1950
GREEN MANSIONS
M-G-M; 1959
CABRIOLA
Columbia; 1966; Spanish

Ferreri, Marco

b. May 11, 1928
Milan, Italy
Contact:
Minister of Tourism
Via Della Ferratella
No. 51
00184 Rome, Italy
06-7732

EL PISITO
1958; Spanish
LOS CHICOS
1959; Spanish
THE WHEELCHAIR
1960; Spanish
LE ITALIANE E L'AMORE
co-director; 1961; Italian
THE CONJUGAL BED
Embassy; 1963; Italian-French
THE APE WOMAN
Embassy; 1964; Italian
CONTROSESSO
co-director; 1964; Italian
OGGI DOMANI E DOPODEMANI
co-director; 1965; Italian
MARCIA NUZIALE
1966; Italian
L'HAREM
1967; Italian
THE MAN WITH THE BALLOONS
Sigma III; 1968; French-Italian
DILLINGER IS DEAD
1969; Italian
THE SEED OF MAN
SRL; 1970; Italian
L'UDIENZA
1971; Italian
LIZA
Horizon; 1972; French-Italian
LA GRANDE BOUFFE
ABKCO; 1973; French-Italian
TOUCHEZ PAS LA FEMME BLANCHE
1974; French-Italian
THE LAST WOMAN
Columbia; 1976; Italian-French
BYE BYE MONKEY
Gaumont; 1978; Italian
CIAO MALE
1978; Italian
STORIES OF ORDINARY MADNESS
Titanus; 1981; Italian

Finney, Albert

b. May 9, 1936
Salford, England

CHARLIE BUBBLES
Regional; 1968; British

Fischer, Max

THE LUCKY STAR
Levitt-Pickman; 1981; Canadian

Fisk, Jack
b. December 19, 1945
Ipava, Illinois
Agent:
Creative Artists Agency
Los Angeles
(213) 277-4545

RAGGEDY MAN
Universal; 1981

Fleischer, Richard
b. December 8, 1916
Brooklyn, New York
Agent:
Phil Gersh Agency
Beverly Hills
(213) 274-6611

CHILD OF DIVORCE
1946
BANJO
RKO Radio; 1947
DESIGN FOR DEATH
1948
SO THIS IS NEW YORK
United Artists; 1948
BODYGUARD
Columbia; 1948
MAKE MINE LAUGHS
RKO Radio; 1949
THE CLAY PIGEON
RKO Radio; 1949
FOLLOW ME QUIETLY
RKO Radio; 1949
TRAPPED
Eagle Lion; 1949
ARMORED CAR ROBBERY
RKO Radio; 1950
THE NARROW MARGIN
RKO Radio; 1952
THE HAPPY TIME
Columbia; 1952
ARENA
M-G-M; 1953
20,000 LEAGUES UNDER THE SEA
Buena Vista; 1954
VIOLENT SATURDAY
20th Century-Fox; 1955
THE GIRL IN THE RED VELVET SWING
20th Century-Fox; 1955
BANDIDO
United Artists; 1956
BETWEEN HEAVEN AND HELL
20th Century-Fox; 1956
THE VIKINGS
United Artists; 1958
THESE THOUSAND HILLS
20th Century-Fox; 1959
COMPULSION
20th Century-Fox; 1959
CRACK IN THE MIRROR
20th Century-Fox; 1960
THE BIG GAMBLE
20th Century-Fox; 1961
BARABBAS
Columbia; 1962; Italian
FANTASTIC VOYAGE
20th Century-Fox; 1966
DR. DOLITTLE
20th Century-Fox; 1967
THE BOSTON STRANGLER
20th Century-Fox; 1968
CHE!
20th Century-Fox; 1969

continued

Fleischer, Richard
continued

TORA! TORA! TORA!
co-director with Kinji Fukasaku;
20th Century-Fox; 1970; U.S.-Japanese
10 RILLINGTON PLACE
Columbia; 1971; British
SEE NO EVIL
Columbia; 1971; British
THE LAST RUN
M-G-M; 1971
THE NEW CENTURIONS
Columbia; 1972
SOYLENT GREEN
M-G-M; 1972
THE DON IS DEAD
Universal; 1973
THE SPIKES GANG
United Artists; 1974
MR. MAJESTYK
United Artists; 1974
MANDINGO
Paramount; 1975
THE INCREDIBLE SARAH
Reader's Digest; 1976; British
CROSSED SWORDS
Warner Brothers; 1978; British
ASHANTI
Columbia; 1979; Swiss-U.S.
THE JAZZ SINGER
AFD; 1980
TOUGH ENOUGH
American Cinema; 1981

Flemyng, Gordon
Contact:
British Film Institute
127 Charing Cross Road
London W.C. 2, England
01-437-4355

SOLD FOR SPARROW
Schoenfield; 1962; British
FIVE TO ONE
Allied Artists; 1963; British
JUST FOR FUN
Columbia; 1963
DR. WHO AND THE DALEKS
Continental; 1966; British
DALEKS - INVASION EARTH 2150 A.D.
Continental; 1966; British
THE SPLIT
M-G-M; 1968
GREAT CATHERINE
Warner Brothers; 1968; British
THE LAST GRENADE
Cinerama Releasing Corporation; 1970; British

Flicker, Theodore J.
Agent:
(213) 550-1060

THE TROUBLEMAKER
Janus; 1964
THE PRESIDENT'S ANALYST
Paramount; 1967
UP IN THE CELLAR
American International; 1970
PLAYMATES
ABC Circle Films; telefeature; 1972
GUESS WHO'S SLEEPING IN MY BED?
ABC Circle Films; telefeature; 1973
JUST A LITTLE INCONVENIENCE
Universal TV; telefeature; 1977
JACOB TWO-TWO MEETS THE HOODED FANG
Cinema Shares International; 1978; Canadian
LAST OF THE GOOD GUYS
Columbia TV; telefeature; 1978
WHERE THE LADIES GO
Universal TV; telefeature; 1980
SOGGY BOTTOM, U.S.A.
Cinemax Marketing & Distribution; 1981

Flynn, John
Home:
574 Latimer Road
Santa Monica, CA 90402
(213) 454-6850
Agent:
I.C.M.
Hollywood
(213) 550-4000

THE SERGEANT
Warner Brothers; 1968
THE JERUSALEM FILE
M-G-M; 1972; U.S.-Israeli
THE OUTFIT
M-G-M; 1974
ROLLING THUNDER
American International; 1978
DEFIANCE
American International; 1980
MARILYN: THE UNTOLD STORY
co-director with Jack Arnold & Lawrence Schiller; Lawrence Schiller Productions; telefeature; 1980
SOME SUNNY DAY
Petersmann-Lottimer Productions; 1982

Fonda, Peter
b. February 23, 1939
New York, New York
Business Manager:
Nanas, Stern, Biels & Co.
Beverly Hills
(213) 273-2501

THE HIRED HAND
Universal; 1971
IDAHO TRANSFER
Cinemation; 1975
WANDA NEVADA
United Artists; 1979

Forbes, Bryan
(Bryan Clarke)
b. July 22, 1926
London, England
Agent:
William Morris Agency
Beverly Hills
(213) 274-7451

WHISTLE DOWN THE WIND
Pathe-America; 1962; British
THE L-SHAPED ROOM
Columbia; 1963; British
SEANCE ON A WET AFTERNOON
Artixo; 1964; British
KING RAT
Columbia; 1965; British
THE WRONG BOX
Columbia; 1966; British
THE WHISPERERS
United Artists; 1967; British
DEADFALL
20th Century-Fox; 1968; British
THE MADWOMAN OF CHAILLOT
Warner Brothers; 1969; British
LONG AGO TOMORROW (The Raging Moon)
Cinema 5; 1971; British
THE STEPFORD WIVES
Columbia; 1975
THE SLIPPER AND THE ROSE: THE STORY OF CINDERELLA
Universal; 1976; British
INTERNATIONAL VELVET
M-G-M/United Artists; 1978; British
SUNDAY LOVERS
co-director with Edouard Molinaro, Dino Risi & Gene Wilder; M-G-M/United Artists; 1981; U.S.-British-Italian-French
WHOSE LITTLE GIRL ARE YOU?
Golden Harvest; 1982; British

Foreman, Carl
b. July 23, 1914
Chicago, Illinois

THE VICTORS
Columbia; 1963

Forman, Milos
b. February 18, 1932
Caslav, Czechoslovakia
Agent:
Robert Lantz
New York City
(212) 751-1207

COMPETITION
Brandon; 1963; Czech
BLACK PETER
Billings; 1964; Czech
LOVES OF A BLONDE
Prominent; 1966; Czech
THE FIREMAN'S BALL
Cinema 5; 1968; Czech

continued

Forman, Milos
continued

TAKING OFF
Universal; 1971
VISIONS OF EIGHT
co-director; Cinema 5; 1973
ONE FLEW OVER THE CUCKOO'S NEST
United Artists; 1976
HAIR
United Artists; 1979
RAGTIME
Paramount; 1981

Fosse, Bob
b. June 23, 1927
Chicago, Illinois
Business:
850 Seventh Avenue
New York, N.Y. 10019
(212) 245-9049
Agent:
I.C.M.
New York City
(212) 556-5600

SWEET CHARITY
Universal; 1969
CABARET
Allied Artists; 1972
LENNY
United Artists; 1974
ALL THAT JAZZ
20th Century-Fox/Columbia; 1979

Fraker, William A.
b. 1923
Los Angeles, California
Home:
2572 Outpost Drive
Hollywood, CA 90068

MONTE WALSH
National General; 1970
A REFLECTION OF FEAR
Columbia; 1973; British
THE LEGEND OF THE LONE RANGER
Universal/AFD; 1981

Francis, Freddie
b. 1917
London, England
Contact:
British Film Institute
127 Charing Cross Road
London W.C. 2, England
01-437-4355

TWO AND TWO MAKE SIX
Union; 1962; British
THE BRAIN (Vengeance)
Garrick; 1962; British-West German
PARANOIAC
Universal; 1963; British
NIGHTMARE
Universal; 1964; British
THE EVIL OF FRANKENSTEIN
Universal; 1964; British
TRAITOR'S GATE
Columbia; 1964; British-West German
DR. TERROR'S HOUSE OF HORRORS
Paramount; 1965; British
HYSTERIA
M-G-M; 1965; British
THE SKULL
Paramount; 1965; British
THE PSYCHOPATH
Paramount; 1966; British
THE DEADLY BEES
Paramount; 1967; British
THEY CAME FROM BEYOND SPACE
Embassy; 1967; British
TORTURE GARDEN
Columbia; 1968; British
DRACULA HAS RISEN FROM THE GRAVE
Warner Brothers; 1969; British
MUMSY, NANNY, SONNY & GIRLY (Girly)
Cinerama Releasing Corporation; 1970; British
TROG
Warner Brothers; 1970; British
THE HAPPENING OF THE VAMPIRE
1971; European
TALES FROM THE CRYPT
Cinerama Releasing Corporation; 1972; British
ASYLUM
Cinerama Releasing Corporation; 1972; British
TALES THAT WITNESS MADNESS
Paramount; 1973; British

continued

Francis, Freddie
continued

THE CREEPING FLESH
Columbia; 1973; British
SON OF DRACULA
Cinemation; 1974; British
CRAZE
Warner Brothers; 1974; British
THE GHOUL
Rank; 1974; British
LEGEND OF THE WEREWOLF
1974; European

Frank, Melvin

b. August 13, 1913
Chicago, Illinois
Home:
1505 San Remo Drive
Pacific Palisades, CA 90272
(213) 459-2771
Agent:
William Morris Agency
Beverly Hills
(213) 274-7451

THE REFORMER AND THE REDHEAD
co-director with Norman Panama; M-G-M; 1950
CALLAWAY WENT THATAWAY
co-director with Norman Panama; M-G-M; 1951
STRICTLY DISHONORABLE
co-director with Norman Panama; M-G-M; 1951
ABOVE AND BEYOND
co-director with Norman Panama; M-G-M; 1952
KNOCK ON WOOD
co-director with Norman Panama;Paramount;1954
THE COURT JESTER
co-director with Norman Panama;Paramount;1956
THAT CERTAIN FEELING
co-director with Norman Panama;Paramount;1956
THE JAYHAWKERS
Paramount; 1959
LI'L ABNER
Paramount; 1959
THE FACTS OF LIFE
United Artists; 1960
STRANGE BEDFELLOWS
Universal; 1965
BUONA SERA, MRS. CAMPBELL
United Artists; 1968
A TOUCH OF CLASS
Avco Embassy; 1973; British
THE PRISONER OF SECOND AVENUE
Warner Brothers; 1975
THE DUCHESS AND THE DIRTWATER FOX
20th Century-Fox; 1976
LOST AND FOUND
Columbia; 1979

Frankenheimer, John

b. February 19, 1930
Malba, New York
Business:
John Frankenheimer
Productions
2800 Olympic Blvd.
Santa Monica, CA 90404
(213) 829-0404
Agent:
I.C.M.
Hollywood
(213) 550-4205

THE YOUNG STRANGER
Allied Artists; 1957
THE YOUNG SAVAGES
United Artists; 1961
ALL FALL DOWN
M-G-M; 1962
BIRDMAN OF ALCATRAZ
United Artists; 1962
THE MANCHURIAN CANDIDATE
United Artists; 1962
SEVEN DAYS IN MAY
Paramount; 1964
THE TRAIN
United Artists; 1965; U.S.-French-Italian
SECONDS
Paramount; 1966
GRAND PRIX
M-G-M; 1966
THE FIXER
M-G-M; 1968; British
THE EXTRAORDINARY SEAMAN
M-G-M; 1969
THE GYPSY MOTHS
M-G-M; 1969
I WALK THE LINE
Columbia; 1970
THE HORSEMEN
Columbia; 1971

continued

Frankenheimer, John
continued

THE ICEMAN COMETH
American Film Theatre; 1973
IMPOSSIBLE OBJECT
Valoria; 1973; French-British
99 AND 44/100% DEAD
20th Century-Fox; 1974
FRENCH CONNECTION II
20th Century-Fox; 1975
BLACK SUNDAY
Paramount; 1976
PROPHECY
Paramount; 1979
THE EQUALS
CBS Theatrical Films; 1982

Franklin, Richard
Contact:
Australian Film Commission
9229 Sunset Blvd.
Los Angeles, CA 90069
(213) 275-7074

BELINDA
Aquarius; 1972; Australian
LOVELAND
Illustrated; 1973; Australian
DICK DOWN UNDER
1974; Australian
THE TRUE STORY OF ESKIMO NELL
Filmways; 1975; Australian
FANTASM
Filmways Australasian; 1977; Australian
PATRICK
Cinema Shares International; 1979; Australian
ROAD GAMES
Avco Embassy; 1981; Australian

Frawley, James
Business:
Maya Films Ltd.
9220 Sunset Blvd.
Los Angeles, CA 90069
(213) 275-3138
Agent:
Herb Tobias & Associates
Los Angeles
(213) 277-6211

THE CHRISTIAN LICORICE STORE
National General; 1971
KID BLUE
20th Century-Fox; 1973
DELANCEY STREET: THE CRISIS WITHIN
Paramount TV; telefeature; 1975
THE BIG BUS
Paramount; 1976
THE MUPPET MOVIE
AFD; 1979; British
THE GREAT AMERICAN TRAFFIC JAM
Ten-Four Productions; telefeature; 1980

Freed, Herb

AWOL
BFB; 1973
HAUNTS
Intercontinental; 1977
BEYOND EVIL
IFI-Scope III; 1980
GRADUATION DAY
IFI-Scope III; 1981

Freedman, Jerrold
Business:
Chesapeake Films, Inc.
9220 Sunset Blvd.
Los Angeles, CA 90069
(213) 275-3138
Agent:
I.C.M.
Hollywood
(213) 550-4000

KANSAS CITY BOMBER
M-G-M; 1972
A COLD NIGHT'S DEATH
ABC Circle Films; telefeature; 1973
BLOOD SPORT
Danny Thomas Productions; telefeature; 1973
THE LAST ANGRY MAN
Screen Gems/Columbia TV; telefeature; 1974
SOME KIND OF MIRACLE
Lorimar Productions; telefeature; 1979
THIS MAN STANDS ALONE
Roger Gimbel Productions/EMI TV/Abby Mann Productions; telefeature; 1979
THE STREETS OF L.A.
George Englund Productions; telefeature; 1979
THE BOY WHO DRANK TOO MUCH
MTM Enterprises; telefeature; 1980
BORDERLINE
AFD: 1980

Friedenberg, Dick
Agent:
Writers & Artists Agency
Beverly Hills
(213) 550-8030

THE DEERSLAYER
Sunn Classic; telefeature; 1978
THE BERMUDA TRIANGLE
Sunn Classic; 1979

Friedkin, David

RIVER OF GOLD
Aaron Spelling Productions; telefeature; 1971

Friedkin, William
b. August 29, 1939
Chicago, Illinois
Agent:
William Morris Agency
Beverly Hills
(213) 274-7451

GOOD TIMES
Columbia; 1967
THE BIRTHDAY PARTY
Continental; 1968; British
THE NIGHT THEY RAIDED MINSKY'S
United Artists; 1968
THE BOYS IN THE BAND
National General; 1970
THE FRENCH CONNECTION
20th Century-Fox; 1971
THE EXORCIST
Warner Brothers; 1973
SORCERER
Universal/Paramount; 1977
THE BRINK'S JOB
Universal; 1978
CRUISING
United Artists/Lorimar; 1980

Freidman, Kim Harlene
Business Manager:
Marty Mickelson
Hollywood
(213) 858-1097

BEFORE AND AFTER
The Konigsberg Company; telefeature; 1979

Fruet, William
Home:
51 Olive Street
Toronto, Ontario M6G 1T7
Canada
(416) 535-3569

WEDDING IN WHITE
Avco Embassy; 1973; Canadian
THE HOUSE BY THE LAKE
American International; 1977; Canadian
SEARCH AND DESTROY
Film Ventures International; 1981
CHATWILL'S VERDICT
1981; Canadian
CRIES IN THE NIGHT
Barry Allen Productions; 1981; Canadian
DEATH BITE
Cinequiety Corporation; 1982; Canadian

Fuest, Robert
b. 1927
London, England
Contact:
Directors Guild of America
Los Angeles
(213) 656-1220

JUST LIKE A WOMAN
Monarch; 1966; British
AND SOON THE DARKNESS
Levitt-Pickman; 1970; British
WUTHERING HEIGHTS
American International; 1971; British
THE ABOMINABLE DR. PHIBES
American International; 1971; British
DR. PHIBES RISES AGAIN
American International; 1972; British
THE LAST DAYS OF MAN ON EARTH (The Final Programme)
New World; 1974; British
THE DEVIL'S RAIN
Bryanston; 1975; U.S.-Mexican
REVENGE OF THE STEPFORD WIVES
Edgar J. Scherick Productions; telefeature; 1980
APHRODITE
Scipion Films; 1982

Fuller, Samuel
b. August 12, 1911
Worcester, Massachusetts
Agent:
Chasin-Park-Citron
Los Angeles
(213) 273-7190

I SHOT JESSE JAMES
Screen Guild; 1949
THE BARON OF ARIZONA
Lippert; 1950
THE STEEL HELMET
Lippert; 1951
FIXED BAYONETS!
20th Century-Fox; 1951
PARK ROW
United Artists; 1952
PICKUP ON SOUTH STREET
20th Century-Fox; 1953
HELL AND HIGH WATER
20th Century-Fox; 1954
HOUSE OF BAMBOO
20th Century-Fox; 1955
RUN OF THE ARROW
20th Century-Fox; 1957
FORTY GUNS
20th Century-Fox; 1957
CHINA GATE
20th Century-Fox; 1957
VERBOTEN!
Columbia; 1958
THE CRIMSON KIMONO
Columbia; 1959
UNDERWORLD U.S.A.
Columbia; 1961
MERRILL'S MARAUDERS
Warner Brothers; 1962
SHOCK CORRIDOR
Allied Artists; 1963
THE NAKED KISS
Allied Artists; 1964
SHARK!
Heritage; 1970; U.S.-Mexican
DEAD PIGEON ON BEETHOVEN STREET
Emerson; 1972; West German
THE BIG RED ONE
United Artists/Lorimar; 1980
WHITE DOG
Paramount; 1982

Funt, Allen
Contact:
Directors Guild of America
New York City
(212) 581-0370

WHAT DO YOU SAY TO A NAKED LADY?
United Artists; 1970
MONEY TALKS
United Artists; 1971

Furie, Sidney J.
b. February 28, 1933
Toronto, Canada
Business:
Furie Productions, Inc.
9169 Sunset Blvd.
Los Angeles, CA 90069
Agent:
Paul Kohner Agency
Hollywood
(213) 550-1060

A DANGEROUS AGE
Ajay; 1959; Canadian
A COOL SOUND FROM HELL
1959; Canadian
DR. BLOOD'S COFFIN
United Artists; 1960; British
THE SNAKE WOMAN
United Artists; 1960; British
NIGHT OF PASSION
Astor; 1961; British
THREE ON A SPREE
United Artists; 1961; British
WONDERFUL TO BE YOUNG!
Paramount; 1961; British
THE BOYS
Gala; 1962; British
THE LEATHER BOYS
Allied Artists; 1964; British
SWINGERS' PARADISE
American International; 1964; British
THE IPCRESS FILE
Universal; 1965; British
THE APPALOOSA
Universal; 1966

continued

Furie, Sidney J.
continued

THE NAKED RUNNER
Warner Brothers; 1967; British
THE LAWYER
Paramount; 1970
LITTLE FAUSS AND BIG HALSY
Paramount; 1970
LADY SINGS THE BLUES
Paramount; 1972
HIT!
Paramount; 1973
SHEILA LEVINE IS DEAD AND LIVING IN NEW YORK
Paramount; 1975
GABLE AND LOMBARD
Universal; 1976
THE BOYS IN COMPANY C
Columbia; 1978
THE ENTITY
American Cinema; 1981

Gage, George
Business:
George Gage Productions
1303 N. Sierra Bonita Avenue
Los Angeles, CA 90046
(213) 874-7400

SKATEBOARD
Universal; 1978

Galfas, Timothy
Agent:
Shapiro-Lichtman Agency
Los Angeles
(213) 557-2244

BOGARD
L-T Films; 1975
THE BLACK STREETFIGHTER
New Line Cinema; 1976
REVENGE FOR A RAPE
Albert S. Ruddy Productions; telefeature; 1976
BLACK FIST
Worldwide; 1977
MANEATERS ARE LOOSE!
Mona Productions/Finnegan Associates; telefeature; 1978
SUNNYSIDE
American International; 1979

Garfein, Jack
b. July 2, 1930
Mukacevo, Czechoslovakia
Business:
Actors & Directors Lab
412 West 42nd Street
New York, N.Y. 10036
(212) 596-5429

THE STRANGE ONE (End as a Man)
Columbia; 1957
SOMETHING WILD
United Artists; 1961

Garland, Patrick

A DOLL'S HOUSE
Paramount; 1973; Canadian-U.S.

Garrett, Lila
Home:
1356 Laurel Way
Beverly Hills, CA 90212
(213) 274-8041
Agent:
Creative Artists Agency
Los Angeles
(213) 277-4545

TERRACES
Charles Fries Productions/Worldvision; telefeature; 1977

Gavras, Costa

See Costa-Gavras

Gershuny, Theodore

LOVE, DEATH
1973
SILENT NIGHT, BLOODY NIGHT
Cannon; 1974
SUGAR COOKIES
Troma; 1977
DEATHOUSE
Cannon; 1981

Gessner, Nicholas

SOMEONE BEHIND THE DOOR
GSF; 1971; French
THE LITTLE GIRL WHO LIVES DOWN THE LANE
American Internationa; 1977; U.S.-Canadian-French
IT RAINED ALL NIGHT THE DAY I LEFT
1981; Canadian

Gethers, Steven
Agent:
Adams, Ray & Rosenberg
Los Angeles
(213) 278-3000

BILLY: PORTRAIT OF A STREET KID
Mark Carliner Productions; telefeature; 1977
DAMIEN...THE LEPER PRIEST
Tomorrow Entertainment; telefeature; 1980
JACQUELINE BOUVIER KENNEDY
ABC Circle Films; telefeature; 1981

Gibson, Alan
Home:
55 Portland Road
London W.11 4LR, England
01-727-0354

GOODBYE GEMINI
Cinerama Releasing Corporation; 1970; British
CRESCENDO
Warner Brothers; 1972; British
DRACULA A.D. 1972
Warner Brothers; 1972; British
COUNT DRACULA AND HIS VAMPIRE BRIDE (Satanic Rites of Dracula)
Dynamite Entertainment; 1978; British
CHECKERED FLAG OR CRASH
Universal; 1978
A WOMAN NAMED GOLDA
Paramount TV; telefeature; 1982

Gibson, Brian
British Film Institute
127 Charing Cross Road
London W.C. 2, England
01-437-4355

BREAKING GLASS
Paramount; 1980; British

Gilbert, Lewis
b. March 6, 1920
London, England
Contact:
Directors Guild of America
Los Angeles
(213) 656-1220

THE LITTLE BALLERINA
General Film Distributors; 1947; British
ONCE A SINNER
Butcher; 1950; British
WALL OF DEATH (There is Another Sun)
Realart; 1951; British
THE SCARLET THREAD
Butcher; 1951; British
HUNDRED HOUR HUNT (Emergency Call)
Greshler; 1952; British
TIME GENTLEMEN PLEASE!
Eros; 1952; British
THE SLASHER (Cosh Boy)
Lippert; 1953; British
JOHNNY ON THE RUN
co-director with Vernon Harris; Associated British Film Distributors/Children's Film Foundation; 1953; British
BREAK TO FREEDOM (Albert R.N.)
United Artists; 1953; British
THE GOOD DIE YOUNG
United Artists; 1954; British

continued

Gilbert, Lewis
continued

THE SEA SHALL NOT HAVE THEM
United Artists; 1954; British
CAST A DARK SHADOW
DCA; 1955; British
REACH FOR THE SKY
Rank; 1956; British
PARADISE LAGOON (The Admirable Crichton)
Columbia; 1957; British
CARVE HER NAME WITH PRIDE
Lopert; 1958; British
A CRY FROM THE STREETS
Tudor; 1959; British
FERRY TO HONG KONG
20th Century-Fox; 1959; British
SINK THE BISMARCK!
20th Century-Fox; 1960; British
SKYWATCH (Light Up the Sky)
Continental; 1960; British
LOSS OF INNOCENCE (The Greengage Summer)
Columbia; 1961; British
DAMN THE DEFIANT! (H.M.S. Defiant)
Columbia; 1962; British
THE SEVENTH DAWN
United Artists; 1964; U.S.-British
ALFIE
Paramount; 1966; British
YOU ONLY LIVE TWICE
United Artists; 1967; British
THE ADVENTURERS
Paramount; 1970
FRIENDS
Paramount; 1971; British-French
PAUL AND MICHELLE
Paramount; 1974; British-French
OPERATION DAYBREAK
Warner Brothers; 1975; British
SEVEN NIGHTS IN JAPAN
EMI; 1976; British-French
THE SPY WHO LOVED ME
United Artists; 1977; British-U.S.
MOONRAKER
United Artists; 1979; British-French

Giler, David
Contact:
Directors Guild of America
Los Angeles
(213) 656-1220

THE BLACK BIRD
Columbia; 1975

Gillard, Stuart
Agent:
Century Artists
Beverly Hills
(213) 273-4366

PARADISE
Avco Embassy; 1981; Canadian

Gilliam, Terry
Contact:
British Film Institute
127 Charing Cross Road
London W.C. 2, England
01-437-4355

MONTY PYTHON AND THE HOLY GRAIL
co-director with Terry Jones; Cinema 5; 1974; British
JABBERWOCKY
Cinema 5; 1977; British
TIME BANDITS
Avco Embassy; 1981; British

Gilroy, Frank D.
Agent:
Ziegler, Diskant, Inc.
Los Angeles
(213) 278-0700

DESPERATE CHARACTERS
ITC; 1971
JOHN O'HARA'S GIBBSVILLE
Columbia TV; telefeature; 1975

continued

Gilroy, Frank D.
continued

THE TURNING POINT OF JIM MALLOY
NBC-TV; telefeature; 1975
FROM NOON TILL THREE
United Artists; 1976
ONCE IN PARIS
Atlantic; 1978
REX STOUT'S NERO WOLFE
Emmett Lavery, Jr. Productions/Paramount TV; telefeature; 1979

Gimbel, Peter
Business:
Blue Gander, Inc.
10 East 63rd Street
New York, N.Y. 10021
(212) 753-9088

BLUE WATER, WHITE DEATH
co-director with James Lipscomb; National General;1971

Ginsberg, Milton Moses

COMING APART
Kaleidoscope; 1969
THE WEREWOLF OF WASHINGTON
Diplomat; 1973

Giraldi, Bob
Contact:
Directors Guild of America
New York City
(212) 581-0370

NATIONAL LAMPOON GOES TO THE MOVIES
co-director with Henry Jaglom; United Artists; 1981

Girard, Bernard
b. 1930
Contact:
Directors Guild of America
Los Angeles
(213) 656-1220

THE GREEN-EYED BLONDE
Warner Brothers; 1957
RIDE OUT FOR REVENGE
United Artists; 1958
AS YOUNG AS WE ARE
Paramount; 1958
THE PARTY CRASHERS
Paramount; 1958
A PUBLIC AFFAIR
Parade; 1962
DEAD HEAT ON A MERRY-GO-ROUND
Paramount; 1966
MAD ROOM
Columbia; 1969
HUNTERS ARE FOR KILLING
Cinema Center; telefeature; 1970
THE HAPPINESS CAGE (The Mind Snatchers)
Cinerama Releasing Corporation; 1972
GONE WITH THE WEST
International Cinefilm; 1975
WE'RE ALL CRAZY NOW
1981

Gladwell, David
Contact:
British Film Institute
127 Charing Cross Road
London W.C. 2, England
01-437-4355

MEMOIRS OF A SURVIVOR
Universal/AFD; 1981; British

Glen, John

FOR YOUR EYES ONLY
United Artists; 1981; British

Glenville, Peter
b. October 28, 1913
London, England
Messages:
(212) PL. 8-0800

THE PRISONER
Columbia; 1955; British
ME AND THE COLONEL
Columbia; 1958
SUMMER AND SMOKE
Paramount; 1961

continued

Glenville, Peter
continued

TERM OF TRIAL
Warner Brothers; 1963; British
BECKET
Paramount; 1964; British
HOTEL PARADISO
M-G-M; 1966; British
THE COMEDIANS
M-G-M; 1967; British

Glickenhaus, Jim

THE ASTROLOGER
Interstar; 1979
THE EXTERMINATOR
Avco Embassy; 1980
THE SOLDIER
Avco Embassy; 1982

Godard, Jean-Luc
b. December 3, 1930
Paris, France
Contact:
Swiss Film Center
7 Spiegel Gasse
8025 Zurich, Switzerland
01-472860

BREATHLESS
Films Around the World; 1960; French
A WOMAN IS A WOMAN
Pathe Contemporary; 1961; French
SEVEN CAPITAL SINS
co-director; Embassy; 1962; French-Italian
MY LIFE TO LIVE
Pathe Contemporary; 1962; French
ROGOPAG
co-director; 1962; French
LE PETIT SOLDAT
West End; 1963; French
LES CARABINIERS
West End; 1963; French
CONTEMPT
Embassy; 1964; French-Italian
LES PLUS BELLES ESCROQUERIES DU MONDE
co-director; 1964; French
BAND OF OUTSIDERS
Royal International; 1964; French
THE MARRIED WOMAN
Royal International; 1964; French
SIX IN PARIS
co-director; 1965; French
ALPHAVILLE
Pathe Contemporary; 1965; French
PIERROT LE FOU
Pathe Contemporary; 1965; French
MASCULINE FEMININE
Royal International; 1966; French-Swedish
MADE IN U.S.A.
1966; French
TWO OR THREE THINGS I KNOW ABOUT HER
New Line Cinema; 1967; French
THE OLDEST PROFESSION
co-director; Goldstone; 1967; Italian-French-West German
FAR FROM VIETNAM
co-director with Alain Resnais, William Klein, Agnes Varda, Joris Ivens & Claude Lelouch; New Yorker; 1967; French
LA CHINOISE
Leacock-Pennebaker; 1967; French
WEEKEND
Grove Press; 1968; French-Italian
UN FILM COMME LES AUTRES
1968; French
AMORE E RABBIA
co-director; 1969; Italian-French
LE GAI SAVOIR
EYR: 1969; French
ONE A.M.
Leacock-Pennebaker; 1969; French; uncompleted
COMMUNICATIONS
1969; French; uncompleted

continued

Godard, Jean-Luc
continued

SYMPATHY FOR THE DEVIL (1 + 1)
New Line Cinema; 1969; British
BRITISH SOUNDS/SEE YOU AT MAO
co-director with Jean-Pierre Gorin; 1969; British; made for television
WIND FROM THE EAST
co-director with Jean-Pierre Gorin; New Line Cinema; 1969; French-Italian-West German
PRAVDA
co-director with Jean-Pierre Gorin; 1969; French-Czech
STRUGGLE IN ITALY
co-director with Jean-Pierre Gorin; RAI-TV; 1970; Italian
TILL VICTORY
co-director with Jean-Pierre Gorin; 1970; French
VLADIMIR AND ROSA
co-director with Jean-Pierre Gorin; 1971; French
TOUT VA BIEN
co-director with Jean-Pierre Gorin; New Yorker; 1973; French-Italian
LETTER TO JANE: INVESTIGATION OF A STILL
co-director with Jean-Pierre Gorin; New Yorker; 1973; French
MOI JE
1973; French
NUMERO DEUX
Zoetrope; 1975; French
LA COMMUNICATION
1976; French; made for television
COMMENT CA VA
1976; French
ICI ET AILLEURS
1977; French
EVERY MAN FOR HIMSELF
New Yorker/Zoetrope; 1980; Swiss

Goddard, Jim

A TALE OF TWO CITIES
Norman Rosemont Productions/Marble Arch Productions; telefeature; 1980

Golan, Menahem
b. May 31, 1929
Tiberias, Israel
Business:
Cannon Group
9911 W. Pico Blvd.
Los Angeles, CA 90035
(213) 553-5978

EL DORADO
1963; Israeli
TRUNK TO CAIRO
American International; 1967; Israeli-West German
TEVYE AND HIS SEVEN DAUGHTERS
Noah; 1968; Israeli
FORTUNA
Trans-American; 1969; Israeli
WHAT'S GOOD FOR THE GOOSE
National Showmanship; 1969; British
MARGO
Cannon; 1970; Israeli
LUPO!
Cannon; 1970; Israeli
QUEEN OF THE ROAD
Noah; 1970; Israeli
KATZ AND KARASSO
Noah; 1971; Israeli
THE GREAT TELEPHONE ROBBERY
Noah; 1972; Israeli
ESCAPE TO THE SUN
Cinevision; 1972; Israeli-West German-French
KAZABLAN
M-G-M; 1973; Israeli
LEPKE
Warner Brothers; 1975
DIAMONDS
Avco Embassy; 1975; U.S.-Israeli-Swiss
THE AMBASSADOR
1976; Israeli

Golan, Menahem
continued

OPERATION THUNDERBOLT
Cinema Shares International; 1978; Israeli
THE URANIUM CONSPIRACY
Noah; 1978; Israeli-West German
THE MAGICIAN OF LUBLIN
Cannon; 1979; Israeli-West German-U.S.
THE APPLE
Cannon; 1980; U.S.-West German
ENTER THE NINJA
Cannon; 1981

Gold, Jack
b. June 28, 1930
London, England
Contact:
British Film Institute
127 Charing Cross Road
London W.C. 2, England
01-437-4355

THE BOFORS GUN
Universal; 1968; British
THE RECKONING
Columbia; 1969; British
CATHOLICS
Sidney Glazier Productions; telefeature; 1973
WHO?
Allied Artists; 1975; British
MAN FRIDAY
Avco Embassy; 1975; British
ACES HIGH
Cinema Shares International; 1977; British
THE MEDUSA TOUCH
Warner Brothers; 1978; British
THE SAILOR'S RETURN
1978; British
THE NAKED CIVIL SERVANT
BBC-TV; telefeature; 1978
CHARLIE MUFFIN
Euston; 1980; British
LITTLE LORD FAUNTLEROY
Norman Rosemont Productions; telefeature; 1980

Goldman, Martin

THE LEGEND OF NIGGER CHARLEY
Paramount; 1972

Goldstone, James
b. June 8, 1931
Los Angeles, California
Agent:
Creative Artists Agency
Los Angeles
(213) 277-4545

SCALPLOCK
Columbia TV; telefeature; 1966
CODE NAME: HERACLITUS
Universal TV; telefeature; 1967
IRONSIDE
Universal TV; telefeature; 1967
SHADOW OVER ELVERON
Universal TV; telefeature; 1968
JIGSAW
Universal; 1968
A MAN CALLED GANNON
Universal; 1969
WINNING
Universal; 1969
A CLEAR AND PRESENT DANGER
Universal TV; telefeature; 1970
BROTHER JOHN
Columbia; 1971
RED SKY AT MORNING
Universal; 1971
CRY PANIC
Spelling-Goldberg Productions; telefeature; 1974
DR. MAX
CBS, Inc.; telefeature; 1974
THINGS IN THEIR SEASON
Tomorrow Entertainment; telefeature; 1974
JOURNEY FROM DARKNESS
Bob Banner Associates; telefeature; 1975
ERIC
Lorimar Productions; telefeature; 1975
SWASHBUCKLER
Universal; 1976

continued

Goldstone, James
continued

ROLLERCOASTER
Universal; 1977
STUDS LONIGAN
Lorimar Productions; television mini-series; 1979
WHEN TIME RAN OUT
Warner Brothers; 1980
KENT STATE
Inter Planetary Productions/Osmond Communications; telefeature; 1981

Gordon, Bert I.
b. September 24, 1922
Kenosha, Wisconsin
Agent:
Phil Gersh Agency
Beverly Hills
(213) 274-6611

KING DINOSAUR
Lippert; 1955
BEGINNING OF THE END
Republic; 1957
CYCLOPS
American International; 1957
THE AMAZING COLOSSAL MAN
American International; 1957
ATTACK OF THE PUPPET PEOPLE
American International; 1958
WAR OF THE COLOSSAL BEAST
American International; 1958
THE SPIDER
American International; 1958
THE BOY AND THE PIRATES
United Artists; 1960
TORMENTED
Allied Artists; 1960
THE MAGIC SWORD
United Artists; 1962
VILLAGE OF THE GIANTS
Embassy; 1965
PICTURE MOMMY DEAD
Embassy; 1966
HOW TO SUCCEED WITH SEX
Medford; 1970
NECROMANCY
American International; 1972
THE MAD BOMBER
Cinemation; 1973
THE POLICE CONNECTION
1973
THE FOOD OF THE GODS
American International; 1976
EMPIRE OF THE ANTS
American International; 1977

Gordon, Michael
b. September 6, 1909
Baltimore, Maryland
Home:
259 N. Layton Drive
Los Angeles, CA 90049
(213) 476-2024
Business:
UCLA Theatre Arts Dept.
405 Hilgard Avenue
Los Angeles, CA 90024
(213) 825-5761

BOSTON BLACKIE GOES HOLLYWOOD
Columbia; 1942
UNDERGROUND AGENT
Columbia; 1942
ONE DANGEROUS NIGHT
Columbia; 1943
CRIME DOCTOR
Columbia; 1943
THE WEB
Universal; 1947
ANOTHER PART OF THE FOREST
Universal; 1948
AN ACT OF MURDER
Universal; 1948
THE LADY GAMBLES
Universal; 1949
WOMAN IN HIDING
Universal; 1950
CYRANO DE BERGERAC
United Artists; 1950
I CAN GET IT FOR YOU WHOLESALE
20th Century-Fox; 1951
THE SECRET OF CONVICT LAKE
20th Century-Fox; 1951

continued

Gordon, Michael
continued

WHEREVER SHE GOES
Mayer-Kingsley; 1953; Australian
PILLOW TALK
Universal; 1959
PORTRAIT IN BLACK
Universal; 1960
BOYS' NIGHT OUT
M-G-M; 1962
FOR LOVE OR MONEY
Universal; 1963
MOVE OVER, DARLING
20th Century-Fox; 1963
A VERY SPECIAL FAVOR
Universal; 1965
TEXAS ACROSS THE RIVER
Universal; 1966
THE IMPOSSIBLE YEARS
M-G-M; 1968
HOW DO I LOVE THEE?
Cinerama Releasing Corporation; 1970

Gordon, Steve
Agent:
William Morris Agency
Beverly Hills
(213) 274-7451

ARTHUR
Orion Pictures/Warner Brothers; 1981

Gordy, Berry
Business:
Motown Records Corp.
6255 Sunset Blvd.
Hollywood, CA 90028
(213) 468-3600

MAHOGANY
Paramount; 1975

Gottlieb, Carl
Agent:
Larry Grossman & Assoc.
Beverly Hills
(213) 550-8127

CAVEMAN
United Artists; 1981

Graham, William A.
Home:
21510 Calle de Barco
Malibu, CA 90265
Agent:
Creative Artists Agency
Los Angeles
(213) 277-4545

THE DOOMSDAY FLIGHT
Universal TV; telefeature; 1966
THE OUTSIDER
Universal TV; telefeature; 1967
WATERHOLE #3
Paramount; 1967
CHANGE OF HABIT
Universal; 1968
THE LEGEND OF CUSTER
20th Century-Fox TV; telefeature; 1968
SUBMARINE X-1
United Artists; 1969; British
TRIAL RUN
Universal TV; telefeature; 1969
THEN CAME BRONSON
Universal TV; telefeature; 1969
THE INTRUDERS
Universal TV; telefeature; 1970
CONGRATULATIONS, IT'S A BOY!
Aaron Spelling Productions; telefeature; 1971
THIEF
Metromedia Productions/Stonehenge Productions; telefeature; 1971
MARRIAGE: YEAR ONE
Universal TV; telefeature; 1971
JIGSAW
Universal TV; telefeature; 1972

continued

Graham, William A.
continued

MAGIC CARPET
Universal TV; telefeature; 1972
HONKY
Jack H. Harris Enterprises; 1972
COUNT YOUR BULLETS (Cry For Me, Billy)
Brut Productions; 1972
BIRDS OF PREY
Tomorrow Entertainment; telefeature; 1973
MR. INSIDE/MR. OUTSIDE
D'Antoni Productions; telefeature; 1973
POLICE STORY
Screen Gems/Columbia TV; telefeature; 1973
SHIRTS/SKINS
M-G-M TV; telefeature; 1973
WHERE THE LILIES BLOOM
United Artists; 1974
TOGETHER BROTHERS
20th Century-Fox; 1974
GET CHRISTIE LOVE!
Wolper Productions; telefeature; 1974
LARRY
Tomorrow Entertainment; telefeature; 1974
TRAPPED BENEATH THE SEA
ABC Circle Films; telefeature; 1974
BEYOND THE BERMUDA TRIANGLE
Playboy Productions; telefeature; 1975
PERILOUS VOYAGE
Universal TV; telefeature; 1976; made in 1968
SHARK KILL
D'Antoni-Weitz Productions; telefeature; 1976
21 HOURS AT MUNICH
Filmways; telefeature; 1976
PART 2 SOUNDER
Gamma III; 1976
MINSTREL MAN
Roger Gimbel Productions/EMI TV; telefeature; 1977
THE AMAZING HOWARD HUGHES
Roger Gimbel Productions/EMI TV; telefeature; 1977
CONTRACT ON CHERRY STREET
Columbia TV; telefeature; 1977
CINDY
John Charles Walters Productions; telefeature; 1978
ONE IN A MILLION: THE RON LeFLORE STORY
Roger Gimbel Productions/EMI TV; telefeature; 1978
AND I ALONE SURVIVED
Jerry Leider/OJL Productions; telefeature; 1978
TRANSPLANT
Time-Life Productions; telefeature; 1979
ORPHAN TRAIN
Roger Gimbel Productions/EMI TV; telefeature; 1979
GUYANA TRAGEDY: THE STORY OF JIM JONES
The Konigsberg Company; telefeature; 1980
RAGE
NBC-TV; telefeature; 1980
HARRY TRACY
1981; Canadian

Grant, Lee
(Lyova Rosenthal)
October 31, 1927
New York, New York
Agent:
William Morris Agency
Beverly Hills
(213) 274-7451

TELL ME A RIDDLE
Filmways; 1980

Grasshoff, Alex
Agent:
Robinson-Weintraub & Assoc.
Los Angeles
(213) 652-5802

YOUNG AMERICANS
Columbia; 1967
JOURNEY TO THE OUTER LIMITS
1974

continued

Grasshoff, Alex
continued

THE LAST DINOSAUR
co-director with Tom Kotani; Rankin-Bass Productions; telefeature; 1977; U.S.-Japanese
SMOKEY AND THE GOODTIME OUTLAWS
Howco International; 1978

Grauman, Walter
b. March 17, 1922
Milwaukee, Wisconsin
Agent:
Broder-Kurland Agency
Hollywood
(213) 274-8291

THE DISEMBODIED
Allied Artists; 1957
LADY IN A CAGE
United Artists; 1964
633 SQUADRON
United Artists; 1964; British
A RAGE TO LIVE
United Artists; 1965
I DEAL IN DANGER
20th Century-Fox; 1966
DAUGHTER OF THE MIND
20th Century-Fox TV; telefeature; 1969
THE LAST ESCAPE
United Artists; 1970
THE OLD MAN WHO CRIED WOLF
Aaron Spelling Productions; telefeature; 1970
CROWHAVEN FARM
Aaron Spelling Productions; telefeature; 1970
THE FORGOTTEN MAN
Walter Grauman Productions; telefeature; 1971
PAPER MAN
20th Century-Fox TV; telefeature; 1971
THEY CALL IT MURDER
20th Century-Fox TV; telefeature; 1971
DEAD MEN TELL NO TALES
20th Century-Fox TV; telefeature; 1971
THE STREETS OF SAN FRANCISCO
QM Productions; telefeature; 1972
MANHUNTER
QM Productions; telefeature; 1974
FORCE FIVE
Universal TV; telefeature; 1975
MOST WANTED
QM Productions; telefeature; 1976
ARE YOU IN THE HOUSE ALONE?
Charles Fries Productions; telefeature; 1978
CRISIS IN MID-AIR
CBS Entertainment; telefeature; 1979
THE GOLDEN GATE MURDERS
Universal TV; telefeature; 1979
THE TOP OF THE HILL
Fellows-Keegan Company/Paramount TV; telefeature; 1980
TO RACE THE WIND
Walter Grauman Productions; telefeature; 1980
THE MEMORY OF EVA RYKER
Irwin Allen Productions; telefeature; 1980
PLEASURE PALACE
Norman Rosemont Productions/Marble Arch Productions; telefeature; 1980
JACQUELINE SUSANN'S VALLEY OF THE DOLLS 1981
20th Century-Fox TV; television mini-series; 1981

Green, Guy
b. 1913
Somerset, England
Paul Kohner Agency
Los Angeles
(213) 550-1060

RIVER BEAT
Lippert; 1954; British
POSTMARK FOR DANGER (Portrait of Alison)
RKO Radio; 1955; British
TEARS FOR SIMON (Lost)
Republic; 1956; British
TRIPLE DECEPTION (House of Secrets)
Rank; 1956; British
THE SNORKEL
Columbia; 1958; British
DESERT PATROL (Sea of Sand)
Universal; 1958; British

continued

Green, Guy
continued

S.O.S. PACIFIC
Universal; 1960; British
THE ANGRY SILENCE
Valiant; 1960; British
THE MARK
Continental; 1961; British
LIGHT IN THE PIAZZA
M-G-M; 1962
DIAMOND HEAD
Columbia; 1963
A PATCH OF BLUE
M-G-M; 1965
A MATTER OF INNOCENCE (Pretty Polly)
Universal; 1968; British
THE MAGUS
20th Century-Fox; 1968; British
A WALK IN THE SPRING RAIN
Columbia; 1970
LUTHER
American Film Theatre; 1974
JACQUELINE SUSANN'S ONCE IS NOT ENOUGH
Paramount; 1975
THE DEVIL'S ADVOCATE
1977; Italian
JENNIFER: A WOMAN'S STORY
Marble Arch Productions; telefeature; 1979
THE INCREDIBLE JOURNEY OF DR. MEG LAUREL
Columbia TV; telefeature; 1979
JIMMY B. & ANDRE
Georgian Bay Productions; telefeature; 1980
INMATES: A LOVE STORY
Henerson-Hirsh Productions/Finnegan Associates; telefeature; 1981

Green, Walon
Agent:
The Ufland Agency
Beverly Hills
(213) 273-9441

SPREE
co-director with Mitchell Leisen; United Producers; 1967
THE HELLSTROM CHRONICLE
Cinema 5; 1971
THE SECRET LIFE OF PLANTS
Paramount; 1978

Greene, David
b. 1924
England
Business:
David Greene Productions
4225 Coldwater Canyon
Studio City, CA 91604
(213) 766-3547
Agent:
Creative Artists Agency
Los Angeles
(213) 277-4545

THE SHUTTERED ROOM
Warner Brothers; 1966; British
SEBASTIAN
Paramount; 1968; British
THE STRANGE AFFAIR
Paramount; 1968; British
I START COUNTING
United Artists; 1969; British
THE PEOPLE NEXT DOOR
Avco Embassy; 1970
MADAME SIN
ITC; telefeature; 1971
GODSPELL
Columbia; 1973
THE COUNT OF MONTE CRISTO
Norman Rosemont Productions/ITC; telefeature; 1975
ELLERY QUEEN
Universal TV; telefeature; 1975
RICH MAN, POOR MAN
co-director with Boris Sagal; Universal TV; television mini-series; 1976
ROOTS
co-director with Marvin J. Chomsky, John Erman & Gilbert Moses; Wolper Productions; television mini-series; 1977
LUCAN
M-G-M TV; telefeature; 1977
THE TRIAL OF LEE HARVEY OSWALD
Charles Fries Productions; telefeature; 1977
GRAY LADY DOWN
Universal; 1978

continued

Greene, David
continued

FRIENDLY FIRE
Marble Arch Productions; telefeature; 1979
A VACATION IN HELL
David Greene Productions/Finnegan Associates; telefeature; 1979
THE CHOICE
David Greene Productions/Finnegan Associates; telefeature; 1981
HARD COUNTRY
Universal/AFD; 1981

Greenspan, Bud
Home:
252 East 61st Street
New York, N.Y. 10021
(212) 838-7565
Business:
Cappy Productions, Inc.
1078 Madison Avenue
New York, N.Y. 10028
(212) 249-1800

WILMA
Cappy Productions; telefeature; 1977

Greenwald, Robert
Business:
Moonlight Productions
2029 Century Park East
Los Angeles, CA 90067
(213) 552-9455
Agent:
I.C.M.
Hollywood
(213) 550-4000

SHARON: PORTRAIT OF A MISTRESS
Moonlight Productions/Paramount TV; telefeature; 1977
KATIE: PORTRAIT OF A CENTERFOLD
Moonlight Productions/Warner Brothers TV; telefeature; 1978
FLATBED ANNIE & SWEETIE PIE: LADY TRUCKERS
Moonlight Productions/Filmways; telefeature; 1979
XANADU
Universal; 1980

Griffith, Charles B.

EAT MY DUST
New World; 1976
UP FROM THE DEPTHS
New World; 1979
DR. HECKLE AND MR. HYPE
Cannon; 1980
SMOKEY BITES THE DUST
New World; 1981

Grofe, Ferde, Jr.

WARKILL
Universal; 1968; Filipino-U.S.
THE PROUD AND THE DAMNED
Prestige; 1972

Grosbard, Ulu
b. January 9, 1929
Antwerp, Belgium
Agent:
I.C.M.
New York City
(212) 556-5600

THE SUBJECT WAS ROSES
M-G-M; 1968
WHO IS HARRY KELLERMAN AND WHY IS HE SAYING THOSE TERRIBLE THINGS ABOUT ME?
National General; 1971
STRAIGHT TIME
Warner Brothers; 1978
TRUE CONFESSIONS
United Artists; 1981

Guenette, Robert
Business:
Robert Guenette Productions
8489 W. 3rd Street
Los Angeles, CA 90048
(213) 658-8450
Agent:
The Sy Fischer Company
Century City
(213) 557-0388

THE TREE
Guenette; 1969
THE MYSTERIOUS MONSTERS
Sunn Classic; 1976
THE AMAZING WORLD OF PSYCHIC PHENOMENA
Sunn Classic; 1976
THE MAN WHO SAW TOMORROW
Warner Brothers; 1981

Guercio, James William
Home:
Caribou Ranch
Nederland, Colorado 80466
(303) 258-3215
Agent:
I.C.M.
Hollywood
(213) 550-4205

ELECTRA GLIDE IN BLUE
United Artists; 1973

Guest, Val
b. 1911
London, England
Contact:
British Film Institute
127 Charing Cross Road
London W.C. 2, England
01-437-4355

MISS LONDON LTD.
General Film Distributors; 1943; British
BEES IN PARADISE
General Film Distributors; 1944; British
GIVE US THE MOON
General Film Distributors; 1944; British
I'LL BE YOUR SWEETHEART
General Film Distributors; 1945; British
JUST WILLIAM'S LUCK
United Artists; 1947; British
WILLIAM COMES TO TOWN
United Artists; 1948; British
MURDER AT THE WINDMILL
Grand National; 1949; British
MISS PILGRIM'S PROGRESS
Grand National; 1950; British
THE BODY SAID NO
Eros; 1950; British
MISTER DRAKE'S DUCK
United Artists; 1951; British
PENNY PRINCESS
Universal; 1952; British
LIFE WITH THE LYONS
Exclusive Films; 1954; British
THE RUNAWAY BUS
Eros; 1954; British
MEN OF SHERWOOD FOREST
Astor; 1954; British
DANCE LITTLE LADY
Renown; 1954; British
THEY CAN'T HANG ME
Independent Film Distributors; 1955; British
THE LYONS IN PARIS
Exclusive Films; 1955; British
BREAK IN THE CIRCLE
20th Century-Fox; 1955; British
THE CREEPING UNKNOWN (The Quatermass Experiment)
United Artists; 1955; British
IT'S A WONDERFUL WORLD
Renown; 1956; British
THE WEAPON
Republic; 1956; British
CARRY ON ADMIRAL
Renown; 1957; British
ENEMY FROM SPACE (Quatermass II)
United Artists; 1957; British
THE ABOMINABLE SNOWMAN OF THE HIMALAYAS
20th Century-Fox; 1957; British
THE CAMP ON BLOOD ISLAND
Columbia; 1958; British
UP THE CREEK
Dominant; 1958; British
FURTHER UP THE CREEK
Warner Brothers; 1958; British
EXPRESSO BONGO
Continental; 1959; British
YESTERDAY'S ENEMY
Columbia; 1959
LIFE IS A CIRCUS
1960; British
HELL IS A CITY
Columbia; 1960; British
STOP ME BEFORE I KILL (The Full Treatment)
Columbia; 1961; British
THE DAY THE EARTH CAUGHT FIRE
Universal; 1962; British

continued

Guest, Val
continued

JIGSAW
Beverly; 1962; British
80,000 SUSPECTS
Rank; 1963; British
CONTEST GIRL (The Beauty Jungle)
Continental; 1964; British
WHERE THE SPIES ARE
M-G-M; 1965; British
CASINO ROYALE
co-director with Ken Hughes, John Huston, Joseph McGrath & Robert Parrish; Columbia; 1967; British
ASSIGNMENT K
Columbia; 1968; British
WHEN DINOSAURS RULED THE EARTH
Warner Brothers; 1969; British
TOOMORROW
FRD; 1970; British
THE PERSUADERS
1971; British
AU PAIR GIRLS
Cannon; 1972; British
CONFESSIONS OF A WINDOW CLEANER
Columbia; 1974; British
KILLER FORCE
American International; 1975; British-Swiss
THE SHILLINGBURY BLOWERS (...And the Band Played On) Inner Circle; 1980; British
DANGEROUS DAVIES - THE LAST DETECTIVE
ITC/Inner Circle/Maidenhead Films; 1981; British

Guillermin, John
b. November 11, 1925
London, England
Agent:
I.C.M.
Hollywood
(213) 550-4000

TORMENT
Adelphi; 1949; British
SMART ALEC
Grand National; 1951; British
TWO ON THE TILES
Grand National; 1951; British
FOUR DAYS
Grand National; 1951; British
BACHELOR IN PARIS (Song of Paris)
Lippert; 1952; British
MISS ROBIN HOOD
Associated British Film Distributors; 1952; British
OPERATION DIPLOMAT
Butcher; 1953; British
ADVENTURE IN THE HOPFIELDS
British Lion/Children's Film Foundation; 1954; British
THE CROWDED DAY
Adelphi; 1954; British
DUST AND GOLD
1955; British
THUNDERSTORM
Allied Artists; 1955; British
TOWN ON TRIAL
Columbia; 1957; British
THE WHOLE TRUTH
Columbia; 1958; British
I WAS MONTY'S DOUBLE
NTA Pictures; 1958; British
TARZAN'S GREATEST ADVENTURE
Paramount; 1959; British-U.S.
THE DAY THEY ROBBED THE BANK OF ENGLAND
M-G-M; 1960; British
NEVER LET GO
Rank; 1960; British
WALTZ OF THE TOREADORS
Continental; 1962; British
TARZAN GOES TO INDIA
M-G-M; 1962; British-U.S.-Swiss
GUNS AT BATASI
20th Century-Fox; 1964; British-U.S.
RAPTURE
International Classics; 1965; British-French

continued

Guillermin, John
continued

THE BLUE MAX
20th Century-Fox; 1966; British-U.S.
P.J.
Universal; 1968
HOUSE OF CARDS
Universal; 1969
THE BRIDGE AT REMAGEN
United Artists; 1969
EL CONDOR
National General; 1970
SKYJACKED
M-G-M; 1972
SHAFT IN AFRICA
M-G-M; 1973
THE TOWERING INFERNO
20th Century-Fox; 1974
KING KONG
Paramount; 1976
DEATH ON THE NILE
Paramount; 1978; British
MR. PATMAN
Film Consortium; 1980; Canadian

Gunn, Bill

STOP
Warner Brothers; 1970
GANJA & HESS
Kelly-Jordan; 1973

Guttfreund, Andre

PARTNERS
Hurricane Gulch; 1981

Guzman, Claudio
Home:
9785 Drake Lane
Beverly Hills, CA 90210
(213) 278-8816

ANTONIO
Guzman Productions; 1973
LINDA LOVELACE FOR PRESIDENT
General Film; 1975
WILLA
co-director with Joan Darling; GJL Productions/ Dove, Inc.; telefeature; 1979
THE HOSTAGE TOWER
Jerry Leider Productions; telefeature; 1980

Hackford, Taylor
Business:
New Visions, Inc.
2049 Century Park East
Los Angeles, CA 90067
(213) 556-8000
Agent:
Creative Artists Agency
Los Angeles
(213) 277-4545

THE IDOLMAKER
United Artists; 1980
AN OFFICER AND A GENTLEMAN
Paramount; 1981

Haggard, Piers
Contact:
British Film Institute
127 Charing Cross Road
London W.C. 2, England
01-437-4355

WEDDING NIGHT
American International; 1970; Irish
THE BLOOD ON SATAN'S CLAW (Satan's Skin)
Cannon; 1971; British
THE QUATERMASS CONCLUSION
Euston; 1979; British
THE FIENDISH PLOT OF DR. FU MANCHU
Orion Pictures/Warner Brothers; 1980; British
VENOM
Paramount; 1982; British

Hagman, Larry
Home:
23750 Malibu Colony
Malibu, CA 90265
Agent:
Creative Artists Agency
Los Angeles
(213) 277-4545

BEWARE! THE BLOB (Son of Blob)
Jack H. Harris Enterprises; 1972

Hagmann, Stuart
Business:
H.I.S.K. Productions
10950 Ventura Blvd.
Studio City, CA 91604
(213) 506-1700

THE STRAWBERRY STATEMENT
M-G-M; 1970
BELIEVE IN ME
M-G-M; 1971
SHE LIVES
ABC Circle Films; telefeature; 1973
TARANTULAS: THE DEADLY CARGO
Alan Landsburg Productions; telefeature; 1977

Hale, William (Billy)
Agent:
William Morris Agency
Beverly Hills
(213) 274-7451
Personal Manager:
Martin Mickelson
Beverly Hills
(213) 858-1097

HOW I SPENT MY SUMMER VACATION
Universal TV; telefeature; 1967
GUNFIGHT IN ABILENE
Universal; 1967
JOURNEY TO SHILOH
Universal; 1968
NIGHTMARE
CBS, Inc.; telefeature; 1974
THE GREAT NIAGARA
Playboy Productions; telefeature; 1974
CROSSFIRE
QM Productions; telefeature; 1975
THE KILLER WHO WOULDN'T DIE
Paramount TV; telefeature; 1976
STALK THE WILD CHILD
Charles Fries Productions; telefeature; 1976
RED ALERT
The Jozak Company/Paramount TV; telefeature; 1977
S.O.S. TITANIC
Roger Gimbel Productions/Argonaut Films Ltd./ EMI Films Ltd.; telefeature; 1979
MURDER IN TEXAS
Dick Clark Productions/Billy Hale Films; telefeature; 1981

Haley, Jack, Jr.
b. October 25, 1933
Business:
1443 Devlin Drive
Los Angeles, CA 90069

NORWOOD
Paramount; 1970
THE LOVE MACHINE
Columbia; 1971
THAT'S ENTERTAINMENT!
M-G-M/United Artists; 1974
THAT'S ENTERTAINMENT, PART 2
co-director with Gene Kelly; M-G-M/United Artists; 1976

Hall, Peter
b. November 22, 1930
Bury St. Edmunds, Suffolk, England
Contact:
British Film Institute
127 Charing Cross Road
London W.C. 2, England
01-437-4355

WORK IS A FOUR LETTER WORD
Universal; 1968; British
A MIDSUMMER NIGHT'S DREAM
1968; British
PERFECT FRIDAY
Chevron; 1970; British
THE HOMECOMING
American Film Theatre; 1973; British
AKENFIELD
Angle Films; 1975; British

Haller, Daniel
b. 1926
Los Angeles, California
Home:
5364 Jed Smith Road
Hidden Hills, CA 91302
(213) 888-7936
Agent:
Irv Schechter
Beverly Hills
(213) 278-8070

DIE, MONSTER, DIE!
American International; 1965; U.S.-British
DEVIL'S ANGELS
American International; 1967
THE WILD RACERS
American International; 1968
PADDY
Allied Artists; 1970; Irish
PIECES OF DREAMS
United Artists; 1970
THE DUNWICH HORROR
American International; 1970

continued

Haller, Daniel
continued

THE DESPERATE MILES
Universal TV; telefeature; 1975
BLACK BEAUTY
Universal TV; television mini-series; 1978
LITTLE MO
Mark VII Ltd./Worldvision; telefeature; 1978
BUCK ROGERS IN THE 25TH CENTURY
Universal; 1979
HIGH MIDNIGHT
The Mirisch Corporation/Universal TV; telefeature; 1979
GEORGIA PEACHES
New World Pictures TV; telefeature; 1980
FOLLOW THAT CAR
New World; 1981
MICKEY SPILLANE'S MARGIN FOR MURDER
Hammer Productions; telefeature; 1981

Hamilton, Guy
b. September, 1922
Paris, France
Agent:
London
01-493-1610

THE RINGER
British Lion; 1952; British
THE INTRUDER
Associated Artists; 1953; British
AN INSPECTOR CALLS
Associated Artists; 1954; British
THE COLDITZ STORY
Republic; 1955; British
CHARLEY MOON
British Lion; 1956; British
STOWAWAY GIRL (Manuela)
Paramount; 1957; British
THE DEVIL'S DISCIPLE
United Artists; 1959; British
A TOUCH OF LARCENY
Paramount; 1960; British
THE BEST OF ENEMIES
Columbia; 1962; Italian-British
MAN IN THE MIDDLE
20th Century-Fox; 1964; British-U.S.
GOLDFINGER
United Artists; 1964; British
THE PARTY'S OVER
Allied Artists; 1966; British
FUNERAL IN BERLIN
Paramount; 1966; British
BATTLE OF BRITAIN
United Artists; 1969; British
DIAMONDS ARE FOREVER
United Artists; 1971; British
LIVE AND LET DIE
United Artists; 1973; British
THE MAN WITH THE GOLDEN GUN
United Artists; 1974; British
FORCE 10 FROM NAVARONE
American International; 1978
THE MIRROR CRACK'D
AFD; 1980; British
EVIL UNDER THE SUN
EMI; 1982; British

Hancock, John
b. February 9, 1939
Kansas City, Missouri
Home:
21531 Deerpath Lane
Malibu, CA 90265
(213) 456-3627
Agent:
Chasin-Park-Citron
(213) 273-7190

LET'S SCARE JESSICA TO DEATH
Paramount; 1971
BANG THE DRUM SLOWLY
Paramount; 1973
BABY BLUE MARINE
Columbia; 1976
CALIFORNIA DREAMING
American International; 1979

Hanson, Curtis

THE LITTLE DRAGONS
Aurora; 1980

Hanwright, Joseph C.
Home:
(208) 726-3594
Business Manager:
Fred Kalmas
Los Angeles
(213) 552-3225

UNCLE JOE SHANNON
United Artists; 1979

Hardy, Joseph
Agent:
Creative Artists Agency
Los Angeles
(213) 277-4545

GREAT EXPECTATIONS
Transcontinental Film Productions; telefeature; 1974; British
A TREE GROWS IN BROOKLYN
20th Century-Fox TV; telefeature; 1974
LAST HOURS BEFORE MORNING
Charles Fries Productions/M-G-M TV; telefeature; 1975
THE SILENCE
Palomar Pictures International; telefeature; 1975
JAMES AT 15
20th Century-Fox TV; telefeature; 1977
THE USERS
Aaron Spelling Productions; telefeature; 1978
LOVE'S SAVAGE FURY
Aaron Spelling Productions; telefeature; 1979
THE SEDUCTION OF MISS LEONA
Edgar J. Scherick Associates; telefeature; 1980
THE DAY THE BUBBLE BURST
20th Century-Fox TV; telefeature; 1981

Hardy, Robin
Contact:
British Film Institute
127 Charing Cross Road
London W.C. 2, England
01-437-4355

THE WICKER MAN
Warner Brothers; 1975; British

Hargrove, Dean
Agent:
Major Talent Agency
Los Angeles
(213) 820-5841

THE MANCHU EAGLE CAPER MYSTERY
United Artists; 1975
THE BIG RIP-OFF
Universal TV; telefeature; 1975
THE RETURN OF THE WORLD'S GREATEST DETECTIVE
Universal TV; telefeature; 1976

Harrington, Curtis
b. September 17, 1928
Los Angeles, California
Agent:
Agency for the Performing Arts
Los Angeles
(213) 273-0744

NIGHT TIDE
Universal; 1963
QUEEN OF BLOOD
American International; 1966
GAMES
Universal; 1967
HOW AWFUL ABOUT ALLAN
Aaron Spelling Productions; telefeature; 1970
WHO SLEW AUNTIE ROO?
American International; 1971; British
WHAT'S THE MATTER WITH HELEN?
United ARtists; 1971
THE CAT CREATURE
Screen Gems/Columbia TV; telefeature; 1973
KILLER BEES
RSO Films; telefeature; 1974
THE KILLING KIND
Media Trend; 1974
THE DEAD DON'T DIE
Douglas S. Cramer Productions; telefeature; 1975
RUBY
Dimension; 1977
DEVIL DOG: THE HOUND OF HELL
Zeitman-Landers-Roberts Productions; telefeature; 1978

Harris, Denny
Business:
Denny Harris Inc.
12152 Olympic Blvd.
Los Angeles, CA
(213) 820-9926

SILENT SCREAM
American Cinema; 1980

Harris, Harry
Business:
Three H. Productions
10999 Riverside Side
N. Hollywood, CA 91602
(213) 769-7822
Agent:
Contemporary-Korman Artists
Beverly Hills
(213) 278-8250

THE RUNAWAYS
Lorimar Productions; telefeature; 1975
THE SWISS FAMILY ROBINSON
Irwin Allen Productions/20th Century-Fox TV; telefeature; 1975
RIVKIN: BOUNTY HUNTER
Chiarascurio Productions/Ten-Four Productions; telefeature; 1981

Harris, James B.
b. August 3, 1928
New York, New York
Business:
Ringer
248½ S. Lasky Drive
Beverly Hills, CA 90212
(213) 273-4270

THE BEDFORD INCIDENT
Columbia; 1965
SOME CALL IT LOVING
Cine Globe; 1973
FAST-WALKING
Lorimar Distributors International; 1981

Harris, Richard
b. October 1, 1932
Limerick, Ireland

THE HERO (Bloomfield)
Avco Embassy; 1972; Israeli-British

Hart, Bruce
Personal Manager:
Scott Shukat
New York City
(212) 582-7614

SOONER OR LATER
Laughing Willow Company/NBC-TV; telefeature; 1979

Hart, Harvey
b. 1928
Toronto, Canada
Business:
Rohar Productions, Ltd.
10 Clarendon Avenue
Toronto M4V 1H9, Ontario
Canada
(416) 962-3436
Agent:
Creative Artists Agency
Los Angeles
(213) 277-4545

BUS RILEY'S BACK IN TOWN
Universal; 1965
DARK INTRUDER
Universal; 1965
SULLIVAN'S EMPIRE
co-director with Thomas Carr; Universal; 1967
THE SWEET RIDE
20th Century-Fox; 1968
THE YOUNG LAWYERS
Paramount TV; telefeature; 1969
FORTUNE AND MEN'S EYES
M-G-M; 1971; Canadian
MAHONEY'S ESTATE
NBC-TV; telefeature; 1972
THE PYX
Cinerama Releasing Corporation; 1973; Canadian
CAN ELLEN BE SAVED?
ABC Circle Films; telefeature; 1974
MURDER OR MERCY
QM Productions; telefeature; 1974
PANIC ON THE 5:22
QM Productions; telefeature; 1974
SHOOT
Avco Embassy; 1976; Canadian
STREET KILLING
ABC Circle Films; telefeature; 1976
THE CITY
QM Productions; telefeature; 1977
GOLDENROD
Talent Associates/Film Funding Ltd. of Canada; telefeature; 1977; U.S.-Canadian

continued

Hart, Harvey
continued

THE PRINCE OF CENTRAL PARK
Lorimar Productions; telefeature; 1977
CAPTAINS COURAGEOUS
Norman Rosemont Productions; telefeature; 1977
STANDING TALL
QM Productions; telefeature; 1978
W.E.B.
NBC-TV; telefeature; 1978
LIKE NORMAL PEOPLE
Christiana Productions/20th Century-Fox TV; telefeature; 1979
THE ALIENS ARE COMING
Woodruff Productions/QM Productions; telefeature; 1980
JOHN STEINBECK'S EAST OF EDEN
Mace Neufeld Productions; television mini-series; 1981
THE HIGH COUNTRY
Crown International; 1981; Canadian
UTILITIES
Robert Cooper Productions; 1981; Canadian

Harvey, Anthony
b. June 3, 1931
London, England
William Morris Agency
Beverly Hills
(213) 274-7451

DUTCHMAN
Continental; 1967; British
THE LION IN WINTER
Avco Embassy; 1968; British
THEY MIGHT BE GIANTS
Universal; 1971
THE GLASS MENAGERIE
Talent Associates; telefeature; 1973
THE ABDICATION
Warner Brothers; 1974; British
THE DISAPPEARANCE OF AIMEE
Tomorrow Entertainment; telefeature; 1976
PLAYERS
Paramount; 1979
EAGLE'S WING
International Picture Show Company; 1980; British
RICHARD'S THINGS
New World; 1981; British

Hayers, Sidney
Agent:
Contemporary-Korman Artists
Beverly Hills
(213) 278-8250

VIOLENT MOMENT
Anglo Amalgamated; 1959; British
THE WHITE TRAP
Anglo Amalgamated; 1959; British
CIRCUS OF HORRORS
American International; 1960; British
THE MALPAS MYSTERY
Anglo Amalgamated; 1960; British
ECHO OF BARBARA
Rank; 1961; British
PAYROLL
Allied Artists; 1961; British
BURN, WITCH, BURN (Night of the Eagle)
American International; 1962; British
THIS IS MY STREET
Anglo Amalgamated; 1963; British
THREE HATS FOR LISA
Anglo Amalgamated; 1963; British
THE TRAP
Rank; 1966; British
FINDERS KEEPERS
United Artists; 1967; British
THE SOUTHERN STAR
Columbia; 1969; French-British
MISTER JERICO
ITC; telefeature; 1970
IN THE DEVIL'S GARDEN (Assault)
Hemisphere; 1971; British
THE FIRECHASERS
Rank; 1971; British
REVENGE
Rank; 1971; British

continued

Hayers, Sidney
continued

ALL COPPERS ARE...
Rank; 1972; British
DEADLY STRANGERS
Fox-Rank; 1974; British
DIAGNOSIS: MURDER
1975; British
WHAT CHANGED CHARLEY FARTHING?
Stirling Gold; 1976; British
INN OF THE FRIGHTENED PEOPLE (Terror From Under the House)
Hemisphere; 1976; British
THE LAST CONVERTIBLE
co-director with Jo Swerling, Jr. & Gus Trikonis; Roy Huggins Productions/Universal TV; television mini-series; 1979
CONDOMINIUM
Universal TV; telefeature; 1980

Hazan, Jack
Contact:
British Film Institute
127 Charing Cross Road
London W.C. 2, England
01-437-4355

A BIGGER SPLASH
co-director with David Mingay; Lagoon Associates; 1975; British
RUDE BOY
co-director with David Mingay; Atlantic; 1980; British

Heffron, Richard
Home:
17419 Revello Drive
Pacific Palisades, CA 90272
Agent:
Creative Artists Agency
Los Angeles
(213) 277-4545

DO YOU TAKE THIS STRANGER?
Universal TV; telefeature; 1971
FILLMORE
20th Century-Fox; 1972
TOMA
Universal TV; telefeature; 1973
OUTRAGE!
ABC Circle Films; telefeature; 1973
NEWMAN'S LAW
Universal; 1974
THE MORNING AFTER
Wolper Productions; telefeature; 1974
THE ROCKFORD FILES
Universal TV; telefeature; 1974
THE CALIFORNIA KID
Universal TV; telefeature; 1974
LOCUSTS
Paramount TV; telefeature; 1974
I WILL FIGHT NO MORE FOREVER
Wolper Productions; telefeature; 1975
DEATH SCREAM
RSO Films; telefeature; 1975
TRACKDOWN
United Artists; 1976
FUTUREWORLD
American International; 1976
YOUNG JOE, THE FORGOTTEN KENNEDY
ABC Circle Films; telefeature; 1977
OUTLAW BLUES
Warner Brothers; 1977
SEE HOW SHE RUNS
CLN Productions; telefeature; 1978
TRUE GRIT: A FURTHER ADVENTURE
Paramount TV; telefeature; 1978
FOOLIN' AROUND
Columbia; 1978
A RUMOR OF WAR
Charles Fries Productions; telefeature; 1980
A WHALE FOR THE KILLING
Playboy Productions/Beowulf Productions; telefeature; 1981
I, THE JURY
American Cinema; 1981

Hellman, Jerome

Business:
68 Malibu Colony Drive
Malibu, CA 90265
(213) 456-3361
Agent:
Creative Artists Agency
Los Angeles
(213) 277-4545

PROMISES IN THE DARK
Orion Pictures/Warner Brothers; 1979

Hellman, Monte

b. 1932
New York, New York
Business:
Monte Hellman Films
265 N. Robertson Blvd.
Beverly Hills, CA 90211
(213) 278-2944
Agent:
William Morris Agency
Beverly Hills
(213) 274-7451

BEAST FROM HAUNTED CAVE
Allied Artists; 1959
BACK DOOR TO HELL
20th Century-Fox; 1964
FLIGHT TO FURY
1965
THE SHOOTING
American International; 1966
RIDE IN THE WHIRLWIND
American International; 1966
TWO-LANE BLACKTOP
Universal; 1971
COCKFIGHTER (Born to Kill)
New World; 1974
CHINA 9 LIBERTY 37
1978; Italian

Hellstrom, Gunnar

Home:
10816 3/4 Lindbrook Drive
Los Angeles, CA 90024
(213) 474-6749
Agent:
Film Artists Management
Hollywood
(213) 656-7590

THE NAME OF THE GAME IS KILL
Universal TV; telefeature; 1968
MARK, I LOVE YOU
The Aubrey Company; telefeature; 1980

Helpern, David, Jr.

I'M A STRANGER HERE MYSELF
October Films; 1974
HOLLYWOOD ON TRIAL
Lumiere; 1976
SOMETHING SHORT OF PARADISE
American International; 1979

Hemmings, David

b. November 18, 1941
Guildford, England
Contact:
British Film Institute
127 Charing Cross Road
London W.C. 2, England
01-437-4355

RUNNING SCARED
Paramount; 1972; British
THE 14
M-G-M/EMI; 1973; British
JUST A GIGOLO
United Artists Classics; 1978; West German
THE SURVIVOR
Hemdale; 1981; Australian
RACE TO THE YANKEE ZEPHYR
Hemdale; 1981; British-New Zealand

Henry, Buck

(Buck Henry Zuckerman)
b. 1930
New York, New York
Agent:
I.C.M.
Hollywood
(213) 550-4000

HEAVEN CAN WAIT
co-director with Warren Beatty; Paramount; 1978
FIRST FAMILY
Warner Brothers; 1980

Henson, Jim

Business:
(212) 794-2400

THE GREAT MUPPET CAPER
Universal/AFD; 1981; British
DARK CRYSTAL
co-director with Frank Oz; Henson Organization Productions/ITC; 1982; British

Herzog, Werner
b. 1942
Sachrang, West Germany
Contact:
Bundesverband Deutscher
Film Produzenten
Langenbeck Str., No. 9
6200 Wiesbaden
West Germany
306 200

DIE FLIEGENDEN ARZTE VON OSTAFRIKA
1968; West German
SIGNS OF LIFE
Werner Herzog Filmproduktion;1968; West German
BEHINDERTE ZUNKUFT
1970; West German
EVEN DWARFS STARTED SMALL
New Line Cinema; 1971; West German
LAND OF SILENCE AND DARKNESS
Werner Herzog Filmproduktion;1972; West German
AGUIRRE, THE WRATH OF GOD
New Yorker; 1973;West German-Mexican-Peruvian
THE MYSTERY OF KASPAR HAUSER (Every Man For Himself and God Against All)
Cinema 5; 1974; West German
HEART OF GLASS
New Yorker; 1976; West German
STROSZEK
New Yorker; 1977; West German
FATA MORGANA
New Yorker; 1978; West German
WOYZECK
New Yorker; 1979; West German
NOSFERATU THE VAMPYRE
20th Century-Fox; 1979; West German-French-U.S.
FITZCARRALDO
New World; 1982

Hessler, Gordon
Agent:
F.A.M.E.
Los Angeles
(213) 656-7590

THE WOMAN WHO WOULDN'T DIE (Catacombs)
Warner Brothers; 1965; British
THE OBLONG BOX
American International; 1969; British
THE LAST SHOT YOU HEAR
20th Century-Fox; 1969; British
SCREAM AND SCREAM AGAIN
American International; 1970; British
CRY OF THE BANSHEE
American International; 1970; British
MURDERS IN THE RUE MORGUE
American International; 1971
EMBASSY
Hemdale; 1973; British
SCREAM, PRETTY PEGGY
Universal TV; telefeature; 1973
SKYWAY TO DEATH
Universal TV; telefeature; 1974
HITCHHIKE!
Universal TV; telefeature; 1974
A CRY IN THE WILDERNESS
Universal TV; telefeature; 1974
BETRAYAL
Metromedia Productions; telefeature; 1974
THE GOLDEN VOYAGE OF SINBAD
Columbia; 1974; British
THE STRANGE POSSESSION OF MRS. OLIVER
The Shpetner Company; telefeature; 1977
SECRETS OF THREE HUNGRY WIVES
Penthouse Productions; telefeature; 1978
KISS MEETS THE PHANTOM OF THE PARK
Hanna-Barbera Productions/KISS Productions; telefeature; 1978
BEGGARMAN, THIEF
Universal TV; telefeature; 1980
THE SECRET WAR OF JACKIE'S GIRLS
Public Arts Productions/Penthouse Productions/ Universal TV; telefeature; 1980

Heston, Charlton
(Charles Carter)
October 4, 1923
Evanston, Illinois

ANTONY AND CLEOPATRA
Rank; 1973; British-Spanish-Swiss
MOTHER LODE
Mother Lode Productions; 1982; Canadian

Heyes, Douglas
Agent:
Frank Cooper Associates
Los Angeles
(213) 277-8422

KITTEN WITH A WHIP
Universal; 1964
BEAU GESTE
Universal; 1966
THE LONELY PROFESSION
Universal TV; telefeature; 1969
POWDERKEG
Filmways/Rodphi; telefeature; 1969
DRIVE HARD, DRIVE FAST
Universal TV; telefeature; 1973; made in 1969
CAPTAINS AND THE KINGS
co-director with Allen Reisner; Universal TV; television mini-series; 1976
ASPEN
Universal TV; television mini-series; 1977
THE FRENCH ATLANTIC AFFAIR
Aaron Spelling Productions/M-G-M TV; telefeature;1979

Hickox, Douglas
Agent:
Shapiro-Lichtman Agency
Los Angeles
(213) 557-2244

IT'S ALL OVER TOWN
British Lion; 1963; British
JUST FOR YOU
Columbia; 1963; British
ENTERTAINING MR. SLOANE
Continental; 1970; British
SITTING TARGET
M-G-M; 1972; British
THEATRE OF BLOOD
United Artists; 1973; British
BRANNIGAN
United Artists; 1975; British
SKY RIDERS
20th Century-Fox; 1976
ZULU DAWN
American Cinema; 1979; British
THE PHOENIX
Mark Carliner Productions; telefeature; 1981

Higgins, Colin
Agent:
Creative Artists Agency
Los Angeles
(213) 277-4545

FOUL PLAY
Paramount; 1978
NINE TO FIVE
20th Century-Fox; 1980
THE BEST LITTLE WHOREHOUSE IN TEXAS
Universal; 1982

Hill, George Roy
b. December 20, 1922
Minneapolis, Minnesota
Business:
Warner Brothers Studios
4000 Warner Blvd.
Burbank, CA 91522
(213) 943-6000

PERIOD OF ADJUSTMENT
M-G-M; 1962
TOYS IN THE ATTIC
United Artists; 1963
THE WORLD OF HENRY ORIENT
United Artists; 1964
HAWAII
United Artists; 1966
THOROUGHLY MODERN MILLIE
Universal; 1967
BUTCH CASSIDY AND THE SUNDANCE KID
20th Century-Fox; 1969
SLAUGHTERHOUSE-FIVE
Universal; 1971
THE STING
Universal; 1973
THE GREAT WALDO PEPPER
Universal; 1975
SLAP SHOT
Universal; 1977
A LITTLE ROMANCE
Orion Pictures/Warner Brothers; 1979; U.S.-French
THE WORLD ACCORDING TO GARP
Warner Brothers; 1982

Hill, Jack
Home:
6856 Farralone AVenue
Canoga Park, CA 91303
(213) 346-0110
Agent:
Robinson-Weintraub & Assoc.
Los Angeles
(213) 653-5802

BLOOD BATH
co-director with Stephanie Rothman; American International; 1966
PIT STOP
Distributors International; 1969
THE BIG DOLL HOUSE
New World; 1971
THE BIG BIRD CAGE
New World; 1972
COFFY
American International; 1973
FOXY BROWN
American International; 1974
THE SWINGING CHEERLEADERS
Centaur; 1974
SWITCHBLADE SISTERS
Centaur; 1975

Hill, James
b. 1919
England
Agent:
The Lantz Office
Los Angeles
(213) 858-1144

THE STOLEN PLANS
Associated British Film Distributors/Children's Film Foundation; 1952; British
THE CLUE OF THE MISSING APE
Associated British Film Distributors/Children's Film Foundation; 1953; British
PERIL FOR THE GUY
British Lion/Children's Film Foundation; 1956; British
MYSTERY IN THE MINE
Children's Film Foundation; 1959; British
THE KITCHEN
British Lion; 1961; British
THE DOCK BRIEF
M-G-M; 1962; British
LUNCH HOUR
Bryanston; 1962; British
SEASIDE SWINGERS (Every Day's A Holiday)
Embassy; 1964; British
A STUDY IN TERROR
Columbia; 1966; British
BORN FREE
Columbia; 1966; British
THE CORRUPT ONES
Warner Brothers; 1967; West German-French-Italian
CAPTAIN NEMO AND THE UNDERWATER CITY
M-G-M; 1970; British
AN ELEPHANT CALLED SLOWLY
American Continental; 1971; British
BLACK BEAUTY
Paramount; 1971; British-West German-Spanish
THE BELSTONE FOX
Cine III; 1973; British
CHRISTIAN THE LION
co-director with Bill Travers; Scotia American; 1974; British
THE WILD AND THE FREE
BSR Productions/Marble Arch Productions; telefeature; 1980

Hill, Walter
b. January 10, 1942
Long Beach, California
Agent:
I.C.M.
Hollywood
(213) 550-4000

HARD TIMES
Columbia; 1975
THE DRIVER
20th Century-Fox; 1978
THE WARRIORS
Paramount; 1979
THE LONG RIDERS
United Artists; 1980
SOUTHERN COMFORT
20th Century-Fox; 1981

Hiller, Arthur
b. November 22, 1923
Edmonton, Canada
Agent:
Phil Gersh Agency
Beverly Hills
(213) 274-6611

THE CARELESS YEARS
United Artists; 1957
THE MIRACLE OF THE WHITE STALLIONS
Buena Vista; 1963

continued

Hiller, Arthur
continued

THE WHEELER DEALERS
M-G-M; 1963
THE AMERICANIZATION OF EMILY
M-G-M; 1964
PROMISE HER ANYTHING
Paramount; 1966
PENELOPE
M-G-M; 1966
TOBRUK
Universal; 1967
THE TIGER MAKES OUT
Columbia; 1967
POPI
United Artists; 1969
THE OUT-OF-TOWNERS
Paramount; 1970
LOVE STORY
Paramount; 1970
PLAZA SUITE
Paramount; 1971
THE HOSPITAL
United Artists; 1971
MAN OF LA MANCHA
United Artists; 1972; Italian-U.S.
THE CRAZY WORLD OF JULIUS VROODER
20th Century-Fox; 1974
THE MAN IN THE GLASS BOOTH
American Film Theatre; 1975
W.C. FIELDS AND ME
Universal; 1976
SILVER STREAK
20th Century-Fox; 1976
THE IN-LAWS
Columbia; 1979
NIGHTWING
Columbia; 1979
MAKING LOVE
20th Century-Fox; 1981
AUTHOR! AUTHOR!
20th Century-Fox; 1982

Hively, Jack B.

THE ADVENTURES OF HUCKLEBERRY FINN
Sunn Classic; telefeature; 1981
CALIFORNIA GOLD RUSH
Sunn Classic; telefeature; 1981

Hodges, Mike
Home:
25 Palace Court
London W.2., England
01-229-6135

GET CARTER
M-G-M; 1971; British
PULP
United Artists; 1972; British
THE TERMINAL MAN
Warner Brothers; 1974
FLASH GORDON
Universal; 1980

Hofsiss, Jack
Contact:
Directors Guild of America
New York City
(212) 581-0370

I'M DANCING AS FAST AS I CAN
Paramount; 1982

Holcomb, Rod
Agent:
Eisenbach-Greene-Duchow
Los Angeles
(213) 659-3420

CAPTAIN AMERICA
Universal TV; telefeature; 1979
MIDNIGHT OFFERINGS
Stephen J. Cannell Productions; telefeature; 1981
THE GREATEST AMERICAN HERO
Stephen J. Cannell Productions; telefeature; 1981

Hooper, Tobe
Contact:
Directors Guild of America
Los Angeles
(213) 656-1220

THE TEXAS CHAINSAW MASSACRE
Bryanston; 1974
EATEN ALIVE
Virgo International; 1977
SALEM'S LOT
Warner Brothers TV; telefeature; 1979
THE FUNHOUSE
Universal; 1981
POLTERGEIST
M-G-M/United Artists; 1982

Hopper, Dennis
b. May 17, 1936
Dodge City, Kansas

EASY RIDER
Columbia; 1969
THE LAST MOVIE
Universal; 1971
OUT OF THE BLUE
Robson Street Productions; 1980; Canadian

Hopper, Jerry
b. July 29, 1907
Guthrie, Oklahoma
Home:
815 Avenida Salvador
San Clemente, CA 92672

THE ATOMIC CITY
Paramount; 1952
HURRICANE SMITH
Paramount; 1952
PONY EXPRESS
Paramount; 1953
ALASKA SEAS
Paramount; 1954
SECRET OF THE INCAS
Paramount; 1954
NAKED ALIBI
Universal; 1954
SMOKE SIGNAL
Universal; 1955
THE PRIVATE WAR OF MAJOR BENSON
Universal; 1955
ONE DESIRE
Universal; 1955
THE SQUARE JUNGLE
Universal; 1956
NEVER SAY GOODBYE
Universal; 1956
TOY TIGER
Universal; 1956
THE MISSOURI TRAVELER
Buena Vista; 1958
BLUEPRINT FOR ROBBERY
Paramount; 1961
MADRON
Four Star-Excelsior; 1970; U.S.-Israeli

Hough, John
b. November 21, 1941
London, England
Business:
Pinewood Studios
Iver Heath, Bucks
England
IVER 700, ext. 540
Agent:
Creative Artists Agency
Los Angeles
(213) 277-4545

WOLFSHEAD
1970; British
SUDDEN TERROR (Eyewitness)
National General; 1971; British
THE PRACTICE
1971; British
TWINS OF EVIL
Universal; 1972; British
TREASURE ISLAND
National General; 1972; British-French-West German-Spanish
THE LEGEND OF HELL HOUSE
20th Century-Fox; 1974
DIRTY MARY CRAZY LARRY
20th Century-Fox; 1974
ESCAPE TO WITCH MOUNTAIN
Buena Vista; 1975
RETURN FROM WITCH MOUNTAIN
Buena Vista; 1978
BRASS TARGET
M-G-M/United Artists; 1978
THE WATCHER IN THE WOODS
Buena Vista; 1980
INCUBUS
Mark Film Productions; 1981; Canadian

Howard, Cy
b. September 27, 1915
Milwaukee, Wisconsin
Home:
10230 Sunset Blvd.
Los Angeles, CA 90024
(213) 276-2615

LOVERS AND OTHER STRANGERS
Cinerama Releasing Corporation; 1970
EVERY LITTLE CROOK AND NANNY
M-G-M; 1972
IT COULDN'T HAPPEN TO A NICER GUY
The Jozak Company; telefeature; 1974

Howard, Ron
b. March 1, 1954
Duncan, Oklahoma
Contact:
Directors Guild of America
Los Angeles
(213) 656-1220

GRAND THEFT AUTO
New World; 1978
COTTON CANDY
Major H Productions; telefeature; 1978
SKYWARD
Major H/Anson Productions; telefeature; 1980

Hudson, Hugh
Contact:
British Film Institute
127 Charing Cross Road
London W.C. 2, England
01-437-4355

CHARIOTS OF FIRE
The Ladd Company/Warner Brothers; 1981; British

Huggins, Roy
Business:
Public Arts, Inc.
1928 Mandeville Canyon
Los Angeles, CA 90049
(213) 476-7892

HANGMAN'S KNOT
Columbia; 1952
THE YOUNG COUNTRY
Universal TV; telefeature; 1970

Hughes, Ken
b. 1922
Liverpool, England
Home:
950 N. King's Road
Los Angeles, CA 90069
(213) 654-2068

WIDE BOY
Realart; 1952; British
HEAT WAVE (The House Across the Lake)
Lippert; 1954; British
BLACK 13
Archway; 1954; British
THE BRAIN MACHINE
RKO Radio; 1955; British
THE CASE OF THE RED MONKEY (Little Red Monkey)
Allied Artists; 1955; British
THE DEADLIEST SIN (Confession)
Allied Artists; 1955; British
THE ATOMIC MAN (Timeslip)
Allied Artists; 1955; British
JOE MACBETH
Columbia; 1956; British
WICKED AS THEY COME
Columbia; 1957; British
THE LONG HAUL
Columbia; 1957; British
JAZZ BOAT
Columbia; 1960; British
IN THE NICK
Columbia; 1960; British
THE TRIALS OF OSCAR WILDE
Kingsley International; 1960; British
PLAY IT COOLER
Columbia; 1961; British
THE SMALL WORLD OF SAMMY LEE
7 Arts; 1963; British
OF HUMAN BONDAGE
M-G-M; 1964; British
ARRIVEDERCI, BABY! (Drop Dead, Darling)
Paramount; 1966; British
CASINO ROYALE
co-director with Val Guest, John Huston, Joseph McGrath & Robert Parrish; Columbia; 1967; British
CHITTY CHITTY BANG BANG
United Artists; 1968; British

continued

Hughes, Ken
continued

CROMWELL
Columbia; 1970; British
THE INTERNECINE PROJECT
Allied Artists; 1974; British
ALFIE DARLING (Oh! Alfie)
1975; British
SEXTETTE
Crown International; 1978
NIGHT SCHOOL (Terror Eyes)
1981

Hunt, Peter
b. 1928
London, England
Home:
2229 Roscomare Road
Los Angeles, CA 90024
Agent:
Shapiro-Lichtman Agency
Hollywood
(213) 557-2244

ON HER MAJESTY'S SECRET SERVICE
United Artists; 1969; British
GOLD
Allied Artists; 1974; British
SHOUT AT THE DEVIL
American International; 1976; British
GULLIVER'S TRAVELS
EMI; 1977; British-Belgian
THE BEASTS ARE ON THE STREETS
Hanna-Barbera Productions; telefeature; 1978
DEATH HUNT
20th Century-Fox; 1981

Hunt, Peter H.
b. December 19, 1938
Pasadena, California
Agent:
Robert Lantz
New York City
(212) 751-2107
Creative Artists Agency
Los Angeles
(213) 277-4545

1776
Columbia; 1972
FLYING HIGH
Mark Carliner Productions; telefeature; 1978
BULLY
Maturo Image; 1978
WHEN SHE WAS BAD...
Ladd Productions/Henry Jaffe Enterprises; telefeature; 1979
RENDEZVOUS HOTEL
Mark Carliner Productions; telefeature; 1979
LIFE ON THE MISSISSIPPI
The Great Amwell Company/Nebraska ETV Network/ WNET-13/Taurus Films; telefeature; 1980
THE PRIVATE HISTORY OF A CAMPAIGN THAT FAILED
Nebraska ETV Network/The Great Amwell Company/ WNET-13; telefeature; 1981

Hunter, Tim

TEX
Buena Vista; 1981

Hurwitz, Harry

THE PROJECTIONIST
Maron Films Limited; 1971
RICHARD
co-director with Lorees Yerby; Billings; 1972
CHAPLINESQUE, MY LIFE AND HARD TIMES
Xanadu; 1972
TWO IN THE BUSH
United Artists; 1981

Hussein, Waris
Agent:
Robert Lantz
New York City
(212) 751-2107

THANK YOU ALL VERY MUCH (A Touch of Love)
Columbia; 1969; British
QUACKSER FORTUNE HAS A COUSIN IN THE BRONX
UMC; 1970; British
MELODY (S.W.A.L.K.)
Levitt-Pickman; 1971; British
THE POSSESSION OF JOEL DELANEY
Paramount; 1972
HENRY VII AND HIS SIX WIVES
Levitt-Pickman; 1973; British
DIVORCE HIS/DIVORCE HERS
World Film Services; telefeature; 1973

continued

Hussein, Waris
continued

AND BABY MAKES SIX
Alan Landsburg Productions; telefeature; 1979
DEATH PENALTY
Brockway Productions/NBC Entertainment; telefeature; 1980
THE HENDERSON MONSTER
Titus Productions; telefeature; 1980
BABY COMES HOME
Alan Landsburg Productions; telefeature; 1980
CALLIE & SON
Rosilyn Heller Productions/Hemdale Presentations/City Films/Motown Pictures Co.; telefeature; 1981

Huston, Jimmy

DEATH DRIVER
Omni; 1977
DARK SUNDAY
Intercontinental; 1978
BUCKSTONE COUNTY PRISON
Film Ventura; 1978
SEABO
E.O. Corporation; 1978
FINAL EXAM
Motion Picture Marketing; 1981

Huston, John
b. August 5, 1906
Nevada, Montana
Agent:
Paul Kohner Agency
Los Angeles
(213) 550-1060

THE MALTESE FALCON
Warner Brothers; 1941
IN THIS OUR LIFE
Warner Brothers; 1942
ACROSS THE PACIFIC
Warner Brothers; 1942
THE TREASURE OF THE SIERRA MADRE
Warner Brothers; 1948
KEY LARGO
Warner Brothers; 1948
WE WERE STRANGERS
Columbia; 1949
THE ASPHALT JUNGLE
M-G-M; 1950
THE RED BADGE OF COURAGE
M-G-M; 1951
THE AFRICAN QUEEN
United Artists; 1952
MOULIN ROUGE
United Artists; 1952; British
BEAT THE DEVIL
United Artists; 1954; British
MOBY DICK
Warner Brothers; 1956; British
HEAVEN KNOWS, MR. ALLISON
20th Century-Fox; 1957
THE BARBARIAN AND THE GEISHA
20th Century-Fox; 1958
THE ROOTS OF HEAVEN
20th Century-Fox; 1958
THE UNFORGIVEN
United Artists; 1960
THE MISFITS
United Artists; 1961
FREUD
Universal; 1962
THE LIST OF ADRIAN MESSENGER
Universal; 1963
NIGHT OF THE IGUANA
M-G-M; 1964
THE BIBLE...In the Beginning
20th Century-Fox; 1966; Italian
REFLECTIONS IN A GOLDEN EYE
Warner Brothers; 1967
CASINO ROYALE
co-director with Val Guest, Ken Hughes, Joseph McGrath & Robert Parrish; Columbia; 1967; British

continued

Huston, John
continued

A WALK WITH LOVE AND DEATH
20th Century-Fox; 1969; British
SINFUL DAVEY
United Artists; 1969; British
THE KREMLIN LETTER
20th Century-Fox; 1970
FAT CITY
Columbia; 1972
THE LIFE AND TIMES OF JUDGE ROY BEAN
National General; 1973
THE MACKINTOSH MAN
Warner Brothers; 1973; U.S.-British
THE MAN WHO WOULD BE KING
Allied Artists; 1975; British
WISE BLOOD
New Line Cinema; 1979
PHOBIA
Paramount; 1981; Canadian
VICTORY
Paramount/Lorimar; 1981
ANNIE
Columbia; 1982

Hutton, Brian G.
b. 1935
New York, New York
Contact:
Directors Guild of America
Los Angeles
(213) 656-1220

WILD SEED
Universal; 1965
THE PAD (...AND HOW TO USE IT)
Universal; 1966
SOL MADRID
M-G-M; 1968
WHERE EAGLES DARE
M-G-M; 1969; British
KELLY'S HEROES
M-G-M; 1970; U.S.-Yugoslavian
X Y & ZEE (Zee & Co.)
Columbia; 1972; British
NIGHT WATCH
Avco Embassy; 1973; British
THE FIRST DEADLY SIN
Filmways; 1980

Huyck, Willard

MESSIAH OF EVIL
International Cinefilm; 1975
FRENCH POSTCARDS
Paramount; 1979

Hyams, Peter
b. July 26, 1943
New York, New York
Agent:
William Morris Agency
Beverly Hills
(213) 274-7451

ROLLING MAN
ABC Circle Films; telefeature; 1972
GOODNIGHT MY LOVE
ABC Circle Films; telefeature; 1972
BUSTING
United Artists; 1974
OUR TIME
Warner Brothers; 1974
PEEEPER
20th Century-Fox; 1976
CAPRICORN ONE
Warner Brothers; 1978
HANOVER STREET
Columbia; 1979
OUTLAND
The Ladd Company/Warner Brothers; 1981

Idle, Eric
Contact:
British Film Institute
127 Charing Cross Road
London W.C. 2, England
01-437-4355

ALL YOU NEED IS CASH
co-director with Gary Weis; NBC-TV;
telefeature;1978; British

Irvin, John
Contact:
Directors Guild of America
Los Angeles
(213) 656-1220

TINKER, TAILOR, SOLDIER, SPY
BBC-TV/Paramount TV; telefeature; 1979; British
THE DOGS OF WAR
United Artists; 1981
GHOST STORY
Universal; 1981

Irving, David

GOOD-BYE, CRUEL WORLD
co-director with Nicholas Niciphor; NSN; 1981

Irving, Richard
Home:
5401 Zelzah Avenue
Encino, CA 91316
(213) 996-6355
Business:
Universal Studios
Universal City, CA 91608
(213) 508-1601

PRESCRIPTION: MURDER
Universal TV; telefeature; 1968
ISTANBUL EXPRESS
Universal TV; telefeature; 1968
BREAKOUT
Universal TV; telefeature; 1970
RANSOM FOR A DEAD MAN
Universal TV; telefeature; 1971
CUTTER
Universal TV; telefeature; 1972
THE SIX-MILLION DOLLAR MAN
Universal TV; telefeature; 1973
THE ART OF CRIME
Universal TV; telefeature; 1975
EXO-MAN
Universal TV; telefeature; 1977
SEVENTH AVENUE
co-director with Russ Mayberry; Universal TV; television mini-series; 1977

Isenberg, Gerald I.
Business:
8383 Wilshire Blvd.
Beverly Hills, CA 90211
(213) 653-4510
Agent:
I.C.M.
Hollywood
(213) 550-4308

SEIZURE: THE STORY OF KATHY MORRIS
The Jozak Company; telefeature; 1980

Israel, Neil
Contact:
Directors Guild of America
Los Angeles
(213) 656-1220

TUNNELVISION
co-director with Brad Swirnoff; World Wide; 1976
AMERICATHON
United Artists; 1979

Ivory, James
b. June 7, 1928
Berkeley, California
Home:
400 East 52nd Street
New York, N.Y. 10022
(212) 759-3694
Business:
Merchant-Ivory Productions
17 West 60th Street
New York, N.Y. 10023
(212) 582-8049
Agent:
Susan Smith Agency
Beverly Hills
(213) 277-8464

THE HOUSEHOLDER
Royal International; 1963; Indian-U.S.
SHAKESPEARE WALLAH
Continental; 1966; Indian
THE GURU
20th Century-Fox; 1969; British-Indian
BOMBAY TALKIE
Dia Films; 1970; Indian
SAVAGES
Angelika; 1972
HELEN - QUEEN OF THE NAUTCH GIRLS
1973; Indian
MAHATMA AND THE MAD BOY
1973; Indian
THE WILD PARTY
American International; 1975
AUTOBIOGRAPHY OF A PRINCESS
Merchant-Ivory Productions; telefeature; 1975
SWEET SOUNDS
1976
ROSELAND
Cinema Shares International; 1977

continued

Ivory, James
continued

THE 5:48
telefeature; 1979
HULLABALOO OVER GEORGIE & BONNIE'S PICTURES
Corinth; 1979
THE EUROPEANS
Levitt-Pickman; 1979; British
JANE AUSTEN IN MANHATTAN
Contemporary; 1980
QUARTET
New World; 1981; British-French

Jackson, Lewis

YOU BETTER WATCH OUT
Edward R. Pressman Productions; 1980

Jacoby, Joseph

SHAME, SHAME, EVERYBODY KNOWS HER NAME
J.E.R.; 1970
HURRY UP OR I'LL BE THIRTY
Avco Embassy; 1973
THE GREAT BANK HOAX
Warner Brothers; 1978

Jaeckin, Just

EMMANUELLE
Columbia; 1974; French
THE STORY OF O
Allied Artists; 1975; French
THE FRENCH WOMAN
Monarch; 1979; French
THE LAST ROMANTIC LOVER
New Line Cinema; 1980; French
LADY CHATTERLEY'S LOVER
Cannon; 1981; French-British

Jaglom, Henry
Business:
International Rainbow Pictures
933 N. La Brea
Hollywood, CA 90038
(213) 851-4811
Agent:
The Ufland Agency
Beverly Hills
(213) 273-9441

A SAFE PLACE
Columbia; 1971
TRACKS
Trio; 1977
SITTING DUCKS
Specialty Films; 1980
NATIONAL LAMPOON GOES TO THE MOVIES
co-director with Bob Giraldi; United Artists; 1981

Jameson, Jerry
Agent:
William Morris Agency
Beverly Hills
(213) 274-7451

BRUTE CORPS
General Films; 1971
THE DIRT GANG
American International; 1972
THE BAT PEOPLE
American International; 1974
HEATWAVE!
Universal TV; telefeature; 1974
THE ELEVATOR
Universal TV; telefeature; 1974
HURRICANE
Metromedia Productions; telefeature; 1974
TERROR ON THE 40TH FLOOR
Metromedia Productions; telefeature; 1974
THE SECRET NIGHT CALLER
Charles Fries Productions/Penthouse Productions; telefeature; 1975
THE DEADLY TOWER
M-G-M TV; telefeature; 1975
THE LIVES OF JENNY DOLAN
Ross Hunter Productions/Paramount TV; telefeature; 1975
THE CALL OF THE WILD
Charles Fries Productions; telefeature; 1976

continued

Jameson, Jerry
continued

THE INVASION OF JOHNSON COUNTY
Roy Huggins Productions/Universal TV; telefeature 1976
AIRPORT '77
Universal; 1977
SUPERDOME
ABC Circle Films; telefeature; 1978
A FIRE IN THE SKY
Bill Driskill Productions; telefeature; 1978
RAISE THE TITANIC
AFD; 1980; British-U.S.
HIGH NOON - PART II: THE RETURN OF WILL KANE
Charles Fries Productions; telefeature; 1980
STAND BY YOUR MAN
Robert Papazian Productions/Peter Guber-Jon Peters Productions; telefeature; 1981

Jarman, Derek
Contact:
British Film Institute
127 Charing Cross Road
London W.C. 2, England
01-437-4355

SEBASTIANE
co-director with Paul Humfress; Discopat; 1977; British
JUBILEE
Libra Films; 1979; British
THE TEMPEST
World Northal; 1980; British

Jarrott, Charles
b. June 6, 1927
London, England
Agent:
William Morris Agency
Beverly Hills
(213) 274-7451

ANNE OF THE THOUSAND DAYS
Universal; 1969; British
MARY, QUEEN OF SCOTS
Universal; 1971; British
LOST HORIZON
Columbia; 1972
THE DOVE
Paramount; 1974
THE LITTLEST HORSE THIEVES (Escape to the Dark)
Buena Vista; 1977; U.S.-British
THE OTHER SIDE OF MIDNIGHT
20th Century-Fox; 1977
THE LAST FLIGHT OF NOAH'S ARK
Buena Vista; 1980
CONDORMAN
Buena Vista; 1981
THE AMATEUR
20th Century-Fox; 1981; Canadian

Jeffries, Lionel
b. 1926
London, England
Contact:
British Film Institute
127 Charing Cross Road
London W.C. 2, England
01-437-4355

THE RAILWAY CHILDREN
Universal; 1971; British
THE AMAZING MR. BLUNDEN
Goldstone; 1972; British
BAXTER!
National General; 1973; British
THE WATER BABIES
1978; British
WOMBLING FREE
1979; British

Jewison, Norman
b. July 21, 1926
Toronto, Canada
Agent:
William Morris Agency
Beverly Hills
(213) 274-7451
Business Manager:
Capell, Flekman, Coyne & Co.
Beverly Hills
(213) 553-0310

40 POUNDS OF TROUBLE
Universal; 1962
THE THRILL OF IT ALL
Universal; 1963
SEND ME NO FLOWERS
Universal; 1964
THE ART OF LOVE
Universal; 1965
THE CINCINNATI KID
M-G-M; 1965
THE RUSSIANS ARE COMING THE RUSSIANS ARE COMING
United Artists; 1966
IN THE HEAT OF THE NIGHT
United Artists; 1967

continued

Jewison, Norman
continued

THE THOMAS CROWN AFFAIR
United Artists; 1968
GAILY, GAILY
United Artists; 1969
FIDDLER ON THE ROOF
United Artists; 1971
JESUS CHRIST SUPERSTAR
Universal; 1973
ROLLERBALL
United Artists; 1975
F.I.S.T.
United Artists; 1978
...AND JUSTICE FOR ALL
Columbia; 1979

Jodorowsky, Alexandro

FANDO AND LIS
Cannon; 1970; Mexican
EL TOPO
ABKCO; 1971; Mexican
HOLY MOUNTAIN
ABKCO; 1974; Mexican
TUSK
Yank Films-Films 21; 1980; French

Johnson, Jed

ANDY WARHOL'S BAD
New World; 1977

Johnson, Ken
Business:
Universal Studios
Universal City, CA 91608
(213) 508-3256

THE INCREDIBLE HULK
Universal TV; telefeature; 1977

Johnson, Lamont
b. 1920
Stockton, California
Agent:
I.C.M.
Hollywood
(213) 550-4000

THIN ICE
20th Century-Fox; 1961
A COVENANT WITH DEATH
Warner Brothers; 1966
KONA COAST
Warner Brothers; 1968
DEADLOCK
Universal TV; telefeature; 1969
THE MACKENZIE BREAK
United Artists; 1970
MY SWEET CHARLIE
Universal TV; telefeature; 1970
A GUNFIGHT
Paramount; 1971
THE GROUNDSTAR CONSPIRACY
Universal; 1972; U.S.-Canadian
YOU'LL LIKE MY MOTHER
Universal; 1972
THAT CERTAIN SUMMER
Universal TV; telefeature; 1972
THE LAST AMERICAN HERO
20th Century-Fox; 1973
VISIT TO A CHIEF'S SON
United Artists; 1974
THE EXECUTION OF PRIVATE SLOVIK
Universal TV; telefeature; 1974
FEAR ON TRIAL
Alan Landsburg Production; telefeature; 1975
LIPSTICK
Paramount; 1976
ONE ON ONE
Warner Brothers; 1977
OFF THE MINNESOTA STRIP
Cherokee Productions/Universal TV; telefeature; 1980

continued

Johnson, Lamont
continued

CATTLE ANNIE AND LITTLE BRITCHES
Universal; 1981
CRISIS AT CENTRAL HIGH
Time-Life TV; telefeature; 1981
ESCAPE FROM IRAN: THE CANADIAN CAPER
Canamedia Productions; telefeature; 1981; Canadian

Jones, Eugene S.
Home:
9545 Hidden Valley Road
Beverly Hills, CA 90210
(213) 278-6155

A FACE OF WAR
Commonwealth; 1968
TWO MEN OF KARAMOJA (The Wild and the Brave)
Tomorrow Entertainment; 1974
HIGH ICE
E.S.J. Productions; telefeature; 1980

Jones, L.Q.
Business:
2144 N. Cahuenga
Hollywood, CA 90068
(213) 463-4426
Agent:
Charter Management
Hollywood
(213) 278-1690

A BOY AND HIS DOG
Pacific Film Enterprises; 1975

Jones, Terry
Contact:
British Film Institute
127 Charing Cross Road
London W.C. 2, England
01-437-4355

MONTY PYTHON AND THE HOLY GRAIL
co-director with Terry Gilliam; Cinema 5; 1974; British
LIFE OF BRIAN
Orion Pictures/Warner Brothers; 1979; British

Jordan, Glenn
Agent:
Creative Artists Agency
Los Angeles
(213) 277-4545
Business Manager:
Bash, Barkin & Gesas
Beverly Hills
(213) 278-7700

FRANKENSTEIN
Dan Curtis Productions; telefeature; 1973
THE PICTURE OF DORIAN GRAY
Dan Curtis Productions; telefeature; 1973
SHELL GAME
Thoroughbred Productions; telefeature; 1975
ONE OF MY WIVES IS MISSING
Spelling-Goldberg Productions; telefeature; 1975
DELTA COUNTY, U.S.A.
Leonard Goldberg Productions/Paramount TV; telefeature; 1977
SUNSHINE CHRISTMAS
Universal TV; telefeature; 1977
THE COURT-MARTIAL OF GEORGE ARMSTRONG CUSTER
NBC-TV; telefeature; 1977
IN THE MATTER OF KAREN ANN QUINLAN
Warren V. Bush Productions; telefeature; 1977
LES MISERABLES
Norman Rosemont Productions/ITV Entertainment; telefeature; 1978
SON RISE: A MIRACLE OF LOVE
Rothman-Wohl Productions/Filmways; telefeature; 1979
THE FAMILY MAN
Time-Life Productions; telefeature; 1979
THE WOMEN'S ROOM
Philip Mandelker Productions/Warner Brothers TV; telefeature; 1980
NEIL SIMON'S ONLY WHEN I LAUGH
Columbia; 1981
THE PRINCESS AND THE CABBIE
Time-Life Productions; telefeature; 1981

Juran, Nathan
b. September 1, 1907
Austria
Home:
623 Via Horquilla
Palos Verdes Estates, CA

THE BLACK CASTLE
Universal; 1952
GUNSMOKE
Universal; 1953
LAW AND ORDER
Universal; 1953

continued

Juran, Nathan
continued

THE GOLDEN BLADE
Universal; 1953
TUMBLEWEED
Universal; 1953
HIGHWAY DRAGNET
Allied Artists; 1954
DRUMS ACROSS THE RIVER
Universal; 1954
THE CROOKED WEB
Columbia; 1955
THE DEADLY MANTIS
Universal; 1957
HELLCATS OF THE NAVY
Columbia; 1957
TWENTY MILLION MILES TO EARTH
Columbia; 1957
THE 7TH VOYAGE OF SINBAD
Columbia; 1958
GOOD DAY FOR A HANGING
Columbia; 1959
FLIGHT OF THE LAST BALLOON
Woolner Brothers; 1961
JACK THE GIANT KILLER
United Artists; 1962
SIEGE OF THE SAXONS
Columbia; 1963; British
FIRST MEN IN THE MOON
Columbia; 1964; British
EAST OF SUDAN
Columbia; 1964; British
LAND RAIDERS
Columbia; 1970
THE BOY WHO CRIED WEREWOLF
Universal; 1973

Jutra, Claude
b. March 11, 1930
Montreal, Canada

MOVEMENT PERPETUEL
co-director with Michel Brault; 1949; Canadian
PIERROT DES BOIS
1954; Canadian
JEUNESSES MUSICALES
1956; Canadian
A CHAIRY TALE
co-director with Norman McLaren; 1957; Canadian
LES MAINS NETTES
1958; Canadian
ANNA LA BONNE
1959; Canadian
FELIX LECLERC - TROUBADOUR
1959; Canadian
LE NIGER - JEUNE REPUBLIQUE
1961; Canadian
LA LUTTE
1961; Canadian
QUEBEC USA
co-director with Michel Brault; 1962; Canadian
LES ENFANTS DU SILENCE
co-director with Michel Brault; 1964; Canadian
A TOUT PRENDE
Lopert; 1966; Canadian
COMMENT SAVOIR
1966; Canadian
WOW!
NFB; 1969; Canadian
MARIE-CHRISTINE
1970; Canadian
MON ONCLE ANTOINE
Gendon; 1972; Canadian
KAMOURASKA
New Line Cinema; 1974; Canadian
TWO SOLITUDES
1978; Canadian
SURFACING
Arista Films; 1981; Canadian
BY DESIGN
BDS Productions; 1981; Canadian

Kaczender, George

Home:
1550 Dr. Penfield Drive
Montreal, Quebec H3E 1C2
Canada
(514) 844-3091
Agent:
The Lantz Office
New York City
(212) 751-2107

DON'T LET THE ANGELS FALL
Kemeny; 1969; Canadian
THE GIRL IN BLUE
Cinerama Releasing Corporation; 1974; Canadian
IN PRAISE OF OLDER WOMEN
Avco Embassy; 1978; Canadian
AGENCY
Taft International; 1980; Canadian
YOUR TICKET IS NO LONGER VALID
1981; Canadian
CHANEL SOLITAIRE
United Film Distribution; 1981; French-British

Kagan, Jeremy Paul

Home:
2024 N. Curson Avenue
Los Angeles, CA 90046
(213) 874-5175
Agent:
Adams, Ray & Rosenberg
Los Angeles
(213) 278-3000

UNWED FATHER
Wolper Productions; telefeature; 1974
JUDGE DEE AND THE MONASTERY MURDERS
ABC Circle Films; telefeature; 1974
KATHERINE
The Jozak Company; telefeature; 1975
HEROES
Universal; 1977
SCOTT JOPLIN
Universal; 1977
THE BIG FIX
Universal; 1978
THE CHOSEN
Landau; 1981

Kanew, Jeff

Business:
Utopia Productions
45 East 89th Street
New York, N.Y. 10028
(212) 722-6968
Agent:
William Morris Agency
New York City
(212) 586-5100

BLACK RODEO
Cinerama Releasing Corporation; 1972
NATURAL ENEMIES
Cinema 5; 1979

Kanin, Garson

b. November 24, 1912
Rochester, New York
Business:
200 West 57th Street
New York, N.Y. 10019

A MAN TO REMEMBER
RKO Radio; 1938
NEXT TIME I MARRY
RKO Radio; 1938
THE GREAT MAN VOTES
RKO Radio; 1939
BACHELOR MOTHER
RKO Radio; 1939
MY FAVORITE WIFE
RKO Radio; 1940
THEY KNEW WHAT THEY WANTED
Columbia; 1940
TOM, DICK AND HARRY
RKO Radio; 1941
THE TRUE GLORY
co-director with Carol Reed; Columbia; 1945
WHERE IT'S AT
United Artists; 1969
SOME KIND OF NUT
United Artists; 1969

Kanter, Hal

b. December 18, 1918
Savannah, Georgia
Agent:
Marvin Moss Agency
Los Angeles
(213) 274-8483

LOVING YOU
Paramount; 1957
I MARRIED A WOMAN
Universal; 1958
ONCE UPON A HORSE
Universal; 1958
FOR THE LOVE OF IT
Charles Fries Productions/Neila Productions; telefeature; 1980

Kaplan, Jonathan
b. November 25, 1947
Paris, France
Agent:
I.C.M.
Hollywood
(213) 550-4000
Business Manager:
Gerwin, Jamner & Pariser
Los Angeles
(213) 655-4410

THE STUDENT TEACHERS
New World; 1973
THE SLAMS
M-G-M; 1973
TRUCK TURNER
American International; 1974
NIGHT CALL NURSES
New World; 1974
WHITE LINE FEVER
Columbia; 1975
MR. BILLION
20th Century-Fox; 1976
OVER THE EDGE
Orion Pictures/Warner Brothers; 1979
THE 11TH VICTIM
Marty Katz Productions/Paramount TV; telefeature; 1979
THE HUSTLER OF MUSCLE BEACH
Furia-Oringer Productions; telefeature; 1980
THE GENTLEMAN BANDIT
Highgate Pictures; telefeature; 1981

Kaplan, Nelly
b. 1931
Buenos Aires, Argentina
Contact:
French Film Office
745 Fifth Avenue
New York, N.Y. 10151
(212) 832-8860

A VERY CURIOUS GIRL
Regional; 1970; French
PAPA LES PETITS BATEAUX
1971; French
NEA
Libra Films; 1976; French
LE SATELLITE DE VENUS
1977; French
AU BONHEUR DES DAMES
1979; French
CHARLES ET LUCIE
Nu-Image; 1980; French

Karlson, Phil
(Philip Karlstein)
b. July 2, 1908
Chicago, Illinois
Agent:
Phil Gersh Agency
Beverly Hills
(213) 274-6611

A WAVE, A WAC AND A MARINE
Monogram; 1944
THERE GOES KELLY
Monogram; 1945
G.I. HONEYMOON
Monogram; 1945
THE SHANGHAI COBRA
Monogram; 1945
DARK ALIBI
Monogram; 1946
LIVE WIVES
Monogram; 1946
THE MISSING LADY
Monogram; 1946
SWING PARADE OF 1946
Monogram; 1946
BEHIND THE MASK
Monogram; 1946
BOWERY BOMBSHELL
Monogram; 1946
WIFE WANTED
Monogram; 1946
BLACK GOLD
Allied Artists; 1947
KILROY WAS HERE
Monogram; 1947
LOUISIANA
Monogram; 1947
ADVENTURES IN SILVERADO
Columbia; 1948
ROCKY
Monogram; 1948
THUNDERHOOF
Columbia; 1948
LADIES OF THE CHORUS
Columbia; 1948

continued

Karlson, Phil
continued

DOWN MEMORY LANE
Eagle Lion; 1949
THE BIG CAT
Eagle Lion; 1949
THE IROQUOIS TRAIL
United Artists; 1950
LORNA DOONE
Columbia; 1951
THE TEXAS RANGERS
Columbia; 1951
MASK OF THE AVENGER
Columbia; 1951
SCANDAL SHEET
Columbia; 1952
KANSAS CITY CONFIDENTIAL
United Artists; 1952
THE BRIGAND
Columbia; 1952
99 RIVER STREET
United Artists; 1953
THEY RODE WEST
Columbia; 1954
HELL'S ISLAND
Paramount; 1955
TIGHT SPOT
Columbia; 1955
FIVE AGAINST THE HOUSE
Columbia; 1955
THE PHENIX CITY STORY
Allied Artists; 1955
THE BROTHERS RICO
Columbia; 1957
GUNMAN'S WALK
Columbia; 1958
HELL TO ETERNITY
Allied Artists; 1960
KEY WITNESS
M-G-M; 1960
THE SECRET WAYS
Universal; 1961
THE YOUNG DOCTORS
United Artists; 1961
THE SCARFACE MOB
Desilu; 1962
KID GALAHAD
United Artists; 1962
RAMPAGE
Warner Brothers; 1963
THE SILENCERS
Columbia; 1966
A TIME FOR KILLING
Columbia; 1967
THE WRECKING CREW
Columbia; 1968
HORNETS' NEST
United Artists; 1970
BEN
Cinerama Releasing Corporation; 1972
WALKING TALL
Cinerama Releasing Corporation; 1973
FRAMED
Paramount; 1974

Karson, Eric
Business:
Karson Films, Inc.
11607 Acama Street
Studio City, CA 91604
(213) 762-1731
Agent:
Phil Gersh Agency
Beverly Hills
(213) 274-6611

DIRT
co-director with Cal Naylor; American Cinema; 1979
THE OCTAGON
American Cinema; 1980

Kasdan, Lawrence
Agent:
Norman Kurland Agency
Los Angeles
(213) 274-8927

BODY HEAT
The Ladd Company/Warner Brothers; 1981

Katselas, Milton
Agent:
Chasin-Park-Citron Agency
Los Angeles
(213) 273-7190

BUTTERFLIES ARE FREE
Columbia; 1972
40 CARATS
Columbia; 1973
REPORT TO THE COMMISSIONER
United Artists; 1975
WHEN YOU COMIN' BACK, RED RYDER?
Columbia; 1979
STRANGERS: THE STORY OF A MOTHER AND A DAUGHTER
Chris-Rose Productions; telefeature; 1979

Katzin, Lee H.
Home:
13425 Java Drive
Beverly Hills, CA 90210
Agent:
Irv Schechter
Beverly Hills
(213) 278-8070
Business Manager:
Norman Greenbaum
Los Angeles
(213) 477-3924

HONDO AND THE APACHES
M-G-M; 1967
HEAVEN WITH A GUN
M-G-M; 1969
WHAT EVER HAPPENED TO AUNT ALICE?
Cinerama Releasing Corporation; 1969
THE PHYNX
Warner Brothers; 1970
LE MANS
National General; 1970
ALONG CAME A SPIDER
20th Century-Fox TV; telefeature; 1970
THE SALZBURG CONNECTION
20th Century-Fox; 1972
VISIONS...
CBS, Inc.; telefeature; 1972
THE VOYAGE OF THE YES
Bing Crosby Productions; telefeature; 1973
THE STRANGER
Bing Crosby Productions; telefeature; 1973
ORDEAL
20th Century-Fox TV; telefeature; 1973
SAVAGES
Spelling-Goldberg Productions; telefeature; 1974
STRANGE HOMECOMING
Alpine Productions/Worldvision; telefeature; 1974
THE LAST SURVIVORS
Bob Banner Associates; telefeature; 1975
SKY HEI$T
Warner Brothers TV; telefeature; 1975
QUEST
David Gerber Productions/Columbia TV; telefeature; 1976
THE MAN FROM ATLANTIS
Solow Production Company; telefeature; 1977
RELENTLESS
CBS, Inc.; telefeature; 1977
THE BASTARD
Universal TV; telefeature; 1978
ZUMA BEACH
Edgar J. Scherick Productions/Warner Brothers TV telefeature; 1978
TERROR OUT OF THE SKY
Alan Landsburg Productions; telefeature; 1978
REVENGE OF THE SAVAGE BEES
telefeature; 1979
SAMURAI
Danny Thomas Productions/Universal TV; telefeature; 1979
DEATH RAY 2000
Woodruff Productions/QM Productions; telefeature; 1981

Kaufer, Jonathan
Contact:
Directors Guild of America
Los Angeles
(213) 656-1220

SOUP FOR ONE
Warner Brothers; 1981

Kaufman, Philip
b. October 23, 1936
Chicago, Illinois
Agent:
Creative Artists Agency
Los Angeles
(213) 277-4545

GOLDSTEIN
co-director with Benjamin Manaster; Altura; 1965
FEARLESS FRANK
American International; 1969
THE GREAT NORTHFIELD, MINNESOTA RAID
Universal; 1972
THE WHITE DAWN
Paramount; 1974
INVASION OF THE BODY SNATCHERS
United Artists; 1978
THE WANDERERS
Orion Pictures/Warner Brothers; 1979

Kaylor, Robert
Agent:
I.C.M.
Hollywood
(213) 653-4143

DERBY
Cinerama Releasing Corporation; 1971
CARNY
United Artists/Lorimar; 1980

Kazan, Elia
(Elia Kazanjoglou)
b. September 7, 1909
Constantinople, Turkey
Business:
850 Seventh Avenue
New York, N.Y. 10019
(212) 246-9714

A TREE GROWS IN BROOKLYN
20th Century-Fox; 1945
SEA OF GRASS
20th Century-Fox; 1947
BOOMERANG!
20th Century-Fox; 1947
GENTLEMAN'S AGREEMENT
20th Century-Fox; 1947
PINKY
20th Century-Fox; 1949
PANIC IN THE STREETS
20th Century-Fox; 1950
A STREETCAR NAMED DESIRE
Warner Brothers; 1951
VIVA ZAPATA!
20th Century-Fox; 1952
MAN ON A TIGHTROPE
20th Century-Fox; 1953
ON THE WATERFRONT
Columbia; 1954
EAST OF EDEN
Warner Brothers; 1955
BABY DOLL
Warner Brothers; 1956
A FACE IN THE CROWD
Warner Brothers; 1957
WILD RIVER
20th Century-Fox; 1960
SPLENDOR IN THE GRASS
Warner Brothers; 1961
AMERICA AMERICA
Warner Brothers; 1963
THE ARRANGEMENT
Warner Brothers; 1969
THE VISITORS
United Artists; 1972
THE LAST TYCOON
Paramount; 1975

Kelljan, Bob
Paul Kohner Agency
Los Angeles
(213) 550-1060

COUNT YORGA, VAMPIRE
American International; 1970
THE RETURN OF COUNT YORGA
American International; 1971

continued

Kelljan, Bob
continued

SCREAM, BLACULA, SCREAM
American International; 1973
ACT OF VENGEANCE
American International; 1974
BLACK OAK CONSPIRACY
New World; 1977
DOG AND CAT
Largo Productions; telefeature; 1977
BEACH PATROL
Spelling-Goldberg Productions; telefeature; 1979

Kelly, Gene
b. August 23, 1912
Pittsburgh, Pennsylvania
Business:
Zoetrope Studios
1040 N. Las Palmas Avenue
Hollywood, CA 90038
(213) 463-7191

ON THE TOWN
co-director with Stanley Donen; M-G-M; 1949
SINGIN' IN THE RAIN
co-director with Stanley Donen; M-G-M; 1952
IT'S ALWAYS FAIR WEATHER
co-director with Stanley Donen; M-G-M; 1955
INVITATION TO THE DANCE
M-G-M; 1956
THE HAPPY ROAD
M-G-M; 1957
THE TUNNEL OF LOVE
M-G-M; 1958
GIGOT
20th Century-Fox; 1962
A GUIDE FOR THE MARRIED MAN
20th Century-Fox; 1967
HELLO, DOLLY!
20th Century-Fox; 1969
THE CHEYENNE SOCIAL CLUB
National General; 1970
THAT'S ENTERTAINMENT, PART 2
new sequences; M-G-M/United Artists; 1976

Kennedy, Burt
b. 1923
Muskegon, Michigan
Home:
13138 Magnolia Blvd.
Sherman Oaks, CA 91403
(213) 986-8759
Agent:
William Morris Agency
Beverly Hills
(213) 274-7451

THE CANADIANS
20th Century-Fox; 1961
MAIL ORDER BRIDE
M-G-M; 1963
THE ROUNDERS
M-G-M; 1965
THE MONEY TRAP
M-G-M; 1966
RETURN OF THE SEVEN
United Artists; 1966
WELCOME TO HARD TIMES
M-G-M; 1967
THE WAR WAGON
Universal; 1967
SUPPORT YOUR LOCAL SHERIFF
United Artists; 1969
YOUNG BILLY YOUNG
United Artists; 1969
THE GOOD GUYS AND THE BAD GUYS
Warner Brothers; 1969
DIRTY DINGUS MAGEE
M-G-M; 1970
SUPPORT YOUR LOCAL GUNFIGHTER
United Artists; 1971
HANNIE CAULDER
Paramount; 1971; British
THE DESERTER
Paramount; 1971; Italian-Yugoslavian
THE TRAIN ROBBERS
Warner Brothers; 1973
SHOOTOUT IN A ONE-DOG TOWN
Hanna-Barbera Productions; telefeature; 1974
SIDEKICKS
Warner Brothers TV; telefeature; 1974
ALL THE KIND STRANGERS
Cinemation TV; telefeature; 1974
THE KILLER INSIDE ME
Warner Brothers; 1976

continued

Kennedy, Burt
continued

HOW THE WEST WAS WON
co-director with Daniel Mann; M-G-M TV; television mini-series; 1977
THE RHINEMANN EXCHANGE
Universal TV; television mini-series; 1977
KATE BLISS & THE TICKER TAPE KID
Aaron Spelling Productions; telefeature; 1978
THE WILD WILD WEST REVISITED
CBS Entertainment; telefeature; 1979
THE CONCRETE COWBOYS
Frankel Films; telefeature; 1979
MORE WILD WILD WEST
CBS Entertainment; telefeature; 1980
WOLF LAKE
Wolf Lake Productions; 1981; Canadian

Kershner, Irvin
b. April 29, 1923
Philadelphia, Pennsylvania
Business:
(213) 275-8795
Agent:
Paul Kohner Agency
Los Angeles
(213) 550-1060

STAKEOUT ON DOPE STREET
Warner Brothers; 1958
THE YOUNG CAPTIVES
Paramount; 1959
THE HOODLUM PRIEST
United Artists; 1961
A FACE IN THE RAIN
Embassy; 1963
THE LUCK OF GINGER COFFEY
Continental; 1964; Canadian
A FINE MADNESS
Warner Brothers; 1966
THE FLIM-FLAM MAN
20th Century-Fox; 1967
LOVING
Columbia; 1970
UP THE SANDBOX
National General; 1972
S*P*Y*S
20th Century-Fox; 1974; British-U.S.
THE RETURN OF A MAN CALLED HORSE
United Artists; 1976
RAID ON ENTEBBE
Edgar J. Scherick Associates/20th Century-Fox TV; telefeature; 1977
EYES OF LAURA MARS
Columbia; 1978
THE EMPIRE STRIKES BACK
20th Century-Fox; 1980

Kessler, Bruce
Home:
4444 Via Marina
Marina del Rey, CA 90291
(213) 823-2394
Agent:
Frank Cooper Agency
Hollywood
(213) 277-8422

ANGELS FROM HELL
American International; 1968
KILLERS THREE
American International; 1968
THE GAY DECEIVERS
Fanfare; 1969
SIMON, KING OF WITCHES
Fanfare; 1971
MURDER IN PEYTON PLACE
20th Century-Fox TV; telefeature; 1977
THE TWO-FIVE
Universal TV; telefeature; 1978
DEATH MOON
Roger Gimbel Productions/EMI TV; telefeature; 1978
CRUISE INTO TERROR
Aaron Spelling Productions; telefeature; 1978

Kibbee, Roland
Agent:
Major Talent Agency
Beverly Hills
(213) 820-5841

THE MIDNIGHT MAN
co-director with Burt Lancaster; Universal; 1974

Kidd, Michael
b. August 12, 1919
Brooklyn, New York
Agent:
William Morris Agency
Beverly Hills
(213) 274-7451

MERRY ANDREW
M-G-M; 1958

King, Allan
b. 1930
Vancouver, Canada
Home:
397 Carlton Street
Toronto, Ontario M5A 2M3
Canada
(416) 964-7284

SKID ROW
1956; Canadian
PORTRAIT OF A HARBOR
1957; Canadian
MOROCCO
1958; Canadian
BULL FIGHT
1959; Canadian
RICKSHAW
1960; Canadian
A MATTER OF PRIDE
1961; Canadian
THE PURSUIT OF HAPPINESS
1962; Canadian
THE PEACEMAKERS
1963; Canadian
BJORN'S INFERNO
1964; Canadian
COMING OF AGE IN IBIZA
1964; Canadian
WARRENDALE
Grove Press; 1968; Canadian
THE NEW WOMAN
1968; Canadian
A MARRIED COUPLE
Aquarius; 1970; Canadian
COME ON CHILDREN
Allan King Associates; 1972; Canadian
WHO HAS SEEN THE WIND
Astral; 1977; Canadian
ONE-NIGHT STAND
1979; Canadian
SILENCE OF THE NORTH
Universal; 1981; Canadian

Kinon, Richard
Agent:
I.C.M.
Hollywood
(213) 550-4308

THE LOVE BOAT
co-director with Alan Myerson; Douglas S. Cramer Productions; telefeature; 1976
THE NEW LOVE BOAT
Douglas S. Cramer Productions;telefeature; 1977
ALOHA PARADISE
Aaron Spelling Productions; telefeature; 1981

Kishon, Ephraim
Contact:
The Israel Film Centre
30 Agron Street
P.O. Box 229
Jerusalem, Israel
02-227241

SALLAH
Palisades International; 1963; Israeli
THE BIG DIG
Canal; 1969; Israeli
THE POLICEMAN
Cinema 5; 1972; Israeli

Kjellin, Alf
b. February 28, 1920
Lund, Sweden
Home:
12630 Mulholland Drive
Beverly Hills, CA 90210
(213) 273-6514
Agent:
I.C.M.
Hollywood
(213) 550-4000

GIRL IN THE RAIN
1955; Swedish
SEVENTEEN YEARS OLD
1957; Swedish
ENCOUNTERS AT DUSK
1957; Swedish
SWINGING AT THE CASTLE
1959; Swedish
ONLY A WAITER
1960; Swedish

continued

Kjellin, Alf
continued

PLEASURE GARDEN
1961; Swedish
SISKA
1962; Swedish
MIDAS RUN
Cinerama Releasing Corporation; 1969
THE McMASTERS
Chevron; 1970
THE DEADLY DREAM
Universal TV; telefeature; 1971
THE GIRLS OF HUNTINGTON HOUSE
Lorimar Productions; telefeature; 1973

Klane, Robert
Contact:
Directors Guild of America
Los Angeles
(213) 656-1220

THANK GOD IT'S FRIDAY
Columbia; 1978

Klein, William
b. 1926
New York, New York
Contact:
French Film Office
745 Fifth Avenue
New York, N.Y.
(212) 832-8860

WHO ARE YOU POLLY MAGGOO?
1966; French
FAR FROM VIETNAM
co-director with Jean-Luc Godard, Joris Ivens, Alain Resnais & Agnes Varda; New Yorker; 1967 French
MISTER FREEDOM
1969; French
FLOAT LIKE A BUTTERFLY - STING LIKE A BEE
1969; French
FESTIVAL PANAFRICAIN
1969; French
ELDRIDGE CLEAVER
1970; French
LE COUPLE TEMOIN
1977; French

Kleiser, Randal
Agent:
I.C.M.
Hollywood
(213) 550-4165

ALL TOGETHER NOW
RSO Films; telefeature; 1975
DAWN: PORTRAIT OF A TEENAGE RUNAWAY
Douglas S. Cramer Productions; telefeature; 1976
THE BOY IN THE PLASTIC BUBBLE
Spelling-Goldberg Productions; telefeature; 1976
THE GATHERING
Hanna-Barbera Productions; telefeature; 1977
GREASE
Paramount; 1978
THE BLUE LAGOON
Columbia; 1980
SUMMER LOVERS
Filmways; 1982

Kobayashi, Masaki
b. February 14, 1916
Hokkaido, Japan
Contact:
Federation of Japanese
Industry, Inc.
Sankei Building
7-2 Otemachi 1-Chome
Chiyoda-Ku
Tokyo, Japan
03-2313897

MY SON'S YOUTH
1952; Japanese
SINCERE HEART
1953; Japanese
ROOM WITH THICK WALLS
1953; Japanese
THREE LOVES
1954; Japanese
SOMEWHERE BENEATH THE WIDE SKY
1954; Japanese
BEAUTIFUL DAYS
1955; Japanese
THE FOUNTAINHEAD
1956; Japanese
I'LL BUY YOU
1956; Japanese
BLACK RIVER
1957; Japanese

continued

Kobayashi, Masaki
continued

THE HUMAN CONDITION, PART I (NO GREATER LOVE)
Shochiku; 1959; Japanese
THE HUMAN CONDITION, PART II (ROAD TO ETERNITY)
Shochiku; 1959; Japanese
THE HUMAN CONDITION, PART III
(A SOLDIER'S PRAYER) Shochiku; 1961; Japanese
THE INHERITANCE
Shochiku; 1962; Japanese
HARAKIRI
Toho; 1962; Japanese
KWAIDAN
Continental; 1964; Japanese
REBELLION
Toho; 1967; Japanese
HYMN TO A TIRED MAN
1968; Japanese
INN OF EVIL
1971; Japanese
FOSSILS
1975; Japanese
GLOWING AUTUMN
1979; Japanese

Koch, Howard W.
b. April 11, 1916
New York, New York
Business:
Paramount Pictures
5451 Marathon Street
Hollywood, CA 90038
(213) 468-5000

SHIELD FOR MURDER
co-director with Edmond O'Brien; United Artists; 1954
BIG HOUSE, U.S.A.
United Artists; 1955
UNTAMED YOUTH
Warner Brothers; 1957
BOP GIRL
United Artists; 1957
JUNGLE HEAT
United Artists; 1957
THE GIRL IN BLACK STOCKINGS
United Artists; 1957
FORT BOWIE
United Artists; 1958
VIOLENT ROAD
Warner Brothers; 1958
FRANKENSTEIN - 1970
Allied Artists; 1958
ANDY HARDY COMES HOME
M-G-M; 1958
THE LAST MILE
United Artists; 1959
BORN RECKLESS
Warner Brothers; 1959
BADGE 373
Paramount; 1973

Kohner, Pancho

THE BRIDGE IN THE JUNGLE
United Artists; 1971; Mexican
MR. SYCAMORE
Film Ventures International; 1975

Korty, John
b. 1936
Indiana
Business:
Korty Films, Inc.
200 Miller Avenue
Mill Valley, CA 94941
(415) 383-6900
Agent:
William Morris Agency
Beverly Hills
(213) 274-7451

CRAZY QUILT
Farallon; 1965
FUNNYMAN
New Yorker; 1967
riverrun
Columbia; 1970
THE PEOPLE
Metromedia Productions/American Zoetrope; telefeature; 1972
GO ASK ALICE
Metromedia Productions; telefeature; 1973
CLASS OF '63
Metromedia Productions/Stonehenge Productions; telefeature; 1973
SILENCE
Cinema Financial of America; 1974

continued

Korty, John
continued

THE AUTOBIOGRAPHY OF MISS JANE PITTMAN
Tomorrow Entertainment; telefeature; 1974
ALEX & THE GYPSY
20th Century-Fox; 1976
FAREWELL TO MANZANAR
Korty Films/Universal TV; telefeature; 1976
WHO ARE THE DE BOLTS?...AND WHERE DID THEY GET 19 KIDS?
1977
FOREVER
Roger Gimbel Productions/EMI TV; telefeature; 1978
OLIVER'S STORY
Paramount; 1979
A CHRISTMAS WITHOUT SNOW
Korty Films/The Konigsberg Company; telefeature; 1980

Kotani, Tom

THE LAST DINOSAUR
co-director with Alex Grasshoff; Rankin-Bass Productions; telefeature; 1977; U.S.-Japanese
THE BERMUDA DEPTHS
Rankin-Bass Productions; telefeature; 1978
THE IVORY APE
Rankin-Bass Productions; telefeature; 1980; U.S.-Japanese
THE BUSHIDO BLADE
Rankin-Bass Productions; 1981; U.S.-Japanese

Kotcheff, Ted
b. April 7, 1931
Toronto, Canada
Agent:
I.C.M.
Hollywood
(213) 550-4000

TIARA TAHITI
Zenith International; 1962; British
LIFE AT THE TOP
Columbia; 1965; British
TWO GENTLEMEN SHARING
American International; 1969; British
OUTBACK (Wake in Fright)
United Artists; 1971; Australian
BILLY TWO HATS
United Artists; 1972; British
THE APPRENTICESHIP OF DUDDY KRAVITZ
Paramount; 1974; Canadian
FUN WITH DICK & JANE
Columbia; 1977
WHO IS KILLING THE GREAT CHEFS OF EUROPE?
Warner Brothers; 1978
NORTH DALLAS FORTY
Paramount; 1979
CAPTURED
Filmways; 1982

Kotto, Yaphet
b. November 15, 1937
New York, New York

THE LIMIT (Time Limit/Speed Limit 65)
Cannon; 1972

Kowalski, Bernard
Home:
17524 Community Street
Northridge, CA 91324
(213) 987-2433
Agent:
Irv Schechter
Beverly Hills
(213) 278-8070

HOT CAR GIRL
Allied Artists; 1958
NIGHT OF THE BLOOD BEAST
American International; 1958
THE GIANT LEECHES
American International; 1959
KRAKATOA, EAST OF JAVA
Cinerama Releasing Corporation; 1969
STILETTO
Avco Embassy; 1969
MACHO CALLAHAN
Avco Embassy; 1970
HUNTERS ARE FOR KILLING
telefeature; 1970
TERROR IN THE SKY
Paramount TV; telefeature; 1971

continued

Kowalski, Bernard
continued

BLACK NOON
Fenady Associates/Screen Gems; telefeature; 1971
WOMEN IN CHAINS
Paramount TV; telefeature; 1972
TWO FOR THE MONEY
Aaron Spelling Productions; telefeature; 1972
THE WOMAN HUNTER
Bing Crosby Productions; telefeature; 1972
SHE CRIED MURDER
telefeature; 1973
Sssssss
Universal; 1973
IN TANDEM
D'Antoni Productions; telefeature; 1974
FLIGHT TO HOLOCAUST
Aycee Productions/First Artists; telefeature; 1977
THE NATIVITY
D'Angelo-Bullock-Allen Productions/20th Century-Fox TV; telefeature; 1978
MARCIANO
ABC Circle Films; telefeature; 1979
TURNOVER SMITH
Wellington Productions; telefeature; 1980
NIGHTSIDE
Stephen J. Cannell Productions/Glen A. Larson Productions/Universal TV; telefeature; 1980

Kramer, Robert

THE EDGE
Film-Makers; 1968
ICE
New Yorker; 1970
MILESTONES
co-director with John Douglas; Stone; 1975

Kramer, Stanley
b. September 23, 1913
New York, New York
Business:
Stanley Kramer Productions
P.O. Box 158
Bellevue, Washington 90889

NOT AS A STRANGER
United Artists; 1955
THE PRIDE AND THE PASSION
United Artists; 1957
THE DEFIANT ONES
United Artists; 1958
ON THE BEACH
United Artists; 1959
INHERIT THE WIND
United Artists; 1960
JUDGMENT AT NUREMBERG
United Artists; 1961
IT'S A MAD, MAD, MAD, MAD WORLD
United Artists; 1963
SHIP OF FOOLS
Columbia; 1965
GUESS WHO'S COMING TO DINNER
Columbia; 1967
THE SECRET OF SANTA VITTORIA
United Artists; 1969
R.P.M.*
Columbia; 1970
BLESS THE BEASTS & CHILDREN
Columbia; 1971
OKLAHOMA CRUDE
Columbia; 1973
THE DOMINO PRINCIPLE
Avco Embassy; 1977
THE RUNNER STUMBLES
20th Century-Fox; 1979

Krasny, Paul
Agent:
Shapiro-Lichtman Agency
Los Angeles
(213) 557-2244

THE D.A.: CONSPIRACY TO KILL
Universal TV/Mark VII Ltd.; telefeature; 1971
THE ADVENTURES OF NICK CARTER
Universal TV; telefeature; 1972
THE LETTERS
co-director with Gene Nelson; ABC Circle Films; telefeature; 1973

continued

Krasny, Paul
continued

CHRISTINA
International Amusements; 1974
BIG ROSE
20th Century-Fox TV; telefeature; 1974
JOE PANTHER
Artists Creation & Associates; 1976
CENTENNIAL
co-director with Harry Falk, Bernard McEveety & Virgil Vogel; Universal TV; television mini-series; 1978
THE ISLANDER
Universal TV; telefeature; 1978
WHEN HELL WAS IN SESSION
Aubrey-Hamner Productions; telefeature; 1979
ALCATRAZ? THE WHOLE SHOCKING STORY
Pierre Cossette Productions; telefeature; 1980
FUGITIVE FAMILY
Aubrey-Hamner Productions; telefeature; 1980
TERROR AMONG US
David Gerber Productions; telefeature; 1981
FLY AWAY HOME
An Lac Productions/Warner Brothers TV; telefeature; 1981

Krish, John
Contact:
British Film Institute
127 Charing Cross Road
London W.C. 2, England
01-437-4355

THE SALVAGE GANG
CFF; 1958; British
THE WILD AFFAIR
Goldstone; 1963; British
THE UNEARTHLY STRANGER
American International; 1964; British
DECLINE AND FALL OF A BIRD WATCHER
20th Century-Fox; 1969; British
THE MAN WHO HAD POWER OVER WOMEN
Avco Embassy; 1971; British
JESUS
co-director with Peter Sykes; Warner Brothers; 1979; British

Kronick, William
Home:
950 N. King's Road
Los Angeles, CA 90069
(213) 656-8150
Business:
William Kronick Productions
8489 W. Third Street
Los Angeles, CA 90048
(213) 651-2810

THE 500-POUND JERK
Wolper Productions; telefeature; 1973

Kronsberg, Jeremy Joe
Contact:
Directors Guild of America
Los Angeles
(213) 656-1220

GOING APE!
Paramount; 1981

Kubrick, Stanley
b. July 26, 1928
Bronx, New York
Attorney:
Louis C. Blau
Beverly Hills
(213) 552-7774

FEAR AND DESIRE
Joseph Burstyn, Inc.; 1954
KILLER'S KISS
United Artists; 1955
THE KILLING
United Artists; 1956
PATHS OF GLORY
United Artists; 1957
SPARTACUS
Universal; 1960
LOLITA
M-G-M; 1962; British
DR. STRANGELOVE OR: HOW I LEARNED TO STOP WORRYING AND LOVE THE BOMB
Columbia; 1964; British

continued

Kubrick, Stanley
continued

2001: A SPACE ODYSSEY
M-G-M; 1968; British
A CLOCKWORK ORANGE
Warner Brothers; 1971; British
BARRY LYNDON
Warner Brothers; 1975; British
THE SHINING
Warner Brothers; 1980; British

Kulik, Buzz
(Seymour Kulik)
b. 1923
New York, New York
Agent:
Herb Tobias
Los Angeles
(213) 277-6211

THE EXPLOSIVE GENERATION
United Artists; 1961
THE YELLOW CANARY
20th Century-Fox; 1963
READY FOR THE PEOPLE
Warner Brothers; 1964
WARNING SHOT
Paramount; 1968
SERGEANT RYKER
Universal; 1968
VILLA RIDES!
Paramount; 1968
RIOT
Paramount; 1969
VANISHED
Universal TV; telefeature; 1971
OWEN MARSHALL, COUNSELOR AT LAW
Universal TV; telefeature; 1971
BRIAN'S SONG
Screen Gems/Columbia TV; telefeature; 1971
TO FIND A MAN (Sex and the Teenager)
Columbia; 1972
INCIDENT ON A DARK STREET
20th Century-Fox TV; telefeature; 1973
PIONEER WOMAN
Filmways; telefeature; 1973
SHAMUS
Columbia; 1973
BAD RONALD
Lorimar Productions; telefeature; 1974
REMEMBER WHEN
Danny Thomas Productions/The Raisin Company; telefeature; 1974
CAGE WITHOUT A KEY
Columbia TV; telefeature; 1975
MATT HELM
Columbia TV; telefeature; 1975
BABE
M-G-M TV; telefeature; 1975
THE LINDBERGH KIDNAPPING CASE
Columbia TV; telefeature; 1976
COREY: FOR THE PEOPLE
Columbia TV; telefeature; 1977
KILL ME IF YOU CAN
Columbia TV; telefeature; 1977
ZIEGFELD: THE MAN AND HIS WOMEN
Frankovich Productions/Columbia TV; telefeature; 1978
FROM HERE TO ETERNITY
Bennett-Katleman Productions/Columbia TV; television mini-series; 1979
THE HUNTER
Paramount; 1980

Kurosawa, Akira
b. March 23, 1910
Tokyo, Japan
Contact:
Federation of Japanese
Industry, Inc.
Sankei Building
7-2 Otemachi 1-Chome
Chiyoda-Ku
Tokyo, Japan
03-2313897

SANSHIRO SUGATA
Toho; 1943; Japanese
THE MOST BEAUTIFUL
Toho; 1944; Japanese
THOSE WHO TREAD ON THE TIGER'S TAIL
Toho; 1945; Japanese
SANSHIRO SUGATA - PART TWO
Toho; 1945; Japanese

continued

Kurosawa, Akira
continued

NO REGRETS FOR OUR YOUTH
Toho; 1946; Japanese
THOSE WHO MAKE TOMORROW
Toho; 1946; Japanese
ONE WONDERFUL SUNDAY
Toho; 1947; Japanese
DRUNKEN ANGEL
Toho; 1948; Japanese
THE QUIET DUEL
Daiei; 1949; Japanese
STRAY DOG
Toho; 1949; Japanese
SCANDAL
Shochiku; 1950; Japanese
RASHOMON
Daiei; 1950; Japanese
THE IDIOT
Shochiku; 1951; Japanese
IKIRU
Toho; 1952; Japanese
SEVEN SAMURAI
Toho; 1954; Japanese
I LIVE IN FEAR
Toho; 1955; Japanese
THE LOWER DEPTHS
Toho; 1957; Japanese
THRONE OF BLOOD
Toho; 1957; Japanese
THE HIDDEN FORTRESS
Toho; 1958; Japanese
THE BAD SLEEP WELL
Toho; 1960; Japanese
YOJIMBO
Toho; 1961; Japanese
SANJURO
Toho; 1962; Japanese
HIGH AND LOW
Toho; 1963; Japanese
RED BEARD
Toho; 1965; Japanese
DODES'KA'DEN
Janus; 1970; Japanese
DERSU UZALA
New World; 1975; Soviet-Japanese
KAGEMUSHA: THE SHADOW WARRIOR
20th Century-Fox; 1980; Japanese

Kurys, Diane
Contact:
French Film Office
745 Fifth Avenue
New York, N.Y. 10151
(212) 832-8860

PEPPERMINT SODA
Gaumont/New Yorker; 1979; French
COCKTAIL MOLOTOV
Putnam Square; 1981; French

Laidman, Harvey
Business:
Disappearing, Inc.
10999 Riverside Drive
Toluca Lake, CA 91602
(213) 769-7822
Agent:
Century Artists Ltd.
Beverly Hills
(213) 273-4366

STEEL COWBOY
Roger Gimbel Productions/EMI TV; telefeature; 1978

Laird, Marlena
Home:
2729 Westshire Drive
Hollywood, CA 90068
(213) 465-6400
Agent:
Irv Schechter
Beverly Hills
(213) 278-8070

FRIENDSHIP, SECRETS AND LIES
co-director with Ann Zane Shanks; Wittman-Riche Productions/Warner Brothers TV; telefeature; 1979

LaLoggia, Frank

FEAR NO EVIL
Avco Embassy; 1981

Lancaster, Burt
b. November 2, 1913
New York, New York

THE MIDNIGHT MAN
co-director with Roland Kibbee; Universal;1974

Landis, John
Business:
Universal Studios
Universal City, CA 91608
(213) 985-4321
Agent:
Paul Kohner Agency
Los Angeles
(213) 550-1060

SCHLOCK
Jack H. Harris Enterprises; 1973
THE KENTUCKY FRIED MOVIE
United Film Distribution; 1977
NATIONAL LAMPOON'S ANIMAL HOUSE
Universal; 1978
THE BLUES BROTHERS
Universal; 1980
AN AMERICAN WEREWOLF IN LONDON
Universal; 1981

Landon, Michael
Business Manager:
Jay Eller
Los Angeles
(213) 277-6408

IT'S GOOD TO BE ALIVE
Metromedia Productions; telefeature; 1974
LITTLE HOUSE ON THE PRAIRIE
NBC Productions; telefeature; 1974
THE LONELIEST RUNNER
NBC Productions; telefeature; 1976
KILLING STONE
Universal TV; telefeature; 1978

Landsburg, Alan
Business:
Alan Landsburg Productions
1554 S. Sepulveda Blvd.
Los Angeles, CA 90025
(213) 473-9641

BLACK WATER GOLD
Metromedia Productions; telefeature; 1970

Lang, Richard
Agent:
Herb Tobias & Associates
Los Angeles
(213) 277-6211

FANTASY ISLAND
Spelling-Goldberg Productions;telefeature;1977
THE HUNTED LADY
QM Productions; telefeature; 1977
NOWHERE TO RUN
MTM Enterprises; telefeature; 1978
NIGHT CRIES
Charles Fries Productions; telefeature; 1978
DR. SCORPION
Universal TV; telefeature; 1978
VEGA$
Aaron Spelling Productions; telefeature; 1978
THE WORD
Charles Fries Productions/Stonehenge Productions;television mini-series; 1978
THE MOUNTAIN MEN
Columbia; 1980
A CHANGE OF SEASONS
20th Century-Fox; 1980

Lathan, Stan
Personal Manager:
The Brillstein Company
Los Angeles
(213) 275-6135

SAVE THE CHILDREN
Paramount; 1973
AMAZING GRACE
United Artists; 1974

Laughlin, Frank
Home:
(213) 476-7262

THE TRIAL OF BILLY JACK
Taylor-Laughlin; 1974
THE MASTER GUNFIGHTER
Taylor-Laughlin; 1975

Laughlin, Tom

b. 1938
Minneapolis, Minnesota
Business:
National Student Film Corp.
4024 Radford Avenue
Studio City, CA 91604
(213) 394-0286

THE PROPER TIME
Lopert; 1960
THE YOUNG SINNER
United Screen Arts; 1965
BORN LOSERS
directed under pseudonym of T.C. Frank; American International; 1967
BILLY JACK
directed under pseudonym of T.C. Frank; Warner Brothers; 1973
BILLY JACK GOES TO WASHINGTON
Taylor-Laughlin; 1978

Laven, Arnold

b. February 23, 1922
Chicago, Illinois
Agent:
Irv Schecter
Beverly Hills
(213) 278-8070

WITHOUT WARNING
United Artists; 1952
VICE SQUAD
United Artists; 1953
DOWN THREE DARK STREETS
United Artists; 1954
THE RACK
M-G-M; 1956
THE MONSTER THAT CHALLENGED THE WORLD
United Artists; 1957
SLAUGHTER ON TENTH AVENUE
Universal; 1957
ANNA LUCASTA
United Artists; 1958
GERONIMO
United Artists; 1962
THE GLORY GUYS
United Artists; 1965
ROUGH NIGHT IN JERICHO
Universal; 1967
SAM WHISKEY
United Artists; 1969

Lazarus, Ashley

FOREVER YOUNG, FOREVER FREE
Universal; 1976; British
GOLDEN RENDEZVOUS
Rank; 1977; British

Leacock, Philip

b. 1917
London, England
Home:
914 Bienveneda Avenue
Pacific Palisades, CA 90272
(213) 454-4188
Agent:
Contemporary-Korman Artists
Beverly Hills
(213) 278-8250

RIDERS OF THE NEW FOREST
Crown; 1946; British
THE BRAVE DON'T CRY
Mayer-Kingsley; 1952; British
APPOINTMENT IN LONDON
Associated Artists; 1953; British
THE LITTLE KIDNAPPERS (The Kidnappers)
United Artists; 1954; British
ESCAPADE
DCA; 1955; British
THE SPANISH GARDENER
Rank; 1956; British
HIGH TIDE AT NOON
Rank; 1957; British
INNOCENT SINNERS
Rank; 1958; British
THE RABBIT TRAP
United Artists; 1959
LET NO MAN WRITE MY EPITAPH
Columbia; 1960
TAKE A GIANT STEP
United Artists; 1960
HAND IN HAND
Columbia; 1961; British
REACH FOR GLORY
Royal International; 1962; British
13 WEST STREET
Columbia; 1962
THE WAR LOVER
Columbia; 1962; British

continued

Leacock, Philip
continued

TAMAHINE
M-G-M; 1964; British
ADAM'S WOMAN
Warner Brothers; 1970; Australian
THE BIRDMEN
Universal TV; telefeature; 1971
WHEN MICHAEL CALLS
Palomar International; telefeature; 1972
THE DAUGHTERS OF JOSHUA CABE
Spelling-Goldberg Productions; telefeature; 1972
BAFFLED!
Arena Productions/ITC; telefeature; 1973
THE GREAT MAN'S WHISKERS
Universal TV; telefeature; 1973
DYING ROOM ONLY
Lorimar Productions; telefeature; 1973
KEY WEST
Warner Brothers TV; telefeature; 1973
KILLER ON BOARD
Lorimar Productions; telefeature; 1977
WILD AND WOOLY
Aaron Spelling Productions; telefeature; 1978
THE CURSE OF KING TUT'S TOMB
Stromberg-Kerby Productions/Columbia TV/H.T.V. West; telefeature; 1980
ANGEL CITY
Factor-Newland Productions; telefeature; 1980
THE TWO LIVES OF CAROL LETNER
Penthouse One Presentations; telefeature; 1981

Leaf, Paul
Home:
924 23rd Street
Santa Monica, CA 90403
(213) 829-2223
Agent:
Creative Artists Agency
Los Angeles
(213) 277-4545

TOP SECRET
Jemmin, Inc./Sheldon Leonard Productions; telefeature; 1978
SERGEANT MATLOVICH VS. THE U.S. AIR FORCE
Tomorrow Entertainment; telefeature; 1978

Lean, David
b. March 25, 1908
Croydon, England

IN WHICH WE SERVE
co-director with Noel Coward; Universal; 1942; British
THIS HAPPY BREED
Universal; 1944; British
BLITHE SPIRIT
United Artists; 1945; British
BRIEF ENCOUNTER
Universal; 1946; British
GREAT EXPECTATIONS
Universal; 1947; British
OLIVER TWIST
United Artists; 1948; British
ONE WOMAN'S STORY (The Passionate Friends)
Universal; 1949; British
MADELEINE
Universal; 1950; British
BREAKING THE SOUND BARRIER (The Sound Barrier)
United Artists; 1952; British
HOBSON'S CHOICE
United Artists; 1954; British
SUMMERTIME (Summer Madness)
United Artists; 1955; British
THE BRIDGE ON THE RIVER KWAI
Columbia; 1957; British
LAWRENCE OF ARABIA
Columbia; 1962; British
DOCTOR ZHIVAGO
M-G-M; 1965; British
RYAN'S DAUGHTER
M-G-M; 1970; British

Lear, Norman
b. July 27, 1922
New Haven, Connecticut
Business:
TAT Communications
1901 Avenue of the Stars
Los Angeles, CA 90067
(213) 553-3600

COLD TURKEY
United Artists; 1971

Lee, Joanna
Business:
Christiana Productions
532 Colorado Avenue
Santa Monica, CA 90401
(213) 451-8171

MIRROR, MIRROR
Christiana Productions; telefeature; 1979
CHILDREN OF DIVORCE
Christiana Productions/Marble Arch Productions; telefeature; 1980

Leeds, Robert
Agent:
Brandon & Rodgers
Los Angeles
(213) 273-6173

RETURN OF THE BEVERLY HILLBILLIES
CBS-TV; telefeature; 1981

Lehman, Ernest
b. 1920
New York, New York
Business Manager:
Henry J. Bamberger
2049 Century Park East
Los Angeles, CA 90067
(213) 553-0581

PORTNOY'S COMPLAINT
Warner Brothers; 1972

Lelouch, Claude
b. October 30, 1937
Paris, France
Contact:
French Film Office
745 Fifth Avenue
New York, N.Y. 10151
(212) 832-8860

LE PROPRE DE L'HOMME
1960; French
L'AMOUR AVEC DES SI
1963; French
LA FEMME SPECTACLE
1964; French
TO BE A CROOK
Comet; 1965; French
LES GRAND MOMENTS
1965; French
A MAN AND A WOMAN
Allied Artists; 1966; French
LIVE FOR LIFE
United Artists; 1967; French
FAR FROM VIETNAM
co-director with Jean-Luc Godard, Joris Ivens, William Klein, Alain Resnais & Agnes Varda; New Yorker; 1967; French
GRENOBLE
co-director with Francois Reichenbach; United Producers of America; 1968; French
LIFE LOVE DEATH
Lopert; 1969; French
LOVE IS A FUNNY THING
United Artists; 1970; French-Italian
THE CROOK
United Artists; 1971; French
SMIC, SMAC, SMOC
GSF; 1971; French
MONEY MONEY MONEY (Adventure is Adventure)
GSF; 1972; French
HAPPY NEW YEAR (The Good Year)
Avco Embassy; 1973; French-Italian
VISIONS OF EIGHT
co-director; Cinema 5; 1973
AND NOW MY LOVE (A Lifetime)
Avco Embassy; 1975; French-Italian
MARRIAGE
1975; French

continued

Lelouch, Claude
continued

CAT AND MOUSE
Quartet; 1975; French
THE GOOD AND THE BAD
Paramount; 1976; French
A SECOND CHANCE (If I Had to Do It All Over Again)
United Artists Classics; 1976; French
ANOTHER MAN, ANOTHER CHANCE
United Artists; 1977; U.S.-French
ROBERT ET ROBERT
Quartet; 1978; French
AN ADVENTURE FOR TWO
1979; French-Canadian

Lemmon, Jack
b. February 8, 1925
Boston, Massachusetts
Business:
Jalem Productions, Inc.
141 El Camino
Beverly Hills, CA 90212
(213) 278-7750
Agent:
William Morris Agency
Beverly Hills
(213) 274-7451

KOTCH
Cinerama Releasing Corporation; 1971

Leo, Malcolm
Home:
10048 Cielo Drive
Beverly Hills, CA 90210
(213) 274-4738
Business:
Solt, Leo Productions
6534 Sunset Blvd.
Hollywood, CA 90028
(213) 464-5193
Agent:
William Morris Agency
Beverly Hills
(213) 274-7451

HEROES OF ROCK AND ROLL
co-director with Andrew Solt; ABC-TV; television documentary; 1979
THIS IS ELVIS
co-director with Andrew Solt; Warner Brothers; 1981

Leonard, Herbert B.
Business:
5300 Fulton Avenue
Van Nuys, CA 91401
(213) 783-0457
Agent:
I.C.M.
Hollywood
(213) 550-4000

THE PERILS OF PAULINE
Universal; 1967
GOING HOME
M-G-M; 1971

Leone, John
Agent:
William Morris Agency
Beverly Hills
(213) 274-7451

THE GREAT SMOKEY ROADBLOCK (The Last of the Cowboys)
Dimension; 1978

Leone, Sergio
b. 1921
Rome, Italy
Contact:
Minister of Tourism
Via Della Ferratella
No. 51
00184 Rome, Italy
06-7732

THE COLOSSUS OF RHODES
M-G-M; 1960; Italian-French-Spanish
A FISTFUL OF DOLLARS
United Artists; 1967; Italian-Spanish-West German
FOR A FEW DOLLARS MORE
United Artists; 1967; Italian-Spanish-West German
THE GOOD, THE BAD AND THE UGLY
United Artists; 1968; Italian

continued

Leone, Sergio
continued

ONCE UPON A TIME IN THE WEST
Paramount; 1969; Italian-U.S.
DUCK! YOU SUCKER (Fistful of Dynamite)
United Artists; 1972; Italian-U.S.
UN GENIO DUE COMPARI E UN POLLO
1975; Italian

Lester, Mark L.
Home:
7932 Mulholland Drive
Los Angeles, CA 90046
(213) 876-7067
Agent:
I.C.M.
Hollywood
(213) 550-4315

STEEL ARENA
L-T; 1973
TRUCK STOP WOMEN
L-T; 1974
THE WAY HE WAS
1975
BOBBI JO AND THE OUTLAW
American International; 1976
STUNTS
New Line Cinema; 1977
GOLD OF THE AMAZON WOMEN
Mi-Ka Productions; telefeature; 1979
ROLLER BOOGIE
United Artists; 1979
CLASS OF 1984
Guerilla High Productions; 1982; Canadian

Lester, Richard
b. January 19, 1932
Philadelphia, Pennsylvania
Business:
Twickenham Film Studios
St. Margarets
Middlesex, England

RING-A-DING RHYTHM (It's Trad, Dad)
Columbia; 1962; British
THE MOUSE ON THE MOON
United Artists; 1963; British
A HARD DAY'S NIGHT
United Artists; 1964; British
THE KNACK...AND HOW TO GET IT
Lopert; 1965; British
HELP!
United Artists; 1965; British
A FUNNY THING HAPPENED ON THE WAY TO THE FORUM
United Artists; 1966
TEENAGE REBELLION (Mondo Teeno)
co-director with Norman Herbert; Trans-American; 1967; British-U.S.
HOW I WON THE WAR
United Artists; 1967; British
PETULIA
Warner Brothers; 1968; U.S.-British
THE BED SITTING ROOM
United Artists; 1969; British
THE THREE MUSKETEERS (THE QUEEN'S DIAMONDS)
20th Century-Fox; 1974; British
JUGGERNAUT
United Artists; 1974; British
THE FOUR MUSKETEERS (MILADY'S REVENGE)
20th Century-Fox; 1975; British
ROYAL FLASH
20th Century-Fox; 1976; British
ROBIN AND MARIAN
Columbia; 1976; British
THE RITZ
Warner Brothers; 1976
BUTCH AND SUNDANCE: THE EARLY DAYS
20th Century-Fox; 1979
CUBA
United Artists; 1979
SUPERMAN II
Warner Brothers; 1981; U.S.-British

Levey, William A.
Business:
The Movie Machine
7471 Melrose Avenue
Los Angeles, CA 90046
(213) 852-0337
Agent:
William Morris Agency
Beverly Hills
(213) 274-7451

BLACKENSTEIN
L.F.G.; 1973
SLUMBER PARTY '57
Cannon; 1977
THE HAPPY HOOKER GOES TO WASHINGTON
Cannon; 1977
SKATETOWN, U.S.A.
Columbia; 1979

Levi, Alan J.
Home:
13417 Inwood Drive
Sherman Oaks, CA 91423
(213) 981-3417
Agent:
William Morris Agency
Beverly Hills
(213) 274-7451

GEMINI MAN
Universal TV; telefeature; 1976
THE RETURN OF THE INCREDIBLE HULK
Universal TV; telefeature; 1977
GO WEST, YOUNG GIRL
Bennett-Katleman Productions/Columbia TV; telefeature; 1978
THE IMMIGRANTS
Universal TV; television mini-series; 1978
THE LEGEND OF THE GOLDEN GUN
Bennett-Katleman Productions/Columbia TV; telefeature; 1979
SCRUPLES
Lou-Step Productions/Warner Brothers TV; television mini-series; 1980
THE LAST SONG
Ron Samuels Productions/Motown Pictures; telefeature; 1980

Levin, Peter
Agent:
Broder-Kurland Agency
Los Angeles
(213) 274-8921
Business Manager:
Lloyd Zeiderman
Los Angeles
(213)

PALMERSTOWN, U.S.A.
Haley-TAT Productions; telefeature; 1980
THE COMEBACK KID
ABC Circle Films; telefeature; 1980
RAPE AND MARRIAGE: THE RIDEOUT CASE
Stonehenge Productions/Blue Greene Productions/ Lorimar Productions; telefeature; 1980

Levin, Sidney
Agent:
Crayton Smith-Ray
Gosnell Agency
Malibu
(213) 456-6641

LET THE GOOD TIMES ROLL
co-director with Robert J. Abel; Columbia; 1973
THE GREAT BRAIN
Osmond; 1978

Levinson, Barry
Contact:
Directors Guild of America
Los Angeles
(213) 656-1220

DINER
M-G-M/United Artists; 1981

Levitt, Gene
Agent:
Adams, Ray & Rosenberg
Hollywood
(213) 278-3000

ANY SECOND NOW
Universal TV; telefeature; 1969
RUN A CROOKED MILE
Universal TV; telefeature; 1969
ALIAS SMITH AND JONES
Universal TV; telefeature; 1971
COOL MILLION
Universal TV; telefeature; 1972
THE PHANTOM OF HOLLYWOOD
M-G-M TV; telefeature; 1974

Levy, Edmond
Home:
135 Central Park West
New York, N.Y. 10023
(212) 595-7666
Business:
(212) PL. 7-1840

MOM, THE WOLFMAN AND ME
Time-Life Productions; telefeature; 1981

Levy, Ralph
Agent:
Irv Schechter
Beverly Hills
(213) 278-8070

BEDTIME STORY
Universal; 1964
DO NOT DISTURB
20th Century-Fox; 1965

Lewis, Jerry
(Joseph Levitch)
b. March 16, 1926
Newark, New Jersey
Business:
Jerry Lewis Films, Inc.
1888 Century Park East
Los Angeles, CA 90067
(213) 552-2200
Agent:
William Morris Agency
Beverly Hills
(213) 274-7451

THE BELLBOY
Paramount; 1960
THE LADIES' MAN
Paramount; 1961
THE ERRAND BOY
Paramount; 1962
THE NUTTY PROFESSOR
Paramount; 1963
THE PATSY
Paramount; 1964
THE FAMILY JEWELS
Paramount; 1965
THREE ON A COUCH
Columbia; 1966
THE BIG MOUTH
Columbia; 1967
ONE MORE TIME
United Artists; 1970; British
WHICH WAY TO THE FRONT?
Warner Brothers; 1970
THE DAY THE CLOWN CRIED
unreleased
HARDLY WORKING
20th Century-Fox; 1981

Lewis, Robert M.
Agent:
William Morris Agency
Beverly Hills
(213) 274-7451
Business Manager:
Frank Rohner
Los Angeles
(213) 274-6182

THE ASTRONAUT
Universal TV; telefeature; 1972
THE ALPHA CAPER
Universal TV; telefeature; 1973
MONEY TO BURN
Universal TV; telefeature; 1973
MESSAGE TO MY DAUGHTER
Metromedia Productions; telefeature; 1973
PRAY FOR THE WILDCATS
ABC Circle Films; telefeature; 1974
THE DAY THE EARTH MOVED
ABC Circle Films; telefeature; 1975
THE INVISIBLE MAN
Universal TV; telefeature; 1975
GUILTY OR INNOCENT: THE SAM SHEPPARD MURDER CASE
Universal TV; telefeature; 1975
THE NIGHT THEY TOOK MISS BEAUTIFUL
Don Kirshner Productions; telefeature; 1977
RING OF PASSION
20th Century-Fox TV; telefeature; 1980
S*H*E
Martin Bregman Productions; telefeature; 1980
IF THINGS WERE DIFFERENT
Bob Banner Associates; telefeature; 1980
ESCAPE
Henry Jaffe Enterprises; telefeature; 1980
A PRIVATE BATTLE
Proctor & Gamble Productions/Robert Halmi Inc.; telefeature; 1980
FALLEN ANGEL
Green-Epstein Productions/Columbia TV; telefeature; 1981
THE MIRACLE OF KATHY LEWIS
Rothman-Wohl Productions/Universal TV; telefeature; 1981

Lieberman, Jeff
Home:
51 Warren Street
Hastings-on-Hudson,
N.Y. 10706

SQUIRM
American International; 1976
BLUE SUNSHINE
Cinema Shares International; 1979
JUST BEFORE DAWN
Picturmedia Limited; 1981

Lieberman, Robert
Business:
Harmony Pictures
2242 Cahuenga Blvd.
Los Angeles, CA 90068
(213) 462-2121
Agent:
Chasin-Park-Citron
Hollywood
(213) 273-7190

FIGHTING BACK
MTM Enterprises; telefeature; 1980

Lindsay-Hogg, Michael
b. May 5, 1940
New York, New York
Contact:
Directors Guild of America
Los Angeles
(213) 656-1220

LET IT BE
United Artists; 1970; British
NASTY HABITS
Brut Productions; 1977; British

Linson, Art
Business:
Universal Pictures
Universal City, CA 91608
(213) 508-1546

WHERE THE BUFFALO ROAM
Universal; 1980

Lisberger, Steven

ANIMALYMPICS
1980
TRON
Buena Vista; 1982

Loach, Kenneth
Contact:
British Film Institute
127 Charing Cross Road
London W.C. 2, England
01-437-4355

POOR COW
National General; 1968; British
KES
United Artists; 1970; British
WEDNESDAY'S CHILD
Cinema 5; 1972; British
BLACK JACK
Boyd's Company; 1979; British
THE GAMEKEEPER
ATV; 1980; British
LOOKS AND SMILES
1981; British

Logan, Joshua
b. October 5, 1908
Texarkana, Texas
Business:
435 East 52nd Street
New York, N.Y. 10022
(212) PL. 2-1910

I MET MY LOVE AGAIN
co-director with Arthur Ripley; United Artists; 1938
MISTER ROBERTS
co-director with John Ford; Warner Brothers; 1955
PICNIC
Columbia; 1956
BUS STOP
20th Century-Fox; 1956
SAYONARA
Warner Brothers; 1957
SOUTH PACIFIC
Magna; 1958
TALL STORY
Warner Brothers; 1960
FANNY
Warner Brothers; 1961
ENSIGN PULVER
Warner Brothers; 1964
CAMELOT
Warner Brothers; 1967
PAINT YOUR WAGON
Paramount; 1969

Lombardo, Louis
Home:
14550 Deervale
Sherman Oaks, CA 91606
(213) 501-5033
Business:
Triple L Productions
1801 Century Park East
Los Angeles, CA 90067
(213) 556-0200

RUSSIAN ROULETTE
Avco Embassy; 1975; U.S.-Canadian

Lommel, Ulli

TENDERNESS OF THE WOLVES
Monument; 1973; West German
BLANK GENERATION
International Harmony; 1979; West German
COCAINE COWBOYS
International Harmony; 1979; West German
THE BOOGEY MAN
Jerry Gross Organization; 1980

London, Jerry
Agent:
Creative Artists Agency
Los Angeles
(213) 277-4545

KILLDOZER
Universal TV; telefeature; 1974
McNAUGHTON'S DAUGHTER
Universal TV; telefeature; 1976
COVER GIRLS
Columbia TV; telefeature; 1977
ARTHUR HAILEY'S WHEELS
Universal TV; television mini-series; 1978
EVENING IN BYZANTIUM
Universal TV; telefeature; 1978
WOMEN IN WHITE
NBC-TV; television mini-series; 1979
SWAN SONG
Renee Valente Productions/Topanga Services Ltd./
20th Century-Fox TV; telefeature; 1980
SHOGUN
Paramount TV/NBC Entertainment; television mini-
series; 1980; U.S.-Japanese
FATHER FIGURE
Finnegan Associates/Time-Life Productions;
telefeature; 1980
THE CHICAGO STORY
Eric Bercovici Productions/M-G-M TV; telefeature
1981

Lord, Jack
(John Joseph Ryan)
b. December 30, 1928
New York, New York
Home:
4999 Kahala Avenue
Honolulu, Hawaii 96816
(808) 737-6060
Business:
Lord & Lady Enterprises
Honolulu, Hawaii 96816
(808) 735-5050

M STATION: HAWAII
Lord & Lady Enterprises; telefeature; 1980

Losey, Joseph
b. January 14, 1909
La Crosse, Wisconsin
Agent:
Georges Beaume
Paris
325 27-59

THE BOY WITH GREEN HAIR
RKO Radio; 1948
THE LAWLESS
Paramount; 1950
M
Columbia; 1951
THE PROWLER
United Artists; 1951
THE BIG NIGHT
United Artists; 1951

Losey, Joseph
continued

STRANGER ON THE PROWL
directed under pseudonym of Andrea Forzano; United Artists; 1952; U.S.-Italian
THE SLEEPING TIGER
directed under pseudonym of Victor Hanbury; Astor; 1954; British
FINGER OF GUILT (The Intimate Stranger)
directed under pseudonym of Joseph Walton; RKO Radio; 1955; British
TIME WITHOUT PITY
Astor; 1956; British
THE GYPSY AND THE GENTLEMAN
Rank; 1958; British
CHANCE MEETING (Blind Date)
Paramount; 1959; British
THE CONCRETE JUNGLE (The Criminal)
Fanfare; 1960; British
THESE ARE THE DAMNED (The Damned)
Columbia; 1961; British
EVA
Times; 1962; French-Italian
THE SERVANT
Landau; 1964; British
KING AND COUNTRY
Allied Artists; 1965; British
MODESTY BLAISE
20th Century-Fox; 1966; British
ACCIDENT
Cinema 5; 1967; British
SECRET CEREMONY
Universal; 1968; British-U.S.
BOOM!
Universal; 1968; British-U.S.
FIGURES IN A LANDSCAPE
National General; 1971; British
THE GO-BETWEEN
Columbia; 1971; British
THE ASSASSINATION OF TROTSKY
Cinerama Releasing Corporation; 1972; French-Italian-British
A DOLL'S HOUSE
Tomorrow Entertainment; 1973; British-French
GALILEO
American Film Theatre; 1975; British-Canadian
THE ROMANTIC ENGLISHWOMAN
New World; 1975; British
MR. KLEIN
Quartet; 1977; French-Italian
LES ROUTES DU SUD
Parafrance; 1978; French
DON GIOVANNI
Gaumont/New Yorker; 1980; French

Lowry, Dick
Business:
PoKoJo Films
704 N. Gardner
Los Angeles, CA 90046
(213) 653-6115
Agent:
I.C.M.
Hollywood
(213) 550-4308

OHMS
Grant-Case-McGrath Enterprises; telefeature; 1980
KENNY ROGERS AS THE GAMBLER
Kragen & Co.; telefeature; 1980
THE JAYNE MANSFIELD STORY
Alan Landsburg Productions; telefeature; 1980
ANGEL DUSTED
NRW Features; telefeature; 1981
COWARD OF THE COUNTY
Kraco Productions; telefeature; 1981
A FEW DAYS IN WEASEL CREEK
Hummingbird Productions/Warner Brothers TV; telefeature; 1981

Loxton, David R.
Home:
935 Park Avenue
New York, N.Y. 10028
(212) 249-0538
Business:
Television Laboratory
WNET/13
356 West 58th Street
New York, N.Y. 10019
(212) 560-3192

THE PHANTOM OF THE OPEN HEARTH
co-director with Fred Barzyk; PBS-TV; telefeature; 1976
CHARLIE SMITH AND THE FRITTER TREE
co-director with Fred Barzyk; PBS-TV; telefeature; 1978
THE LATHE OF HEAVEN
co-director with Fred Barzyk; The Television Laboratory/WNET-13/Taurus Film; telefeature; 1980

Lucas, George
1945
Modesto, California
Business:
Lucasfilm Ltd.
P.O. Box 668
San Anselmo, CA 94960

THX 1138
Warner Brothers; 1971
AMERICAN GRAFFITI
Universal; 1973
STAR WARS
20th Century-Fox; 1977

Lumet, Sidney
b. June 25, 1924
Philadelphia, Pennsylvania
Agent:
I.C.M.
Hollywood
(213) 550-4264

TWELVE ANGRY MEN
United Artists; 1957
STAGE STRUCK
RKO Radio; 1958
THAT KIND OF WOMAN
Paramount; 1959
THE FUGITIVE KIND
United Artists; 1960
A VIEW FROM THE BRIDGE
Allied Artists; 1961; French-Italian
LONG DAY'S JOURNEY INTO NIGHT
Embassy; 1962
FAIL SAFE
Columbia; 1964
THE PAWNBROKER
Landau/Allied Artists; 1965
THE HILL
M-G-M; 1965; British
THE GROUP
United Artists; 1966
THE DEADLY AFFAIR
Columbia; 1967; British
BYE BYE BRAVERMAN
Warner Brothers; 1968
THE SEA GULL
Warner Brothers; 1968; British
THE APPOINTMENT
M-G-M; 1969
LAST OF THE MOBILE HOT-SHOTS
Warner Brothers; 1970
KING: A FILMED RECORD...MONTGOMERY TO MEMPHIS
co-director with Joseph L. Mankiewicz; Maron Films Limited; 1970
THE ANDERSON TAPES
Columbia; 1971
CHILD'S PLAY
Paramount; 1972
THE OFFENSE
United Artists; 1973; British
SERPICO
Paramount; 1973
LOVIN' MOLLY
Columbia; 1974
MURDER ON THE ORIENT EXPRESS
Paramount; 1974; British
DOG DAY AFTERNOON
Warner Brothers; 1975
NETWORK
M-G-M/United Artists; 1976
EQUUS
United Artists; 1977; British
THE WIZ
Universal; 1978
JUST TELL ME WHAT YOU WANT
Columbia; 1980
PRINCE OF THE CITY
Orion Pictures/Warner Brothers; 1981
DEATHTRAP
Warner Brothers; 1982

Luraschi, Tony

THE OUTSIDER
Paramount; 1980; U.S.-Irish

Lynch, David
Agent:
Creative Artists Agency
Los Angeles
(213) 277-4545

ERASERHEAD
Libra Films; 1978
THE ELEPHANT MAN
Paramount; 1980; British-U.S.

Lynch, Paul
Home:
33 Harboursquare, #3223
Toronto, Ontario
Canada
(416) 961-1595/929-0516

THE HARD PART
1974; Canadian
BLOOD AND GUTS
Ambassador; 1978; Canadian
PROM NIGHT
Avco Embassy; 1980; Canadian
HUMONGOUS
Avco Embassy; 1982; Canadian

Lyne, Adrian
Contact:
Directors Guild of America
Los Angeles
(213) 656-1220

FOXES
United Artists; 1980

Mackendrick, Alexander
b. 1912
Boston, Massachusetts

TIGHT LITTLE ISLAND (Whiskey Galore!)
Rank; 1949; British
THE MAN IN THE WHITE SUIT
Rank; 1951; British
CRASH OF SILENCE (Mandy)
Universal; 1952; British
HIGH AND DRY (The Maggie)
Universal; 1954; British
THE LADYKILLERS
Continental; 1956; British
SWEET SMELL OF SUCCESS
United Artists; 1957
A BOY TEN FEET TALL (Sammy Going South)
Paramount; 1963; British
A HIGH WIND IN JAMAICA
20th Century-Fox; 1965; British
DON'T MAKE WAVES
M-G-M; 1967

Mackenzie, John
Contact:
British Film Institute
127 Charing Cross Road
London W.C. 2, England
01-437-4355

UNMAN, WITTERING & ZIGO
Paramount; 1971; British
ONE BRIEF SUMMER
Cinevision; 1972; British
MADE
International Co-Productions; 1975; British
THE LONG GOOD FRIDAY
Handmade Films; 1980; British

Mailer, Norman
b. January 31, 1923
Long Branch, New Jersey

WILD 90
Supreme Mix; 1968
BEYOND THE LAW
Grove Press; 1968
MAIDSTONE
Supreme Mix; 1971

Malick, Terrence
b. 1945
Texas
Agent:
Evarts Ziegler
Hollywood
(213) 278-0070

BADLANDS
Warner Brothers; 1974
DAYS OF HEAVEN
Paramount; 1978

Malle, Louis
b. October 30, 1932
Thumeries, France

FONTAINE DE VAUCLUSE
1953; French
STATION 307
1955; French
THE SILENT WORLD
co-director with Jacques-Yves Cousteau; Columbia; 1956; French
FRANTIC (Lift to the Scaffold)
Times; 1957; French
THE LOVERS
Zenith International; 1958; French
ZAZIE (Zazie in the Metro)
Astor; 1960; French
A VERY PRIVATE AFFAIR
M-G-M; 1962; French-Italian
THE FIRE WITHIN
Governor; 1963; French
VIVA MARIA!
United Artists; 1965; French-Italian
THE THIEF OF PARIS
Lopert; 1967; French-Italian
SPIRITS OF THE DEAD
co-director with Federico Fellini & Roger Vadim; American International; 1969; French-Italian
CALCUTTA
1969; French
PHANTOM INDIA
1969; television documentary; French
MURMUR OF THE HEART
Palomar; 1971; French
HUMAIN TROP HUMAIN
New Yorker; 1972; French
LACOMBE LUCIEN
20th Century-Fox; 1974; French-Italian-West German
BLACK MOON
20th Century-Fox; 1975; French
PRETTY BABY
Paramount; 1978
ATLANTIC CITY
Paramount; 1981; Canadian-French
MY DINNER WITH ANDRE
New Yorker; 1981

Malmuth, Bruce
Business:
Soularview
9981 Robbins Drive
Beverly Hills, CA 90212
(213) 277-4555
Agent:
Marvin Moss
Beverly Hills
(213) 274-8483

FORE PLAY
co-director with John G. Avildsen & Robert McCarty; Cinema National; 1975
NIGHTHAWKS
Universal; 1981

Mandel, Robert

RIDERS ON THE STORM
Warner Brothers; 1982

Manduke, Joseph
Agent:
Film Artists Management
Los Angeles
(213) 656-7590

JUMP
Cannon; 1971
CORNBREAD, EARL AND ME
American International; 1975
KID VENGEANCE
Irwin Yablans; 1977; U.S.-Israeli
BEATLEMANIA
American Cinema; 1981

Mankiewicz, Francis

LES BONS DEBARRAS (GOOD RIDDANCE)
IFEX Film; 1981; Canadian

Mankiewicz, Joseph L.
b. February 11, 1909
Wilkes-Barre, Pennsylvania
Business Manager:
Arthur B. Greene
New York City
(212) 867-9050

DRAGONWYCK
20th Century-Fox; 1946
SOMEWHERE IN THE NIGHT
20th Century-Fox; 1946
THE LATE GEORGE APLEY
20th Century-Fox; 1947
THE GHOST AND MRS. MUIR
20th Century-Fox; 1947
ESCAPE
20th Century-Fox; 1948
A LETTER TO THREE WIVES
20th Century-Fox; 1949
HOUSE OF STRANGERS
20th Century-Fox; 1949
NO WAY OUT
20th Century-Fox; 1950
ALL ABOUT EVE
20th Century-Fox; 1950
PEOPLE WILL TALK
20th Century-Fox; 1951
FIVE FINGERS
20th Century-Fox; 1952
JULIUS CAESAR
M-G-M; 1953
THE BAREFOOT CONTESSA
United Artists; 1954; U.S.-Italian
GUYS AND DOLLS
M-G-M; 1955
THE QUIET AMERICAN
United Artists; 1958
SUDDENLY LAST SUMMER
Columbia; 1960
CLEOPATRA
20th Century-Fox; 1963
THE HONEY POT
United Artists; 1967; British-U.S.-Italian
THERE WAS A CROOKED MAN
Warner Brothers; 1970
KING: A FILMED RECORD...MONTGOMERY TO MEMPHIS
co-director with Sidney Lumet; Maron Films Limited; 1970
SLEUTH
20th Century-Fox; 1972; British

Mankiewicz, Tom
Contact:
Directors Guild of America
Los Angeles
(213) 656-1220

HART TO HART
Spelling-Goldberg Productions; telefeature; 1979

Mann, Abby
(Abraham Goodman)
b. 1927
Philadelphia, Pennsylvania
Agent:
William Morris Agency
Beverly Hills
(213) 274-7451

KING
Abby Mann Productions/Filmways; television mini-series; 1978

Mann, Daniel
b. August 8, 1912
New York, New York
Agent:
Grossman-Stalmaster Agency
Hollywood
(213) 657-3040
Business Manager:
The Berke Management Co.
Encino
(213) 990-2631

COME BACK, LITTLE SHEBA
Paramount; 1952
ABOUT MRS. LESLIE
Paramount; 1954
THE ROSE TATTOO
Paramount; 1955
I'LL CRY TOMORROW
M-G-M; 1955
TEAHOUSE OF THE AUGUST MOON
M-G-M; 1956
HOT SPELL
Paramount; 1958

continued

Mann, Daniel
continued

THE LAST ANGRY MAN
Columbia; 1959
THE MOUNTAIN ROAD
Columbia; 1960
BUTTERFIELD 8
M-G-M; 1960
ADA
M-G-M; 1961
FIVE FINGER EXERCISE
Columbia; 1962
WHO'S GOT THE ACTION?
Paramount; 1962
WHO'S BEEN SLEEPING IN MY BED?
Paramount; 1963
JUDITH
Paramount; 1965; U.S.-British-Israeli
OUR MAN FLINT
20th Century-Fox; 1966
FOR LOVE OF IVY
Cinerama Releasing Corporation; 1968
A DREAM OF KINGS
National General; 1969
WILLARD
Cinerama Releasing Corporation; 1971
THE REVENGERS
National General; 1972; U.S.-Mexican
INTERVAL
Avco Embassy; 1973; U.S.-Mexican
MAURIE (Big Mo)
National General; 1973
LOST IN THE STARS
American Film Theatre; 1974
JOURNEY INTO FEAR
Stirling Gold; 1976; Canadian
HOW THE WEST WAS WON
co-director with Burt Kennedy; M-G-M TV; television mini-series; 1977
MATILDA
American International; 1978
PLAYING FOR TIME
Syzygy Productions; telefeature; 1980
THE DAY THE LOVING STOPPED
Monash-Zeitman Productions; telefeature; 1981

Mann, Delbert
b. January 30, 1920
Lawrence, Kansas
Agent:
William Morris Agency
Beverly Hills
(213) 274-7451

MARTY
United Artists; 1955
THE BACHELOR PARTY
United Artists; 1957
DESIRE UNDER THE ELMS
Paramount; 1958
SEPARATE TABLES
United Artists; 1959
MIDDLE OF THE NIGHT
Columbia; 1959
THE DARK AT THE TOP OF THE STAIRS
Warner Brothers; 1960
THE OUTSIDER
Universal; 1961
LOVER, COME BACK
Universal; 1962
THAT TOUCH OF MINK
Universal; 1962
A GATHERING OF EAGLES
Universal; 1963
DEAR HEART
Warner Brothers; 1964
QUICK BEFORE IT MELTS
M-G-M; 1965
MISTER BUDDWING
M-G-M; 1966
FITZWILLY
United Artists; 1967
HEIDI
Omnibus Productions; telefeature; 1968

Mann, Delbert
continued

THE PINK JUNGLE
Universal; 1968
DAVID COPPERFIELD
Omnibus Productions/Sagittarius Productions; telefeature; 1970; British-U.S.
KIDNAPPED
American International; 1971; British
JANE EYRE
Omnibus Productions/Sagittarius Productions; telefeature; 1971; British-U.S.
SHE WAITS
Metromedia Productions; telefeature; 1972
NO PLACE TO RUN
ABC Circle Films; telefeature; 1972
THE MAN WITHOUT A COUNTRY
Norman Rosemont Productions; telefeature; 1973
A GIRL NAMED SOONER
Frederick Brogger Associates/20th Century-Fox TV; telefeature; 1975
BIRCH INTERVAL
Gamma III; 1976
FRANCIS GARY POWERS: THE TRUE STORY OF THE U-2 SPY INCIDENT
Charles Fries Productions; telefeature; 1976
TELL ME MY NAME
Talent Associates; telefeature; 1977
BREAKING UP
Time-Life Productions; telefeature; 1978
LOVE'S DARK RIDE
Mark VII Ltd./Worldvision; telefeature; 1978
HOME TO STAY
Time-Life Productions; telefeature; 1978
THOU SHALT NOT COMMIT ADULTERY
Edgar J. Scherick Associates; telefeature; 1978
TORN BETWEEN TWO LOVERS
Alan Landsburg Productions; telefeature; 1979
ALL QUIET ON THE WESTERN FRONT
Norman Rosemont Productions/Marble Arch Productions; telefeature; 1979
TO FIND MY SON
Green-Epstein Productions/Columbia TV; telefeature; 1980
NIGHT CROSSING
Buena Vista; 1982

Mann, Michael
Agent:
The Paul Kohner Agency
Los Angeles
(213) 550-1060

THE JERICHO MILE
ABC Circle Films; telefeature; 1979
THIEF
United Artists; 1981

Marcel, Terry
Contact:
British Film Institute
127 Charing Cross Road
London W.C. 2, England
01-437-4355

THERE GOES THE BRIDE
Vanguard; 1980; British
HAWK THE SLAYER
ITC; 1980; British

March, Alex
Contact:
Directors Guild of America
Los Angeles
(213) 656-1220

THE DANGEROUS DAYS OF KIOWA JONES
M-G-M TV; telefeature; 1966
PAPER LION
United Artists; 1968
THE BIG BOUNCE
Warner Brothers; 1969
FIREHOUSE
Metromedia Productions/Stonehenge Productions; telefeature; 1972
MASTERMIND
Goldstone; 1977

Margolin, Stuart
Agent:
The Paul Kohner Agency
Los Angeles
(213) 550-1060

SUDDENLY, LOVE
Ross Hunter Productions; telefeature; 1978
A SHINING SEASON
Green-Epstein Productions/T-M Productions/ Columbia TV; telefeature; 1979

Markowitz, Robert
Agent:
I.C.M.
Hollywood
(213) 550-4000

THE STORYTELLER
Universal TV; telefeature; 1977
THE DEADLIEST SEASON
Titus Productions; telefeature; 1977
VOICES
M-G-M/United Artists; 1979
THE WALL
Time-Life Productions; telefeature; 1981

Marks, Arthur
Business:
ARM Service Company
P.O. Box 1305
Woodland Hills, CA 91365
(213) 887-1007
Agent:
Jim Jacobson Agency
Los Angeles
(213) 275-0804

CLASS OF '74
General Film Corporation; 1972
BONNIE'S KIDS
General Film Corporation; 1973
THE ROOM MATES
General Film Corporation; 1973
DETROIT 9000
General Film Corporation; 1973
A WOMAN FOR ALL MEN
General Film Corporation; 1975
BUCKTOWN
American International; 1975
FRIDAY FOSTER
American International; 1975
J.D.'S REVENGE
American International; 1976
THE MONKEY HUSTLE
American International; 1976

Marquand, Richard
b. Wales

SEARCH FOR THE NILE
BBC-TV; television mini-series
THE LEGACY
Universal; 1979
BIRTH OF THE BEATLES
Dick Clark Productions; telefeature; 1979; British-U.S.
EYE OF THE NEEDLE
United Artists; 1981; U.S.-British

Martin, Charles
Business:
Forward Films
8033 Sunset Blvd.
Los Angeles, CA 90046
(213) 277-5843

NO LEAVE TO LOVE
M-G-M; 1946
MY DEAR SECRETARY
United Artists; 1948
DEATH OF A SCOUNDREL
RKO Radio; 1956
IF HE HOLLERS, LET HIM GO
Cinerama Releasing Corporation; 1968
HOW TO SEDUCE A WOMAN
Cinerama Releasing Corporation; 1974
ONE MAN JURY
Cal-Am Artists; 1978
DEAD ON ARRIVAL
Cinema Shares International; 1979

Martinson, Leslie H.
Home:
2288 Coldwater Canyon
Beverly Hills, CA 90210
(213) 271-4127
Agent:
Shapiro-Lichtman Agency
Hollywood
(213) 550-2244

THE ATOMIC KID
Republic; 1954
HOT ROD GIRL
American International; 1956
HOT ROD RUMBLE
Allied Artists; 1957

continued

Martinson, Leslie H.
continued

LAD: A DOG
co-director with Aram Avakian; Warner Brothers; 1961
PT 109
Warner Brothers; 1963
BLACK GOLD
Warner Brothers; 1963
F.B.I. CODE 98
Warner Brothers; 1964
FOR THOSE WHO THINK YOUNG
United Artists; 1964
BATMAN
20th Century-Fox; 1966
FATHOM
20th Century-Fox; 1967
THE CHALLENGERS
Universal TV; telefeature; 1970
MRS. POLLIFAX - SPY
United Artists; 1971
HOT TO STEAL AN AIRPLANE
Universal TV; telefeature; 1971
ESCAPE FROM ANGOLA
Doty-Dayton; 1976
CRUISE MISSILE
1978
RESCUE FROM GILLIGAN'S ISLAND
Sherwood Schwartz Productions; telefeature; 1978

Maslansky, Paul
Business Manager:
Leah Lynn Broidy
Los Angeles
(213) 474-2795

SUGAR HILL
American International; 1974

Mastroianni, Armand

HE KNOWS YOU'RE ALONE
M-G-M/United Artists; 1980

Matthau, Walter
(Walter Matuschanskavasky)
b. October 1, 1920
New York, New York

GANGSTER STORY
RCIP-States Rights; 1960

Maxwell, Ronald F.
Agent:
I.C.M.
Hollywood
(213) 550-4000

VERNA: USO GIRL
PBS-TV; telefeature; 1978
LITTLE DARLINGS
Paramount; 1980
THE NIGHT THE LIGHTS WENT OUT IN GEORGIA
Avco Embassy; 1981

May, Elaine
(Elaine Berlin)
b. April 21, 1932
Philadelphia, Pennsylvania
Contact:
Directors Guild of America
New York City
(212) 581-0370

A NEW LEAF
Paramount; 1971
THE HEARTBREAK KID
20th Century-Fox; 1972
MIKEY AND NICKY
Paramount; 1977

Mayberry, Russ
Agent:
Herb Tobias & Associates
Los Angeles
(213) 277-6211

THE JESUS TRIP
EMCO; 1971
PROBE
Warner Brothers TV; telefeature; 1972
A VERY MISSING PERSON
Universal TV; telefeature; 1972

continued

Mayberry, Russ
continued

FER-DE-LANCE
Leslie Stevens Productions; telefeature; 1974
SEVENTH AVENUE
co-director with Richard Irving; Universal TV; television mini-series; 1977
STONESTREET: WHO KILLED THE CENTERFOLD MODEL?
Universal TV; telefeature; 1977
THE 3,000 MILE CHASE
Universal TV; telefeature; 1977
THE YOUNG RUNAWAYS
NBC-TV; telefeature; 1978
THE MILLION DOLLAR DIXIE DELIVERY
NBC-TV; telefeature; 1978
THE REBELS
Universal TV; television mini-series; 1979
UNIDENTIFIED FLYING ODDBALL
Buena Vista; 1979
THE $5.20 AN HOUR DREAM
Thompson-Sagal Productions/Big Deal Inc./Finnegan Associates; telefeature; 1980
MARRIAGE IS ALIVE AND WELL
Lorimar Productions; telefeature; 1980
REUNION
Barry Weitz Films; telefeature; 1980
A MATTER OF LIFE AND DEATH
Big Deal, Inc./Ravens' Claw Productions/Lorimar Productions; telefeature; 1981
SIDNEY SHORR
Hajeno Productions/Warner Brothers TV; telefeature; 1981

Maysles, Albert
b. November 26, 1926
Brookline, Massachusetts

PSYCHIATRY IN RUSSIA
1955
YOUTH IN POLAND
co-director with David Maysles; 1957
SHOWMAN
co-director with David Maysles; 1962
WHAT'S HAPPENING: THE BEATLES IN THE USA
co-director with David Maysles; 1964
MEET MARLON BRANDO
co-director with David Maysles; 1965
WITH LOVE FROM TRUMAN
co-director with David Maysles; 1966
SALESMAN
co-director with David Maysles & Charlotte Zwerin; Maysles Film; 1969
GIMME SHELTER
co-director with David Maysles & Charlotte Zwerin; Cinema 5; 1971
CHRISTO'S VALLEY CURTAIN
co-director with David Maysles & Ellen Giffard; 1972
GREY GARDENS
co-director with David Maysles, Ellen Hovde & Muffie Meyer; 1975
RUNNING FENCE
co-director with David Maysles; 1977

Maysles, David
b. January 10, 1932
Brookline, Massachusetts

YOUTH IN POLAND
co-director with Albert Maysles; 1957
SHOWMAN
co-director with Albert Maysles; 1962
WHAT'S HAPPENING: THE BEATLES IN THE USA
co-director with Albert Maysles; 1964
MEET MARLON BRANDO
co-director with Albert Maysles; 1965
WITH LOVE FROM TRUMAN
co-director with Albert Maysles; 1966
SALESMAN
co-director with Albert Maysles & Charlotte Zwerin; Maysles Film; 1969

continued

Maysles, David
continued

GIMME SHELTER
co-director with Albert Maysles & Charlotte Zwerin; Cinema 5; 1971
CHRISTO'S VALLEY CURTAIN
co-director with David Maysles & Ellen Giffard; 1972
GREY GARDENS
co-director with Albert Maysles, Ellen Hovde & Muffie Meyer; 1975
RUNNING FENCE
co-director with Albert Maysles; 1977

Mazursky, Paul
b. April 25, 1930
Brooklyn, New York
Agent:
I.C.M.
Hollywood
(213) 550-4000

BOB & CAROL & TED & ALICE
Columbia; 1969
ALEX IN WONDERLAND
M-G-M; 1970
BLUME IN LOVE
Warner Brothers; 1973
HARRY AND TONTO
20th Century-Fox; 1974
NEXT STOP, GREENWICH VILLAGE
20th Century-Fox; 1976
AN UNMARRIED WOMAN
20th Century-Fox; 1978
WILLIE AND PHIL
20th Century-Fox; 1980
TEMPEST
Columbia; 1982

McCarty, Robert
Home:
222 West 83rd Street
New York, N.Y. 10024
(212) 580-1034

I COULD NEVER HAVE SEX WITH A MAN WHO HAS SO LITTLE REGARD FOR MY HUSBAND
Cinema 5; 1973
FORE PLAY
co-director with John G. Avildsen & Bruce Malmuth Cinema National; 1975

McCowan, George
Agent:
The Blake Agency
Beverly Hills
(213) 278-6885

THE MONK
Thomas-Spelling Productions; telefeature; 1969
THE BALLAD OF ANDY CROCKER
Thomas-Spelling Productions; telefeature; 1969
CARTER'S ARMY
Thomas-Spelling Productions; telefeature; 1970
THE LOVE WAR
Thomas-Spelling Productions; telefeature; 1970
THE OVER-THE-HILL GANG RIDES AGAIN
Thomas-Spelling Productions; telefeature; 1970
RUN, SIMON, RUN
Aaron Spelling Productions; telefeature; 1970
LOVE, HATE, LOVE
Aaron Spelling Productions; telefeature; 1971
CANNON
QM Productions; telefeature; 1971
THE FACE OF FEAR
QM Productions; telefeature; 1971
IF TOMORROW COMES
Aaron Spelling Productions; telefeature; 1971
WELCOME HOME, JOHNNY BRISTOL
Cinema Center; telefeature; 1972
THE MAGNIFICENT SEVEN RIDE!
United Artists; 1972
FROGS
American International; 1972
MURDER ON FLIGHT 502
Spelling-Goldberg Productions; telefeature; 1975
SHADOW OF THE HAWK
Columbia; 1976; Canadian
RETURN TO FANTASY ISLAND
Spelling-Goldberg Productions; telefeature; 1978
THE RETURN OF THE MOD SQUAD
Thomas-Spelling Productions; telefeature; 1979
THE SHAPE OF THINGS TO COME
Film Ventures International; 1979; Canadian
NEVER TRUST AN HONEST THIEF
1981; Canadian

McDougall, Don
Agent:
Film Artists Enterprise
Hollywood
(213) 656-7590

ESCAPE TO MINDANAO
Universal TV; telefeature; 1968
WILD WOMEN
Aaron Spelling Productions; telefeature; 1970
THE HEIST
Paramount TV; telefeature; 1972
THE MARK OF ZORRO
20th Century-Fox; telefeature; 1974
THE MISSING ARE DEADLY
Lawrence Gordon Productions;telefeature; 1975

McDowall, Roddy
b. September 17, 1928
London, England

TAM LIN (The Devil's Widow)
American International; 1971

McEveety, Bernard
Agent:
Conway-Penny Agency
Los Angeles
(213) 271-8133

RIDE BEYOND VENGEANCE
Columbia; 1966
A STEP OUT OF LINE
Cinema Center; telefeature; 1971
THE BROTHERHOOD OF SATAN
Columbia; 1971
KILLER BY NIGHT
Cinema Center; telefeature; 1972
NAPOLEON AND SAMANTHA
Buena Vista; 1972
ONE LITTLE INDIAN
Buena Vista; 1973
THE BEARS AND I
Buena Vista; 1974
THE MACAHANS
Albert S. Ruddy Productions/M-G-M TV; telefeature 1976
THE HOSTAGE HEART
Andrew J. Fenady Associates/M-G-M TV; telefeature 1977
DONOVAN'S KID
NBC-TV; telefeature; 1979
CENTENNIAL
co-director with Harry Falk, Paul Krasny & Virgil Vogel; Universal TV; television mini-series; 1979
ROUGHNECKS
Douglas Netter Productions/Metromedia Producers Corporation; telefeature; 1980

McEveety, Vincent
Home:
14561 Mulholland Drive
Los Angeles, CA 90024
(213) 783-4674

THIS SAVAGE LAND
telefeature; 1968
FIRECREEK
Warner Brothers; 1968
CUTTER'S TRAIL
CBS Studio Center; telefeature; 1970
THE MILLION DOLLAR DUCK
Buena Vista; 1971
THE BISCUIT EATER
Buena Vista; 1972
CHARLEY AND THE ANGEL
Buena Vista; 1972
WONDER WOMAN
Warner Brothers TV; telefeature; 1974
SUPERDAD
Buena Vista; 1974
THE CASTAWAY COWBOY
Buena Vista; 1974
THE STRONGEST MAN IN THE WORLD
Buena Vista; 1975
THE LAST DAY
Paramount TV; telefeature; 1975
THE TREASURE OF MATECUMBE
Buena Vista; 1976
GUS
Buena Vista; 1976
HERBIE GOES TO MONTE CARLO
Buena Vista; 1976

continued

McEveety, Vincent
continued

THE APPLE DUMPLING GANG RIDES AGAIN
Buena Vista; 1979
HERBIE GOES BANANAS
Buena Vista; 1980
AMY
Buena Vista; 1981

McGavin, Darren
b. May 7, 1922
Spokane, Washington
Agent:
William Morris Agency
Beverly Hills
(213) 274-7451

HAPPY MOTHER'S DAY - LOVE, GEORGE
Cinema 5; 1973

McGoohan, Patrick
b. 1928
New York, New York
Contact:
Directors Guild of America
Los Angeles
(213) 656-1220

CATCH MY SOUL
Cinerama Releasing Corporation; 1974

McGrath, Joseph
Contact:
British Film Institute
127 Charing Cross Road
London W.C. 2, England
01-437-4355

CASINO ROYALE
co-director with Val Guest, Ken Hughes, John Huston & Robert Parrish; Columbia; 1967; British
30 IS A DANGEROUS AGE, CYNTHIA
Columbia; 1968; British
THE BLISS OF MRS. BLOSSOM
Paramount; 1969; British
THE MAGIC CHRISTIAN
Commonwealth United; 1970; British
DIGBY, THE BIGGEST DOG IN THE WORLD
Cinerama Releasing Corporation; 1974; British
THE GREAT McGONAGALL
Scotia American; 1975; British
I'M NOT FEELING MYSELF TONIGHT
1976; British
THE STRANGE CASE OF THE END OF CIVILIZATION AS WE KNOW IT
1978; telefeature; British
RISING DAMP
1980; British

McGuane, Thomas
Home:
Hoffman Route
Livingston, Montana 59047
Agent:
I.C.M.
Hollywood
(213) 550-4000

92 IN THE SHADE
United Artists; 1975

McLaglen, Andrew V.
b. July 28, 1920
London, England
Agent:
Contemporary-Korman Artists
Beverly Hills
(213) 278-8250

GUN THE MAN DOWN
United Artists; 1956
MAN IN THE VAULT
Universal; 1956
THE ABDUCTORS
20th Century-Fox; 1957
FRECKLES
20th Century-Fox; 1960
THE LITTLE SHEPHERD OF KINGDOM COME
20th Century-Fox; 1961
McLINTOCK!
United Artists; 1963
SHENANDOAH
Universal; 1965

continued

McLaglen, Andrew V.
continued

THE RARE BREED
  Universal; 1966
MONKEYS, GO HOME!
  Buena Vista; 1967
THE WAY WEST
  United Artists; 1967
THE BALLAD OF JOSIE
  Universal; 1968
THE DEVIL'S BRIGADE
  United Artists; 1968
BANDOLERO!
  20th Century-Fox; 1968
HELLFIGHTERS
  Universal; 1969
THE UNDEFEATED
  20th Century-Fox; 1969
CHISUM
  Warner Brothers; 1970
ONE MORE TRAIN TO ROB
  Universal; 1971
FOOLS' PARADE
  Columbia; 1971
something big
  National General; 1971
CAHILL, U.S. MARSHAL
  Warner Brothers; 1973
MITCHELL
  Allied Artists; 1975
THE LOG OF THE BLACK PEARL
  Universal TV/Mark VII Ltd.; telefeature; 1975
STOWAWAY TO THE MOON
  20th Century-Fox TV; telefeature; 1975
BANJO HACKETT: ROAMIN' FREE
  Bruce Lansbury Productions/Columbia TV; telefeature; 1976
THE LAST HARD MEN
  20th Century-Fox; 1976
MURDER AT THE WORLD SERIES
  ABC Circle Films; telefeature; 1977
SERGEANT STEINER (Breakthrough)
  Palladium/Rapid; 1978; West German
THE WILD GEESE
  Allied Artists; 1979; British
ffolkes
  Universal; 1980; British
THE SEA WOLVES
  Paramount/Lorimar; 1981; British
THE BLUE AND THE GRAY
  Larry White Productions; Lou Reda Productions/ Columbia TV; television mini-series; 1982

Medak, Peter

Home:
1415 N. Genesee
Los Angeles, CA 90046
(213) 874-6530
Agent:
The Paul Kohner Agency
Los Angeles
(213) 550-1060
Anthony Jones Peters
London
01-839-2556

NEGATIVES
  Continental; 1968; British
A DAY IN THE DEATH OF JOE EGG
  Columbia; 1972; British
THE RULING CLASS
  Avco Embassy; 1972; British
THE THIRD GIRL FROM THE LEFT
  Playboy Productions; telefeature; 1973
GHOST IN THE NOONDAY SUN
  Columbia; 1974; British
THE ODD JOB
  Columbia; 1978; British
THE CHANGELING
  AFD; 1980; British
THE BABYSITTER
  Moonlight Productions/Filmways; telefeature; 1980
ZORRO, THE GAY BLADE
  20th Century-Fox; 1981
MISTRESS OF PARADISE
  Lorimar Productions; telefeature; 1981

Medford, Don
Home:
1956 Bentley Avenue S.
Los Angeles, CA 90025
(213) 473-3439
Agent:
Irv Schechter
Beverly Hills
(213) 278-8070

TO TRAP A SPY
M-G-M; 1966
THE HUNTING PARTY
United Artists; 1970
INCIDENT IN SAN FRANCISCO
QM Productions; telefeature; 1971
THE ORGANIZATION
United Artists; 1971
THE NOVEMBER PLAN
1976
THE CLONE MASTER
Mel Ferber Productions/Paramount TV; telefeature; 1978
COACH OF THE YEAR
A. Shane Company; telefeature; 1980

Melendez, Bill

A BOY NAMED CHARLIE BROWN
National General; 1968
SNOOPY, COME HOME
National General; 1972
DICK DEADEYE, OR DUTY DONE
Intercontinental; 1976; British
RACE FOR YOUR LIFE, CHARLIE BROWN
Paramount; 1978
BON VOYAGE, CHARLIE BROWN (AND DON'T COME BACK!)
Paramount; 1980

Mendeluk, George
Business:
World Classic Pictures
6263 Topia Drive
Malibu, CA 90265
(213) 457-9911/457-5591

STONE COLD DEAD
Dimension; 1979; Canadian
THE KIDNAPPING OF THE PRESIDENT
Crown International; 1980; Canadian

Merrill, Kieth
Home:
11930 Rhus Ridge Road
Los Altos Hills, CA 94022
(415) 941-4456

THE GREAT AMERICAN COWBOY
Sun International; 1974
THREE WARRIORS
United Artists; 1978
TAKE DOWN
Buena Vista; 1979
WINDWALKER
Pacific International; 1980
HARRY'S WAR
Taft International; 1981

Metzger, Radley
b. 1930

DARK ODYSSEY
co-director with William Kyriaskys; ERA; 1961
DICTIONARY OF SEX
1964
THE DIRTY GIRLS
1965
THE ALLEY CATS
1966
CARMEN, BABY
Audubon; 1967; U.S.-Yugoslavian-West German
THERESE AND ISABELLE
Audubon; 1968; West German-U.S.
CAMILLE 2000
Audubon; 1969; Italian
THE LICKERISH QUARTET
Audubon; 1970; U.S.-Italian-West German
LITTLE MOTHER
Audubon; 1972
SCORE
Audubon; 1973
NAKED CAME THE STRANGER
directed under pseudonym of Henry Paris; Catalyst; 1975

continued

Metzger, Radley
continued

THE PRIVATE AFTERNOONS OF PAMELA MANN
directed under pseudonym of Henry Paris; Hudson Valley; 1975
THE IMAGE
Audubon; 1976
THE OPENING OF MISTY BEETHOVEN
directed under pseudonym of Henry Paris; Catalyst; 1976
BARBARA BROADCAST
directed under pseudonym of Henry Paris; Crescent; 1977
THE CAT AND THE CANARY
1978

Meyer, Nicholas
Home:
2109 Stanley Hills Drive
Los Angeles, CA 90046

TIME AFTER TIME
Orion Pictures/Warner Brothers; 1979
STAR TREK II
Paramount; 1982

Meyer, Russ
b. 1923
Oakland, California
Business:
RM Films International
P.O. Box 3748
Hollywood, CA 90028
(213) 466-7791

THE IMMORAL MR. TEAS
Pedram; 1959
EVE AND THE HANDYMAN
Eve; 1961
EROTICA
1961
THE IMMORAL WEST AND HOW IT WAS LOST
1962
EUROPE IN THE RAW
1963
HEAVENLY BODIES
1963
KISS ME QUICK!
1964
LORNA
Eve; 1965
ROPE OF FLESH
Eve; 1965
FANNY HILL: MEMOIRS OF A WOMAN OF PLEASURE
Pan World; 1965; U.S.-West German
MOTOR PSYCHO
Eve; 1965
FASTER PUSSYCAT, KILL! KILL!
Eve; 1965
MONDO TOPLESS
Eve; 1966
GOOD MORNING...AND GOODBYE
Eve; 1967
COMMON LAW CABIN
Eve; 1967
FINDERS KEEPERS, LOVERS WEEPERS
Eve; 1968
RUSS MEYER'S VIXEN
Eve; 1968
CHERRY, HARRY AND RAQUEL
Eve; 1969
BEYOND THE VALLEY OF THE DOLLS
20th Century-Fox; 1970
THE SEVEN MINUTES
20th Century-Fox; 1971
SWEET SUZY! (Blacksnake)
Signal 166; 1973
SUPERVIXENS
RM Films; 1975
RUSS MEYER'S UP!
RM Films; 1976
BENEATH THE VALLEY OF THE ULTRAVIXENS
RM Films; 1979

Michaels, Richard
Agent:
Adams, Ray & Rosenberg
Los Angeles
(213) 278-3000

HOW COME NOBODY'S ON OUR SIDE?
American Films Ltd.; 1975
DEATH IS NOT THE END
Libert Films International; 1976

continued

Michaels, Richard
continued

ONCE AN EAGLE
co-director with E.W. Swackhamer; Universal TV; television mini-series; 1976
CHARLIE COBB: NICE NIGHT FOR HANGING
Universal TV; telefeature; 1977
HAVING BABIES II
The Jozak Company; telefeature; 1977
THE REACH OF LOVE
telefeature; 1978
LEAVE YESTERDAY BEHIND
ABC Circle Films; telefeature; 1978
MY HUSBAND IS MISSING
Bob Banner Associates; telefeature; 1978
...AND YOUR NAME IS JONAH
Charles Fries Productions; telefeature; 1979
ONCE UPON A FAMILY
Universal TV; telefeature; 1980
THE PLUTONIUM INCIDENT
Time-Life Productions; telefeature; 1980
SCARED STRAIGHT! ANOTHER STORY
Golden West TV; telefeature; 1980
BERLIN TUNNEL 21
Cypress Point Productions/Filmways; telefeature; 1981

Mihalka, George
Home:
2030 Closse, #4
Montreal, Quebec H3H 1Z9
Canada
(514) 937-4740

MY BLOODY VALENTINE
Paramount; 1981; Canadian
PICK-UP SUMMER
Film Ventures International; 1981; Canadian

Miles, Christopher
b. April 19, 1939
London, England
Contact:
British Film Institute
127 Charing Cross Road
London W.C. 2, England
01-437-4355

THE VIRGIN AND THE GYPSY
Chevron; 1970; British
TIME FOR LOVING
Hemdale; 1972; British
THE MAIDS
American Film Theatre; 1975; British-Canadian
THAT LUCKY TOUCH
Allied Artists; 1975; British
PRIEST OF LOVE
Filmways; 1981; British

Milius, John
Contact:
Directors Guild of America
Los Angeles
(213) 656-1220

DILLINGER
American International; 1973
THE WIND AND THE LION
M-G-M/United Artists; 1975
BIG WEDNESDAY
Warner Brothers; 1978
CONAN
Universal; 1982

Millar, Stuart
b. 1929
New York, New York
Home:
300 Central Park West
New York, N.Y. 10024
(212) 873-5515

WHEN THE LEGENDS DIE
20th Century-Fox; 1972
ROOSTER COGBURN
Universal; 1975

Miller, David
b. November 28, 1909
Paterson, New Jersey
Home:
1843 Thayer Avenue
Los Angeles, CA 90025
(213) 474-8542
Agent:
Phil Gersh Agency
Beverly Hills
(213) 274-6611

BILLY THE KID
M-G-M; 1941
SUNDAY PUNCH
M-G-M; 1942
FLYING TIGERS
Republic; 1942
TOP O' THE MORNING
Paramount; 1948

continued

Miller, David
continued

LOVE HAPPY
United Artists; 1949
OUR VERY OWN
RKO Radio; 1950
SATURDAY'S HERO
Columbia; 1951
SUDDEN FEAR
RKO Radio; 1952
TWIST OF FATE (The Beautiful Stranger)
United Artists; 1954; British
DIANE
M-G-M; 1956
THE OPPOSITE SEX
M-G-M; 1956
THE STORY OF ESTHER COSTELLO
Columbia; 1957
HAPPY ANNIVERSARY
United Artists; 1959
MIDNIGHT LACE
Universal; 1961
BACK STREET
Universal; 1961
LONELY ARE THE BRAVE
Universal; 1962
CAPTAIN NEWMAN, M.D.
Universal; 1964
HAMMERHEAD
Columbia; 1968; British
HAIL, HERO!
National General; 1969
EXECUTIVE ACTION
National General; 1973
BITTERSWEET LOVE
Avco Embassy; 1976
LOVE FOR RENT
Warren V. Bush Productions; telefeature; 1979
THE BEST PLACE TO BE
Ross Hunter Productions; telefeature; 1979
GOLDIE AND THE BOXER
Orenthal Productions/Columbia TV; telefeature; 1979
GOLDIE AND THE BOXER GO TO HOLLYWOOD
Orenthal Productions/Columbia TV; telefeature; 1981

Miller, George
Contact:
Australian Film Commission
9229 Sunset Blvd.
Los Angeles, CA 90069
(213) 275-7074

MAD MAX
American International; 1980; Australian
MAD MAX II
1982; Australian

Miller, Jonathan

TAKE A GIRL LIKE YOU
Columbia; 1970; British

Miller, Michael

STREET GIRLS
New World; 1975
JACKSON COUNTY JAIL
New World; 1976
OUTSIDE CHANCE
New World Productions/Miller-Begun Productions; telefeature; 1978
SILENT RAGE
Columbia; 1982

Miller, Robert Ellis
b. 1927
Agent:
The Paul Kohner Agency
Los Angeles
(213) 550-1060

ANY WEDNESDAY
Warner Brothers; 1966
SWEET NOVEMBER
Warner Brothers; 1967

continued

Miller, Robert Ellis
continued

THE HEART IS A LONELY HUNTER
Warner Brothers; 1968
THE BUTTERCUP CHAIN
Warner Brothers; 1970; British
THE GIRL FROM PETROVKA
Universal; 1974
JUST AN OLD SWEET SONG
MTM Enterprises; telefeature; 1976
ISHI: THE LAST OF HIS TRIBE
Edward & Mildred Lewis Productions; telefeature; 1978
THE BALTIMORE BULLET
Avco Embassy; 1980
MADAME X
Levenback-Riche Productions/Universal TV; telefeature; 1981

Miller, Walter C.
Home:
2401 Crest View Drive
Los Angeles, CA 90046
(213) 656-2819

THE BORROWERS
Walt DeFaria Productions/20th Century-Fox; telefeature; 1973

Mills, Reginald

PETER RABBIT & TALES OF BEATRIX POTTER
M-G-M; 1971; British

Miner, Steve
Agent:
Marvin Moss Agency
Beverly Hills
(213) 274-8483

FRIDAY THE 13TH PART 2
Paramount; 1981

Mingay, David
Contact:
British Film Institute
127 Charing Cross Road
London W.C. 2, England
01-437-4355

A BIGGER SPLASH
co-director with Jack Hazan; Lagoon Associates; 1975; British
RUDE BOY
co-director with Jack Hazan; Atlantic; 1980; British

Minnelli, Vincente
b. February 28, 1910
Chicago, Illinois
Home:
812 N. Crescent Drive
Beverly Hills, CA 90210
(213) 276-8128
Agent:
The Paul Kohner Agency
Los Angeles
(213) 550-1060

CABIN IN THE SKY
M-G-M; 1943
I DOOD IT
M-G-M; 1943
MEET ME IN ST. LOUIS
M-G-M; 1944
YOLANDA AND THE THIEF
M-G-M; 1945
THE CLOCK
M-G-M; 1945
ZIEGFELD FOLLIES
M-G-M; 1946
TILL THE CLOUDS ROLL BY
co-director with Richard Whorf; M-G-M; 1946
UNDERCURRENT
M-G-M; 1946
THE PIRATE
M-G-M; 1948
MADAME BOVARY
M-G-M; 1949
FATHER OF THE BRIDE
M-G-M; 1950
AN AMERICAN IN PARIS
M-G-M; 1951
FATHER'S LITTLE DIVIDEND
M-G-M; 1951
THE BAD AND THE BEAUTIFUL
M-G-M; 1952

continued

Minnelli, Vincente
continued

THE STORY OF THREE LOVES
M-G-M; 1953
THE BAND WAGON
M-G-M; 1953
THE LONG, LONG TRAILER
M-G-M; 1954
BRIGADOON
M-G-M; 1954
THE COBWEB
M-G-M; 1955
KISMET
M-G-M; 1955
LUST FOR LIFE
M-G-M; 1956
TEA AND SYMPATHY
M-G-M; 1956
DESIGNING WOMAN
M-G-M; 1957
GIGI
M-G-M; 1958
THE RELUCTANT DEBUTANTE
M-G-M; 1958
SOME CAME RUNNING
M-G-M; 1959
HOME FROM THE HILL
M-G-M; 1960
BELLS ARE RINGING
M-G-M; 1960
THE FOUR HORSEMEN OF THE APOCALYPSE
M-G-M; 1962
TWO WEEKS IN ANOTHER TOWN
M-G-M; 1962
THE COURTSHIP OF EDDIE'S FATHER
M-G-M; 1963
GOODBYE, CHARLIE
20th Century-Fox; 1964
THE SANDPIPER
M-G-M; 1965
ON A CLEAR DAY YOU CAN SEE FOREVER
Paramount; 1970
A MATTER OF TIME
American International; 1976; U.S.-Italian

Mizrahi, Moshe
Contact:
French Film Office
745 Fifth Avenue
New York, N.Y. 10151
(212) 832-8860

I LOVE YOU ROSA
Leisure Media; 1973; Israeli
THE HOUSE ON CHELOUCHE STREET
Productions Unlimited; 1974; Israeli
DAUGHTERS! DAUGHTERS!
Steinmann-Baxter; 1975; Israeli
RACHEL'S MAN
Allied Artists; 1976; Israeli
MADAME ROSA (La Vie Devant Soi)
Atlantic; 1978; French
I SENT A LETTER TO MY LOVE
Atlantic; 1981; French

Moessinger, David
Agent:
The Richland Agency
Los Angeles
(213) 553-1257

MOBILE TWO
Universal TV/Mark VII Ltd.; telefeature; 1975

Molinaro, Edouard
b. May 13, 1928
Bordeaux, France
Contact:
French Film Office
New York, N.Y. 10151
(212) 832-8860

BACK TO THE WALL
Ellis; 1958; French
THE ROAD TO SHAME
1959; French
A MISTRESS FOR THE SUMMER
1960; French
THE PASSION OF SLOW FIRE
Trans-Lux; 1961; French

continued

Molinaro, Edouard
continued

SEVEN CAPITAL SINS
co-director; Embassy; 1962; French-Italian
LES ENNEMIS
1962; French
ARSENE LUPIN CONTRE ARSENE LUPIN
1962; French
A RAVISHING IDIOT
1964; French
MALE HUNT
Pathe Contemporary; 1965; French-Italian
QUAND PASSENT LES FAISANS
1965; French
TO COMMIT A MURDER
Cinerama Releasing Corporation; 1967; French-Italian-West German
OSCAR
1968; French
HIBERNATUS
1969; French
MON ONCLE BENJAMIN
1969; French
LA LIBERTEEN CROUPE
1970; French
LES AVEUX LES PLUS DOUX
1971; French
LA MANDARINE
1972; French
A PAIN IN THE A--
Corwin-Mahler; 1973; French
THE HOSTAGES
Gaumont; 1973; French
L'IRONIE DU SORT
1974; French
THE PINK TELEPHONE
S.J. International; 1975; French
DRACULA PERE ET FILS
1976; French
MAN IN A HURRY
1977; French
LA CAGE AUX FOLLES
United Artists; 1979; French-Italian
SUNDAY LOVERS
co-director with Bryan Forbes, Dino Risi & Gene Wilder; M-G-M/United Artists; 1981;U.S.-British-Italian-French
LA CAGE AUX FOLLES II
United Artists; 1981; French-Italian

Monicelli, Mario
b. May 15, 1915
Rome, Italy
Contact:
Minister of Tourism
Via Della Ferratella
No. 51
00184 Rome, Italy
06-7732

AL DIAVOLO LA CELEBRITA
co-director with Steno; 1949; Italian
TOTO CERCA CASA
co-director with Steno; 1950; Italian
VITA DA CANI
co-director with Steno; 1950; Italian
E ARRIVATO IL CAVALIERE
co-director with Steno; 1950; Italian
COPS AND ROBBERS
co-director with Steno; 1951; Italian
TOTO E I RE DI ROMA
co-director with Steno; 1952; Italian
LE INFEDELI
co-director with Steno; 1953; Italian
PROIBITO
1954; Italian
TOTO E CAROLINA
1955; Italian
UN EROE DEI NOSTRI TEMPI
1955; Italian
DONATELLA
1956; Italian
THE TAILOR'S MAID
Trans-Lux; 1957; Italian
IL MEDICO E LO STREGONE
1957; Italian

continued

Monicelli, Mario
continued

BIG DEAL ON MADONNA STREET
United Motion Picture Organization; 1958; Italian
THE GREAT WAR
United Artists; 1959; Italian
THE PASSIONATE THIEF
Embassy; 1960; Italian
BOCCACCIO '70
co-director with Federico Fellini, Vittorio De Sica & Luchino Visconti; Embassy; 1962; Italian
THE ORGANIZER
Continental; 1963; Italian-French-Yugoslavian
HIGH INFIDELITY
co-director; Magna; 1964; Italian-French
CASANOVA '70
Embassy; 1965; Italian-French
L'ARMATA BRANCALEONE
1965; Italian
THE QUEENS
co-director; Royal International; 1966; Italian-French
GIRL WITH A GUN
1968; Italian
CAPRICCIO ALL'ITALIANA
co-director; 1968; Italian
TO'E MORTA LA NONNA
1969; Italian
LE COPPIE
co-director; 1970; Italian
BRANCALEONE ALLE CROCIATE
1970; Italian
LADY LIBERTY (Mortadella)
United Artists; 1971; Italian
VOGLIAMO DI COLONNELLI
1973; Italian
ROMANZO POPOLARE
1975; Italian
MY FRIENDS
Cineriz; 1975; Italian
CARO MICHELE
1976; Italian
SIGNORE E SIGNORI - BUONANOTTE
co-director; 1976; Italian
LA GODURIA
co-director; 1976; Italian
UN BORGHESE PICCOLO PICCOLO
1977; Italian
VIVA ITALIA!
co-director with Nino Risi & Ettore Scola; Cinema 5; 1978; Italian
LOVERS AND LIARS (Travels With Anita)
Summit; 1979; Italian

Moore, Richard
Home:
(213) 459-4593
Business:
(213) 651-5180
Agent:
Adams, Ray & Rosenberg
Hollywood
(213) 278-3000

CIRCLE OF IRON
Avco Embassy; 1979

Moore, Robert
Agent:
The Artist's Agency
Beverly Hills
(213) 278-3200

THURSDAY'S GAME
ABC Circle Films; telefeature; 1974; filmed in 1971
CAT ON A HOT TIN ROOF
NBC-TV; telefeature; 1974
MURDER BY DEATH
Columbia; 1976
THE CHEAP DETECTIVE
Columbia; 1978
CHAPTER TWO
Columbia; 1980

Mora, Philippe
Contact:
Directors Guild of America
Los Angeles
(213) 656-1220

SWASTIKA
Cinema 5; 1974; British
BROTHER, CAN YOU SPARE A DIME?
Dimension; 1975; Canadian
MAD DOG (Mad Dog Morgan)
Cinema Shares International; 1976; Australian
THE BEAST WITHIN
United Artists; 1981

Morris, Howard
b. September 4, 1919
New York, New York
Business Manager:
E.B.M.
Beverly Hills
(213) CR. 8-6700

WHO'S MINDING THE MINT?
Columbia; 1967
WITH SIX YOU GET EGGROLL
National General; 1968
DON'T DRINK THE WATER
Avco Embassy; 1969
GOIN' COCONUTS
Osmond; 1978

Morrissey, Paul
b. 1939
New York, New York

FLESH
Warhol; 1968
TRASH
Warhol; 1970
ANDY WARHOL'S WOMEN
Warhol; 1971
HEAT
Warhol; 1972
L'AMOUR
co-director with Andy Warhol; Altura; 1973
ANDY WARHOL'S FRANKENSTEIN
Bryanston; 1974; Italian-French
ANDY WARHOL'S DRACULA
Bryanston; 1974; Italian-French
THE HOUND OF THE BASKERVILLES
Atlantic; 1979; British
MADAME WANG'S
1981

Morrow, Vic
b. February 14, 1932
Bronx, New York
Agent:
Contemporary-Korman Artists
Beverly Hills
(213) 278-8250

A MAN CALLED SLEDGE
Columbia; 1971

Moses, Gilbert
Agent:
Shapiro-Lichtman Agency
Los Angeles
(213) 557-2244

WILLIE DYNAMITE
Universal; 1974
ROOTS
co-director with Marvin J. Chomsky, John Erman & David Greene; Wolper Productions; television mini-series; 1977
THE GREATEST THING THAT ALMOST HAPPENED
Charles Fries Productions; telefeature; 1977
THE FISH THAT SAVED PITTSBURGH
United Artists/Lorimar; 1979

Moses, Harry
Contact:
Directors Guild of America
New York City
(212) 581-0370

THORNWELL
MTM Enterprises; telefeature; 1981

Moxey, John Llewellyn
b. 1920
Hurlingham, England
Personal Manager:
General Management Corp.
Beverly Hills
(213) 274-8805

HORROR HOTEL (City of the Dead)
Trans-World; 1960; British
FOXHOLE IN CAIRO
Paramount; 1961; British
DEATH TRAP
Anglo Amalgamated; 1962; British

continued

Moxey, John Llewellyn
continued

THE 20,000 POUND KISS
Anglo Amalgamated; 1963; British
RICOCHET
Warner-Pathe; 1963; British
DOWNFALL
Embassy; 1964; British
FACE OF A STRANGER
Warner-Pathe; 1964; British
STRANGLER'S WEB
Embassy; 1965; British
PSYCHO-CIRCUS (Circus of Fear)
American International; 1967; British
THE TORMENTOR
ITC; 1967; British
SAN FRANCISCO INTERNATIONAL AIRPORT
Universal TV; telefeature; 1970
THE HOUSE THAT WOULD NOT DIE
Aaron Spelling Productions; telefeature; 1970
ESCAPE
Paramount TV; telefeature; 1971
THE LAST CHILD
Aaron Spelling Productions; telefeature; 1971
A TASTE OF EVIL
Aaron Spelling Productions; telefeature; 1971
THE DEATH OF ME YET!
Aaron Spelling Productions; telefeature; 1971
THE NIGHT STALKER
ABC, Inc.; telefeature; 1972
HARDCASE
Hanna-Barbera Productions; telefeature; 1972
THE BOUNTY MAN
ABC Circle Films; telefeature; 1972
HOME FOR THE HOLIDAYS
ABC Circle Films; telefeature; 1972
GENESIS II
Warner Brothers TV; telefeature; 1973
THE STRANGE AND DEADLY OCCURENCE
Metromedia Productions; telefeature; 1974
WHERE HAVE ALL THE PEOPLE GONE?
Metromedia Productions; telefeature; 1974
FOSTER AND LAURIE
Charles Fries Productions; telefeature; 1975
CHARLIE'S ANGELS
Spelling-Goldberg Productions;telefeature;1976
CONSPIRACY OF TERROR
Lorimar Productions; telefeature; 1976
NIGHTMARE IN BADHAM COUNTY
ABC Circle Films; telefeature; 1976
SMASH-UP ON INTERSTATE 5
Filmways; telefeature; 1976
PANIC IN ECHO PARK
Edgar J. Scherick Associates; telefeature; 1977
INTIMATE STRANGERS
Charles Fries Productions; telefeature; 1977
THE PRESIDENT'S MISTRESS
Stephen Friedman/King's Road Productions; telefeature; 1978
THE COURAGE AND THE PASSION
David Gerber Productions/Columbia TV; telefeature;1978
SANCTUARY OF FEAR
Marble Arch Productions; telefeature; 1979
THE POWER WITHIN
Aaron Spelling Productions; telefeature; 1979
THE SOLITARY MAN
Universal TV; telefeature; 1979
EBONY, IVORY AND JADE
Frankel Films; telefeature; 1979
THE CHILDREN OF AN LAC
Charles Fries Productions; telefeature; 1980
THE MATING SEASON
Highgate Pictures; telefeature; 1980
NO PLACE TO HIDE
Metromedia Producers Corporation; telefeature; 1981
THE VIOLATION OF SARAH McDAVID
CBS Entertainment; telefeature; 1981
KILLJOY
Lorimar Productions; telefeature; 1981

Moyle, Alan
Contact:
Directors Guild of America
New York City
(212) 581-0370

THE RUBBER GUN
Schuman-Katzka; 1978; Canadian
TIMES SQUARE
AFD; 1980

Mulligan, Robert
b. August 23, 1925
Bronx, New York
Agent:
William Morris Agency
Beverly Hills
(213) 274-7451

FEAR STRIKES OUT
Paramount; 1957
THE RAT RACE
Paramount; 1960
THE GREAT IMPOSTER
Universal; 1961
COME SEPTEMBER
Universal; 1961
THE SPIRAL ROAD
Universal; 1962
TO KILL A MOCKINGBIRD
Universal; 1962
LOVE WITH THE PROPER STRANGER
Paramount; 1964
BABY, THE RAIN MUST FALL
Columbia; 1965
INSIDE DAISY CLOVER
Warner Brothers; 1966
UP THE DOWN STAIRCASE
Warner Brothers; 1967
THE STALKING MOON
National General; 1969
THE PURSUIT OF HAPPINESS
Columbia; 1971
SUMMER OF '42
Warner Brothers; 1971
THE OTHER
20th Century-Fox; 1972
THE NICKEL RIDE
20th Century-Fox; 1975
BLOODBROTHERS
Warner Brothers; 1979
SAME TIME, NEXT YEAR
Universal; 1979

Murakami, Jimmy T.

BATTLE BEYOND THE STARS
New World; 1979

Murray, Don
b. July 39, 1929
Hollywood, California

THE CROSS AND THE SWITCHBLADE
Dick Ross; 1970

Mutrux, Floyd
Contact:
Directors Guild of America
Los Angeles
(213) 656-1220

DUSTY AND SWEETS McGEE
Warner Brothers; 1971
aloha, bobby and rose
Columbia; 1975
AMERICAN HOT WAX
Paramount; 1978
THE HOLLYWOOD KNIGHTS
Columbia; 1980

Myerson, Alan
Personal Manager:
Shapiro-West
Beverly Hills
(213) 278-8896

STEELYARD BLUES
Warner Brothers; 1973
THE LOVE BOAT
co-director with Richard Kinon; Douglas S. Cramer Productions; telefeature; 1976
PRIVATE LESSONS
Jensen Farley Pictures; 1981

Nadel, Arthur H.
Business:
Filmation Studios
18107 Sherman Way
Reseda, CA 91335
(213) 345-7414
Attorney:
Siegel & Brifman
Los Angeles
(213) 552-9681

CLAMBAKE
United Artists; 1967
UNDERGROUND
United Artists; 1970

Nagy, Ivan
Agent:
I.C.M.
Hollywood
(213) 550-4000

BAD CHARLESTON CHARLIE
International Cinema; 1973
DEADLY HERO
Avco Embassy; 1976
MIND OVER MURDER
Paramount TV; telefeature; 1979
ONCE UPON A SPY
David Gerber Productions/Columbia TV; telefeature; 1980
MIDNIGHT LACE
Four R Productions/Universal TV; telefeature; 1981
A GUN IN THE HOUSE
Channing-Debin-Locke Company;telefeature;1981

Nankin, Michael
Business:
4333 Vantage Avenue
Studio City, CA 91604
(213) 769-2863
Agent:
The Phil Gersh Agency
Beverly Hills
(213) 274-6611

MIDNIGHT MADNESS
co-director with David Wechter; Buena Vista; 1981

Narizzano, Silvio
b. 1927
Montreal, Canada
Home:
8400 De Longpre
Los Angeles, CA 90069
(213) 654-9548
Agent:
William Morris Agency
Beverly Hills
(213) 274-7451

DIE! DIE! MY DARLING! (Fanatic)
Columbia; 1965; British
GEORGY GIRL
Columbia; 1967; British
BLUE
Paramount; 1968; British
LOOT
Cinevision; 1972; British
REDNECK
International Amusements; 1975
THE SKY IS FALLING
1976; Canadian
WHY SHOOT THE TEACHER
Quartet; 1977; Canadian
COME BACK, LITTLE SHEBA
Granada Television, Ltd.; telefeature; 1977; U.S.-British
THE CLASS OF MISS MacMICHAEL
Brut Productions; 1979; British
STAYING ON
Granada Television, Ltd.; telefeature; 1980; British

Naylor, Cal
Home:
17606 Posetano Road
Pacific Palisades, CA 90272
(213) 454-7229

DIRT
co-director with Eric Karson; American Cinema; 1979

Neame, Ronald
b. 1911
London, England
Home:
2317 Kimridge Road
Beverly Hills, CA 90210
(213) 271-2970

TAKE MY LIFE
Eagle Lion; 1947; British
THE GOLDEN SALAMANDER
Eagle Lion; 1950; British

continued

Neame, Ronald
continued

THE PROMOTER (The Card)
Universal; 1952; British
MAN WITH A MILLION (The Million Pound Note)
United Artists; 1954; British
THE MAN WHO NEVER WAS
20th Century-Fox; 1956
THE SEVENTH SIN
M-G-M; 1957
WINDOM'S WAY
Rank; 1958; British
THE HORSE'S MOUTH
United Artists; 1959; British
TUNES OF GLORY
Lopert; 1960; British
ESCAPE FROM ZAHRAIN
Paramount; 1962
I COULD GO ON SINGING
United Artists; 1963; British
THE CHALK GARDEN
Universal; 1964; British
MISTER MOSES
United Artists; 1965
A MAN COULD GET KILLED
co-director with Cliff Owen; Universal; 1966
GAMBIT
Universal; 1966
THE PRIME OF MISS JEAN BRODIE
20th Century-Fox; 1969; British
SCROOGE
National General; 1970; British
THE POSEIDON ADVENTURE
20th Century-Fox; 1972
THE ODESSA FILE
Columbia; 1974; British-West German
METEOR
American International; 1979
HOPSCOTCH
Avco Embassy; 1980
FIRST MONDAY IN OCTOBER
Paramount; 1981

Needham, Hal
Business:
3518 Cahuenga Blvd. West
Hollywood, CA 90068
(213) 876-8052
Agent:
Chasin-Park-Citron
Los Angeles
(213) 273-7190

SMOKEY AND THE BANDIT
Universal; 1977
HOOPER
Warner Brothers; 1978
THE VILLAIN
Columbia; 1979
DEATH CAR ON THE FREEWAY
Shpetner Productions; telefeature; 1979
STUNTS UNLIMITED
Lawrence Gordon Productions/Paramount TV; telefeature; 1980
SMOKEY AND THE BANDIT, PART II
Universal; 1980
THE CANNONBALL RUN
20th Century-Fox; 1981
MEGAFORCE
20th Century-Fox; 1982

Nelson, Gary
Contact:
Directors Guild of America
Los Angeles
(213) 656-1220

MOLLY AND LAWLESS JOHN
Producers Distribution Corporation; 1972
SANTEE
Crown International; 1973
THE GIRL ON THE LATE, LATE SHOW
Screem Gems/Columbia TV; telefeature; 1974
MEDICAL STORY
David Gerber Productions/Columbia TV; telefeature; 1975
PANACHE
Warner Brothers TV; telefeature; 1976
WASHINGTON: BEHIND CLOSED DOORS
Paramount TV; television mini-series; 1977

continued

Nelson, Gary
continued

FREAKY FRIDAY
Buena Vista; 1977
TO KILL A COP
David Gerber Productions/Columbia TV; telefeature; 1978
THE BLACK HOLE
Buena Vista; 1979
THE PRIDE OF JESSE HALLAM
The Konigsberg Company; telefeature; 1981
JIMMY THE KID
Zephyr Productions; 1982

Nelson, Gene
(Gene Berg)
b. March 24, 1920
Seattle, Washington
Home:
3431 Vinton Avenue
Los Angeles, CA 90034
(213) 837-0484
Agent:
Contemporary-Korman Artists
Los Angeles
(213) 278-8250

HAND OF DEATH
20th Century-Fox; 1962
HOOTENANNY HOOT
M-G-M; 1962
KISSIN' COUSINS
M-G-M; 1964
YOUR CHEATIN' HEART
M-G-M; 1964
HARUM SCARUM
M-G-M; 1965
THE COOL ONES
Warner Brothers; 1967
WAKE ME WHEN THE WAR IS OVER
Thomas-Spelling Productions; telefeature; 1969
THE LETTERS
co-director with Paul Krasny; ABC Circle Films; telefeature; 1973

Nelson, Ralph
b. August 12, 1916
New York, New York
Agent:
Chasin-Park-Citron
Los Angeles
(213) 273-7190

REQUIEM FOR A HEAVYWEIGHT
Coumbia; 1962
LILIES OF THE FIELD
United Artists; 1963
SOLDIER IN THE RAIN
Allied Artists; 1963
FATE IS THE HUNTER
20th Century-Fox; 1964
FATHER GOOSE
Universal; 1964
ONCE A THIEF
M-G-M; 1965
DUEL AT DIABLO
United Artists; 1966
COUNTERPOINT
Universal; 1968
CHARLY
Cinerama Releasing Corporation; 1968
...tick...tick...tick
M-G-M; 1970
SOLDIER BLUE
Avco Embassy; 1970
FLIGHT OF THE DOVES
Columbia; 1971; British
THE WRATH OF GOD
M-G-M; 1972
THE WILBY CONSPIRACY
United Artists; 1975; British
EMBRYO
Cine Artists; 1976
A HERO AIN'T NOTHIN' BUT A SANDWICH
New World; 1977
LADY OF THE HOUSE
co-director with Vincent Sherman; Metromedia Productions; telefeature; 1978
BECAUSE HE'S MY FRIEND
1979
CHRISTMAS LILIES OF THE FIELD
Rainbow Productions/Osmond Productions; telefeature; 1979
YOU CAN'T GO HOME AGAIN
CBS Entertainment; telefeature; 1979

Newell, Mike

THE MAN IN THE IRON MASK
Norman Rosemont Productions/ITC; telefeature; 1977; U.S.-British
THE AWAKENING
Orion Pictures/Warner Brothers; 1980
BAD BLOOD
Southern Pictures/New Zealand Film Commission; 1981; New Zealand

Newland, John
Business:
The Factor-Newland
Production Corporation
4000 Warner Blvd.
Burbank, CA 91505
(213) 943-6000
Agent:
Herb Tobias & Assoc.
Los Angeles
(213) 277-6211

THAT NIGHT
Universal; 1957
THE VIOLATORS
Universal; 1957
THE SPY WITH MY FACE
M-G-M; 1966
MY LOVER, MY SON
M-G-M; 1970; British
THE DEADLY HUNT
Four Star International; telefeature; 1971
CRAWLSPACE
Titus Productions; telefeature; 1972
DON'T BE AFRAID OF THE DARK
Lorimar Productions; telefeature; 1973
WHO FEARS THE DEVIL (The Legend of Hillbilly John) Jack H. Harris Enterprises; 1974
A SENSITIVE, PASSIONATE MAN
Factor-Newland Production Corporation; telefeature; 1977
OVERBOARD
Factor-Newland Production Corporation; telefeature; 1978
THE SUICIDE'S WIFE
Factor-Newland Production Corporation; telefeature; 1979

Newley, Anthony
b. September 24, 1931
London, England

CAN HIERONYMOUS MERKIN EVER FORGET MERCY HUMPPE AND FIND TRUE HAPPINESS?
Regional; 1969; British
SUMMERTREE
Columbia; 1971

Newman, Paul
b. January 26, 1925
Cleveland, Ohio
Contact:
Directors Guild of America
New York City
(212) 581-0370

RACHEL, RACHEL
Warner Brothers; 1968
SOMETIMES A GREAT NOTION (Never Give An Inch)
Universal; 1971
THE EFFECT OF GAMMA RAYS ON MAN-IN-THE-MOON MARIGOLDS
20th Century-Fox; 1973
THE SHADOW BOX
The Shadow Box Film Company; telefeature; 1980

Nichols, Mike
(Michael Igor Peschkowsky)
b. November 6, 1931
Berlin, Germany
Agent:
I.C.M.
New York City
(212) 556-6810
Attorney:
Rosenfeld, Meyer & Susman
Beverly Hills
(213) 858-7700

WHO'S AFRAID OF VIRGINIA WOOLF?
Warner Brothers; 1966
THE GRADUATE
Avco Embassy; 1967
CATCH-22
Paramount; 1970
CARNAL KNOWLEDGE
Avco Embassy; 1971
THE DAY OF THE DOLPHIN
Avco Embassy; 1973
THE FORTUNE
Columbia; 1975
GILDA LIVE
Warner Brothers; 1980

Nicholson, Jack
b. April 22, 1937
Neptune, New Jersey
Agent:
The Artists Agency
Beverly Hills
(213) 278-3200
Business Manager:
Guild Management Corp.
Los Angeles
(213) 277-9711

DRIVE, HE SAID
Columbia; 1971
GOIN' SOUTH
Paramount; 1979

Niciphor, Nicholas

GOOD-BYE, CRUEL WORLD
co-director with David Irving; NSN; 1981

Norton, B.W.L.
Agent:
William Morris Agency
Beverly Hills
(213) 274-7451

CISCO PIKE
Columbia; 1971
GARGOYLES
Tomorrow Entertainment; telefeature; 1972
MORE AMERICAN GRAFFITI
Universal; 1979

Nosseck, Noel
Agent:
Chasin-Park-Citron
Los Angeles
(213) 273-7190

BEST FRIENDS
Crown International; 1973
LAS VEGAS LADY
Crown International; 1976
YOUNGBLOOD
American International; 1978
DREAMER
20th Century-Fox; 1979
KING OF THE MOUNTAIN
Universal; 1981
RETURN OF THE REBELS
Moonlight Productions/Filmways; telefeature; 1981

Noyce, Phillip
Contact:
Australian Film Commission
9229 Sunset Blvd.
Los Angeles, CA 90069
(213) 275-7074

BACKROADS
Cinema Ventures; 1978; Australian
NEWSFRONT
New Yorker; 1979; Australian
HEATWAVE
Heatwave Films; 1981; Australian

Nunn, Trevor

HEDDA
Brut Productions; 1975; British

Nyby, Christian, III
Home:
1030 Green Lane
La Canada, CA 91011
(213) 790-0754
Agent:
Eisenbach-Greene-Duchow
Hollywood
(213) 659-3420

THE RANGERS
Universal TV/Mark VII Ltd.; telefeature; 1974
PINE CANYON IS BURNING
Universal TV; telefeature; 1977

Oboler, Arch
b. December 7, 1909
Chicago, Illinois

BEWITCHED
M-G-M; 1945
STRANGE HOLIDAY
Producers Releasing Corporation; 1946
THE ARNELO AFFAIR
M-G-M; 1947

continued

Oboler, Arch
continued

FIVE
Columbia; 1951
BWANA DEVIL
United Artists; 1952
THE TWONKY
United Artists; 1953
1 + 1: EXPLORING THE KINSEY REPORTS
1961; U.S.-Canadian
THE BUBBLE
Arch Oboler; 1967

O'Brien, Edmond
b. September 10, 1915
New York, New York
Agent:
Paul Kohner Agency
Los Angeles
(213) 550-1060

SHIELD FOR MURDER
co-director with Howard Koch; United Artists; 1954
MAN TRAP
Paramount; 1961

O'Connell, Jack

GREENWICH VILLAGE STORY
Lion International; 1963
REVOLUTION
Lopert; 1968
SWEDISH FLY GIRLS (Christa)
American International; 1971; U.S.-Danish

O'Connolly, James
Contact:
British Film Institute
127 Charing Cross Road
London W.C. 2, England
01-437-4355

THE HI-JACKERS
Butcher; 1964; British
SMOKESCREEN
Butcher; 1964; British
THE LITTLE ONES
Columbia; 1965; British
BERSERK!
Columbia; 1968; British
THE VALLEY OF GWANGI
Warner Brothers; 1969; British
SOPHIE'S PLACE (Crooks and Coronets)
Warner Brothers; 1969; British
HORROR ON SNAPE ISLAND
Fanfare; 1972; British
MISTRESS PAMELA
Fanfare; 1974; British

O'Donoghue, Michael

MR. MIKE'S MONDO VIDEO
New Line Cinema; 1979

O'Hara, Gerry
b. 1924
Boston, Lincolnshire, England
Contact:
British Film Institute
127 Charing Cross Road
London W.C. 2, England
01-437-4355

MODELS, INC. (That Kind of Girl)
Mutual; 1963; British
A GAME FOR THREE LOSERS
Embassy; 1963; British
THE PLEASURE GIRLS
Times; 1965; British
MAROC 7
Paramount; 1966; British
AMSTERDAM AFFAIR
Lippert; 1968; 1968
FIDELIA
1970; British
ALL THE RIGHT NOISES
20th Century-Fox; 1971; British
THE BRUTE
1976; British
LEOPARD IN THE SNOW
New World; 1978; Canadian
THE BITCH
1979; British

O'Herlihy, Michael
b. Ireland
Agent:
Contemporary-Korman Artists
Beverly Hills
(213) 278-8250

THE FIGHTING PRINCE OF DONEGAL
Buena Vista; 1966; British-U.S.
THE ONE AND ONLY GENUINE, ORIGINAL FAMILY BAND
Buena Vista; 1967
SMITH!
Buena Vista; 1969
DEADLY HARVEST
CBS, Inc.; telefeature; 1972
YOUNG PIONEERS
ABC Circle Films; telefeature; 1976
KISS ME, KILL ME
Columbia TV; telefeature; 1976
YOUNG PIONEERS' CHRISTMAS
ABC Circle Films; telefeature; 1976
PETER LUNDY AND THE MEDICINE HAT STALLION
Ed Friendly Productions; telefeature; 1977
BACKSTAIRS AT THE WHITE HOUSE
Ed Friendly Productions; television mini-series;1979
THE FLAME IS LOVE
Ed Friendly Productions/Friendly-O'Herlihy Ltd.;telefeature; 1979
DALLAS COWBOYS CHEERLEADERS II
Aubrey-Hamner Productions; telefeature; 1980
DETOUR TO TERROR
Orenthal Productions/Playboy Productions/Columbia TV; telefeature; 1980
THE GREAT CASH GIVEAWAY GETAWAY
Penthouse Productions/Cine Guarantors Inc.; telefeature; 1980
CRY OF THE INNOCENT
Tara Productions; telefeature; 1980
DESPERATE VOYAGE
Barry Weitz Films/Joe Wizan TV Productions; telefeature; 1980
A TIME FOR MIRACLES
ABC Circle Films; telefeature; 1980
THE MILLION DOLLAR FACE
Nephi-Hamner Productions; telefeature; 1981

O'Horgan, Tom

FUTZ
Commonwealth United; 1969
RHINOCEROS
American Film Theatre; 1974

Oliansky, Joel
Agent:
Adams, Ray & Rosenberg
Los Angeles
(213) 278-3000

THE COMPETITION
Columbia; 1980

Olivier, Laurence
b. May 22, 1907
Dorking, England
Contact:
British Film Institute
127 Charing Cross Road
London W.C. 2, England
01-437-4355

HENRY V
Rank; 1945; British
HAMLET
Universal; 1946; British
RICHARD III
Lopert; 1956; British
THE PRINCE AND THE SHOWGIRL
Warner Brothers; 1957; U.S.-British
THREE SISTERS
American Film Theatre; 1974; British

Olmi, Ermanno
b. July 24, 1931
Bergamo, Italy
Contact:
Minister of Tourism
Via Della Ferratella
No. 51
00184 Rome, Italy
06-7732

TIME STOOD STILL
Sezione Cinema Edison Volta; 1959; Italian
THE SOUND OF TRUMPETS
Janus; 1961; Italian
THE FIANCES
Janus; 1963; Italian

continued

Olmi, Ermanno
continued

AND THERE CAME A MAN
Brandon; 1965; Italian
ONE FINE DAY
Cinema Spa/Italnoleggio; 1968; Italian
THE SCAVENGERS
RAI-TV/Produzione Palumbo; telefeature; 1969; Italian
DURING THE SUMMER
RAI-TV; telefeature; 1971; Italian
THE CIRCUMSTANCE
RAI-TV/Italnoleggio;telefeature;1974;Italian
THE TREE OF WOODEN CLOGS
New Yorker; 1979; Italian;made for television

O'Neal, Ron
b. September 1, 1937
Utica, New York

SUPERFLY T.N.T.
Paramount; 1973

Ophuls, Marcel
b. 1927
Frankfurt, Germany

LOVE AT TWENTY
co-director; Embassy; 1962; French-Italian-Japanese-Polish-West German
BANANA PEEL
Pathe Contemporary; 1965; French-Italian
FEU A VOLONTE
1965; French-Italian
THE SORROW AND THE PITY
Cinema 5; 1972; French-Swiss-West German
A SENSE OF LOSS
Cinema 5; 1972; U.S.-Swiss
THE MEMORY OF JUSTICE
Paramount; 1976; British-West German

O'Steen, Sam
Agent:
The Ufland Agency
Beverly Hills
(213) 273-9441

A BRAND NEW LIFE
Tomorrow Entertainment; telefeature; 1973
I LOVE YOU, GOODBYE
Tomorrow Entertainment; telefeature; 1974
QUEEN OF THE STARDUST BALLROOM
Tomorrow Entertainment; telefeature; 1975
HIGH RISK
Danny Thomas Productions-M-G-M TV;telefeature; 1976
SPARKLE
Warner Brothers; 1976
LOOK WHAT'S HAPPENED TO ROSEMARY'S BABY
Paramount TV; telefeature; 1976
THE BEST LITTLE GIRL IN THE WORLD
Aaron Spelling Productions; telefeature; 1981

Oswald, Gerd
b. June 9, 1916
Berlin, Germany
Home:
237A Spalding Drive
Beverly Hills, CA 90212
(213) 553-7150
Agent:
Irving Salkow Agency
Beverly Hills
(213) 276-3141

A KISS BEFORE DYING
United Artists; 1956
THE BRASS LEGEND
United Artists; 1956
CRIME OF PASSION
United Artists; 1957
FURY AT SHOWDOWN
United Artists; 1957
VALERIE
United Artists; 1957
PARIS HOLIDAY
United Artists; 1958
SCREAMING MIMI
Columbia; 1958
THE DAY THE RAINS CAME
1959; West German
BRAINWASHED
Allied Artists; 1960; West German
THE SCARLET EYE
1963; Italian-French

continued

Oswald, Gerd
continued

AGENT FOR H.A.R.M.
Universal; 1966
80 STEPS TO JONAH
Warner Brothers; 1969
BUNNY O'HARE
American International; 1971
TO THE BITTER END
1975; Australian-West German

Oury, Gerard
(Max-Gerard Houry Tannenbaum)
b. 1919
Paris, France
Contact:
French Film Office
745 Fifth Avenue
New York, N.Y. 10151
(212) 832-8860

LA MAIN CHAUDE
1960; French
THE MENACE
Warner Brothers; 1961; French
CRIME DOES NOT PAY
Embassy; 1962; French-Italian
THE SUCKER
Royal International; 1966; French-Italian
DON'T LOOK NOW...WE'RE BEING SHOT AT
Cinepix; 1966; British-French
THE BRAIN
Paramount; 1969
DELUSIONS OF GRANDEUR
Joseph Green Pictures; 1971; French
THE MAD ADVENTURES OF 'RABBI' JACOB
20th Century-Fox; 1974; French-Italian
LA CARAPATE
1978; French

Owen, Cliff
b. April 22, 1919
London, England
Contact:
British Film Institute
127 Charing Cross Road
London W.C. 2, England
01-437-4355

OFFBEAT
1961; British
A PRIZE OF ARMS
British Lion; 1961; British
THE WRONG ARM OF THE LAW
Continental; 1963; British
A MAN COULD GET KILLED
co-director with Ronald Neame; Universal; 1966
THAT RIVIERA TOUCH
Continental; 1966; British
WHAT HAPPENED AT CAMPO GRANDE? (The Magnificent Two) Alan Enterprises; 1967; British
THE VENGEANCE OF SHE
20th Century-Fox; 1968; British
STEPTOE AND SON
1972; British
THE BAWDY ADVENTURES OF TOM JONES
Universal; 1975; British
GET CHARLIE TULLY
1976; British

Page, Anthony
Business Manager:
Richard M. Rosenthal
Los Angeles
(213) 820-8585

INADMISSABLE EVIDENCE
Paramount; 1968; British
PUEBLO
telefeature; 1973
THE MISSILES OF OCTOBER
ABC-TV; telefeature; 1974
COLLISION COURSE
ABC-TV; telefeature; 1975
ALPHA BETA
Cine III; 1976; British
F. SCOTT FITZGERALD IN HOLLYWOOD
Titus Productions; telefeature; 1976
I NEVER PROMISED YOU A ROSE GARDEN
New World; 1977
ABSOLUTION
Bulldog Productions; 1979; British
THE LADY VANISHES
Rank; 1979; British
F.D.R.: THE LAST YEAR
NBC-TV; telefeature; 1980

Pakula, Alan J.
b. April 7, 1928
New York, New York
Agent:
William Morris Agency
Beverly Hills
(213) 274-7451

THE STERILE CUCKOO
Paramount; 1969
KLUTE
Warner Brothers; 1971
LOVE AND PAIN and the whole damned thing
Columbia; 1973; British-U.S.
THE PARALLAX VIEW
Paramount; 1974
ALL THE PRESIDENT'S MEN
Warner Brothers; 1976
COMES A HORSEMAN
United Artists; 1978
STARTING OVER
Paramount; 1979
ROLLOVER
Orion Pictures/Warner Brothers; 1981

Palmer, Tony
Contact:
British Film Institute
127 Charing Cross Road
London W.C. 2, England
01-437-4355

200 MOTELS
co-director with Frank Zappa; United Artists; 1971; British
BIRD ON A WIRE
EMI; 1974; British
THE SPACE MOVIE
International Harmony; 1980; British

Paltrow, Bruce
Business:
MTM Enterprises
4024 Radford Avenue
Studio City, CA 91604
(213) 760-5000
Agent:
I.C.M.
Hollywood
(213) 550-4000

A LITTLE SEX
Universal; 1982

Panama, Norman
b. April 21, 1914
Chicago, Illinois
Agent:
Phil Gersh Agency
Beverly Hills
(213) 274-6611
Attorney:
Leon Kaplan
Beverly Hills
(213) 274-8011

THE REFORMER AND THE REDHEAD
co-director with Melvin Frank; M-G-M; 1950
STRICTLY DISHONORABLE
co-director with Melvin Frank; M-G-M; 1951
CALLAWAY WENT THATAWAY
co-director with Melvin Frank; M-G-M; 1951
ABOVE AND BEYOND
co-director with Melvin Frank; M-G-M; 1952
KNOCK ON WOOD
co-director with Melvin Frank; Paramount;1954
THE COURT JESTER
co-director with Melvin Frank; Paramount;1956
THAT CERTAIN FEELING
co-director with Melvin Frank; Paramount;1956
THE TRAP
Paramount; 1959
THE ROAD TO HONG KONG
United Artists; 1962
NOT WITH MY WIFE, YOU DON'T!
Warner Brothers; 1966
HOW TO COMMIT MARRIAGE
Cinerama Releasing Corporation; 1969
THE MALTESE BIPPY
M-G-M; 1969
COFFEE, TEA OR ME?
CBS, Inc.; telefeature; 1973
I WILL, I WILL...FOR NOW
20th Century-Fox; 1976
BARNABY AND ME
Trans-Atlantic Enterprises; 1978

Paris, Jerry
b. July 25, 1925
San Francisco, California
Agent:
Creative Artists Agency
Los Angeles
(213) 277-4545

DON'T RAISE THE BRIDGE - LOWER THE RIVER
Columbia; 1968; British
NEVER A DULL MOMENT
Buena Vista; 1968

continued

Paris, Jerry
continued

HOW SWEET IT IS!
National General; 1968
VIVA MAX!
Commonwealth United; 1969
THE GRASSHOPPER
National General; 1969
BUT I DON'T WANT TO GET MARRIED!
Aaron Spelling Productions; telefeature; 1970
THE FEMINIST AND THE FUZZ
Screen Gems/Columbia TV; telefeature; 1970
TWO ON A BENCH
Universal TV; telefeature; 1971
WHAT'S A NICE GIRL LIKE YOU...?
Universal TV; telefeature; 1971
STAR SPANGLED GIRL
Paramount; 1971
CALL HER MOM
Screen Gems/Columbia TV; telefeature; 1972
EVIL ROY SLADE
Universal TV; telefeature; 1972
THE COUPLE TAKES A WIFE
Universal TV; telefeature; 1972
EVERY MAN NEEDS ONE
ABC Circle Films; telefeature; 1972
ONLY WITH MARRIED MEN
Spelling-Goldberg Productions; telefeature; 1974
HOW TO BREAK UP A HAPPY DIVORCE
Charles Fries Productions; telefeature; 1976
MAKE ME AN OFFER
ABC Circle Films; telefeature; 1980
LEO AND LOREE
United Artists; 1980

Parker, Alan
b. England
Agent:
William Morris Agency
Beverly Hills
(213) 274-7451

BUGSY MALONE
Paramount; 1976; British
MIDNIGHT EXPRESS
Columbia; 1978; British
FAME
M-G-M/United Artists; 1980
SHOOT THE MOON
M-G-M/United Artists; 1982
PINK FLOYD - THE WALL
M-G-M/United Artists; 1982; British

Parks, Gordon
b. November 30, 1912
Fort Scott, Kansas
Home:
860 U.N. Plaza
New York, N.Y. 10017
Agent:
I.C.M.
Hollywood
(213) 550-4000

THE LEARNING TREE
Warner Brothers; 1969
SHAFT
M-G-M; 1971
SHAFT'S BIG SCORE!
M-G-M; 1972
THE SUPER COPS
M-G-M; 1974
LEADBELLY
Paramount
SUPER COPS
CBS-TV; telefeature; 1976

Parone, Edward
Agent:
William Morris Agency
Beverly Hills
(213) 274-7451

PROMISE HIM ANYTHING...
ABC Circle Films; telefeature; 1975
LETTERS FROM FRANK
The Jozak Company/Cypress Point Productions; telefeature; 1979

Parrish, Robert
b. January 4, 1916
Columbus, Georgia
Business Manager:
Jess S. Morgan & Co.
(213) 651-1601

CRY DANGER
RKO Radio; 1951
THE MOB
Columbia; 1951

continued

Parrish, Robert
continued

THE SAN FRANCISCO STORY
Warner Brothers; 1952
ASSIGNMENT - PARIS
Columbia; 1952
MY PAL GUS
20th Century-Fox; 1952
SHOOT FIRST (Rough Shoot)
United Artists; 1953; British
THE PURPLE PLAIN
United Artists; 1954; British
LUCY GALLANT
Paramount; 1955
FIRE DOWN BELOW
Columbia; 1957
SADDLE THE WIND
M-G-M; 1957
THE WONDERFUL COUNTRY
United Artists; 1959
IN THE FRENCH STYLE
Columbia; 1963; French-U.S.
UP FROM THE BEACH
20th Century-Fox; 1965
CASINO ROYALE
co-director with Val Guest, Ken Hughes, John Huston & Joseph McGrath; Columbia; 1967; British
THE BOBO
Warner Brothers; 1967; British
DUFFY
Columbia; 1968; British
JOURNEY TO THE FAR SIDE OF THE SUN
Universal; 1969; British
A TOWN CALLED BASTARD (A Town Called Hell)
Scotia International; 1971; British-Spanish
THE DESTRUCTORS (The Marseilles Contract)
American International; 1974; British-French

Passer, Ivan
b. Czechoslovakia
Attorney:
Egon Dumler
New York City
(212) PL. 9-4580

INTIMATE LIGHTING
Altura; 1969; Czech
BORN TO WIN
United Artists; 1971
LAW AND DISORDER
Columbia; 1974
CRIME AND PASSION
American International; 1976
SILVER BEARS
Columbia; 1978
CUTTER'S WAY (Cutter and Bone)
United Artists Classics; 1981

Paul, Steven

FALLING IN LOVE AGAIN
International Picture Show Company; 1980

Paulsen, David
Home:
11645 Woodbridge
Studio City, CA 91604

SAVAGE WEEKEND
1978
SCHIZOID
Cannon; 1980

Pearce, Richard
Home:
767 Paseo Miramar
Pacific Palisades, CA 90271
Agent:
William Morris Agency
Beverly Hills
(213) 274-7451

THE GARDENER'S SON
PBS-TV; telefeature; 1976
SIEGE
Titus Productions; telefeature; 1978
NO OTHER LOVE
Tisch-Avnet Productions; telefeature; 1979
HEARTLAND
Levitt-Pickman; 1979
THRESHOLD
Paragon Productions; 1981; Canadian

Peckinpah, Sam
b. February 21, 1925
Fresno, California
Agent:
Chasin-Park-Citron
Los Angeles
(213) 273-7190
Business Manager:
Kip Dellinger
Hollywood
(213) 273-1410

THE DEADLY COMPANIONS
Pathe-American; 1961
RIDE THE HIGH COUNTRY
M-G-M; 1962
MAJOR DUNDEE
Columbia; 1965
THE WILD BUNCH
Warner Brothers; 1969
THE BALLAD OF CABLE HOGUE
Warner Brothers; 1970
STRAW DOGS
Cinerama Releasing Corporation; 1972; British
THE GETAWAY
National General; 1972
JUNIOR BONNER
Cinerama Releasing Corporation; 1973
PAT GARRETT & BILLY THE KID
M-G-M; 1973
BRING ME THE HEAD OF ALFREDO GARCIA
United Artists; 1974
THE KILLER ELITE
United Artists; 1975
CROSS OF IRON
Avco Embassy; 1977; British-West German
CONVOY
United Artists; 1978

Peerce, Larry
b. Bronx, New York
Agent:
Creative Artists Agency
Los Angeles
(213) 277-4545

ONE POTATO, TWO POTATO
Cinema 5; 1964
THE BIG T.N.T. SHOW
American International; 1966
THE INCIDENT
20th Century-Fox; 1967
GOODBYE, COLUMBUS
Paramount; 1969
THE SPORTING CLUB
Avco Embassy; 1971
A SEPARATE PEACE
Paramount; 1972
ASH WEDNESDAY
Paramount; 1973
THE STRANGER WHO LOOKS LIKE ME
Filmways; telefeature; 1974
THE OTHER SIDE OF THE MOUNTAIN
Universal; 1975
TWO-MINUTE WARNING
Universal; 1976
THE OTHER SIDE OF THE MOUNTAIN - PART 2
Universal; 1978
THE BELL JAR
Avco Embassy; 1979
WHY WOULD I LIE?
M-G-M/United Artists; 1980

Peeters, Barbara

THE DARK SIDE OF TOMORROW
co-director with Jacque Beerson; Able; 1970
BURY ME AN ANGEL
New World; 1972
SUMMER SCHOOL TEACHERS
New World; 1975
JUST THE TWO OF US
Boxoffice International; 1975
STARHOPS
First American; 1978
HUMANOIDS FROM THE DEEP
New World; 1980

Penn, Arthur
b. September 27, 1922
Philadelphia, Pennsylvania

THE LEFT HANDED GUN
Warner Brothers; 1958
THE MIRACLE WORKER
United Artists; 1962

continued

Penn, Arthur
continued
Business:
Florin Productions
1860 Broadway
New York, N.Y. 10023
(212) 582-1470
Agent:
I.C.M.
New York City
(212) 556-5600

MICKEY ONE
Columbia; 1965
THE CHASE
Columbia; 1966
BONNIE AND CLYDE
Warner Brothers; 1967
ALICE'S RESTAURANT
United Artists; 1969
LITTLE BIG MAN
National General; 1970
NIGHT MOVES
Warner Brothers; 1975
THE MISSOURI BREAKS
United Artists; 1976
FOUR FRIENDS
Filmways; 1981

Penn, Leo
Agent:
James McHugh, Jr. Agency
Los Angeles
(213) OL. 1-2770

QUARANTINED
Paramount TV; telefeature; 1970
TESTIMONY OF TWO MEN
co-director with Larry Yust; Universal TV; television mini-series; 1977
THE DARK SECRET OF HARVEST HOME
Universal TV; telefeature; 1978
MURDER IN MUSIC CITY
Frankel Films; telefeature; 1979
HELLINGER'S LAW
Universal TV; telefeature; 1981

Peppard, George
b. October 1, 1928
Detroit, Michigan
Home:
Box 1643
Beverly Hills, CA 90210
(213) 652-6622
Agent:
William Morris Agency
Beverly Hills
(213) 274-7451

FIVE DAYS FROM HOME
Universal; 1977

Perrier, Etienne
Contact:
French Film Office
745 Fifth Avenue
New York, N.Y. 10151
(212) 832-8860

BOBOSSE
1959; Belgian
MEURTRE EN 45 TOURS
1960; Belgian
BRIDGE TO THE SUN
M-G-M; 1961; U.S.-French
SWORDSMAN OF SIENA
M-G-M; 1962; Italian-French
DIS-MOI QUI TUER
1965; Belgian
DES GARCONS ET DES FILLES
1968; French
RUBLO DE LOS CARAS
1969
WHEN EIGHT BELLS TOLL
Cinerama Releasing Corporation; 1971; British
ZEPPELIN
Warner Brothers; 1971; British
A MURDER IS A MURDER...IS A MURDER
Levitt-Pickman; 1974; French
LA MAIN A COUPER
1974; French

Perry, Frank
b. 1930
New York, New York
Business:
Frank Perry Films
667 Madison Avenue
New York, N.Y. 10021
(212) 759-5714

DAVID AND LISA
Continental; 1962
LADYBUG, LADYBUG
United Artists; 1963
THE SWIMMER
Columbia; 1968

continued

Perry, Frank
continued

LAST SUMMER
Allied Artists; 1969
TRILOGY
Allied Artists; 1969; made for television
DIARY OF A MAD HOUSEWIFE
Universal; 1970
DOC
United Artists; 1971
PLAY IT AS IT LAYS
Universal; 1972
MAN ON A SWING
Paramount; 1974
RANCHO DeLUXE
United Artists; 1975
DUMMY
The Konigsberg Company/Warner Brothers TV; telefeature; 1979
SKAG
NBC-TV; telefeature; 1980
MOMMIE DEAREST
Paramount; 1981
MONSIGNORE
20th Century-Fox; 1982

Persky, Bill
Agent:
Creative Artists Agency
Los Angeles
(213) 277-4545

ROLL, FREDDY, ROLL!
ABC Circle Films; telefeature; 1974
HOW TO PICK UP GIRLS!
King-Hitzig Productions; telefeature; 1978
SERIAL
Paramount; 1980

Petri, Elio
b. January 29, 1929
Rome, Italy
Contact:
Minister of Tourism
Via Della Ferratella
No. 51
00184 Rome, Italy
06-7732

THE ASSASSIN (The Lady Killer of Rome)
Manson Distributing Corporation; 1961; Italian-French
I GIORNI CONTATI
1962; Italian
IL MAESTRO DI VIGEVANO
1963; Italian
HIGH INFIDELITY
co-director; Magna; 1965; Italian-French
THE TENTH VICTIM
Embassy; 1965; Italian
WE STILL KILL THE OLD WAY
Lopert; 1967; Italian
A QUIET PLACE IN THE COUNTRY
United Artists; 1968; Italian-French
INVESTIGATION OF A CITIZEN ABOVE SUSPICION
Columbia; 1970; Italian
THE WORKING CLASS GOES TO HEAVEN (Lulu the Tool)
1971; Italian
LA PROPRIETA NON E PIEU EN FURTO
1973; Italian
TODO MODO
1976; Italian

Petrie, Daniel
b. 1920
Agent:
I.C.M.
Hollywood
(213) 550-4135

THE BRAMBLE BUSH
Warner Brothers; 1960
A RAISIN IN THE SUN
Columbia; 1961
THE MAIN ATTRACTION
M-G-M; 1962
STOLEN HOURS
United Artists; 1963
THE IDOL
Embassy; 1966; British
THE SPY WITH A COLD NOSE
Embassy; 1966; British
SILENT NIGHT, LONELY NIGHT
Universal TV; telefeature; 1969
THE CITY
Universal TV; telefeature; 1971

continued

Petrie, Daniel
continued

A HOWLING IN THE WOODS
Universal TV; telefeature; 1971
MOON OF THE WOLF
Filmways; telefeature; 1972
HEC RAMSEY
Universal TV/Mark VII Ltd.; telefeature; 1972
TROUBLE COMES TO TOWN
ABC Circle Films; telefeature; 1973
THE NEPTUNE FACTOR
20th Century-Fox; 1973; Canadian
MOUSEY
Universal TV/Associated British Films; telefeature; 1974; U.S.-British
THE GUN AND THE PULPIT
Danny Thomas Productions; telefeature; 1974
BUSTER AND BILLIE
Columbia; 1974
RETURNING HOME
Lorimar Productions/Samuel Goldwyn Productions; telefeature; 1975
ELEANOR AND FRANKLIN
Talent Associates; telefeature; 1976
SYBIL
Lorimar Productions; telefeature; 1976
LIFEGUARD
Paramount; 1976
ELEANOR AND FRANKLIN: THE WHITE HOUSE YEARS
Talent Associates; telefeature; 1977
THE QUINNS
Daniel Wilson Productions; telefeature; 1977
THE BETSY
Allied Artists; 1978
RESURRECTION
Universal; 1980
FORT APACHE, THE BRONX
20th Century-Fox; 1981

Pevney, Joseph
b. 1920
New York, New York
Agent:
Herb Tobias & Assoc.
Los Angeles
(213) 277-6211

SHAKEDOWN
Universal; 1950
UNDERCOVER GIRL
Universal; 1950
AIR CADET
Universal; 1951
IRON MAN
Universal; 1951
THE LADY FROM TEXAS
Universal; 1951
THE STRANGE DOOR
Universal; 1951
MEET DANNY WILSON
Universal; 1952
FLESH AND FURY
Universal; 1952
JUST ACROSS THE STREET
Universal; 1952
BECAUSE OF YOU
Universal; 1952
DESERT LEGION
Universal; 1953
IT HAPPENS EVERY THURSDAY
Universal; 1953
BACK TO GOD'S COUNTRY
Universal; 1953
YANKEE PASHA
Universal; 1954
PLAYGIRL
Universal; 1954
THREE RING CIRCUS
Paramount; 1954
SIX BRIDGES TO CROSS
Universal; 1955
FOXFIRE
Universal; 1955
FEMALE ON THE BEACH
Universal; 1955

continued

Pevney, Joseph
continued

AWAY ALL BOATS
Universal; 1956
CONGO CROSSING
Universal; 1956
ISTANBUL
Universal; 1956
TAMMY AND THE BACHELOR
Universal; 1957
THE MIDNIGHT STORY
Universal; 1957
MAN OF A THOUSAND FACES
Universal; 1957
TWILIGHT FOR THE GODS
Universal; 1958
TORPEDO RUN
M-G-M; 1958
CASH McCALL
Warner Brothers; 1960
THE PLUNDERERS
Allied Artists; 1960
THE CROWDED SKY
Warner Brothers; 1960
PORTRAIT OF A MOBSTER
Warner Brothers; 1961
THE NIGHT OF THE GRIZZLY
Paramount; 1966
MY DARLING DAUGHTERS' ANNIVERSARY
Universal TV; telefeature; 1973
WHO IS THE BLACK DAHLIA?
Douglas S. Cramer Productions; telefeature; 1975
MYSTERIOUS ISLAND OF BEAUTIFUL WOMEN
Alan Landsburg Productions; telefeature; 1977

Peyser, John
Home:
19721 Redwing Street
Woodland Hills, CA 91364
(213) 884-7730
Agent:
Shapiro-Lichtman Agency
Los Angeles
(213) 557-2244

HONEYMOON WITH A STRANGER
20th Century-Fox TV; telefeature; 1969
CENTER FOLD GIRLS
Dimension; 1974
STUNT SEVEN
Martin Poll Productions; telefeature; 1979

Philips, Lee
Agent:
Shapiro-Lichtman Agency
Los Angeles
(213) 557-2244

GETTING AWAY FROM IT ALL
Palomar Pictures International; telefeature; 1972
THE GIRL MOST LIKELY TO...
ABC Circle Films; telefeature; 1973
THE STRANGER WITHIN
Lorimar Productions; telefeature; 1974
THE RED BADGE OF COURAGE
20th Century-Fox TV; telefeature; 1974
SWEET HOSTAGE
Brut Productions; telefeature; 1975
LOUIS ARMSTRONG - CHICAGO STYLE
Charles Fries Productions; telefeature; 1975
JAMES A. MICHENER'S DYNASTY
David Paradine TV; telefeature; 1976
WANTED: THE SUNDANCE WOMAN
20th Century-Fox TV; telefeature; 1976
THE SPELL
Charles Fries Productions; telefeature; 1977
THE WAR BETWEEN THE TATES
Talent Associates; telefeature; 1977
SPECIAL OLYMPICS
Roger Gimbel Productions/EMI TV; telefeature; 1978
THE COMEDY COMPANY
Merrit Malloy-Jerry Adler Productions; telefeature; 1978
SALVAGE
Bennett-Katleman Productions/Columbia TV; telefeature; 1979

continued

Philips, Lee
continued

VALENTINE
Malloy-Philips Productions/Edward S. Feldman Company; telefeature; 1979
HARDHAT AND LEGS
Syzygy Productions; telefeature; 1980
CRAZY TIMES
Kayden-Gleason Productions/George Reeves Productions/Warner Brothers TV; telefeature; 1981
ON THE RIGHT TRACK
20th Century-Fox; 1981

Pierce, Charles B.

THE LEGEND OF BOGGY CREEK
Howco International; 1973
BOOTLEGGERS
Howco International; 1974
WINTERHAWK
Howco International; 1975
THE WINDS OF AUTUMN
Howco International; 1976
THE TOWN THAT DREADED SUNDOWN
American International; 1977
GREYEAGLE
American International; 1977
THE NORSEMEN
American International; 1978
THE EVICTORS
American International; 1979

Pierson, Frank
Agent:
Adams, Ray & Rosenberg
Hollywood
(213) 278-3000

THE LOOKING GLASS WAR
Columbia; 1970; British
THE NEON CEILING
Universal TV; telefeature; 1971
A STAR IS BORN
Warner Brothers; 1976
KING OF THE GYPSIES
Paramount; 1978

Pinter, Harold
b. October 10, 1930
London, England

BUTLEY
American Film Theatre; 1974; British

Pintoff, Ernest
b. December 15, 1931
Watertown, Connecticut
Agent:
Century Artists
Beverly Hills
(213) 273-4366

HARVEY MIDDLEMAN, FIREMAN
Columbia; 1965
WHO KILLED MARY WHAT'S'ERNAME?
Cannon; 1971
DYNAMITE CHICKEN
EYR; 1972
HUMAN FEELINGS
Crestview Productions/Worldvision; telefeature;1978
JAGUAR LIVES
American International; 1979
LUNCH WAGON
Seymour Borde Associates; 1981
ST. HELENS
Davis/Panzer Productions; 1981

Pogostin, S. Lee
Agent:
Paul Kohner Agency
Los Angeles
(213) 550-1060

HARD CONTRACT
20th Century-Fox; 1969

Poitier, Sidney

b. February 20, 1924
Miami, Florida
Business:
Verdon Productions
9350 Wilshire Blvd.
Beverly Hills, CA 90212
(213) 274-7253
Agent:
Creative Artists Agency
Los Angeles
(213) 277-4545

BUCK AND THE PREACHER
Columbia; 1972
A WARM DECEMBER
National General; 1973
UPTOWN SATURDAY NIGHT
Warner Brothers; 1974
LET'S DO IT AGAIN
Warner Brothers; 1975
A PIECE OF THE ACTION
Warner Brothers; 1977
STIR CRAZY
Columbia; 1980
HANKY PANKY
Columbia; 1982

Polanski, Roman

b. August 18, 1933
Paris, France
Contact:
Directors Guild of America
Los Angeles
(213) 656-1220

KNIFE IN THE WATER
Kanawha; 1963; Polish
THE BEAUTIFUL SWINDLERS
co-director with Ugo Grigoretti, Claude Chabrol & Hiromichi Horikawa; Jack Ellis; 1964; French-Italian-Japanese-Dutch
REPULSION
Royal International; 1965; British
CUL-DE-SAC
Sigma III; 1966; British
THE FEARLESS VAMPIRE KILLERS, OR PARDON ME BUT YOUR TEETH ARE IN MY NECK (Dance of the Vampires)
M-G-M; 1967; British
ROSEMARY'S BABY
Paramount; 1968
MACBETH
Columbia; 1971; British
WHAT?
Avco Embassy; 1973; Italian-French-West German
CHINATOWN
Paramount; 1974
THE TENANT
Paramount; 1976; French-U.S.
TESS
Columbia; 1980; French-British

Pollack, Barry

COOL BREEZE
M-G-M; 1972
THIS IS A HIJACK
Fanfare; 1973

Pollack, Sydney

b. July 1, 1934
South Bend, Indiana
Business:
Mirage Productions
4000 Warner Blvd.
Burbank, CA 91522
(213) 943-6000
Agent:
Creative Artists Agency
Los Angeles
(213) 277-4545

THE SLENDER THREAD
Paramount; 1965
THIS PROPERTY IS CONDEMNED
Paramount; 1966
THE SCALPHUNTERS
United Artists; 1968
CASTLE KEEP
Columbia; 1969
THEY SHOOT HORSES, DON'T THEY?
Cinerama Releasing Corporation; 1969
JEREMIAH JOHNSON
Warner Brothers; 1972
THE WAY WE WERE
Columbia; 1973
THE YAKUZA
Warner Brothers; 1975
3 DAYS OF THE CONDOR
Paramount; 1975
BOBBY DEERFIELD
Columbia; 1977
THE ELECTRIC HORSEMAN
Columbia; 1979
ABSENCE OF MALICE
Columbia; 1981

Polonsky, Abraham
b. December 5, 1910
New York, New York
Agent:
Phil Gersh Agency
Beverly Hills
(213) 274-6611

FORCE OF EVIL
M-G-M; 1948
TELL THEM WILLIE BOY IS HERE
Universal; 1969
ROMANCE OF A HORSETHIEF
Allied Artists; 1971

Pontecorvo, Gillo
b. November 19, 1919
Pisa, Italy
Contact:
Minister of Tourism
Via Della Ferratella
No. 51
00184 Rome, Italy
06-7732

DIE WINDROSE
co-director; 1956; East German
LA GRANDE STRADA AZZURRA
1957; Italian
KAPO
1960; Italian
BATTLE OF ALGIERS
Rizzoli; 1967; Italian-Algerian
BURN!
United Artists; 1970; Italian-French
CRISTO NON VOLEVA MORIRE
1972; Italian
OPERATION OGRO
1979; Italian
TUNNEL
1979; Italian

Post, Ted
b. March 31, 1918
Brooklyn, New York
Business:
T.P. Films Ltd.
10889 Wilshire Blvd.
Los Angeles, CA 90024
(213) 820-2521
Agent:
Phil Gersh Agency
Beverly Hills
(213) 274-6611

THE PEACEMAKER
United Artists; 1956
THE LEGEND OF TOM DOOLEY
Columbia; 1959
HANG 'EM HIGH
United Artists; 1968
BENEATH THE PLANET OF THE APES
20th Century-Fox; 1970
NIGHT SLAVES
Bing Crosby Productions; telefeature; 1970
DR. COOK'S GARDEN
Paramount TV; telefeature; 1970
YUMA
Aaron Spelling Productions; telefeature; 1971
FIVE DESPERATE WOMEN
Aaron Spelling Productions; telefeature; 1971
DO NOT FOLD, SPINDLE OR MUTILATE
Lee Rich Productions; telefeature; 1971
THE BRAVOS
Universal TV; telefeature; 1972
SANDCASTLES
Metromedia Productions; telefeature; 1972
THE BABY
Scotia International; 1973; British
THE HARRAD EXPERIMENT
Cinerama Releasing Corporation; 1973
MAGNUM FORCE
Warner Brothers; 1973
WHIFFS
20th Century-Fox; 1975
GOOD GUYS WEAR BLACK
American Cinema; 1978
GO TELL THE SPARTANS
Avco Embassy; 1978
DIARY OF A TEENAGE HITCHHIKER
Shpetner Company; telefeature; 1979
THE GIRLS IN THE OFFICE
ABC Circle Films; telefeature; 1979
NIGHTKILL
Cine Artists; telefeature; 1980
CAGNEY & LACEY
Mace Neufeld Productions/Filmways; telefeature; 1981

Potterton, Gerald

HEAVY METAL
Columbia; 1981; Canadian

Powell, Michael

b. September 30, 1905
Canterbury, England
Business:
Zoetrope Studios
1040 N. Las Palmas Avenue
Hollywood, CA 90038
(213) 463-7191

TWO CROWDED HOURS
1931; British
MY FRIEND THE KING
1931; British
RYNOX
1931; British
THE RASP
1931; British
THE STAR REPORTER
1931; British
HOTEL SPLENDIDE
1932; British
BORN LUCKY
1932; British
C.O.D.
1932; British
HIS LORDSHIP
1932; British
THE FIRE RAISERS
1933; British
THE NIGHT OF THE PARTY
1934; British
RED ENSIGN
1934; British
SOMETHING ALWAYS HAPPENS
1934; British
THE GIRL IN THE CROWD
1934; British
SOME DAY
1935; British
LAZYBONES
1935; British
HER LAST AFFAIR
1935; British
THE LOVE TEST
1935; British
THE PRICE OF A SONG
1935; British
THE PHANTOM LIGHT
1935; British
THE BROWN WALLET
1936; British
CROWN VS. STEVENS
1936; British
THE MAN BEHIND THE MASK
1936; British
THE EDGE OF THE WORLD
1937; British
U-BOAT 29 (The Spy in Black)
Columbia; 1939; British
THE LION HAS WINGS
co-director with Brian Desmond Hurst & Adrian Brunel; 1939; British
THE THIEF OF BAGDAD
co-director with Ludwig Berger & Tim Whelan; United Artists; 1940; British
CONTRABAND (Blackout)
Anglo-American; 1940; British
THE FORTY-NINTH PARALLEL (The Invaders)
Columbia; 1941; British
ONE OF OUR AIRCRAFT IS MISSING
co-director with Emeric Pressburger; United Artists; 1942; British
THE VOLUNTEER
co-director with Emeric Pressburger; 1943; British
THE LIFE AND DEATH OF COLONEL BLIMP
co-director with Emeric Pressburger; Archers-General; 1943; British
A CANTERBURY TALE
co-director with Emeric Pressburger; 1944; British
I KNOW WHERE I'M GOING
co-director with Emeric Pressburger; Universal; 1945; British

continued

Powell, Michael
continued

STAIRWAY TO HEAVEN (A Matter of Life and Death)
co-director with Emeric Pressburger; Universal; 1946; British
BLACK NARCISSUS
co-director with Emeric Pressburger; Universal; 1947; British
THE RED SHOES
co-director with Emeric Pressburger; Eagle Lion; 1948; British
THE SMALL BACK ROOM (Hour of Glory)
co-director with Emeric Pressburger; Snader Productions; 1948; British
THE WILD HEART (Gone to Earth)
co-director with Emeric Pressburger; RKO Radio; 1950; British
THE ELUSIVE PIMPERNEL
co-director with Emeric Pressburger; 1950; British
THE TALES OF HOFFMANN
co-director with Emeric Pressburger; Lopert; 1951; British
OH ROSALINDA! (Fledermaus '55)
co-director with Emeric Pressburger; 1955; British
PURSUIT OF THE GRAF SPEE (The Battle of the River Plate)
co-director with Emeric Pressburger; Rank; 1956; British
NIGHT AMBUSH (Ill Met by Moonlight)
co-director with Emeric Pressburger; Rank; 1957; British
HONEYMOON (Luna de Miel)
RKO Radio; 1958; Spanish
PEEPING TOM
Astor; 1960; British
THE QUEEN'S GUARDS
20th Century-Fox; 1961; British
BLUEBEARD'S CASTLE
1964; British
THEY'RE A WEIRD MOB
1966; Australian
AGE OF CONSENT
Columbia; 1970; Australian
THE TEMPEST
1974; Greek-British

Preece, Michael
Home:
12233 Everglade Street
Mar Vista, CA 90066
(213) 390-6414
Business:
Charbridge Productions
1901 Avenue of the Stars
Los Angeles, CA 90067
(213) 277-9511
Agent:
Herb Tobias & Assoc.
Hollywood
(213) 277-6211

THE PRIZE FIGHTER
New World; 1979
PARADISE CONNECTION
Woodruff Productions/QM Productions; telefeature; 1979

Preminger, Otto
b. December 5, 1906
Vienna, Austria
Business:
Sigma Productions, Inc.
129 East 64th Street
New York, N.Y. 10021
(212) 535-6001

DIE GROSSE LIEBE
1931; Austrian-German
UNDER YOUR SPELL
20th Century-Fox; 1936
DANGER - LOVE AT WORK
20th Century-Fox; 1937
MARGIN FOR ERROR
20th Century-Fox; 1943
IN THE MEANTIME, DARLING
20th Century-Fox; 1944
LAURA
20th Century-Fox; 1944

continued

Preminger, Otto
continued

A ROYAL SCANDAL
20th Century-Fox; 1945
FALLEN ANGEL
20th Century-Fox; 1945
CENTENNIAL SUMMER
20th Century-Fox; 1946
FOREVER AMBER
20th Century-Fox; 1947
DAISY KENYON
20th Century-Fox; 1947
THE FAN
20th Century-Fox; 1949
WHIRLPOOL
20th Century-Fox; 1950
WHERE THE SIDEWALK ENDS
20th Century-Fox; 1950
THE 13TH LETTER
20th Century-Fox; 1951
ANGEL FACE
RKO Radio; 1953
THE MOON IS BLUE
United Artists; 1953
RIVER OF NO RETURN
20th Century-Fox; 1954
CARMEN JONES
20th Century-Fox; 1955
THE MAN WITH THE GOLDEN ARM
United Artists; 1955
THE COURT-MARTIAL OF BILLY MITCHELL
Warner Brothers; 1955
SAINT JOAN
United Artists; 1957
BONJOUR TRISTESSE
Columbia; 1958
PORGY AND BESS
Columbia; 1959
ANATOMY OF A MURDER
Columbia; 1959
EXODUS
United Artists; 1960
ADVISE AND CONSENT
Columbia; 1962
THE CARDINAL
Columbia; 1963
IN HARM'S WAY
Paramount; 1964
BUNNY LAKE IS MISSING
Columbia; 1965; British
HURRY SUNDOWN
Paramount; 1967
SKIDOO
Paramount; 1968
TELL ME THAT YOU LOVE ME, JUNIE MOON
Paramount; 1970
SUCH GOOD FRIENDS
Paramount; 1971
ROSEBUD
United Artists; 1975
THE HUMAN FACTOR
United Artists; 1979; British

Pressman, Michael
Home:
8635 Lookout Mountain Ave.
Los Angeles, CA 90046
(213) 654-7996
Agent:
Creative Artists Agency
Los Angeles
(213) 277-4545

THE GREAT TEXAS DYNAMITE CHASE
New World; 1976
THE BAD NEWS BEARS IN BREAKING TRAINING
Paramount; 1977
LIKE MOM, LIKE ME
CBS Entertainment; telefeature; 1978
BOULEVARD NIGHTS
Warner Brothers; 1979
THOSE LIPS, THOSE EYES
United Artists; 1980
SOME KIND OF HERO
Paramount; 1981

Prince, Harold

SOMETHING FOR EVERYONE
National General; 1970; British
A LITTLE NIGHT MUSIC
New World; 1978; Austrian-U.S.

Pyun, Albert

THE SWORD AND THE SORCERER
Group 1; 1982

Quested, John
Contact:
British Film Institute
127 Charing Cross Road
London W.C. 2, England
01-437-4355

LOOPHOLE
M-G-M/United Artists; 1981; British

Quine, Richard
b. November 12, 1920
Detroit, Michigan
Agent:
Creative Artists Agency
Los Angeles
(213) 277-4545
Business Manager:
Laney, Weidenbaum & Ryder
Beverly Hills
(213) 277-7611

LEATHER GLOVES
co-director with William Asher; Columbia; 1948
SUNNY SIDE OF THE STREET
Columbia; 1951
PURPLE HEART DIARY
Columbia; 1951
SOUND OFF
Columbia; 1952
RAINBOW 'ROUND MY SHOULDER
Columbia; 1952
ALL ASHORE
Columbia; 1953
SIREN OF BAGDAD
Columbia; 1953
CRUISIN' DOWN THE RIVER
Columbia; 1953
DRIVE A CROOKED ROAD
Columbia; 1954
PUSHOVER
Columbia; 1954
SO THIS IS PARIS
Universal; 1955
MY SISTER EILEEN
Columbia; 1955
THE SOLID GOLD CADILLAC
Columbia; 1956
FULL OF LIFE
Columbia; 1957
OPERATION MAD BALL
Columbia; 1957
BELL, BOOK AND CANDLE
Columbia; 1958
IT HAPPENED TO JANE
Columbia; 1959
STRANGERS WHEN WE MEET
Columbia; 1960
THE WORLD OF SUZIE WONG
Paramount; 1960
THE NOTORIOUS LANDLADY
Columbia; 1962
PARIS WHEN IT SIZZLES
Paramount; 1964
SEX AND THE SINGLE GIRL
Warner Brothers; 1965
HOW TO MURDER YOUR WIFE
United Artists; 1965
SYNANON
Columbia; 1965
OH DAD, POOR DAD, MOMMA'S HUNG YOU IN THE CLOSET AND I'M FEELING SO SAD
Paramount; 1967
HOTEL
Warner Brothers; 1967
A TALENT FOR LOVING
1969
THE MOONSHINE WAR
M-G-M; 1970

continued

Quine, Richard
continued

"W"
Cinerama Releasing Corporation; 1974; British
THE SPECIALISTS
Mark VII Ltd./Universal TV; telefeature; 1975
THE PRISONER OF ZENDA
Universal; 1979

Quinn, Anthony
b. April 21, 1915
Chihuahua, Mexico

THE BUCCANEER
Paramount; 1959

Quintero, Jose
Agent:
The Lantz Office
New York City
(212) 751-2107

THE ROMAN SPRING OF MRS. STONE
Warner Brothers; 1961

Rae, Michael

LASERBLAST
Irwin Yablans; 1978

Rafelson, Bob
b. 1934
New York, New York
Business:
1400 N. Fuller Avenue
Hollywood, CA 90046

HEAD
Columbia; 1968
FIVE EASY PIECES
Columbia; 1970
THE KING OF MARVIN GARDENS
Columbia; 1972
STAY HUNGRY
United Artists; 1976
THE POSTMAN ALWAYS RINGS TWICE
Paramount/Lorimar; 1981

Raffill, Stewart

THE TENDER WARRIOR
Safari; 1971
THE ADVENTURES OF THE WILDERNESS FAMILY
Pacific International; 1975
ACROSS THE GREAT DIVIDE
Pacific International; 1976
THE SEA GYPSIES
Warner Brothers; 1978
HIGH RISK
American Cinema; 1981

Rafkin, Alan
Home:
10701 Wilshire Blvd.
Los Angeles, CA 90024
(213) 475-9952
Personal Manager:
The Brillstein Company
Hollywood
(213) 275-6135

SKI PARTY
American International; 1965
THE GHOST AND MR. CHICKEN
Universal; 1966
THE RIDE TO HANGMAN'S TREE
Universal; 1967
NOBODY'S PERFECT
Universal; 1968
THE SHAKIEST GUN IN THE WEST
Universal; 1968
ANGEL IN MY POCKET
Universal; 1969
HOW TO FRAME A FIGG
Universal; 1971
LET'S SWITCH
Universal TV; telefeature; 1975

Rakoff, Alvin
Business:
Jara Productions Ltd.
1 The Orchard
Chiswick
London W41JZ, England
01-994-1269

ON FRIDAY AT 11
British
CROSSPLOT
British
WORLD IN MY POCKET
M-G-M; 1962; West German-French-Italian

continued

Rakoff, Alvin
continued

THE COMEDY MAN
Continental; 1964; British
HOFFMAN
Levitt-Pickman; 1971; British
SAY HELLO TO YESTERDAY
Cinerama Releasing Corporation; 1971; British
THE ADVENTURES OF DON QUIXOTE
Universal TV/BBC-TV; telefeature; 1973; U.S.-British
KING SOLOMON'S TREASURE
1978
CITY ON FIRE!
Avco Embassy; 1979; Canadian
DEATH SHIP
Avco Embassy; 1980; Canadian
DIRTY TRICKS
Avco Embassy; 1981; Canadian

Ramis, Harold
Business Manager:
David Kahn
Chicago
(312) 236-2351

CADDYSHACK
Orion Pictures/Warner Brothers; 1980

Rapper, Irving
b. 1898
London, England
Home:
7250 Franklin Avenue
Los Angeles, CA 90046
(213) 876-6000

SHINING VICTORY
Warner Brothers; 1941
ONE FOOT IN HEAVEN
Warner Brothers; 1941
THE GAY SISTERS
Warner Brothers; 1942
NOW, VOYAGER
Warner Brothers; 1942
THE ADVENTURES OF MARK TWAIN
Warner Brothers; 1944
THE CORN IS GREEN
Warner Brothers; 1945
RHAPSODY IN BLUE
Warner Brothers; 1945
DECEPTION
Warner Brothers; 1946
THE VOICE OF THE TURTLE
Warner Brothers; 1947
ANNA LUCASTA
Columbia; 1949
THE GLASS MENAGERIE
Warner Brothers; 1950
ANOTHER MAN'S POISON
United Artists; 1952; British
BAD FOR EACH OTHER
Columbia; 1954
FOREVER FEMALE
Paramount; 1954
STRANGE INTRUDER
Allied Artists; 1956
THE BRAVE ONE
Universal; 1956
MARJORIE MORNINGSTAR
Warner Brothers; 1958
THE MIRACLE
Warner Brothers; 1959
THE STORY OF JOSEPH AND HIS BRETHREN
English Language Version; Colorama; 1960; Italian
PONTIUS PILATE
U.S. Films; 1962; Italian-French
THE CHRISTINE JORGENSEN STORY
United Artists; 1970
BORN AGAIN
Avco Embassy; 1978

Rash, Steve
Business:
Innovisions, Inc.
11751 Mississippi Avenue
Los Angeles, CA 90025
(213) 478-3523

THE BUDDY HOLLY STORY
Columbia; 1978
UNDER THE RAINBOW
Orion Pictures/Warner Brothers; 1981

Ray, Satyajit
b. May 2, 1921
Calcutta, India

PATHER PANCHALI
Harrison; 1955; Indian
APARAJITO
Harrison; 1956; Indian
PARAS PATHAR
1957; Indian
THE MUSIC ROOM
Harrison; 1958; Indian
THE WORLD OF APU
Harrison; 1959; Indian
DEVI
Harrison; 1960; Indian
RABINDRANATH TAGORE
1961; Indian
TWO DAUGHTERS
Janus; 1961; Indian
KANCHENJUNGHA
Harrison; 1962; Indian
EXPEDITION
1962; Indian
THE BIG CITY
1963; Indian
CHARULATA, THE LONELY WIFE
Trans-World; 1964; Indian
THE COWARD AND THE SAINT
1966; Indian
THE HERO
1966; Indian
THE ZOO
1967; Indian
THE ADVENTURES OF GOOPY AND BAGHA
Purnima Pictures; 1968; Indian
DAYS AND NIGHTS IN THE FOREST
Pathe Contemporary; 1970; Indian
THE ADVERSARY
Audio Brandon; 1971; Indian
SIMABADDHA
1972; Indian
DISTANT THUNDER
Cinema 5; 1973; Indian
THE MIDDLEMAN
Bauer International;
THE CHESS PLAYERS
Creative; 1977; Indian
THE KINGDOM OF DIAMONDS
1980; Indian

Redford, Robert
(Charles Robert Redford)
b. August 18, 1937
Santa Monica, California

ORDINARY PEOPLE
Paramount; 1980

Reeve, Geoffrey
Contact:
British Film Institute
127 Charing Cross Road
London W.C. 2, England
01-437-4355

PUPPET ON A CHAIN
co-director with Don Sharp;Cinerama Releasing Corporation; 1972; British
CARAVAN TO VACCARES
Bryanston; 1976; British-French

Reichert, Mark

UNION CITY
Kinesis; 1980

Reichenbach, Francois
b. July 3, 1922
Paris, France
Contact:
French Film Office
745 Fifth Avenue
New York, N.Y.
(212) 832-8860

L'AMERIQUE INSOLITE
1960; French
THE WINNER
1961; French
LES AMOUREAUX DU "FRANCE"
co-director with Pierre Grimblat; 1963; French
GRENOBLE
co-director with Claude Lelouch; 1968; French

continued

Reichenbach, Francois
continued

MEXICO MEXICO
1969; French
ARTHUR RUBINSTEIN: LOVE OF LIFE
co-director with Gerard Patris; 1970; French
L'INDISCRETE
1970; French
MEDICINE BALL CARAVAN
Warner Brothers; 1971; French-U.S.
YEHUDI MENUHIN - ROAD OF LIGHT
co-director with Bernard Gavoty; 1971; French
LA RAISON DU PLUS FOU
co-director; 1973; French
DON'T YOU HEAR THE DOGS BARK?
1975; Mexican
SEX O'CLOCK
1976
ANOTHER WAY TO LOVE
1976; French
PELE
1977; French

Reid, Alastair
Contact:
British Film Institute
127 Charing Cross Road
London W.C. 2, England
01-437-4355

BABY LOVE
Avco Embassy; 1969; British
THE NIGHT DIGGER
M-G-M; 1971; British

Reiner, Carl
b. March 20, 1922
Bronx, New York
Personal Manager:
Shapiro-West & Assoc.
Beverly Hills
(213) 278-8896

ENTER LAUGHING
Columbia; 1967
THE COMIC
Columbia; 1969
WHERE'S POPPA?
United Artists; 1970
THE ONE AND ONLY
Paramount; 1978
OH, GOD!
Warner Brothers; 1978
THE JERK
Universal; 1979
DEAD MEN DON'T WEAR PLAID
Aspen Film Society; 1982

Reisner, Allen
Home:
(213) 274-2844
Agent:
William Morris Agency
Beverly Hills
(213) 274-7451

ST. LOUIS BLUES
Paramount; 1958
ALL MINE TO GIVE (The Day They Gave Babies Away)
Universal; 1958
TO DIE IN PARIS
co-director with Charles Dubin; Universal TV: telefeature; 1968
YOUR MONEY OR YOUR WIFE
Brentwood Productions; telefeature; 1972
CAPTAINS AND THE KINGS
co-director with Douglas Heyes; Universal TV; television mini-series; 1976
MARY JANE HARPER CRIED LAST NIGHT
Paramount TV; telefeature; 1977
COPS AND ROBIN
Paramount TV; telefeature; 1978
THE LOVE TAPES
Christiana Productions/M-G-M TV; telefeature; 1980

Reisz, Karel
b. July 21, 1926
Ostrava, Czechoslovakia
Agent:
William Morris Agency
Beverly Hills
(213) 274-7451

WE ARE THE LAMBETH BOYS
Rank; 1958; British
SATURDAY NIGHT AND SUNDAY MORNING
Continental; 1961; British
NIGHT MUST FALL
Embassy; 1964; British

continued

Reisz, Karel
continued

MORGAN! (Morgan: A Suitable Case for Treatment)
Cinema 5; 1966; British
ISADORA (The Loves of Isadora)
Universal; 1969; British
THE GAMBLER
Paramount; 1974
WHO'LL STOP THE RAIN
United Artists; 1978
THE FRENCH LIEUTENANT'S WOMAN
United Artists; 1981; British

Reitherman, Wolfgang
Business:
Walt Disney Productions
500 S. Buena Vista Street
Burbank, CA 91521
(213) 845-3141

101 DALMATIONS
co-director with Hamilton S. Luke & Clyde Geronimi; Buena Vista; 1961
THE SWORD IN THE STONE
Buena Vista; 1963
THE JUNGLE BOOK
Buena Vista; 1967
THE ARISTOCATS
Buena Vista; 1970
ROBIN HOOD
Buena Vista; 1973
THE RESCUERS
Buena Vista; 1977

Reitman, Ivan
Contact:
Directors Guild of America
Los Angeles
(213) 277-4545

FOXY LADY
Ivan Reitman Productions; 1971; Canadian
CANNIBAL GIRLS
American International; 1973; Canadian
MEATBALLS
Paramount; 1979; Canadian
STRIPES
Columbia; 1981

Resnais, Alain
b. June 3, 1922
Vannes, France
Contact:
French Film Office
745 Fifth Avenue
New York, N.Y. 10151
(212) 832-8860

HIROSHIMA, MON AMOUR
Zenith; 1959; French
LAST YEAR AT MARIENBAD
Astor; 1961; French-Italian
MURIEL
Lopert; 1963; French-Italian
LA GUERRE EST FINIE
Brandon; 1966; French-Swedish
FAR FROM VIETNAM
co-director with Jean-Luc Godard, William Klein, Claude Lelouch, Agnes Varda & Joris Ivens; New Yorker; 1967; French
JE T'AIME, JE T'AIME
New Yorker; 1968; French-Spanish
STAVISKY
Cinemation; 1974; French
PROVIDENCE
Cinema 5; 1977; French-Swiss
MON ONCLE D'AMERIQUE
New World; 1980; French

Reynolds, Burt
b. February 11, 1936
Waycross, Georgia
Business:
8730 Sunset Blvd.
Los Angeles, CA 90069
(213) 652-6005
Personal Manager:
Dick Clayton
Los Angeles
(213) 659-5186

GATOR
United Artists; 1976
THE END
United Artists; 1978
SHARKY'S MACHINE
Orion Pictures/Warner Brothers; 1982

Rich, David Lowell
b. 1923(?)
Business:
Boulder Brook, Inc.
9000 Sunset Blvd.
Los Angeles, CA 90069
(213) 273-9050
Agent:
Shapiro-Lichtman Agency
Los Angeles
(213) 557-2244

NO TIME TO BE YOUNG
Columbia; 1957
SENIOR PROM
Columbia; 1958
HEY BOY! HEY GIRL!
Columbia; 1959
HAVE ROCKET, WILL TRAVEL
Columbia; 1959
SEE HOW THEY RUN
Universal TV; telefeature; 1964
MADAME X
Universal; 1966
THE PLAINSMAN
Universal; 1966
ROSIE!
Universal; 1967
WINGS OF FIRE
Universal TV; telefeature; 1967
THE BORGIA STICK
Universal TV; telefeature; 1967
A LOVELY WAY TO DIE
Universal; 1968
THREE GUNS FOR TEXAS
co-director with Paul Stanley & Earl Bellamy; Universal; 1968
MARCUS WELBY, M.D.
Universal; telefeature; 1969
EYE OF THE CAT
Universal; 1969
THE MASK OF SHEBA
M-G-M TV; telefeature; 1970
BERLIN AFFAIR
Universal TV; telefeature; 1970
THE SHERIFF
Screen Gems/Columbia TV; telefeature; 1971
ASSIGNMENT: MUNICH
M-G-M TV; telefeature; 1972
LIEUTENANT SCHUSTER'S WIFE
Universal TV; telefeature; 1972
ALL MY DARLING DAUGHTERS
Universal TV; telefeature; 1972
THAT MAN BOLT
co-director with Henry Levin; Universal; 1972
THE JUDGE AND JAKE WYLER
Universal TV; telefeature; 1972
SET THIS TOWN ON FIRE
Universal TV;telefeature;1973;filmed in 1969
THE HORROR AT 37,000 FEET
CBS, Inc.; telefeature; 1973
BROCK'S LAST CASE
Talent Associates/Universal TV; telefeature; 1973
CRIME CLUB
CBS, Inc.; telefeature; 1973
BEG, BORROW...OR STEAL
Universal TV; telefeature; 1973
SATAN'S SCHOOL FOR GIRLS
Spelling-Goldberg Productions; telefeature; 1973
RUNAWAY!
Universal TV; telefeature; 1973
DEATH RACE
Universal TV; telefeature; 1973
THE CHADWICK FAMILY
Universal TV; telefeature; 1974
THE SEX SYMBOL
Screen Gems/Columbia; telefeature; 1974
ALOHA MEANS GOODBYE
Universal TV; telefeature; 1974
THE DAUGHTERS OF JOSHUA CABE RETURN
Spelling-Goldberg Productions; telefeature; 1975
ADVENTURES OF THE QUEEN
20th Century-Fox TV; telefeature; 1975
YOU LIE SO DEEP, MY LOVE
Universal TV; telefeature; 1975

continued

Rich, David Lowell
continued

BRIDGER
Universal TV; telefeature; 1976
THE SECRET LIFE OF JOHN CHAPMAN
The Jozak Company; telefeature; 1976
THE STORY OF DAVID
co-director with Alex Segal; ABC-TV; telefeature; 1976
SST - DEATH FLIGHT
ABC Circle Films; telefeature; 1977
RANSOM FOR ALICE!
Universal TV; telefeature; 1977
TELETHON
ABC Circle Films; telefeature; 1977
THE DEFECTION OF SIMAS KUDIRKA
The Jozak Company/Paramount TV; telefeature; 1978
A FAMILY UPSIDE DOWN
Ross Hunter-Jacques Mapes Film/Paramount TV; telefeature; 1978
LITTLE WOMEN
Universal TV; telefeature; 1978
THE CONCORDE - AIRPORT '79
Universal; 1979
NURSE
Robert Halmi Productions; telefeature; 1980
ENOLA GAY
The Production Company/Viacom; telefeature; 1980
CHU CHU AND THE PHILLY FLASH
20th Century-Fox; 1981

Rich, John
b. July 6, 1925
Rockaway Beach, New York
Business:
John Rich Productions
4151 Prospect Avenue
Los Angeles, CA 90027
(213) 557-7777
Business Manager:
Marvin Freedman
Los Angeles
(213) 277-0700

WIVES AND LOVERS
Paramount; 1963
THE NEW INTERNS
Columbia; 1964
ROUSTABOUT
Paramount; 1964
BOEING BOEING
Paramount; 1965
EASY COME, EASY GO
Paramount; 1967

Rich, Richard
Business:
Walt Disney Productions
500 S. Buena Vista Street
Burbank, CA 91521
(213) 845-3141

THE FOX AND THE HOUND
co-director with Art Stevens & Ted Berman; Buena Vista; 1981

Richards, Dick
Agent:
William Morris Agency
Beverly Hills
(213) 274-7451

THE CULPEPPER CATTLE CO.
20th Century-Fox; 1972
RAFFERTY AND THE GOLD DUST TWINS
Warner Brothers; 1975
FAREWELL, MY LOVELY
Avco Embassy; 1975
MARCH OR DIE
Columbia; 1977; British
DEATH VALLEY
Universal; 1981

Richards, Lloyd
Business:
O'Heill Center
1860 Broadway
New York, N.Y. 10023
(212) 246-1485

ROOTS: THE NEXT GENERATIONS
co-director with John Erman, Charles S. Dubin & Georg Stanford Brown; Wolper Productions; television mini-series; 1979

Richardson, Tony

(Cecil Antonio Richardson)
b. June 5, 1928
Shipley, England
Business:
1478 N. Kings Road
Los Angeles, CA 90069

LOOK BACK IN ANGER
Warner Brothers; 1958; British
THE ENTERTAINER
Continental; 1960; British
SANCTUARY
20th Century-Fox; 1961
A TASTE OF HONEY
Continental; 1962; British
THE LONELINESS OF THE LONG DISTANCE RUNNER
Continental; 1962; British
TOM JONES
Lopert; 1963; British
THE LOVED ONE
M-G-M; 1965
MADEMOISELLE
Lopert; 1966; French-British
THE SAILOR FROM GIBRALTER
Lopert; 1967; British
THE CHARGE OF THE LIGHT BRIGADE
United Artists; 1968; British
LAUGHTER IN THE DARK
Lopert; 1969; British-French
HAMLET
Columbia; 1969; British
NED KELLY
United Artists; 1970; British
A DELICATE BALANCE
American Film Theatre; 1973
DEAD CERT
United Artists; 1973; British
JOSEPH ANDREWS
Paramount; 1977; British
A DEATH IN CANAAN
Chris-Rose Productions/Warner Brothers TV; telefeature; 1978
THE BORDER
Universal; 1982

Richert, William

Contact:
Directors Guild of America
Los Angeles
(213) 656-1220

FIRST POSITION
Roninfilm; 1973
WINTER KILLS
Avco Embassy; 1979
THE AMERICAN SUCCESS COMPANY (Success)
Columbia; 1979

Risi, Dino

b. December 23, 1917
Milan, Italy
Contact:
Minister of Tourism
Via Della Ferratella
No. 51
00184 Rome, Italy
06-7732

VACANZE COL GANGSTER
1952; Italian
IL VIALE DELLA SPERANZA
1953; Italian
LOVE IN THE CITY
co-director; Italian Films Export; 1953; Italian
THE SIGN OF VENUS
1955; Italian
SCANDAL IN SORRENTO
DCA; 1955; Italian-French
POOR BUT BEAUTIFUL
Trans-Lux; 1956; Italian
LA NONNA SABELLA
1957; Italian
BEAUTIFUL BUT POOR
1957; Italian
VENEZIA LA LUNA E TU
1958; Italian
POVERI MILIONARI
1959; Italian
IL VEDOVO
1959; Italian
LOVE AND LARCENY
Major Film; 1960; Italian-French
UN AMORE A ROMA
1960; Italian
BEHIND CLOSED DOORS
1960; Italian

continued

Risi, Dino
continued

A DIFFICULT LIFE
1961; Italian
THE EASY LIFE
Embassy; 1962; Italian
IL GIOVEDI
1962; Italian
15 FROM ROME
McAbee; 1963; Italian-French
IL GAUCHO
1964; Italian
BAMBOLE!
co-director; Royal Films International; 1965; Italian
I COMPLESSI
co-director; 1965; Italian
WEEKEND, ITALIAN STYLE
Marvin; 1966; Italian-French-Spanish
I NOSTRI MARITI
co-director; 1966; Italian
TREASURE OF SAN GENNARO
Paramount; 1966; Italian-French-West German
THE TIGER AND THE PUSSYCAT
Embassy; 1967; Italian-U.S.
IL PROFETA
1967; Italian
STRAZIAMI MA DI BACI SAZIAMI
1968; Italian
VEDO NUDO
1969; Italian
IL GIOVANE NORMALE
1969; Italian
THE PRIEST'S WIFE
Warner Brothers; 1970; Italian-French
NOI DONNE SIAMO FATTE COSI
1971; Italian
IN NOME DEL POPOLO ITALIANO
1972; Italian
MORDI E FUGGI
1973; Italian
HOW FUNNY CAN SEX BE?
In-Frame; 1973; Italian
DUCK A L'ORANGE
1975; Italian
SCENT OF A WOMAN
20th Century-Fox; 1976; Italian
THE PROPHET
Joseph Green Pictures; 1976; Italian
THE CAREER OF A CHAMBERMAID
1976; Italian
ANIMA PERSA
1977; Italian
LA STANZA DEL VESCOVO
1977; Italian
VIVA ITALIA!
co-director with Mario Monicelli & Ettore Scola;Cinema 5; 1978; Italian
PRIMO AMORE
1978; Italian
CARO PAPA
1979; Italian-French-Canadian
SUNDAY LOVERS
co-director with Bryan Forbes, Edouard Molinaro & Gene Wilder; M-G-M/United Artists; 1980; U.S.-British-Italian-French

Ritchie, Michael
b. 1938
Waukesha, Wisconsin
Business:
Miracle Pictures
22 Miller Avenue
Mill Valley, CA 94941
(415) 383-2564
Business Manager:
Marvin Freedman
Los Angeles
(213) 277-4545

THE OUTSIDER
Universal TV; telefeature; 1967
THE SOUND OF ANGER
Universal TV; telefeature; 1968
DOWNHILL RACER
Paramount; 1969
PRIME CUT
National General; 1972
THE CANDIDATE
Warner Brothers; 1972

continued

Ritchie, Michael
continued

SMILE
United Artists; 1975
THE BAD NEWS BEARS
Paramount; 1976
SEMI-TOUGH
United Artists; 1978
AN ALMOST PERFECT AFFAIR
Paramount; 1979
THE ISLAND
Universal; 1980
DIVINE MADNESS
The Ladd Company/Warner Brothers; 1980

Ritt, Martin
b. March 2, 1920
New York, New York
Agent:
Chasin-Park-Citron
Los Angeles
(213) 273-7190

EDGE OF THE CITY
M-G-M; 1957
NO DOWN PAYMENT
20th Century-Fox; 1957
THE LONG HOT SUMMER
M-G-M; 1958
THE BLACK ORCHID
Paramount; 1959
THE SOUND AND THE FURY
20th Century-Fox; 1959
FIVE BRANDED WOMEN
Paramount; 1960; Italian-Yugoslavian-U.S.
PARIS BLUES
United Artists; 1961
HEMINGWAY'S ADVENTURES OF A YOUNG MAN
20th Century-Fox; 1962
HUD
Paramount; 1963
THE OUTRAGE
M-G-M; 1964
THE SPY WHO CAME IN FROM THE COLD
Paramount; 1965; British
HOMBRE
20th Century-Fox; 1967
THE BROTHERHOOD
Paramount; 1968
THE MOLLY MAGUIRES
Paramount; 1970
THE GREAT WHITE HOPE
20th Century-Fox; 1970
SOUNDER
20th Century-Fox; 1972
PETE 'N' TILLIE
Universal; 1972
CONRACK
20th Century-Fox; 1974
THE FRONT
Columbia; 1976
CASEY'S SHADOW
Columbia; 1978
NORMA RAE
20th Century-Fox; 1979
BACK ROADS
Warner Brothers; 1981

Rivers, Joan
Personal Manager:
Katz-Gallin-Morey
Los Angeles
(213) 273-4210

RABBIT TEST
Avco Embassy; 1978

Robbe-Grillet, Alain
b. August 18, 1922
Brest, France
Contact:
French Film Office
745 Fifth Avenue
New York, N.Y. 10151
(212) 832-8860

L'IMMORTELLE
Grove Press; 1963; French
TRANS-EUROP-EXPRESS
Trans-American; 1967; French
THE MAN WHO LIES
Grove Press; 1968; French-Czech

continued

Robbe-Grillet, Alain
continued

EDEN AND AFTER
1970; French-Czech
LES GOMMES
1972; French
GLISSEMENTS PROGRESSIFS DU PLAISIR
1973; French
LE JEU AVEC LE FEU
1975; Italian-French
PIEGE A FOURRURE
1977; French

Robbie, Seymour
Home:
9980 Liebe Drive
Beverly Hills, CA 90210
(213) 274-6713

C.C. AND COMPANY
Avco Embassy; 1970
MARCO
Cinerama Releasing Corporation; 1974

Robbins, Jerome
(Jerome Rabinowitz)
b. October 11, 1918
Weehawken, New Jersey
Contact:
Directors Guild of America
New York City
(212) 581-0370

WEST SIDE STORY
co-director with Robert Wise; United Artists; 1961

Robbins, Matthew
Contact:
Directors Guild of America
Los Angeles
(213) 656-1220

CORVETTE SUMMER
M-G-M/United Artists; 1978
DRAGONSLAYER
Paramount; 1981; U.S.-British

Robert, Yves
b. June 19, 1920
Saumur, France
Contact:
French Film Office
745 Fifth Avenue
New York, N.Y. 10151
(212) 832-8860

LES HOMMES NE PENSENT QU'A CA
1954; French
SIGNE ARSENE LUPIN
1959; French
LA FAMILLE FENOUILLARD
1961; French
WAR OF THE BUTTONS
1962; French
BEBERT ET L'OMNIBUS
1963; French
LES COPAINS
1964; French
MONNAIE DE SINGE
1965; French
VERY HAPPY ALEXANDER (Alexander)
Cinema 5; 1968; French
CLERAMBARD
1969; French
THE TALL BLOND MAN WITH ONE BLACK SHOE
Cinema 5; 1972; French
SALUT L'ARTISTE
Exxel; 1973; French
RETURN OF THE TALL BLOND MAN WITH ONE BLACK SHOE
Lanir Releasing; 1974; French
PARDON MON AFFAIRE (An Elephant Ca Trompe Enormement)
First Artists; 1977; French
PARDON MON AFFAIRE, TOO! (Nous Irons Tous Au Paradis)
First Artists; 1978; French

Roberts, Alan

THE ZODIAC COUPLES
co-director with Bob Stein; SAE; 1970
PANORAMA BLUE
Ellman Film Enterprises; 1974

continued

Roberts, Alan
continued

YOUNG LADY CHATTERLEY
1976
THE HAPPY HOOKER GOES HOLLYWOOD
Cannon; 1980

Robertson, Cliff
b. September 9, 1925
La Jolla, California
Agent:
I.C.M.
Hollywood
(213) 550-4000

J.W. COOP
Columbia; 1972
THE PILOT
Summit Features; 1981

Robertson, Hugh A.
Home:
208A Terrace Vale Road
Good Wood Park
Trinidad, West Indies
637-5994
Business:
Sharc Productions Ltd.
1 Valleton Avenue
Maraval
Trinidad, West Indies
62-26580
Agent:
Ron Mutchnick
Los Angeles
(213) 659-3294

MELINDA
M-G-M; 1972
BIM
Sharc Productions; 1976; West Indian

Roddam, Franc

QUADROPHENIA
World Northal; 1979; British

Roeg, Nicolas
b. 1928
London, England
Home:
2 Oxford-Cambridge
Mansions
Old Marylebone Road
London N.W. 1, England
262-8612
Agent:
Robert Littman
Hollywood
(213) 274-6054

PERFORMANCE
co-director with Donald Cammell; Warner Brothers; 1970; British
WALKABOUT
20th Century-Fox; 1971; British-Australian
DON'T LOOK NOW
Paramount; 1974; British-Italian
THE MAN WHO FELL TO EARTH
Cinema 5; 1976; British
BAD TIMING/A SENSUAL OBSESSION
World Northal; 1980; British

Roemer, Michael
b. January 1, 1928
Berlin, Germany

A TOUCH OF THE TIMES
1949
CORTILE CASCINO
unreleased
NOTHING BUT A MAN
Cinema 5; 1965
DYING
PBS-TV; television documentary; 1976
PILGRIM, FAREWELL
Post Mills Productions; 1980

Rogosin, Lionel
b. 1924
New York, New York

ON THE BOWERY
Film Representations; 1957
COME BACK, AFRICA
Rogosin; 1959
GOOD TIMES, WONDERFUL TIMES
Rogosin; 1966

continued

Rogosin, Lionel
continued

BLACK ROOTS
1970
BLACK FANTASY
Impact; 1972
WOODCUTTERS OF THE DEEP SOUTH
1973

Rohmer, Eric
(Jean-Marie Maurice Scherer)
b. April 4, 1920
Nancy, France
Contact:
French Film Office
745 Fifth Avenue
New York, N.Y. 10151
(212) 832-8860

THE SIGN OF LEO
1959; French
LA CARRIERE DE SUZANNE
Films du Losange; 1963; French
SIX IN PARIS
co-director; 1965; French
LA COLLECTIONNEUSE
Pathe Contemporary; 1967; French
MY NIGHT AT MAUD'S
Pathe Contemporary; 1970; French
CLAIRE'S KNEE
Columbia; 1971; French
CHLOE IN THE AFTERNOON
Columbia; 1972; French
THE MARQUISE OF O...
New Line Cinema; 1976; French-West German
PERCEVAL
Gaumont/New Yorker; 1978; French
THE AVIATOR'S WIFE
Gaumont/New Yorker; 1981; French

Roley, Sutton
Home:
777 Arden Road
Pasadena, CA 91106
(213) 449-2491
Business:
The Sutton Roley Organization
6311 Romaine Street
Hollywood, CA 90038
(213) 462-0730

SWEET, SWEET RACHEL
ABC, Inc.; telefeature; 1971
THE LONERS
Fanfare; 1972
SNATCHED
ABC Circle Films; telefeature; 1973
SATAN'S TRIANGLE
Danny Thomas Productions; telefeature; 1975
CHOSEN SURVIVORS
Columbia; 1974

Romero, Eddie

THE RAIDERS OF LEYTE GULF
Hemisphere; 1963; Filipino-U.S.
MORE WITCH DOCTOR
20th Century-Fox; 1964; Filipino-U.S.
THE WALLS OF HELL
co-director with Gerardo De Leon; Hemisphere; 1964; U.S.-Filipino
THE RAVAGERS
Hemisphere; 1965; U.S.-Filipino
BEAST OF BLOOD
Marvin; 1971; U.S.-Filipino
BLACK MAMA, WHITE MAMA
American International; 1973; U.S.-Filipino
BEYOND ATLANTIS
Dimension; 1973; U.S.-Filipino
SAVAGE SISTERS
American International; 1974; U.S.-Filipino
THE WOMAN HUNT
New World; 1975; U.S.-Filipino
SUDDEN DEATH
Topar; 1977; U.S.-Filipino

Romero, George A.

NIGHT OF THE LIVING DEAD
Continental; 1968
THERE'S ALWAYS VANILLA
Cambist; 1972
THE CRAZIES
Cambist; 1972
HUNGRY WIVES
Jack H. Harris Enterprises; 1973

continued

Romero, George A.
continued

MARTIN
Libra Films; 1978
DAWN OF THE DEAD
United Film Distribution; 1979
KNIGHTRIDERS
United Film Distribution; 1981

Rooks, Conrad

CHAPPAQUA
Regional; 1968
SIDDHARTHA
Columbia; 1973

Rose, Les
Home:
17 Maple Avenue
Toronto, Ontario
Canada
(416) 960-1829
Agent:
Jeanine Edward-Fif Oscard
New York City
(212) 764-1100

THREE CARD MONTE
Arista; 1977; Canadian
TITLE SHOT
Arista; 1979; Canadian
HOG WILD
Avco Embassy; 1980; Canadian
GAS
Paramount; 1981; Canadian

Rose, Mickey

STUDENT BODIES
Paramount; 1981

Rosen, Martin

WATERSHIP DOWN
Avco Embassy; 1978
THE PLAGUE DOGS
Avco Embassy; 1981

Rosenberg, Stuart
b. 1928
New York, New York
Agent:
William Morris Agency
Beverly Hills
(213) 274-7451

MURDER, INC.
co-director with Burt Balaban; 20th Century-Fox; 1960
QUESTION 7
De Rochemont; 1961; U.S.-West German
FAME IS THE NAME OF THE GAME
Universal TV; telefeature; 1966
ASYLUM FOR A SPY
Universal TV; telefeature; 1967
COOL HAND LUKE
Warner Brothers; 1967
THE APRIL FOOLS
National General; 1969
MOVE
20th Century-Fox; 1970
WUSA
Paramount; 1970
POCKET MONEY
National General; 1972
THE LAUGHING POLICEMAN
20th Century-Fox; 1973
THE DROWNING POOL
Warner Brothers; 1975
VOYAGE OF THE DAMNED
Avco Embassy; 1977; British
LOVE AND BULLETS
AFD; 1979
THE AMITYVILLE HORROR
American International; 1979
BRUBAKER
20th Century-Fox; 1980

Rosenthal, Rick
Contact:
Directors Guild of America
Los Angeles
(213) 656-1220

HALLOWEEN II
Universal; 1981

Rosi, Francesco
b. November 15, 1922
Naples, Italy
Contact:
Minister of Tourism
Via Della Ferratella
No. 51
00184 Rome, Italy
06-7732

THE CHALLENGE
1958; Italian
I MAGLIARI
1959; Italian
SALVATORE GIULIANO
1962; Italian
HANDS OVER THE CITY
1963; Italian
THE MOMENT OF TRUTH
Rizzoli; 1965; Italian-Spanish
MORE THAN A MIRACLE
M-G-M; 1967; Italian-French
UOMINI CONTRO
1970; Italian-Yugoslavian
THE MATTEI AFFAIR
Paramount; 1973; Italian
LUCKY LUCIANO
Avco Embassy; 1974; Italian
IL CONTESTO
1975; Italian
ILLUSTRIOUS CORPSES
1976; Italian-French
EBOLI (Christ Stopped at Eboli)
Franklin Media; 1980; Italian
THREE BROTHERS
New World; 1981; Italian

Ross, Herbert
b. May 13, 1927
New York, New York
Agent:
William Morris Agency
Beverly Hills
(213) 274-7451

GOODBYE, MR. CHIPS
M-G-M; 1969; British
THE OWL AND THE PUSSYCAT
Columbia; 1970
T.R. BASKIN
Paramount; 1971
PLAY IT AGAIN, SAM
Paramount; 1972
THE LAST OF SHEILA
Warner Brothers; 1973
FUNNY LADY
Columbia; 1975
THE SUNSHINE BOYS
M-G-M/United Artists; 1975
THE SEVEN-PER-CENT SOLUTION
Universal; 1976; British
THE TURNING POINT
20th Century-Fox; 1977
THE GOODBYE GIRL
Warner Brothers; 1977
CALIFORNIA SUITE
Columbia; 1978
NIJINSKY
Paramount; 1980
PENNIES FROM HEAVEN
M-G-M/United Artists; 1981
I OUGHT TO BE IN PICTURES
20th Century-Fox; 1982

Roth, Bobby

INDEPENDENCE DAY
1977
THE BOSS' SON
Circle Associates; 1980
MYSTIQUE
Aura; 1981

Rothman, Stephanie

BLOOD BATH
co-director with Jack Hill; American International 1966
IT'S A BIKINI WORLD
American International; 1967
THE STUDENT NURSES
New World; 1970

continued

Rothman, Stephanie
continued

THE VELVET VAMPIRE
New World; 1971
GROUP MARRIAGE
Dimension; 1973
THE WORKING GIRLS
Dimension; 1974

Rouse, Russell
b. 1916
New York, New York
Attorney:
Covey & Covey
Los Angeles
(213) 272-0074

THE WELL
co-director with Leo Popkin; United Artists; 1951
THE THIEF
United Artists; 1952
WICKED WOMAN
United Artists; 1954
NEW YORK CONFIDENTIAL
Warner Brothers; 1955
THE FASTEST GUN ALIVE
M-G-M; 1956
HOUSE OF NUMBERS
Columbia; 1957
THUNDER IN THE SUN
Paramount; 1959
A HOUSE IS NOT A HOME
Embassy; 1964
THE OSCAR
Embassy; 1966
THE CAPER OF THE GOLDEN BULLS
Embassy; 1967

Ruben, Joseph

THE SISTER-IN-LAW
Crown International; 1975
THE POM-POM GIRLS
Crown International; 1976
JOYRIDE
American International; 1977
OUR WINNING SEASON
American International; 1978
GORP
American International; 1980

Rudolph, Alan
Agent:
I.C.M.
Hollywood
(213) 550-4000
Business Manager:
W. Goldstein
Encino
(213) 783-7671

WELCOME TO L.A.
Lions Gate; 1977
REMEMBER MY NAME
Lagoon Associates; 1979
ROADIE
United Artists; 1980
ENDANGERED SPECIES
M-G-M/United Artists; 1982

Rush, Richard
b. 1930
Business:
The Rush Organization
821 Stradella Road
Bel Air, CA 90024
(213) 472-1246
Agent:
I.C.M.
Hollywood
(213) 550-4000

TOO SOON TO LOVE
Universal; 1960
OF LOVE AND DESIRE
20th Century-Fox; 1963
THE FICKLE FINGER OF FATE
Pro International; 1967
THUNDER ALLEY
American International; 1967
HELL'S ANGELS ON WHEELS
American International; 1967
A MAN CALLED DAGGER
M-G-M; 1968
PSYCH-OUT
American International; 1968
THE SAVAGE SEVEN
American International; 1968
GETTING STRAIGHT
Columbia; 1970
FREEBIE AND THE BEAN
Warner Brothers; 1974
THE STUNT MAN
20th Century-Fox; 1980

Russell, Ken
b. July 3, 1927
Southampton, England
Contact:
Directors Guild of America
Los Angeles
(213) 656-1220

FRENCH DRESSING
Warner-Pathe; 1963; British
BILLION DOLLAR BRAIN
United Artists; 1967; British
WOMEN IN LOVE
United Artists; 1970; British
THE MUSIC LOVERS
United Artists; 1971; British
THE DEVILS
Warner Brothers; 1971; British
THE BOY FRIEND
M-G-M; 1971; British
SAVAGE MESSIAH
M-G-M; 1972; British
MAHLER
Mayfair; 1974; British
TOMMY
Columbia; 1975; British
LISZTOMANIA
Warner Brothers; 1975; British
VALENTINO
United Artists; 1977; British
ALTERED STATES
Warner Brothers; 1980

Rydell, Mark
b. 1934
Contact:
Directors Guild of America
Los Angeles
(213) 656-1220

THE FOX
Claridge; 1968
THE REIVERS
National General; 1969
THE COWBOYS
Warner Brothers; 1972
CINDERELLA LIBERTY
20th Century-Fox; 1974
HARRY AND WALTER GO TO NEW YORK
Columbia; 1976
THE ROSE
20th Century-Fox; 1979
ON GOLDEN POND
Universal/AFD; 1981

Sachs, William

SECRETS OF THE GODS
Film Ventures International; 1976
THERE IS NO THIRTEEN
Film Ventures International; 1977
THE INCREDIBLE MELTING MAN
American International; 1977
VAN NUYS BLVD.
Crown International; 1979
GALAXINA
Crown International; 1980

St. Jacques, Raymond
(James Arthur Johnson)
b. 1930
Hartford, Connecticut

BOOK OF NUMBERS
Avco Embassy; 1973

Saks, Gene
b. November 8, 1921
New York, New York
Attorney:
Arthur J. Klein
New York City
(212) 688-6040

BAREFOOT IN THE PARK
Paramount; 1966
THE ODD COUPLE
Paramount; 1968
CACTUS FLOWER
Columbia; 1969
LAST OF THE RED HOT LOVERS
Paramount; 1972
MAME
Warner Brothers; 1974

Salter, James

THREE
United Artists; 1969; British

Sanders, Denis
b. January 21, 1929
New York, New York
Business:
SRS Productions
4224 Ellenita Avenue
Tarzana, CA 91356
(213) 873-3171

CRIME AND PUNISHMENT, U.S.A.
Allied Artists; 1959
WAR HUNT
United Artists; 1961
ONE MAN'S WAY
United Artists; 1964
SHOCK TREATMENT
20th Century-Fox; 1964
ELVIS - THAT'S THE WAY IT IS
M-G-M; 1970
SOUL TO SOUL
Cinerama Releasing Corporation; 1971
INVASION OF THE BEE GIRLS
Centaur; 1973

Sandrich, Jay
Home:
(213) 392-7357
Agent:
Creative Artists Agency
Los Angeles
(213) 277-4545

THE CROOKED HEARTS
Lorimar Productions; telefeature; 1972
WHAT ARE BEST FRIENDS FOR?
ABC Circle Films; telefeature; 1973
NEIL SIMON'S SEEMS LIKE OLD TIMES
Columbia; 1980

Sangster, Jimmy
b. 1924
England
Contact:
British Film Institute
127 Charing Cross Road
London W.C. 2, England
01-437-4355

THE HORROR OF FRANKENSTEIN
Levitt-Pickman; 1970; British
LUST FOR A VAMPIRE
American Continental; 1971; British
FEAR IN THE NIGHT
International Co-Productions; 1972; British

Sarafian, Richard C.
b. 1925
New York, New York
Agent:
Agency for the Performing Arts
Los Angeles
(213) 273-0744

TERROR AT BLACK FALLS
Beckman; 1962
ANDY
Universal; 1965
SHADOW ON THE LAND
Screen Gems/Columbia TV; telefeature; 1968
RUN WILD, RUN FREE
Columbia; 1969; British
FRAGMENT OF FEAR
Columbia; 1971; British
MAN IN THE WILDERNESS
Warner Brothers; 1971
VANISHING POINT
20th Century-Fox; 1971
LOLLY-MADONNA XXX
M-G-M; 1973
THE MAN WHO LOVED CAT DANCING
M-G-M; 1973
ONE OF OUR OWN
Universal TV; telefeature; 1975
THE NEXT MAN
Allied Artists; 1976
A KILLING AFFAIR
Columbia TV; telefeature; 1977
SUNBURN
Paramount; 1979; U.S.-British
DISASTER ON THE COASTLINER
Moonlight Productions/Filmways; telefeature; 1979
THE GOLDEN MOMENT: AN OLYMPIC LOVE STORY
Don Ohlmeyer Productions/Telepictures Corporation; telefeature; 1980
THE GANGSTER CHRONICLES
Universal TV; telefeature; 1981
SPLENDOR IN THE GRASS
Katz-Gallin Productions/Half-Pint Productions; telefeature; 1981

Sargent, Joseph
b. 1925
Jersey City, New Jersey
Business:
Joseph Sargent Productions
Hollywood
(213) 769-5407
Agent:
Shapiro-Lichtman Agency
Hollywood
(213) 557-2244

ONE SPY TOO MANY
M-G-M; 1966
THE HELL WITH HEROES
Universal; 1968
THE SUNSHINE PATRIOT
Universal TV; telefeature; 1968
THE IMMORTAL
Paramount TV; telefeature; 1969
COLOSSUS: THE FORBIN PROJECT
Universal; 1970
TRIBES
20th Century-Fox TV; telefeature; 1970
MAYBE I'LL COME HOME IN THE SPRING
Metromedia Productions; telefeature; 1971
LONGSTREET
Paramount TV; telefeature; 1971
MAN ON A STRING
Screen Gems/Columbia TV; telefeature; 1972
THE MAN
Paramount; 1972
THE MARCUS-NELSON MURDERS
Universal TV; telefeature; 1973
THE MAN WHO DIED TWICE
Cinema Center; telefeature; 1973; filmed in 1970
SUNSHINE
Universal TV; telefeature; 1973
WHITE LIGHTNING
United Artists; 1973
THE TAKING OF PELHAM 1-2-3
United Artists; 1974
HUSTLING
Filmways; telefeature; 1975
FRIENDLY PERSUASION
International TV Productions/Allied Artists; telefeature; 1975
THE NIGHT THAT PANICKED AMERICA
Paramount TV; telefeature; 1975
MacARTHUR
Universal; 1977
GOLDENGIRL
Avco Embassy; 1979
AMBER WAVES
Time-Life Productions; telefeature; 1980
COAST TO COAST
Paramount; 1980
FREEDOM
Hill-Mandelker Films; telefeature; 1981
THE MANIONS OF AMERICA
co-director with Charles S. Dubin; Roger Gimbel Productions/EMI Films/Argonaut Films Ltd.; television mini-series; 1981

Sarne, Michael
b. August 6, 1939
London, England

LE ROUTE DE ST. TROPEZ
1966; French
JOANNA
20th Century-Fox; 1968; British
MYRA BRECKINRIDGE
20th Century-Fox; 1970

Satlof, Ron
Business:
Metaphor Productions
155 N. LaPeer Drive
Los Angeles, CA 90048
(213) 278-2351
Agent:
David Shapira Agency
Beverly Hills
(213) 278-2742

BENNY & BARNEY: LAS VEGAS UNDERCOVER
Universal TV; telefeature; 1977
WAIKIKI
Aaron Spelling Productions; telefeature; 1980
THE MURDER THAT WOULDN'T DIE
Universal TV; telefeature; 1980

Saura, Carlos
b. January 4, 1932
Huesca, Spain
Contact:
Secretary of State for
Tourism
Alcala 44
Madrid, Spain
91-2228370

THE HOOLIGANS
1962; Spanish
LAMENT FOR A BANDIT
1964; Spanish
THE HUNT
Trans-Lux; 1966; Spanish
PEPPERMINT FRAPPE
1967; Spanish
STRESS EN TRES TRES
1968; Spanish
HONEYCOMB
CineGlobe; 1969; Spanish
THE GARDEN OF DELIGHTS
Perry/Fleetwood; 1970; Spanish
ANNA AND THE WOLVES
1973; Spanish
COUSIN ANGELICA
New Yorker; 1974; Spanish
CRIA!
Jason Allen; 1976; Spanish
ELISA MY LOVE
1977; Spanish

Sautet, Claude
b. February 23, 1924
Montrouge, France
Contact:
French Film Office
745 Fifth Avenue
New York, N.Y. 10151
(212) 832-8860

BONJOUR SOURIRE
Vox; 1955; French
THE BIG RISK
United Artists; 1960; French-Italian
GUNS FOR THE DICTATOR
1965; French
THE THINGS OF LIFE
Columbia; 1970; French
MAX ET LES FERRAILLEURS
1971; French
CESAR AND ROSALIE
Cinema 5; 1972; French-Italian-West German
VINCENT, FRANCOIS, PAUL AND THE OTHERS
Joseph Green Pictures; 1974; French-Italian
MADO
Joseph Green Pictures; 1976; French
A SIMPLE STORY
Quartet; 1979; French
A BAD SON
1980; French

Sayles, John
Contact:
Writers Guild of America
Los Angeles
(213) 550-1000

RETURN OF THE SECAUCUS SEVEN
Libra Films/Specialty; 1980

Schaefer, George
b. December 16, 1920
Wallingford, Connecticut
Home:
1040 Woodland Drive
Beverly Hills, CA 90210
Business:
Compass Productions
1801 Avenue of the Stars
Los Angeles, CA 90067
(213) 553-6205
Agent:
Chasin-Park-Citron
Los Angeles
(213) 273-7190

PENDULUM
Columbia; 1969
GENERATION
Avco Embassy; 1969
DOCTORS' WIVES
Columbia; 1971
A WAR OF CHILDREN
Tomorrow Entertainment; telefeature; 1972
F. SCOTT FITZGERALD AND "THE LAST OF THE BELLES"
Titus Productions; telefeature; 1974
ONCE UPON A SCOUNDREL
Image International; 1974; U.S.-Mexican
IN THIS HOUSE OF BREDE
Tomorrow Entertainment; telefeature; 1975
AMELIA EARHART
Universal TV; telefeature; 1976
TRUMAN AT POTSDAM
NBC-TV; telefeature; 1976
THE GIRL CALLED HATTER FOX
Roger Gimbel Productions/EMI TV; telefeature; 1978

continued

Schaefer, George
continued

FIRST YOU CRY
MTM Enterprises; telefeature; 1978
AN ENEMY OF THE PEOPLE
Warner Brothers; 1978
WHO'LL SAVE OUR CHILDREN?
Time-Life Productions; telefeature; 1978
BLIND AMBITION
Time-Life Productions; television mini-series; 1979
MAYFLOWER: THE PILGRIMS' ADVENTURE
Syzygy Productions; telefeature; 1979
THE BUNKER
Time-Life Productions/SFP France/Antenne 2 France; telefeature; 1981; U.S.-French
THE PEOPLE VS. JEAN HARRIS
PKO Television; telefeature; 1981

Schaffner, Franklin J.
b. May 30, 1920
Tokyo, Japan
Agent:
Chasin-Park-Citron
Los Angeles
(213) 273-7190

THE STRIPPER
20th Century-Fox; 1962
THE BEST MAN
United Artists; 1964
THE WAR LORD
Universal; 1965
THE DOUBLE MAN
Warner Brothers; 1968; British
PLANET OF THE APES
20th Century-Fox; 1968
PATTON
20th Century-Fox; 1970
NICHOLAS AND ALEXANDRA
Columbia; 1971; British
PAPILLON
Allied Artists; 1973
ISLANDS IN THE STREAM
Paramount; 1977
THE BOYS FROM BRAZIL
20th Century-Fox; 1978
SPHINX
Orion Pictures/Warner Brothers; 1981
YES, GIORGIO
M-G-M/United Artists; 1982

Schain, Don
Home:
1817 N. Fuller Avenue
Los Angeles, CA 90046
Business:
Derio Productions, Inc.
7942 Mulholland Drive
Hollywood, CA 90046
(213) 851-8140

GINGER
Joseph Brenner Associates; 1971
THE ABDUCTORS
Joseph Brenner Associates; 1972
A PLACE CALLED TODAY
Avco Embassy; 1972
GIRLS ARE FOR LOVING
Continental; 1973
TOO HOT TO HANDLE
Derio Productions; 1978

Schatzberg, Jerry
b. New York, New York
Agent:
William Morris Agency
Beverly Hills
(213) 274-7451

PUZZLE OF A DOWNFALL CHILD
Universal; 1970
PANIC IN NEEDLE PARK
20th Century-Fox; 1971
SCARECROW
Warner Brothers; 1973
SWEET REVENGE (Dandy, The All-American Girl)
M-G-M/United Artists; 1976
THE SEDUCTION OF JOE TYNAN
Universal; 1979
HONEYSUCKLE ROSE
Warner Brothers; 1980

Scheerer, Robert
Agent:
FCA Agency, Inc.
Los Angeles
(213) 277-8422

HANS BRINKER
NBC-TV; telefeature; 1969
ADAM AT SIX A.M.
National General; 1970

continued

Scheerer, Robert
continued

THE WORLD'S GREATEST ATHLETE
Buena Vista; 1973
POOR DEVIL
Paramount TV; telefeature; 1973
TARGET RISK
Universal TV; telefeature; 1975
IT HAPPENED AT LAKEWOOD MANOR
Alan Landsburg Productions; telefeature; 1977
HAPPILY EVER AFTER
Tri-Media II,Inc./Hamel-Somers Entertainment; telefeature; 1978
HOW TO BEAT THE HIGH COST OF LIVING
American International; 1980

Schell, Maximilian
b. December 8, 1930
Vienna, Austria

FIRST LOVE
UMC; 1970; Swiss-West German
THE PEDESTRIAN
Cinerama Releasing Corporation; 1974; West German-Swiss-Israeli
END OF THE GAME
20th Century-Fox; 1976; West German-Italian
TALES FROM THE VIENNA WOODS
Arabella Film/MFG Film-Seitz/Solaris Film-Bayerischer Rundfunk; 1979; Austrian-West German

Schellerup, Henning

THE BLACK BUNCH
Entertainment Pyramid; 1973
SWEET JESUS, PREACHER MAN
M-G-M; 1973
THE BLACK ALLEYCATS
Entertainment Pyramid; 1974
THE TIME MACHINE
Sunn Classic; telefeature; 1978
IN SEARCH OF HISTORIC JESUS
Sunn Classic; 1979
BEYOND DEATH'S DOOR
Sunn Classic; 1979
THE LEGEND OF SLEEPY HOLLOW
Sunn Classic; 1979
THE ADVENTURES OF NELLIE BLY
Sunn Classic; telefeature; 1981

Schepisi, Fred
Contact:
Directors Guild of America
Los Angeles
(213) 656-1220

THE DEVIL'S PLAYGROUND
Entertainment Marketing; 1976; Australian
THE CHANT OF JIMMIE BLACKSMITH
New Yorker; 1980; Australian
BARBAROSA
Universal/AFD; 1981

Schiller, Lawrence J.
Business:
P.O. Box 5345
Beverly Hills, CA 90210
(213) 462-2284
Agent:
William Morris Agency
Beverly Hills
(213) 274-7451

THE LEXINGTON EXPERIENCE
Corda; 1971
THE AMERICAN DREAMER
co-director with L.M. Kit Carson; EYR; 1971
HEY, I'M ALIVE!
Charles Fries Productions/Worldvision; telefeature; 1975
MARILYN: THE UNTOLD STORY
co-director with Jack Arnold & John Flynn; Lawrence Schiller Productions; telefeature; 1980
THE EXECUTIONER'S SONG
Lawrence Schiller Productions; telefeature; 1982

Schlatter, George
Business:
Schlatter Productions
8321 Beverly Blvd.
Los Angeles, CA 90048
(213) 655-1400
Agent:
William Morris Agency
Beverly Hills
(213) 274-7451

NORMAN...IS THAT YOU?
M-G-M/United Artists; 1976

Schlesinger, John
b. 1926
London, England
Agent:
William Morris Agency
Beverly Hills
(213) 274-7451

A KIND OF LOVING
Continental; 1962; British
BILLY LIAR
Continental; 1963; British
DARLING
Embassy; 1965; British
FAR FROM THE MADDING CROWD
M-G-M; 1967; British
MIDNIGHT COWBOY
United Artists; 1969
SUNDAY BLOODY SUNDAY
United Artists; 1970; British
VISIONS OF EIGHT
co-director; Cinema 5; 1973
THE DAY OF THE LOCUST
Paramount; 1975
MARATHON MAN
Paramount; 1976
YANKS
Universal; 1979; British-U.S.
HONKY TONK FREEWAY
Universal/AFD; 1981

Schlondorff, Volker
b. 1939
Wiesbaden, Germany
Contact:
Bundesverband Deutscher
Film Produzenten
Langenbeck Str., No. 9
6200 Wiesbaden
West Germany
306 200

YOUNG TORLESS
Kanawha; 1966; West German-French
A DEGREE OF MURDER
Universal; 1967; West German
MICHAEL KOHLHAAS
Columbia; 1969; West German
THE SUDDEN WEALTH OF THE POOR PEOPLE OF KOMBACH
New Yorker; 1971; West German
DIE MORAL DER RUTH HALBFASS
1972; West German
A FREE WOMAN
New Yorker; 1972; West German
SUMMER LIGHTNING
1972; West German
UBERNACHTUNG IN TIROL
1974; West German
THE LOST HONOR OF KATHARINE BLUM
New World; 1975; West German
DER FANGSCHUSS
1976; West German
COUP DE GRACE
Cinema 5; 1978; West German
DAS ZWEITE ERWACHEN DI CHRISTINA KLAGE
1978; West German
DEUTSCHLAND IM HERBST
co-director; 1978; West German
THE TIN DRUM
New World; 1980; West German
THE FORGERY
Bioskop-Argos-Artemis-UA; 1981; West German

Schmoeller, David
Agent:
Shapiro-Lichtman Agency
Los Angeles
(213) 557-2244

TOURIST TRAP
Compass International; 1979
THE SEDUCTION
Avco Embassy; 1981

Schnitzer, Robert A.

NO PLACE TO HIDE
American Films Ltd.; 1975
THE PREMONITION
Avco Embassy; 1976

Schrader, Paul
b. 1946
Grand Rapids, Michigan
Agent:
I.C.M.
Hollywood
(213) 550-4000

BLUE COLLAR
Universal; 1978
HARDCORE
Columbia; 1979
AMERICAN GIGOLO
Paramount; 1980
THE CAT PEOPLE
Universal; 1982

Schroeder, Barbet
b. August 26, 1941
Teheran, Iran
Contact:
French Film Office
745 Fifth Avenue
New York, N.Y. 10151
(212) 832-8860

MORE
Cinema 5; 1969; Luxembourg
THE VALLEY (OBSCURED BY CLOUDS)
Lagoon Associates; 1972; French
IDI AMIN DADA
Tinc; 1974; French
MAITRESSE
Tinc; 1976; French
KOKO, A TALKING GORILLA
New Yorker; 1978; French

Schultz, Michael
b. November 10, 1938
Milwaukee, Wisconsin
Agent:
Eisenbach, Greene, Duchow
Los Angeles
(213) 659-3420

TOGETHER FOR DAYS
Olas; 1973
HONEYBABY, HONEYBABY
Kelly-Jordan; 1974
COOLEY HIGH
American International; 1975
CAR WASH
Universal; 1976
GREASED LIGHTNING
Warner Brothers; 1977
WHICH WAY IS UP?
Universal; 1978
SGT. PEPPER'S LONELY HEARTS CLUB BAND
Universal; 1978
SCAVENGER HUNT
20th Century-Fox; 1979
CARBON COPY
Avco Embassy; 1981

Schumacher, Joel
Agent:
I.C.M.
Hollywood
(213) 550-4000

THE VIRGINIA HILL STORY
RSO Films; telefeature; 1974
AMATEUR NIGHT AT THE DIXIE BAR & GRILL
Motown/Universal TV; telefeature; 1979
THE INCREDIBLE SHRINKING WOMAN
Universal; 1981

Scola, Ettore
b. 1931
Trevico, Italy
Contact:
Minister of Tourism
Via Della Ferratella
No. 51
00184 Rome, Italy
06-7732

LET'S TALK ABOUT WOMEN
Embassy; 1964; Italian-French
LA CONGIUNTURA
1965; Italian
THRILLING
co-director; 1966; Italian
THE DEVIL IN LOVE
Warner Brothers; 1966; Italian
IL PROFETA
1967; Italian
RIUSCIRANNO I NOSTRI EROI A TROVARE L'AMICO
MISTERIOSAMENTE SCOMPARSO IN AFRICA?
1968; Italian
IL COMMISSARIO PEPE
1969; Italian

continued

Scola, Ettore
continued

THE PIZZA TRIANGLE (A Drama of Jealousy and Other Things)
Warner Brothers; 1970; Italian-Spanish
ROCCO PAPALEO
Rumson; 1971; Italian
LA PIU BELLA SERATA DELLA MIA VITA
1972; Italian
WE ALL LOVED EACH OTHER SO MUCH
Cinema 5; 1975; Italian
DOWN AND DIRTY
New Line Cinema; 1976; Italian
SIGNORE E SIGNORI - BUONANOTTE
co-director; 1976; Italian
A SPECIAL DAY
Cinema 5; 1977; Italian
VIVA ITALIA!
co-director with Mario Monicelli & Dino Risi; Cinema 5; 1978; Italian
CHE SI DICE A ROMA
1979; Italian
THE TERRACE
Dean Film; 1980; Italian
PASSIONE D'AMORE
Massfilm; 1981; Italian-French

Scorsese, Martin
b. November 17, 1942
Flushing, New York
Agent:
The Ufland Agency
Beverly Hills
(213) 273-9441

WHO'S THAT KNOCKING AT MY DOOR?
Joseph Brenner Associates; 1968
BOXCAR BERTHA
American International; 1972
MEAN STREETS
Warner Brothers; 1973
ALICE DOESN'T LIVE HERE ANYMORE
Warner Brothers; 1974
ITALIANAMERICAN
1974
TAXI DRIVER
Columbia; 1976
NEW YORK, NEW YORK
United Artists; 1977
AMERICAN BOY
1978
THE LAST WALTZ
United Artists; 1978
RAGING BULL
United Artists; 1980
THE KING OF COMEDY
20th Century-Fox; 1982

Scott, George C.
b. October 18, 1927
Wise, Virginia
Agent:
Jane Deacy Agency, Inc.
New York City
(212) 752-4865
Business Manager:
Matthew Alexander, Inc.
New York City
(212) 755-1317

RAGE
Warner Brothers; 1972
THE SAVAGE IS LOOSE
Campbell Devon; 1974

Scott, Oz
Contact:
Directors Guild of America
Los Angeles
(213) 656-1220

BUSTIN' LOOSE
Universal; 1981

Scott, Ridley
b. England
Contact:
Directors Guild of America
Los Angeles
(213) 656-1220

THE DUELLISTS
Paramount; 1978; British
ALIEN
20th Century-Fox; 1979; U.S.-British
BLADE RUNNER
The Ladd Company/Warner Brothers; 1982

Seidelman, Arthur Allan
Home:
(213) 479-5846
(212) 580-9438
Business Manager:
Barry Rosenthal
Boston
(617) 261-1000

CHILDREN OF RAGE
LSF; 1975; U.S.-Israeli
ECHOES
1981

Sembene, Ousmene

THE MONEY ORDER
1968; Senegalese
BLACK GIRL
New Yorker; 1969; Senegalese
BOROM SARRET
New Yorker; 1969; Senegalese
MANDABI
Grove Press; 1970; Senegalese
EMITAI
New Yorker; 1973; Senegalese
XALA
New Yorker; 1976; Senegalese
CEDDO
New Yorker; 1978; Senegalese

Senensky, Ralph
Agent:
Shapiro-Lichtman Agency
Hollywood
(213) 557-2244

A DREAM FOR CHRISTMAS
Lorimar Productions; telefeature; 1973
THE FAMILY KOVACK
Playboy Productions; telefeature; 1974
DEATH CRUISE
Spelling-Goldberg Productions; telefeature; 1974
THE FAMILY NOBODY WANTED
Universal TV; telefeature; 1975
THE NEW ADVENTURES OF HEIDI
Pierre Cossette Enterprises; telefeature; 1978
DYNASTY
Aaron Spelling Productions/Fox-Cat Productions; telefeature; 1981

Sgarro, Nicholas
Agent:
Century Artists
Beverly Hills
(213) 273-4366
Business Manager:
Geneva Management
Beverly Hills
(213) 271-5295

THE HAPPY HOOKER
Cannon; 1975
THE MAN WITH THE POWER
Universal TV; telefeature; 1977

Shah, Krishna
Home:
P.O. Box 64515
Los Angeles, CA 90064

RIVALS
Avco Embassy; 1972
THE RIVER NIGER
Cine Artists; 1976
SHALIMAR
1978; U.S.-Indian
CINEMA-CINEMA
Shahab Ahmed Productions; 1980; Indian

Shanks, Ann Zane
Contact:
Directors Guild of America
Los Angeles
(213) 656-1220

FRIENDSHIPS, SECRETS AND LIES
co-director with Marlene Laird; Wittman-Riche Productions/Warner Brothers TV; telefeature; 1979

Shapiro, Ken
Home:
2044 Stanley Hills Drive
Los Angeles, CA 90046
(213) 654-7471

THE GROOVE TUBE
Levitt-Pickman; 1974
MODERN PROBLEMS
20th Century-Fox; 1981

Shapiro, Melvin
Contact:
Directors Guild of America
Los Angeles
(213) 656-1220

SAMMY STOPS THE WORLD
Elkins; 1979

Sharman, Jim

SUMMER OF SECRETS
Greater Union Film Distribution; 1976; Australian
THE ROCKY HORROR PICTURE SHOW
20th Century-Fox; 1976; British
THE NIGHT THE PROWLER
1978; Australian
SHOCK TREATMENT
20th Century-Fox; 1981; British

Sharp, Don
b. April, 1922
Hobart, Tasmania
Contact:
British Film Institute
127 Charing Cross Road
London W.C. 2, England
01-437-4355

THE STOLEN AIRLINER
British Lion/Children's Film Foundation; 1955; British
THE ADVENTURES OF HAL 5
Children's Film Foundation; 1958; British
THE IN-BETWEEN AGE
Allied Artists; 1958; British
THE PROFESSIONALS
American International; 1960; British
IT'S ALL HAPPENING (The Dream Maker)
Universal; 1963; British
KISS OF THE VAMPIRE
Universal; 1963; British
THE DEVIL-SHIP PIRATES
Columbia; 1964; British
WITCHCRAFT
20th Century-Fox; 1964; British
THE FACE OF FU MANCHU
7 Arts; 1965; British
CURSE OF THE FLY
20th Century-Fox; 1965; British
RASPUTIN - THE MAD MONK (I Killed Rasputin)
20th Century-Fox; 1966; British-French-Italian
BANG, BANG, YOU'RE DEAD! (Our Man in Marrakesh)
American International; 1966; British
THE BRIDES OF FU MANCHU
7 Arts; 1966; British
LINDA
Bryanston; 1966; British
THOSE FANTASTIC FLYING FOOLS (Blast Off)
American International; 1967; British
TASTE OF EXCITEMENT
Crispin; 1968; British
THE VIOLENT ENEMY
1969; British
PUPPET ON A CHAIN
co-director with Geoffrey Reeve; Cinerama Releasing Corporation; 1972; British
THE DEATH WHEELERS (Psychomania)
Scotia International; 1973; British
DARK PLACES
Cinerama Releasing Corporation; 1974; British
HENNESSY
American International; 1975; British
CALLAN
Cinema National; 1975; British
THE FOUR FEATHERS
Norman Rosemont Productions/Trident Films, Ltd.; telefeature; 1978; U.S.-British
THE 39 STEPS
International Picture Show Company; 1978; British
BEAR ISLAND
Taft International; 1980; Canadian-British

Shavelson, Melville
b. April 1, 1917
Brooklyn, New York
Business:
Llenroc Productions
1801 Avenue of the Stars
Los Angeles, CA 90067
(213) 277-0700
Agent:
William Morris Agency
Beverly Hills
(213) 274-7451

THE SEVEN LITTLE FOYS
Paramount; 1955
BEAU JAMES
Paramount; 1957
HOUSEBOAT
Paramount; 1958
THE FIVE PENNIES
Paramount; 1959
IT STARTED IN NAPLES
Paramount; 1960
ON THE DOUBLE
Paramount; 1961
THE PIGEON THAT TOOK ROME
Paramount; 1962
A NEW KIND OF LOVE
Paramount; 1963
CAST A GIANT SHADOW
United Artists; 1966
YOURS, MINE AND OURS
United Artists; 1968
THE WAR BETWEEN MEN AND WOMEN
National General; 1972
MIXED COMPANY
United Artists; 1974
THE LEGEND OF VALENTINO
Spelling-Goldberg Productions;telefeature; 1975
THE GREAT HOUDINIS
ABC Circle Films; telefeature; 1976
IKE
co-director with Boris Sagal; ABC Circle Films;
television mini-series; 1979

Shea, Jack
Agent:
Major Talent Agency
Los Angeles
(213) 820-5841

DAYTON'S DEVILS
Commonwealth United; 1968
THE MONITORS
Commonwealth United; 1969

Shebib, Donald
Business:
Eudon Films Ltd.
312 Wright Avenue
Toronto, Ontario
M6R 1L9 Canada
(416) 536-8969

GOIN' DOWN THE ROAD
Chevron; 1970; Canadian
RIP-OFF
Alliance; 1971; Canadian
BETWEEN FRIENDS
1973; Canadian
SECOND WIND
Health and Entertainment Corporation of America;
1976; Canadian
FIGHTING MEN
1977; Canadian
FISH HAWK
Avco Embassy; 1981; Canadian
HEARTACHES
Rising Star; 1981; Canadian

Sheldon, James
Home:
9428 Lloydcrest Drive
Beverly Hills, CA 90210
(213) 275-2210
Agent:
Contemporary-Korman Agency
Beverly Hills
(213) 278-8250

GIDGET GROWS UP
Screen Gems/Columbia TV; telefeature; 1969
WITH THIS RING
The Jozak Company/Paramount TV; telefeature; 1978
THE GOSSIP COLUMNIST
Universal TV; telefeature; 1980

Sheldon, Sidney
b. 1917
Chicago, Illinois
Agent:
Creative Artists Agency
Los Angeles
(213) 277-4545

DREAM WIFE
M-G-M; 1953
THE BUSTER KEATON STORY
Paramount; 1957

Sher, Jack
b. March 16, 1913
Minneapolis, Minnesota
Home:
9520 Dalegrove Drive
Beverly Hills, CA 90210
(213) 273-2091
Agent:
William Morris Agency
Beverly Hills
(213) 274-7451

FOUR GIRLS IN TOWN
Universal; 1957
KATHY O'
Universal; 1958
THE WILD AND THE INNOCENT
Universal; 1959
THE THREE WORLDS OF GULLIVER
Columbia; 1960; British
LOVE IN A GOLDFISH BOWL
Paramount; 1961

Sherin, Edwin
Business:
484 West 43rd Street
New York, N.Y. 10036
(212) 695-7469
Agent:
William Morris Agency
New York City
(212) 586-5100

VALDEZ IS COMING
United Artists; 1971
MY OLD MAN'S PLACE (Glory Boy)
Cinerama Releasing Corporation; 1972

Sherman, Gary

RAW MEAT (Death Line)
American International; 1973
DEAD AND BURIED
Avco Embassy; 1981
VICE SQUAD
Avco Embassy; 1981

Sherman, George
b. July 14, 1908
New York, New York
Attorney:
Sylvan Covey
Hollywood
(213) 272-0074

WILD HORSE RODEO
Republic; 1938
THE PURPLE VIGILANTES
Republic; 1938
OUTLAWS OF SONORA
Republic; 1938
RIDERS OF THE BLACK HILLS
Republic; 1938
PALS OF THE SADDLE
Republic; 1938
OVERLAND STAGE RAIDERS
Republic; 1938
RHYTHM OF THE SADDLE
Republic; 1938
SANTA FE STAMPEDE
Republic; 1938
RED RIVER RANGE
Republic; 1938
MEXICALI ROSE
Republic; 1939
THE NIGHT RIDERS
Republic; 1939
THREE TEXAS STEERS
Republic; 1939
WYOMING OUTLAW
Republic; 1939
COLORADO SUNSET
Republic; 1939
NEW FRONTIER
Republic; 1939
COWBOYS FROM TEXAS
Republic; 1939
THE KANSAS TERRORS
Republic; 1939
ROVIN' TUMBLEWEEDS
Republic; 1939
SOUTH OF THE BORDER
Republic; 1939
GHOST VALLEY RAIDERS
Republic; 1940
ONE MAN'S LAW
Republic; 1940

continued

Sherman, George
continued

THE TULSA KID
Republic; 1940
TEXAS TERRORS
Republic; 1940
COVERED WAGON DAYS
Republic; 1940
ROCKY MOUNTAIN RANGERS
Republic; 1940
UNDER TEXAS SKIES
Republic; 1940
THE TRAIL BLAZERS
Republic; 1940
LONE STAR RAIDERS
Republic; 1940
FRONTIER VENGEANCE
Republic; 1940
WYOMING WILDCAT
Republic; 1941
THE PHANTOM COWBOY
Republic; 1941
TWO GUN SHERIFF
Republic; 1941
DESERT BANDIT
Republic; 1941
KANSAS CYCLONE
Republic; 1941
DEATH VALLEY OUTLAWS
Republic; 1941
A MISSOURI OUTLAW
Republic; 1941
CITADEL OF CRIME
Republic; 1941
THE APACHE KID
Republic; 1941
ARIZONA TERRORS
Republic; 1942
STAGECOACH EXPRESS
Republic; 1942
JESSE JAMES JR.
Republic; 1942
THE CYCLONE KID
Republic; 1942
THE SOMBRERO KID
Republic; 1942
X MARKS THE SPOT
Republic; 1942
LONDON BLACKOUT MURDERS
Republic; 1942
THE PURPLE V
Republic; 1943
THE MANTRAP
Republic; 1943
THE WEST SIDE KID
Republic; 1943
MYSTERY BROADCAST
Republic; 1943
THE LADY AND THE MONSTER
Republic; 1944
STORM OVER LISBON
Republic; 1944
THE CRIME DOCTOR'S COURAGE
Columbia; 1945
THE GENTLEMAN MISBEHAVES
Columbia; 1946
RENEGADES
Columbia; 1946
TALK ABOUT A LADY
Columbia; 1946
THE BANDIT OF SHERWOOD FOREST
co-director with Henry Levin; Columbia; 1946
PERSONALITY KID
Columbia; 1947
SECRETS OF THE WHISTLER
Columbia; 1947
LAST OF THE REDMEN
Columbia; 1947
RELENTLESS
Columbia; 1948

continued

Sherman, George
continued

BLACK BART
Universal; 1948
RIVER LADY
Universal; 1948
LARCENY
Universal; 1948
RED CANYON
Universal; 1949
CALAMITY JANE AND SAM BASS
Universal; 1949
YES SIR, THAT'S MY BABY
Universal; 1949
SWORD IN THE DESERT
Universal; 1949
SPY HUNT
Universal; 1950
THE SLEEPING CITY
Universal; 1950
FEUDIN', FUSSIN' AND A-FIGHTIN'
Universal; 1950
COMANCHE TERRITORY
Universal; 1950
TOMAHAWK
Universal; 1951
TARGET UNKNOWN
Universal; 1951
THE RAGING TIDE
Universal; 1951
THE GOLDEN HORDE
Universal; 1951
STEEL TOWN
Universal; 1952
AGAINST ALL FLAGS
Universal; 1952
THE BATTLE AT APACHE PASS
Universal; 1952
BACK AT THE FRONT
Universal; 1952
THE LONE HAND
Universal; 1953
WAR ARROW
Universal; 1953
VEILS OF BAGDAD
Universal; 1953
BORDER RIVER
Universal; 1954
DAWN AT SOCORRO
Universal; 1954
CHIEF CRAZY HORSE
Universal; 1955
COUNT THREE AND PRAY
Universal; 1955
THE TREASURE OF PANCHO VILLA
Universal; 1955
COMANCHE
United Artists; 1956
REPRISAL!
Columbia; 1956
THE HARD MAN
Columbia; 1957
THE LAST OF THE FAST GUNS
Universal; 1958
TEN DAYS TO TULARA
United Artists; 1958
THE SON OF ROBIN HOOD
20th Century-Fox; 1959
THE FLYING FONTAINES
Columbia; 1959
HELL BENT FOR LEATHER
Universal; 1960
FOR THE LOVE OF MIKE
20th Century-Fox; 1960
THE ENEMY GENERAL
Columbia; 1960
THE WIZARD OF BAGHDAD
20th Century-Fox; 1960
THE FIERCEST HEART
20th Century-Fox; 1961

continued

Sherman, George
continued

PANIC BUTTON
Gorton; 1964
MURIETA
Warner Brothers; 1965; Spanish
SMOKY
20th Century-Fox; 1966
BIG JAKE
National General; 1971

Sherman, Vincent
b. July 16, 1906
Vienna, Georgia
Home:
6355 Sycamore Meadows Drive
Malibu, CA 90265
(213) 457-2229
Agent:
Creative Artists Agency
Los Angeles
(213) 277-4545

THE RETURN OF DOCTOR X
Warner Brothers; 1939
SATURDAY'S CHILDREN
Warner Brothers; 1940
THE MAN WHO TALKED TOO MUCH
Warner Brothers; 1940
FLIGHT FROM DESTINY
Warner Brothers; 1941
UNDERGROUND
Warner Brothers; 1941
ALL THROUGH THE NIGHT
Warner Brothers; 1942
THE HARD WAY
Warner Brothers; 1942
OLD ACQUAINTANCE
Warner Brothers; 1943
IN OUR TIME
Warner Brothers; 1944
MR. SKEFFINGTON
Warner Brothers; 1945
PILLOW TO POST
Warner Brothers; 1945
NORA PRENTISS
Warner Brothers; 1947
THE UNFAITHFUL
Warner Brothers; 1947
THE ADVENTURES OF DON JUAN
Warner Brothers; 1949
THE HASTY HEART
Warner Brothers; 1949
BACKFIRE
Warner Brothers; 1950
THE DAMNED DON'T CRY
Warner Brothers; 1950
HARRIET CRAIG
Columbia; 1950
GOODBYE, MY FANCY
Warner Brothers; 1951
LONE STAR
M-G-M; 1952
AFFAIR IN TRINIDAD
Columbia; 1952
DIFENDO IL MIO AMORE
1956; Italian
THE GARMENT JUNGLE
Columbia; 1957
THE NAKED EARTH
20th Century-Fox; 1959
THE YOUNG PHILADELPHIANS
Warner Brothers; 1959
ICE PALACE
Warner Brothers; 1960
A FEVER IN THE BLOOD
Warner Brothers; 1961
THE SECOND TIME AROUND
20th Century-Fox; 1961
THE YOUNG REBEL (Cervantes)
American International; 1968; Italian-Spanish-French
THE LAST HURRAH
O'Connor-Becker Productions/Columbia TV; telefeature; 1977
LADY OF THE HOUSE
co-director with Ralph Nelson; Metromedia Productions; telefeature; 1978

continued

Sherman, Vincent
continued

WOMEN AT WEST POINT
Green-Epstein Productions/Alan Sacks Productions; telefeature; 1979
BOGIE: THE LAST HERO
Charles Fries Productions; telefeature; 1980
THE DREAM MERCHANTS
Columbia TV; telefeature; 1980
TROUBLE IN HIGH TIMBER COUNTRY
Witt-Thomas Productions/Warner Brothers TV; telefeature; 1980

Sidaris, Andy

Business:
The Sidaris Company
1891 Carla Ridge
Beverly Hills, CA 90210
(213) 275-6282

THE RACING SCENE
Filmways; 1970
SEVEN
American International; 1979

Sidney, George

b. October 4, 1916
Long Island City, New York
Business:
9301 Wilshire Blvd.
Beverly Hills, CA 90210
(213) 550-7434

FREE AND EASY
M-G-M; 1941
PACIFIC RENDEZVOUS
M-G-M; 1942
PILOT NO. 5
M-G-M; 1943
THOUSANDS CHEER
M-G-M; 1943
BATHING BEAUTY
M-G-M; 1944
ANCHORS AWEIGH
M-G-M; 1945
THE HARVEY GIRLS
M-G-M; 1946
HOLIDAY IN MEXICO
M-G-M; 1946
CASS TIMBERLANE
M-G-M; 1947
THE THREE MUSKETEERS
M-G-M; 1948
THE RED DANUBE
M-G-M; 1949
KEY TO THE CITY
M-G-M; 1950
ANNIE GET YOUR GUN
M-G-M; 1950
SHOW BOAT
M-G-M; 1951
SCARAMOUCHE
M-G-M; 1952
YOUNG BESS
M-G-M; 1953
KISS ME KATE
M-G-M; 1953
JUPITER'S DARLING
M-G-M; 1955
THE EDDY DUCHIN STORY
Columbia; 1956
JEANNE EAGELS
Columbia; 1957
PAL JOEY
Columbia; 1957
WHO WAS THAT LADY?
Columbia; 1960
PEPE
Columbia; 1960
BYE BYE BIRDIE
Columbia; 1963
A TICKLISH AFFAIR
M-G-M; 1963
VIVA LAS VEGAS
M-G-M; 1964
THE SWINGER
Paramount; 1966
HALF A SIXPENCE
Paramount; 1968; British

Siegel, Don

b. October 26, 1912
Chicago, Illinois
Business Manager:
Capell, Flekman, Coyne & Co.
Beverly Hills
(213) 553-0310

THE VERDICT
Warner Brothers; 1946
NIGHT UNTO NIGHT
Warner Brothers; 1949
THE BIG STEAL
RKO Radio; 1949
DUEL AT SILVER CREEK
Universal; 1952
NO TIME FOR FLOWERS
RKO Radio; 1952
COUNT THE HOURS
RKO Radio; 1953
CHINA VENTURE
Columbia; 1953
RIOT IN CELL BLOCK 11
Allied Artists; 1954
PRIVATE HELL 36
Filmmakers; 1954
AN ANNAPOLIS STORY
Allied Artists; 1955
INVASION OF THE BODY SNATCHERS
Allied Artists; 1956
CRIME IN THE STREETS
Allied Artists; 1956
BABY FACE NELSON
Allied Artists; 1957
SPANISH AFFAIR
Paramount; 1958; Spanish
THE LINEUP
Columbia; 1958
THE GUN RUNNERS
United Artists; 1958
HOUND DOG MAN
20th Century-Fox; 1959
EDGE OF ETERNITY
Columbia; 1959
FLAMING STAR
20th Century-Fox; 1960
HELL IS FOR HEROES
Paramount; 1962
THE KILLERS
Universal; 1964
THE HANGED MAN
Universal TV; telefeature; 1964
STRANGER ON THE RUN
Universal TV; telefeature; 1967
MADIGAN
Universal; 1968
COOGAN'S BLUFF
Universal; 1968
DEATH OF A GUNFIGHTER
co-director with Robert Totten; both directed under pseudonym of Allen Smithee; Universal; 1969
TWO MULES FOR SISTER SARA
Universal; 1970; U.S.-Mexican
THE BEGUILED
Universal; 1971
DIRTY HARRY
Warner Brothers; 1972
CHARLEY VARRICK
Universal; 1973
THE BLACK WINDMILL
Universal; 1974; British
THE SHOOTIST
Paramount; 1976
TELEFON
M-G-M/United Artists; 1977
ESCAPE FROM ALCATRAZ
Paramount; 1979
ROUGH CUT
Paramount; 1980
JINXED
United Artists; 1982

Siegel, Robert J.

PARADES
Cinerama Releasing Corporation; 1972

Silver, Joan Micklin
Business:
Midwest Film Productions
600 Madison Avenue
New York, N.Y. 10022
(212) 355-0282
Agent:
I.C.M.
New York City
(212) 556-5600

HESTER STREET
Midwest Film Productions; 1975
BETWEEN THE LINES
Midwest Film Productions; 1977
HEAD OVER HEELS
United Artists; 1979

Silver, Raphael D.
Business:
Midwest Film Productions
600 Madison Avenue
New York, N.Y. 10022
(212) 355-0282

ON THE YARD
Midwest Film Productions; 1979

Silverstein, Elliot
b. 1927
Boston, Massachusetts
Agent:
The Paul Kohner Agency
Los Angeles
(213) 550-1060

BELLE SOMMARS
Columbia; 1962
CAT BALLOU
Columbia; 1965
THE HAPPENING
Columbia; 1967
A MAN CALLED HORSE
National General; 1970
DEADLY HONEYMOON (Nightmare Honeymoon)
M-G-M; 1974
THE CAR
Universal; 1977

Simon, Francis

THE CHICKEN CHRONICLES
Avco Embassy; 1977

Simmons, Anthony
Contact:
British Film Institute
127 Charing Cross Road
London W.C. 2, England
01-437-4355

YOUR MONEY OR YOUR WIFE
Rank; 1960; British
FOUR IN THE MORNING
West One; 1965; British
THE OPTIMISTS (The Optimists of Nine Elms)
Paramount; 1973; British
BLACK JOY
Kastner-Milchan; 1977; British

Sinatra, Frank
b. December 12, 1915
Hoboken, New Jersey

NONE BUT THE BRAVE
Warner Brothers; 1964; U.S.-Japanese

Sinclair, Andrew
Contact:
British Film Institute
127 Charing Cross Road
London W.C. 2, England
01-437-4355

UNDER MILK WOOD
Altura; 1973; British
BLUE BLOOD
Mallard Productions; 1975; British

Singer, Alexander
b. 1932
New York, New York
Agent:
I.C.M.
Hollywood
(213) 550-4000

A COLD WIND IN AUGUST
Lopert; 1961
PSYCHE 59
Royal International; 1964; British
LOVE HAS MANY FACES
Columbia; 1965
CAPTAIN APACHE
Scotia International; 1971; British
GLASS HOUSES
Columbia; 1972
THE FIRST 36 HOURS OF DR. DURANT
Columbia TV; telefeature; 1975

continued

Singer, Alexander
continued

TIME TRAVELERS
Irwin Allen Productions/20th Century-Fox TV; telefeature; 1976
THE MILLION DOLLAR RIP-OFF
Charles Fries Productions; telefeature; 1976
HUNTERS OF THE REEF
Writers Company Productions/Paramount TV; telefeature; 1978

Sitowitz, Hal
Agent:
Adams, Ray & Rosenberg
Los Angeles
(213) 278-3000

A LAST CRY FOR HELP
Myrt-Hal Productions/Viacom; telefeature; 1979

Sjoman, Vilgot
(David Harald Vilgot Sjoman)
b. December 2, 1924
Stockholm, Sweden
Contact:
Swedish Film Institute
P.O. Box 27126
S-10252 Stockholm
Sweden
08-630510

THE SWEDISH MISTRESS
1962; Swedish
491
Peppercorn-Wormser; 1964; Swedish
THE DRESS
1964; Swedish
MY SISTER, MY LOVE
Sigma III; 1966; Swedish
STIMULANTIA
co-director; 1967; Swedish
I AM CURIOUS (YELLOW)
Grove Press; 1967; Swedish
I AM CURIOUS (BLUE)
Grove Press; 1968; Swedish
YOU'RE LYING
Grove Press; 1969; Swedish
BLUSHING CHARLIE
1970; Swedish
THE KARLSSON BROTHERS
1972; Swedish
TILL SEX DO US PART
Astro; 1973; Swedish
A HANDFUL OF LOVE
1974; Swedish
THE GARAGE
1975; Swedish
TABOO
1977; Swedish
LINUS AND THE MYSTERIOUS RED BRICK HOUSE
Svensk Filminstitutet; 1979; Swedish

Skolimowski, Jerzy
b. May 5, 1938
Warsaw, Poland

IDENTIFICATION MARKS: NONE
New Yorker; 1964; Polish
WALKOVER
New Yorker; 1965; Polish
BARRIER
Film Polski; 1966; Polish
LE DEPART
Pathe Contemporary; 1967; Belgian
HANDS UP!
1967; Polish
DIALOGUE
co-director; 1968; Czech
THE ADVENTURES OF GIRARD
United Artists; 1969; British-Swiss
DEEP END
Paramount; 1971; British-West German
KING, QUEEN, KNAVE
Avco Embassy; 1972; West German-British
THE SHOUT
Films Inc.; 1979; British

Slate, Lane
Contact:
Directors Guild of America
Los Angeles
(213) 656-1220

CLAY PIGEON
co-director with Tom Stern; M-G-M; 1971
DEADLY GAME
M-G-M TV; telefeature; 1977

Smight, Jack
b. March 9, 1926
Minneapolis, Minnesota
Agent:
Chasin-Park-Citron
Los Angeles
(213) 273-7190

I'D RATHER BE RICH
Universal; 1964
THE THIRD DAY
Warner Brothers; 1965
HARPER
Warner Brothers; 1966
KALEIDOSCOPE
Warner Brothers; 1966; British
THE SECRET WAR OF HARRY FRIGG
Universal; 1968
NO WAY TO TREAT A LADY
Paramount; 1968
STRATEGY OF TERROR
Universal; 1969; made for television
THE ILLUSTRATED MAN
Warner Brothers; 1969
RABBIT, RUN
Warner Brothers; 1970
THE TRAVELING EXECUTIONER
M-G-M; 1970
THE SCREAMING WOMAN
Universal TV; telefeature; 1972
BANACEK: DETOUT TO NOWHERE
Universal TV; telefeature; 1972
THE LONGEST NIGHT
Universal TV; telefeature; 1972
PARTNERS IN CRIME
Universal TV; telefeature; 1973
DOUBLE INDEMNITY
Universal TV; telefeature; 1973
LINDA
Universal TV; telefeature; 1973
FRANKENSTEIN: THE TRUE STORY
Universal TV; telefeature; 1973
AIRPORT 1975
Universal; 1974
MIDWAY
Universal; 1976
DAMNATION ALLEY
20th Century-Fox; 1977
ROLL OF THUNDER, HEAR MY CRY
Tomorrow Entertainment; telefeature; 1978
FAST BREAK
Columbia; 1979
LOVING COUPLES
20th Century-Fox; 1980

Smith, Howard
Business:
The Village Voice
842 Broadway
New York, N.Y. 10003
(212) 475-3300

MARJOE
co-director with Sarah Kernochan;Cinema 5;1972
GIZMO!
New Line Cinema; 1977

Sole, Alfred
Contact:
Directors Guild of America
Los Angeles
(213) 656-1220

ALICE, SWEET ALICE (Communion/Holy Terror)
Allied Artists; 1977
TANYA'S ISLAND
IFEX Film; 1981; Canadian
THURSDAY THE 12TH
Paramount; 1981

Solt, Andrew
Home:
1301 N. Harper Avenue
Los Angeles, CA 90046
Business:
Solt-Leo Productions
6534 Sunset Blvd.
Los Angeles, CA 90028
(213) 464-5193
Agent:
William Morris Agency
Beverly Hills
(213) 274-7451

HEROES OF ROCK AND ROLL
co-director with Malcolm Leo; ABC-TV; television documentary; 1979
THIS IS ELVIS
co-director with Malcolm Leo; Warner Brothers; 1981

Sontag, Susan

DUET FOR CANNIBALS
Grove Press; 1969; Swedish
BROTHER CARL
New Yorker; 1972; Swedish
PROMISED LANDS
New Yorker; 1974; French

Spangler, Larry G.

THE SOUL OF NIGGER CHARLEY
Paramount; 1973
A KNIFE FOR THE LADIES
Bryanston; 1974
THE LIFE AND TIMES OF XAVIERA HOLLANDER
Mature; 1974
JOSHUA
Lone Star; 1976

Sperling, Karen

MAKE A FACE
Sperling; 1971

Spielberg, Steven
b. 1947
Cincinnati, Ohio
Agent:
I.C.M.
Hollywood
(213) 550-4000

NIGHT GALLERY
co-director with Boris Sagal & Barry Shear;
Universal TV; telefeature; 1969
DUEL
Universal TV; telefeature; 1971
SOMETHING EVIL
Belford Productions/CBS International;
telefeature; 1972
SAVAGE
Universal TV; telefeature; 1973
THE SUGARLAND EXPRESS
Universal; 1974
JAWS
Universal; 1975
CLOSE ENCOUNTERS OF THE THIRD KIND
Columbia; 1977
1941
Universal/Columbia; 1979
RAIDERS OF THE LOST ARK
Paramount; 1981
A BOY'S LIFE
Universal; 1982

Spottiswoode, Roger
Home:
364 Sumach Street
Toronto, Ontario M4X 1V4
Canada
(416) 961-9977

TERROR TRAIN
20th Century-Fox; 1980; Canadian
THE PURSUIT OF D.B. COOPER
Universal; 1981

Spradlin, G. D.
Agent:
The Mishkin Agency
Los Angeles
(213) 274-5261

THE ONLY WAY HOME
Regional; 1972

Spry, Robin
Home:
5330 Durocher
Montreal, Quebec H2V 3Y1
Canada
(514) 277-1503

PROLOGUE
Vaudeo; 1970; Canadian
ONE MAN
Baxter; 1977; Canadian
DRYING UP THE STREETS
CBS; 1978; Canadian
SUZANNE
1981; Canadian
HIT AND RUN
Agora Productions; 1981; Canadian

Stallone, Sylvester
b. 1946
New York, New York
Personal Manager:
Herb Nanas Organization
Beverly Hills
(213) 858-7049

PARADISE ALLEY
Universal; 1978
ROCKY II
United Artists; 1979
ROCKY III
United Artists; 1981

Stanley, Paul
Agent:
David Shapira & Assoc.
Beverly Hills
(213) 278-2742

CRY TOUGH
United Artists; 1959
THREE GUNS FOR TEXAS
co-director with David Lowell Rich & Earl Bellamy; Universal; 1968
SOLE SURVIVOR
Cinema Center; telefeature; 1969
RIVER OF MYSTERY
Universal TV; telefeature; 1971
NICKY'S WORLD
Tomorrow Entertainment; telefeature; 1974
CRISIS IN SUN VALLEY
Columbia TV; telefeature; 1978
THE ULTIMATE IMPOSTER
Universal TV; telefeature; 1979

Starr, Ringo
(Richard Starkey)
b. July 7, 1940
Liverpool, England

BORN TO BOOGIE
M-G-M/EMI; 1972; British

Starrett, Jack
Business:
4342 Bakman Street
N. Hollywood, CA 91605
(213) 506-5466
Agent:
Rodney Sheldon Agency
Los Angeles
(213) 275-9599

RUN, ANGEL, RUN!
Fanfare; 1969
THE LOSERS
Fanfare; 1970
CRY BLOOD, APACHE
Golden Eagle International; 1970
NIGHT CHASE
Cinema Center; telefeature; 1970
THE STRANGE VENGEANCE OF ROSALIE
20th Century-Fox; 1972
SLAUGHTER
American International; 1972
CLEOPATRA JONES
Warner Brothers; 1973
GRAVY TRAIN (The Dion Brothers)
Columbia; 1974
RACE WITH THE DEVIL
20th Century-Fox; 1975
A SMALL TOWN IN TEXAS
American International; 1976
FINAL CHAPTER - WALKING TALL
American International; 1977
ROGER & HARRY: THE MITERA TARGET
Bruce Lansbury Productions/Columbia TV; telefeature; 1977
NOWHERE TO HIDE
Mark Carliner Productions/Viacom; telefeature; 1977
THADDEUS ROSE AND EDDIE
CBS, Inc.; telefeature; 1978
BIG BOB JOHNSON AND HIS FANTASTIC SPEED CIRCUS
Playboy Productions/Paramount TV; telefeature; 1978
MR. HORN
Lorimar Productions; telefeature; 1979
SURVIVAL OF DANA
EMI TV; telefeature; 1979
A TEXAS LEGEND
Aura; 1981

Stein, Jeff

THE KIDS ARE ALRIGHT
New World; 1979; British

Steinberg, David
Contact:
Directors Guild of America
Los Angeles
(213) 656-1220

PATERNITY
Paramount; 1981

Stern, Leonard B.
Business:
Heyday Productions, Inc.
300 Colgems Square
Burbank, CA 91505
(213) 946-3000
Business Manager:
Gerwin, Jamner & Pariser
Los Angeles
(213) 652-0222

ONCE UPON A DEAD MAN
Universal TV; telefeature; 1971
THE SNOOP SISTERS
Universal TV; telefeature; 1972
JUST YOU AND ME, KID
Columbia; 1979

Stern, Sandor
Business:
9116½ Pico Blvd.
Los Angeles, CA 90035
(213) 275-0180
Agent:
I.C.M.
Hollywood
(213) 550-4000

THE SEEDING OF SARAH BURNS
Michael Klein Productions; telefeature; 1979

Stern, Steven Hilliard
Home:
4321 Clear Valley Drive
Encino, CA 91436
(213) 788-3607
Agent:
I.C.M.
Hollywood
(213) 550-4000

B.S. I LOVE YOU
20th Century-Fox; 1971
NEITHER BY DAY NOR BY NIGHT
Motion Pictures International; 1972; U.S.-Israeli
THE HARRAD SUMMER
Cinerama Releasing Corporation; 1974
ESCAPE FROM BOGEN COUNTY
Paramount TV; telefeature; 1977
THE GHOST OF FLIGHT 401
Paramount TV; telefeature; 1978
DOCTORS' PRIVATE LIVES
David Gerber Productions/Columbia TV; telefeature; 1978
GETTING MARRIED
Paramount TV; telefeature; 1978
FAST FRIENDS
Columbia TV; telefeature; 1979
ANATOMY OF A SEDUCTION
Moonlight Productions/Filmways; telefeature; 1979
YOUNG LOVE, FIRST LOVE
Lorimar Productions; telefeature; 1979
RUNNING
Columbia; 1979; Canadian-U.S.
PORTRAIT OF AN ESCORT
Moonlight Productions/Filmways; telefeature; 1980
THE DEVIL AND MAX DEVLIN
Buena Vista; 1981
MIRACLE ON ICE
Moonlight Productions/Filmways; telefeature; 1981

Stevens, Art
Business:
Walt Disney Productions
500 S. Buena Vista Street
Burbank, CA 91521
(213) 845-3141

THE FOX AND THE HOUND
co-director with Ted Berman & Richard Rich; Buena Vista; 1981

Stevens, Leslie

b. February 3, 1924
Washington, D.C.
Business:
Leslie Stevens Productions
1107 Glendon Avenue
Los Angeles, CA 90024
(213) 479-2770

PRIVATE PROPERTY
Citation; 1960
INCUBUS
1961
HERO'S ISLAND
United Artists; 1962
DELLA
Four Star; 1964
FANFARE FOR A DEATH SCENE
Four Star; 1967
I LOVE A MYSTERY
Universal TV; telefeature; 1973; filmed in 1967

Stevenson, Robert

b. 1905
London, England
Business:
Walt Disney Productions
500 S. Buena Vista Street
Burbank, CA 91521
(213) 845-3141

HAPPILY EVER AFTER
Gaumont-British; 1932; British
FALLING FOR YOU
Woolf and Freedman Film Service; 1933; British
JACK OF ALL TRADES
Gaumont-British; 1936; British
NINE DAYS A QUEEN (Tudor Rose)
Gaumont-British; 1936; British
THE MAN WHO LIVED AGAIN (The Man Who Changed His Mind)
Gaumont-British; 1936; British
KING SOLOMON'S MINES
Gaumont-British; 1937; British
NON-STOP NEW YORK
General Film Distributors; 1937; British
TO THE VICTOR (Owd Bob)
Gaumont-British; 1938; British
THE WARE CASE
Associated British Film Distributors; 1939; British
A YOUNG MAN'S FANCY
Associated British Film Distributors; 1939; British
RETURN TO YESTERDAY
Associated British Film Distributors; 1939; British
TOM BROWN'S SCHOOLDAYS
RKO Radio; 1940
BACK STREET
Universal; 1941
JOAN OF PARIS
RKO Radio; 1942
FOREVER AND A DAY
co-director with Rene Clair, Edmund Goulding, Cedric Hardwicke, Frank Lloyd, Victor Saville & Herbert Wilcox; RKO Radio; 1943
JANE EYRE
RKO Radio; 1944
DISHONORED LADY
United Artists; 1947
TO THE ENDS OF THE EARTH
RKO Radio; 1948
THE WOMAN ON PIER 13 (I Married A Communist)
RKO Radio; 1949
WALK SOFTLY, STRANGER
RKO Radio; 1950
MY FORBIDDEN PAST
RKO Radio; 1951
THE LAS VEGAS STORY
RKO Radio; 1952
JOHNNY TREMAIN
Buena Vista; 1957
OLD YELLER
Buena Vista; 1957
DARBY O'GILL AND THE LITTLE PEOPLE
Buena Vista; 1959
KIDNAPPED
Buena Vista; 1960; British-U.S.
THE ABSENT-MINDED PROFESSOR
Buena Vista; 1960
IN SEARCH OF THE CASTAWAYS
Buena Vista; 1962; British-U.S.

continued

Stevenson, Robert
continued

SON OF FLUBBER
Buena Vista; 1963
THE MISADVENTURES OF MERLIN JONES
Buena Vista; 1964
MARY POPPINS
Buena Vista; 1964
THE MONKEY'S UNCLE
Buena Vista; 1965
THAT DARN CAT
Buena Vista; 1965
THE GNOME-MOBILE
Buena Vista; 1967
BLACKBEARD'S GHOST
Buena Vista; 1968
THE LOVE BUG
Buena Vista; 1969
BEDKNOBS AND BROOMSTICKS
Buena Vista; 1971
HERBIE RIDES AGAIN
Buena Vista; 1974
THE ISLAND AT THE TOP OF THE WORLD
Buena Vista; 1974
ONE OF OUR DINOSAURS IS MISSING
Buena Vista; 1975; U.S.-British
THE SHAGGY D.A.
Buena Vista; 1976

Stone, Andrew, L.
b. July 16, 1902
Oakland, California
Home:
10478 Wyton Drive
Los Angeles, CA 90024
(213) 279-2427
Agent:
Calven Agency
Los Angeles
(213) 652-3380

DREARY HOUSE
1928
SOMBRAS DE GLORIA
Sono Arts; 1930
HELL'S HEADQUARTERS
Capitol; 1932
THE GIRL SAID NO
Grand National; 1937
STOLEN HEAVEN
Paramount; 1938
SAY IT IN FRENCH
Paramount; 1938
THE GREAT VICTOR HERBERT
Paramount; 1939
THERE'S MAGIC IN MUSIC
Paramount; 1941
STORMY WEATHER
20th Century-Fox; 1943
HI DIDDLE DIDDLE
RKO Radio; 1943
SENSATIONS OF 1945
United Artists; 1944
BEDSIDE MANNER
United Artists; 1945
THE BACHELOR'S DAUGHTER
United Artists; 1946
FUN ON A WEEKEND
United Artists; 1947
HIGHWAY 301
Warner Brothers; 1950
CONFIDENCE GIRL
United Artists; 1951
THE STEEL TRAP
20th Century-Fox; 1952
A BLUEPRINT FOR MURDER
20th Century-Fox; 1953
THE NIGHT HOLDS TERROR
Columbia; 1955
JULIE
M-G-M; 1956
CRY TERROR!
M-G-M; 1958
THE DECKS RAN RED
M-G-M; 1958
THE LAST VOYAGE
M-G-M; 1960
RING OF FIRE
M-G-M; 1961

continued

Stone, Andrew L.
continued

THE PASSWORD IS COURAGE
M-G-M; 1963; British
NEVER PUT IT IN WRITING
Allied Artists; 1964; British
THE SECRET OF MY SUCCESS
M-G-M; 1965; British
SONG OF NORWAY
Cinerama Releasing Corporation; 1970
THE GREAT WALTZ
M-G-M; 1972

Stone, Oliver
Business:
Ixtlan, Inc.
9025 Wilshire Blvd.
Beverly Hills, CA 90211
(213) 858-1276
Agent:
William Morris Agency
Beverly Hills
(213) 274-7451

SEIZURE
Cinerama Releasing Corporation; 1974; Canadian
THE HAND
Orion Pictures/Warner Brothers; 1981

Strick, Joseph
b. 1923
Pittsburgh, Pennsylvania
Home:
266 River Road
Grandview, N.Y. 10960
(914) 359-9527
Business:
Trans-Lux Corporation
625 Madison Avenue
New York, N.Y. 10022
(212) 751-3110

MUSCLE BEACH
co-director with Irving Lerner; 1948
THE BIG BREAK
1953
THE SAVAGE EYE
co-director with Ben Maddow & Sidney Meyers; Trans-Lux; 1959
THE BALCONY
Continental; 1963
ULYSSES
Continental; 1967
TROPIC OF CANCER
Paramount; 1970
ROAD MOVIE
Grove Press; 1974
A PORTRAIT OF THE ARTIST AS A YOUNG MAN
Mahler; 1979

Stuart, Mel
Home:
11508 Thurston Circle
Los Angeles, CA 90049
(213) 476-2634

IF IT'S TUESDAY, THIS MUST BE BELGIUM
United Artists; 1969
I LOVE MY WIFE
Universal; 1970
WILLY WONKA AND THE CHOCOLATE FACTORY
Paramount; 1971
ONE IS A LONELY NUMBER
M-G-M; 1972
WATTSTAX
Columbia; 1973
BRENDA STARR
Wolper Productions; telefeature; 1976
MEAN DOG BLUES
American International; 1978
RUBY AND OSWALD
Alan Landsburg Productions; telefeature; 1978
THE TRIANGLE FACTORY FIRE SCANDAL
Alan Landsburg Productions/Don Kirshner Productions; telefeature; 1979
THE CHISHOLMS
Alan Landsburg Productions; television mini-series; 1979
THE WHITE LIONS
Alan Landsburg Productions; 1979
SOPHIA LOREN: HER OWN STORY
Roger Gimbel Productions/EMI TV; telefeature; 1980

Sturges, John

b. January 3, 1911
Oak Park, Illinois
Business:
The Alpha Corporation
13063 Ventura Blvd.
N. Hollywood, CA 91604
(213) 788-5750
Agent:
William Morris Agency
Beverly Hills
(213) 274-7451

THUNDERBOLT
co-director with William Wyler; Monogram; 1945
THE MAN WHO DARED
Columbia; 1946
SHADOWED
Columbia; 1946
ALIAS MR. TWILIGHT
Columbia; 1946
FOR THE LOVE OF RUSTY
Columbia; 1947
KEEPER OF THE BEES
Columbia; 1947
BEST MAN WINS
Columbia; 1948
THE SIGN OF THE RAM
Columbia; 1948
THE WALKING HILLS
Columbia; 1949
THE CAPTURE
RKO Radio; 1950
MYSTERY STREET
M-G-M; 1950
RIGHT CROSS
M-G-M; 1950
THE MAGNIFICENT YANKEE
M-G-M; 1951
KIND LADY
M-G-M; 1951
THE PEOPLE AGAINST O'HARA
M-G-M; 1951
IT'S A BIG COUNTRY
co-director with Charles Vidor, Richard Thorpe, Don Hartman, Don Weis, Clarence Brown & William Wellman; M-G-M; 1952
THE GIRL IN WHITE
M-G-M; 1952
JEOPARDY
M-G-M; 1953
FAST COMPANY
M-G-M; 1953
ESCAPE FROM FORT BRAVO
M-G-M; 1953
BAD DAY AT BLACK ROCK
M-G-M; 1955
UNDERWATER!
RKO Radio; 1955
THE SCARLET COAT
M-G-M; 1955
BACKLASH
M-G-M; 1956
GUNFIGHT AT THE O.K. CORRAL
Paramount; 1957
THE LAW AND JAKE WADE
M-G-M; 1958
THE OLD MAN AND THE SEA
Warner Brothers; 1958
LAST TRAIN FROM GUN HILL
Paramount; 1959
NEVER SO FEW
M-G-M; 1959
THE MAGNIFICENT SEVEN
United Artists; 1960
BY LOVE POSSESSED
United Artists; 1961
SERGEANTS 3
United Artists; 1962
A GIRL NAMED TAMIKO
Paramount; 1963
THE GREAT ESCAPE
United Artists; 1963
THE SATAN BUG
United Artists; 1965
THE HALLELUJAH TRAIL
United Artists; 1965
HOUR OF THE GUN
United Artists; 1967
ICE STATION ZEBRA
M-G-M; 1968

continued

Sturges, John
continued

MAROONED
Columbia; 1969
JOE KIDD
Universal; 1972
CHINO (The Valdez Horses)
Intercontinental; 1973; Italian-Spanish-French
McQ
Warner Brothers; 1974
THE EAGLE HAS LANDED
Columbia; 1977; British

Summers, Jeremy
Contact:
British Film Institute
127 Charing Cross Road
London W.C. 2, England
01-437-4355

FERRY CROSS THE MERSEY
United Artists; 1965; British
HOUSE OF 1,000 DOLLS
American International; 1967; British
THE VENGEANCE OF FU MANCHU
Warner Brothers; 1968; British
TOURIST
Castle Combe Productions/Paramount TV; telefeature; 1980

Swackhamer, E. W.
Agent:
Shapiro-Lichtman Agency
Los Angeles
(213) 557-2244

IN NAME ONLY
Screen Gems/Columbia TV; telefeature; 1969
MAN AND BOY
Levitt-Pickman; 1972
GIDGET GETS MARRIED
Screen Gems/Columbia TV; telefeature; 1972
DEATH SENTENCE
Spelling-Goldberg Productions;telefeature;1974
DEATH AT LOVE HOUSE
Spelling-Goldberg Productions;telefeature;1976
ONCE AN EAGLE
co-director with Richard Michaels;Universal TV; television mini-series; 1976
NIGHT TERROR
Charles Fries Productions; telefeature; 1977
SPIDER-MAN
Charles Fries Productions; telefeature; 1977
THE DAIN CURSE
Martin Poll Productions; television mini-series; 1978
THE WINDS OF KITTY HAWK
Charles Fries Productions; telefeature; 1978
VAMPIRE
MTM Enterprises; telefeature; 1979
THE DEATH OF OCEAN VIEW PARK
Furia-Oringer Productions/Playboy Productions; telefeature; 1979
REWARD
Jerry Adler Productions/Espirit Enterprises/ Lorimar Productions; telefeature; 1980
TENSPEED AND BROWN SHOE
Stephen J. Cannell Productions; telefeature; 1980
THE OKLAHOMA CITY DOLLS
I.K.E. Productions/Columbia TV; telefeature; 1981
LONGSHOT
G.G. Productions; 1981

Swerling, Jo, Jr.
Agent:
Adams, Ray & Rosenberg
Los Angeles
(213) 278-3000

THE LAST CONVERTIBLE
co-director with Sidney Hayers & Gus Trikonis; Roy Huggins Productions/Universal TV; television mini-series; 1979

Swift, David
b. 1919
Minneapolis, Minnesota
Agent:
I.C.M.
Hollywood
(213) 550-4000

POLYANNA
Buena Vista; 1960
THE PARENT TRAP
Buena Vista; 1961
THE INTERNS
Columbia; 1962

continued

Swift, David
continued

LOVE IS A BALL
United Artists; 1963
UNDER THE YUM YUM TREE
Columbia; 1963
GOOD NEIGHBOR SAM
Columbia; 1964
HOW TO SUCCEED IN BUSINESS WITHOUT REALLY TRYING
United Artists; 1967

Swimmer, Saul

FORCE OF IMPULSE
Sutton; 1961
MRS. BROWN, YOU'VE GOT A LOVELY DAUGHTER
M-G-M; 1968; British
COMETOGETHER
Allied Artists; 1971; U.S.-Italian
THE CONCERT FOR BANGLADESH
20th Century-Fox; 1972
THE BLACK PEARL
Diamond; 1977

Swirnoff, Brad

TUNNELVISION
co-director with Neil Israel; World Wide; 1976

Syberberg, Hans-Jurgen
Contact:
Bundesverband Deutscher
Film Produzenten
Langenbeck Str., No. 9
6200 Wiesbaden
West Germany
306 200

KARL MAY
7MS Film Gesellschaft; 1976; West German
WINIFRED WAGNER
Bauer International; 1978; West German
LUDWIG: REQUIEM FOR A VIRGIN KING
Zoetrope; 1980; West German
HITLER: A FILM FROM GERMANY
Zoetrope; 1980; West German

Sykes, Peter
Contact:
British Film Institute
127 Charing Cross Road
London W.C. 2, England
01-437-4355

THE COMMITTEE
Planet; 1968; British
DEMONS OF THE MIND
M-G-M/EMI; 1972; British
THE HOUSE IN NIGHTMARE PARK
M-G-M/EMI; 1973; British
STEPTOE AND SON RIDE AGAIN
M-G-M/EMI; 1973; British
LEGEND OF SPIDER FOREST (Venom)
New Line Cinema; 1974; British
TO THE DEVIL A DAUGHTER
EMI; 1976; British
CRAZY HOUSE
Constellation; 1977; British
JESUS
co-director with John Krish; Warner Brothers; 1979; British
THE SEARCH FOR ALEXANDER THE GREAT
Time-Life Productions/Video Arts TV Productions; television mini-series; 1981; U.S.-British

Sylbert, Paul
Home:
One Buttonwood Square
Box 304
Philadelphia, PA 19130
(215) 564-0314
Agent:
Ziegler Associates
Los Angeles
(213) 278-0070

THE STEAGLE
Avco Embassy; 1971

Szwarc, Jeannot
b. France
Business:
Terpsichore Productions
10100 Santa Monica Blvd.
Los Angeles, CA 90067
(213) 553-8200
Agent:
Shapiro-Lichtman Agency
Los Angeles
(213) 557-2244

NIGHT OF TERROR
Paramount TV; telefeature; 1972
THE WEEKEND NUN
Paramount TV; telefeature; 1972
THE DEVIL'S DAUGHTER
Paramount TV; telefeature; 1973
YOU'LL NEVER SEE ME AGAIN
Universal TV; telefeature; 1973
LISA, BRIGHT AND DARK
Bob Banner Associates; telefeature; 1973
A SUMMER WITHOUT BOYS
Playboy Productions; telefeature; 1973
THE SMALL MIRACLE
NBC-TV; telefeature; 1973
EXTREME CLOSE-UP
National General; 1973
CRIME CLUB
Universal TV; telefeature; 1975
BUG
Paramount; 1975
CODE NAME: DIAMOND HEAD
QM Productions; telefeature; 1977
JAWS 2
Universal; 1978
SOMEWHERE IN TIME
Universal; 1980
ENIGMA
Filmcrest International; 1982; British-French

Tacchella, Jean-Charles
b. 1926
France
Contact:
French Film Office
745 Fifth Avenue
New York, N.Y. 10151
(212) 832-8860

VOYAGE TO GRAND TARTARIE
New Line Cinema; 1974; French
COUSIN COUSINE
Libra Films; 1977; French
THE BLUE COUNTRY
1978; French
IT'S A LONG TIME THAT I'VE LOVED YOU (Soupcon)
Durham/Pike; 1979; French

Tanner, Alain
b. 1929
Geneva, Switzerland
Contact:
Swiss National Tourist
Office
42 Talacker
8001 Zurich
Switzerland
01-2115377

CHARLES, DEAD OR ALIVE
New Yorker; 1969; Swiss-French
LA SALAMANDRE
New Yorker; 1971; Swiss
LA RETOUR D'AFRIQUE
1972; Swiss
THE MIDDLE OF THE WORLD
New Yorker; 1974; Swiss
JONAH WHO WILL BE 25 IN THE YEAR 2000
New Yorker; 1976; Swiss
MESSIDOR
New Yorker; 1979; Swiss

Taradash, Daniel
b. January 29, 1913
Louisville, Kentucky
Agent:
I.C.M.
Hollywood
(213) 550-4000

STORM CENTER
Columbia; 1956

Tarkovsky, Andrei
b. 1932
Moscow, U.S.S.R.

MY NAME IS IVAN
Shore International; 1962; Soviet
ANDREI RUBLEV
Columbia; 1971; Soviet
SOLARIS
1972; Soviet
THE MIRROR
1978; Soviet

Tati, Jacques
(Jacques Tatischeff)
b. October 9, 1908
Le Pecq, France
Contact:
French Film Office
745 Fifth Avenue
New York, N.Y. 10151
(212) 832-8860

JOUR DE FETE
Mayer-Kingsley; 1949; French
MR. HULOT'S HOLIDAY
GBD International; 1953; French
MY UNCLE
Continental; 1958; French
PLAYTIME
Continental; 1968; French
TRAFFIC
Columbia; 1971; French
PARADE
telefeature; 1974; French

Tavernier, Bertrand
b. April 25, 1941
Lyons, France
Contact:
French Film Office
745 Fifth Avenue
New York, N.Y. 10151
(212) 832-8860

THE CLOCKMAKER OF ST. PAUL
Joseph Green Pictures; 1974; French
LET JOY REIGN SUPREME
Specialty; 1975; French
THE JUDGE AND THE ASSASSIN
1976; French
SPOILED CHILDREN
1977; French
FEMMES FATALES
1979; French
DEATH WATCH
Gaumont; 1980; French
UNE SEMAINE DE VACANCES
1981; French

Taylor, Don
b. December 13, 1920
Freeport, Pennsylvania
Contact:
Directors Guild of America
Hollywood
(213) 656-1220

EVERYTHING'S DUCKY
Columbia; 1961
RIDE THE WILD SURF
Columbia; 1964
JACK OF DIAMONDS
M-G-M; 1967; U.S.-West German
SOMETHING FOR A LONELY MAN
Universal TV; telefeature; 1968
THE FIVE MAN ARMY
M-G-M; 1970; Italian
WILD WOMEN
Aaron Spelling Productions; telefeature; 1970
ESCAPE FROM THE PLANET OF THE APES
20th Century-Fox; 1971
HEAT OF ANGER
Metromedia Productions; telefeature; 1972
TOM SAWYER
United Artists; 1973
NIGHT GAMES
Paramount TV; telefeature; 1974
HONKY TONK
M-G-M TV; telefeature; 1974
ECHOES OF A SUMMER
Cine Artists; 1976; U.S.-Canadian
THE MAN-HUNTER
Universal TV; telefeature; 1976; filmed in 1968
THE GREAT SCOUT AND CATHOUSE THURSDAY
American International; 1976
A CIRCLE OF CHILDREN
Edgar J. Scherick Productions/20th Century-Fox TV; telefeature; 1977
THE ISLAND OF DR. MOREAU
American International; 1977
DAMIEN - OMEN II
20th Century-Fox; 1978
THE GIFT
The Jozak Company/Cypress Point Productions/ Paramount TV; telefeature; 1979
THE FINAL COUNTDOWN
United Artists; 1980
THE PROMISE OF LOVE
Pierre Cossette Productions; telefeature; 1980
BROKEN PROMISE
telefeature; 1981
RED FLAG: THE ULTIMATE GAME
Marble Arch Productions; telefeature; 1981

Taylor, Jud
Contact:
Directors Guild of America
Hollywood
(213) 656-1220

FADE-IN
  Paramount; 1968
WEEKEND OF TERROR
  Paramount TV; telefeature; 1970
SUDDENLY SINGLE
  Chris-Rose Productions; telefeature; 1971
REVENGE
  Mark Carliner Productions; telefeature; 1971
THE ROOKIES
  Aaron Spelling Productions; telefeature; 1972
SAY GOODBYE, MAGGIE COLE
  Spelling-Goldberg Productions; telefeature; 1972
HAWKINS ON MURDER
  Arena-Leda Productions/M-G-M TV; telefeature; 1973
WINTER KILL
  Andy Griffith Enterprises/M-G-M TV; telefeature; 1974
THE DISAPPEARANCE OF FLIGHT 412
  Cinemobile Productions; telefeature; 1975
SEARCH FOR THE GODS
  Warner Brothers TV; telefeature; 1975
FUTURE COP
  Paramount TV; telefeature; 1976
RETURN TO EARTH
  King-Hitzig Productions; telefeature; 1976
WOMAN OF THE YEAR
  M-G-M TV; telefeature; 1976
TAIL GUNNER JOE
  Universal TV; telefeature; 1977
MARY WHITE
  Radnitz/Mattel Productions; telefeature; 1977
CHRISTMAS MIRACLE IN CAUFIELD, U.S.A.
  20th Century-Fox TV; telefeature; 1977
THE LAST TENANT
  Titus Productions; telefeature; 1978
LOVEY: A CIRCLE OF CHILDREN, PART II
  Time-Life Productions; telefeature; 1978
FLESH AND BLOOD
  The Jozak Company/Cypress Point Productions/ Paramount TV; telefeature; 1979
CITY IN FEAR
  directed under pseudonym of Allen Smithee; Trans World International; telefeature; 1980
ACT OF LOVE
  Cypress Point Productions/Paramount TV; telefeature; 1980

Teague, Lewis
Agent:
Phil Gersh Agency
Beverly Hills
(213) 274-6611

DIRTY O'NEIL
  co-director with Howard Freen; American International; 1974
THE LADY IN RED
  New World; 1979
ALLIGATOR
  Group 1; 1980

Tewkesbury, Joan
Agent:
I.C.M.
Hollywood
(213) 550-4000

OLD BOYFRIENDS
  Avco Embassy; 1979
THE TENTH MONTH
  Joe Hamilton Productions; telefeature; 1979
THE ACORN PEOPLE
  Rollins-Joffe-Morra-Brezner Productions; telefeature; 1980

Tewksbury, Peter
b. 1924

SUNDAY IN NEW YORK
  M-G-M; 1964
EMIL AND THE DETECTIVES
  Buena Vista; 1964
DOCTOR, YOU'VE GOT TO BE KIDDING
  M-G-M; 1967
STAY AWAY, JOE
  M-G-M; 1968

continued

Tewksbury, Peter
continued

THE TROUBLE WITH GIRLS
M-G-M; 1969
SECOND CHANCE
Metromedia Productions; telefeature; 1972

Thomas, Gerald
b. December 10, 1920
Hull, England
Contact:
British Film Institute
127 Charing Cross Road
London W.C. 2, England
01-437-4355

CIRCUS FRIENDS
1956; British
TIMELOCK
DCA; 1957; British
THE CIRCLE (The Vicious Circle)
Kassler; 1957; British
CHAIN OF EVENTS
1958; British
CARRY ON SERGEANT
Governor; 1958; British
CARRY ON NURSE
Governor; 1959; British
PLEASE TURN OVER
Columbia; 1959; British
WATCH YOUR STERN
Magna; 1960; British
BEWARE OF CHILDREN (No Kidding)
American International; 1960; British
CARRY ON CONSTABLE
Governor; 1960; British
ROOMMATES (Raising the Wind)
Herts-Lion International; 1961; British
CARRY ON CRUISING
Governor; 1962; British
THE SWINGIN' MAIDEN (The Iron Maiden)
Columbia; 1962; British
NURSE ON WHEELS
Janus; 1963; British
CARRY ON SPYING
Governor; 1964; British
CARRY ON CLEO
Governor; 1964; British
THE BIG JOB
1966; British
FOLLOW THAT CAMEL
Schoenfeld Film Distributing; 1967; British
CARRY ON AT YOUR CONVENIENCE
1971; British
CARRY ON ENGLAND
Fox-Rank; 1976; British
CARRY ON EMMANNUELLE
1978; British

Thomas, Ralph
b. August 10, 1915
Hull, England
Contact:
British Film Institute
127 Charing Cross Road
London W.C. 2, England
01-437-4355

HELTER SKELTER
General Film Distributors; 1949; British
ONCE UPON A DREAM
General Film Distributors; 1949; British
TRAVELLER'S JOY
General Film Distributors; 1949; British
THE CLOUDED YELLOW
General Film Distributors; 1950; British
ISLAND RESCUE (Appointment with Venus)
Universal; 1951; British
THE ASSASSIN (The Venetian Bird)
United Artists; 1952; British
THE DOG AND THE DIAMONDS
Associated British Film Distributors/Children's Film Foundation; 1953; British
A DAY TO REMEMBER
Republic; 1953; British
DOCTOR IN THE HOUSE
Republic; 1954; British
MAD ABOUT MEN
General Film Distributors; 1954; British
DOCTOR AT SEA
Republic; 1955; British
ABOVE US THE WAVES
Republic; 1955; British

continued

Thomas, Ralph
continued

THE IRON PETTICOAT
M-G-M; 1956; British-U.S.
CHECKPOINT
Rank; 1956; British
DOCTOR AT LARGE
Universal; 1957; British
CAMPBELL'S KINGDOM
Rank; 1957; British
A TALE OF TWO CITIES
Rank; 1958; British
THE WIND CANNOT READ
20th Century-Fox; 1958; British
THE 39 STEPS
20th Century-Fox; 1959; British
UPSTAIRS AND DOWNSTAIRS
20th Century-Fox; 1959; British
CONSPIRACY OF HEARTS
Paramount; 1960; British
DOCTOR IN LOVE
Governor; 1960; British
NO LOVE FOR JOHNNIE
Embassy; 1961; British
NO, MY DARLING DAUGHTER
Zenith; 1961; British
A PAIR OF BRIEFS
Rank; 1962; British
YOUNG AND WILLING (The Wild and the Willing)
Universal; 1962; British
DOCTOR IN DISTRESS
Governor; 1963; British
AGENT 8 3/4 (Hot Enough for June)
Continental; 1963; British
McGUIRE, GO HOME! (The High Bright Sun)
Continental; 1964; British
CARNABY, M.D. (Doctor in Clover)
Continental; 1965; British
DEADLIER THAN THE MALE
Universal; 1966; British
SOME GIRLS DO
United Artists; 1968; British
THE HIGH COMMISSIONER (Nobody Runs Forever)
Cinerama Releasing Corporation; 1968; British
DOCTOR IN TROUBLE
Rank; 1970; British
PERCY
M-G-M; 1971; British
QUEST FOR LOVE
Rank; 1971; British
IT'S A 2'6" ABOVE THE GROUND WORLD
British Lion; 1972; British
THE LOVE BAN
1973; British
IT'S NOT THE SIZE THAT COUNTS (Percy's Progress)
Joseph Brenner Associates; 1974; British
A NIGHTINGALE SANG IN BERKELEY SQUARE
1980; British

Thomas, Ralph L.
Business:
365 Markham Street
Toronto, Ontario M6G 2K8
Canada
(416) 922-8700

TYLER
CBC; telefeature; 1977; Canadian
CEMENTHEAD
CBC; telefeature; 1978; Canadian
A PAID VACATION
CBC; telefeature; 1979; Canadian
TICKET TO HEAVEN
United Artists Classics; 1981; Canadian

Thompson, J. Lee
b. 1914
Bristol, England
Home:
21932 W. Pacific Coast
Highway
Malibu, CA 90265
Agent:
Chasin-Park-Citron
Los Angeles
(213) 273-7190

MURDER WITHOUT CRIME
Associated British Picture Corporation; 1950; British
THE YELLOW BALLOON
Allied Artists; 1952; British
THE WEAK AND THE WICKED
Allied Artists; 1954; British

continued

Thompson, J. Lee
continued

COCKTAILS IN THE KITCHEN (For Better or Worse)
Associated British Picture Corporation; 1954; British
AS LONG AS THEY'RE HAPPY
Rank; 1955; British
AN ALLIGATOR NAMED DAISY
Rank; 1955; British
BLONDE SINNER (Yield to the Night)
Allied Artists; 1956; British
THE GOOD COMPANIONS
Rank; 1957; British
WOMAN IN A DRESSING GOWN
Warner Brothers; 1957; British
DESERT ATTACK (Ice Cold in Alex)
20th Century-Fox; 1958; British
NO TREES IN THE STREET
Associated British Picture Corporation; 1959; British
TIGER BAY
Continental; 1959; British
FLAME OVER INDIA (North West Frontier)
20th Century-Fox; 1959; British
I AIM AT THE STARS
Columbia; 1960; U.S.-West German
THE GUNS OF NAVARONE
Columbia; 1961; U.S.-British
CAPE FEAR
Universal; 1962
TARAS BULBA
United Artists; 1962
KINGS OF THE SUN
United Artists; 1963
WHAT A WAY TO GO!
20th Century-Fox; 1964
JOHN GOLDFARB, PLEASE COME HOME
20th Century-Fox; 1965
RETURN FROM THE ASHES
United Artists; 1965; British-U.S.
EYE OF THE DEVIL
M-G-M; 1967; British
BEFORE WINTER COMES
Columbia; 1969; British
THE CHAIRMAN
20th Century-Fox; 1969; British
MACKENNA'S GOLD
Columbia; 1969
BROTHERLY LOVE (Country Dance)
M-G-M; 1970; British
CONQUEST OF THE PLANET OF THE APES
20th Century-Fox; 1972
A GREAT AMERICAN TRAGEDY
Metromedia Productions; telefeature; 1972
BATTLE FOR THE PLANET OF THE APES
20th Century-Fox; 1973
HUCKLEBERRY FINN
United Artists; 1974
THE BLUE KNIGHT
Lorimar Productions; telefeature; 1975
THE REINCARNATION OF PETER PROUD
American International; 1975
ST. IVES
Warner Brothers; 1976
WIDOW
Lorimar Productions; telefeature; 1976
THE WHITE BUFFALO
United Artists; 1977
THE GREEK TYCOON
Universal; 1978
THE PASSAGE
United Artists; 1979; British
CABOBLANCO
Avco Embassy; 1981
HAPPY BIRTHDAY TO ME
Columbia; 1981; Canadian
CODE RED
Irwin Allen Productions/Columbia TV; telefeature 1981

Thompson, Robert C.
Agent:
Irv Schechter
Los Angeles
(213) 278-8070

BUD AND LOU
Bob Banner Associates; telefeature; 1978

Thorpe, Jerry
Home:
865 S. Bundy Drive
Los Angeles, CA 90049
Business:
Glenn-Thorpe Productions
CBS Studio Center
4024 Radford Avenue
Studio City, CA 91604
(213) 760-5201
Agent:
Major Talent Agency
Los Angeles
(213) 820-5841

THE VENETIAN AFFAIR
M-G-M; 1968
DAY OF THE EVIL GUN
M-G-M; 1968
DIAL HOT LINE
Universal TV; telefeature; 1970
LOCK, STOCK AND BARREL
Universal TV; telefeature; 1971
THE CABLE CAR MURDER
Warner Brothers TV; telefeature; 1971
KUNG FU
Warner Brothers TV; telefeature; 1972
COMPANY OF KILLERS
Universal; 1972
SMILE JENNY, YOU'RE DEAD
Warner Brothers TV; telefeature; 1974
THE DARK SIDE OF INNOCENCE
Warner Brothers TV; telefeature; 1976
I WANT TO KEEP MY BABY
CBS, Inc.; telefeature; 1976
THE POSSESSED
Warner Brothers TV; telefeature; 1977
STICKIN' TOGETHER
Blinn-Thorpe Productions/Viacom; telefeature; 1978
A QUESTION OF LOVE
Viacom; telefeature; 1978
THE LAZARUS SYNDROME
Blinn-Thorpe Productions/Viacom; telefeature; 1979
ALL GOD'S CHILDREN
Blinn-Thorpe Productions/Viacom; telefeature; 1980

Till, Eric
Home:
62 Chaplin Crescent
Toronto, Ontario M5P 1A3
Canada
(416) 488-4068

A GREAT BIG THING
Argo Films; 1967; British
HOT MILLIONS
M-G-M; 1968; British
THE WALKING STICK
M-G-M; 1970; British
A FAN'S NOTES
Warner Brothers; 1971; Canadian
ALL THINGS BRIGHT AND BEAUTIFUL (It Shouldn't Happen to a Vet)
World Northal; 1978; British
WILD HORSE HANK
1979; Canadian
AN AMERICAN CHRISTMAS CAROL
ABC-TV; telefeature; 1979
MARY AND JOSEPH: A STORY OF FAITH
Lorimar Productions/CIP-Europaische Treuhand AG; telefeature; 1979; U.S.-West German
IMPROPER CHANNELS
Crown International; 1981; Canadian
IF YOU COULD SEE WHAT I HEAR
Cypress Grove; 1981; Canadian

Toback, James
Home:
11 East 87th Street
New York, N.Y. 10028
(212) 427-5606
Agent:
I.C.M.
Hollywood
(213) 550-4000

FINGERS
Brut Productions; 1978
LOVE AND MONEY
Paramount/Lorimar; 1981

Topper, Burt
Business:
(213) 651-1320
Agent:
Ben Conway
Hollywood
(213) 271-8133

HELL SQUAD
American International; 1958
TANK COMMANDOS
American International; 1959
THE DIARY OF A HIGH SCHOOL BRIDE
American International; 1959
WAR IS HELL
Allied Artists; 1964
THE STRANGLER
Allied Artists; 1964
THE DEVIL'S 8
American International; 1968
THE HARD RIDE
American International; 1971
THE DAY THE LORD GOT BUSTED
American; 1976

Tors, Ivan
b. June 12, 1916
Budapest, Hungary
Business:
Universal Studios
Universal City, CA 91608
(213) 508-2423

RHINO!
M-G-M; 1964
ZEBRA IN THE KITCHEN
M-G-M; 1965

Totten, Robert
Business:
Tottenbob Productions
(213) 788-4242
Agent:
Herb Tobias & Assoc.
Los Angeles
(213) 277-6211

THE QUICK AND THE DEAD
Beckman; 1963
DEATH OF A GUNFIGHTER
co-director with Don Siegel; both directed under pseudonym of Allen Smithee; Universal; 1967
THE WILD COUNTRY
Buena Vista; 1971
THE RED PONY
Universal TV/Omnibus Productions; telefeature; 1973
HUCKLEBERRY FINN
ABC Circle Films; telefeature; 1975
PONY EXPRESS RIDER
Doty-Dayton; 1976
THE SACKETTS
Douglas Netter Enterprises/M.B. Scott Productions/Shalako Enterprises; telefeature; 1979

Towne, Robert
Contact:
Directors Guild of America
Los Angeles
(213) 656-1220

PERSONAL BEST
1981

Townsend, Bud
Home:
5917 Blairstone Drive
Culver City, CA 90230
(213) 870-1559
Agent:
Phil Gersh Agency
Beverly Hills
(213) 274-6611

NIGHTMARE IN WAX
Crown International; 1969
THE FOLKS AT RED WOLF INN (Terror House)
Scope III; 1972
ALICE IN WONDERLAND
General National Enterprises; 1976
COACH
Crown International; 1978

Tramont, Jean-Claude
Agent:
I.C.M.
Hollywood
(213) 550-4000

FOCAL POINT
Warner Brothers-Columbia; 1977; French
ALL NIGHT LONG
Universal; 1981

Trent, John
Home:
50 Dale Avenue
Toronto, Canada
(416) 924-8863
Agent:
Phil Gersh Agency
Beverly Hills
(213) 274-6611

THE BUSHBABY
M-G-M; 1970; British
HOMER
National General; 1970; Canadian
THE MAN WHO WANTED TO LIVE FOREVER
Palomar Pictures International; telefeature; 1970
JALNA
CBC/Thames TV; telefeature; 1972; British
SUNDAY IN THE COUNTRY
American International; 1973; British
IT SEEMED LIKE A GOOD IDEA AT THE TIME
Selective Cinema; 1974; Canadian
FIND THE LADY
Danton; 1975; Canadian
RIEL
CBC; telefeature; 1977; Canadian
CROSSBAR
CBS; telefeature; 1978; Canadian
MIDDLE AGE CRAZY
20th Century-Fox; 1980; Canadian-U.S.
MISDEAL
1981; Canadian

Trikonis, Gus
Agent:
Herb Tobias & Assoc.
Los Angeles
(213) 277-6211

FIVE THE HARD WAY
Fantascope; 1969
THE SWINGING BARMAIDS
Premiere; 1975
SUPERCOCK
Hagen-Wayne; 1975
NASHVILLE GIRL
New World; 1976
MOONSHINE COUNTY EXPRESS
New World; 1977
NEW GIRL IN TOWN
New World; 1977
THE EVIL
New World; 1978
THE DARKER SIDE OF TERROR
Shaner-Ramrus Productions/Bob Banner Associates; telefeature; 1979
SHE'S DRESSED TO KILL
Grant-Case-McGrath Enterprises/Barry Weitz Productions; telefeature; 1979
THE LAST CONVERTIBLE
co-director with Sidney Hayers & Jo Swerling, Jr.; Roy Huggins Productions/Universal TV; television mini-series; 1979
FLAMINGO ROAD
MF Productions/Lorimar Productions; telefeature; 1980
TOUCHED BY LOVE
Columbia; 1980
ELVIS AND THE BEAUTY QUEEN
David Gerber Productions/Columbia TV; telefeature; 1981
TAKE THIS JOB AND SHOVE IT
Avco Embassy; 1981
TWIRL
Charles Fries Productions; telefeature; 1981

Troell, Jan
b. July 23, 1931
Limhamn, Skane, Sweden
Contact:
Swedish Film Institute
P.O. Box 27126
S-10252 Stockholm
Sweden
08-630510

4 X 4
co-director; 1965; Swedish-Finnish-Norwegian-Danish
HERE'S YOUR LIFE
Brandon; 1966; Swedish
EENY, MEENY, MINY, MO (Who Saw Him Die?)
Svensk Filmindustri; 1968; Swedish
THE EMIGRANTS
Warner Brothers; 1972; Swedish
THE NEW LAND (Unto A Good Land)
Warner Brothers; 1973; Swedish
ZANDY'S BRIDE
Warner Brothers; 1974

continued

Troell, Jan
continued

BANG!
1977; Swedish
THE FLIGHT OF THE EAGLE
1978; Swedish
HURRICANE
Paramount; 1979

Truffaut, Francois
b. February 6, 1932
Paris, France
Contact:
French Film Office
745 Fifth Avenue
New York, N.Y. 10151
(212) 832-8860

THE 400 BLOWS
Zenith; 1959; French
SHOOT THE PIANO PLAYER
Astor; 1960; French
JULES AND JIM
Janus; 1961; French
LOVE AT TWENTY
co-director; Embassy; 1962; French-Italian-Japanese-Polish-West German
THE SOFT SKIN
Cinema 5; 1964; French
FAHRENHEIT 451
Universal; 1967; British
THE BRIDE WORE BLACK
Lopert; 1968; French-Italian
STOLEN KISSES
Lopert; 1969; French
MISSISSIPPI MERMAID
United Artists; 1970; French-Italian
THE WILD CHILD
United Artists; 1970; French
BED AND BOARD
Columbia; 1971; French
TWO ENGLISH GIRLS
Janus; 1972; French
SUCH A GORGEOUS KID LIKE ME
Columbia; 1973; French
DAY FOR NIGHT (La Nuit Americaine)
Warner Brothers; 1973; French-Italian
THE STORY OF ADELE H.
New World; 1975; French
SMALL CHANGE
New World; 1976; French
THE MAN WHO LOVED WOMEN
Cinema 5; 1977; French
THE GREEN ROOM
New World; 1978; French
LOVE ON THE RUN
New World; 1979; French
THE LAST METRO
United Artists Classics; 1980; French
THE WOMAN NEXT DOOR
United Artists Classics; 1981; French

Trumbull, Douglas
Business:
(213) 823-0433

SILENT RUNNING
Universal; 1972
BRAINSTORM
M-G-M/United Artists; 1982

Tuchner, Michael
b. England
Agent:
The Paul Kohner Agency
Los Angeles
(213) 550-1060
Douglas Rae Management
London
01-836-3903

VILLAIN
M-G-M; 1971; British
FEAR IS THE KEY
Paramount; 1973; British
MR. QUILP
Avco Embassy; 1975; British
THE LIKELY LADS
EMI; 1976; British
SUMMER OF MY GERMAN SOLDIER
Highgate Productions; telefeature; 1978
HAYWIRE
Pando Productions/Warner Brothers TV; telefeature; 1980
THE HUNCHBACK OF NOTRE DAME
Norman Rosemont Productions; telefeature; 1982

Turman, Lawrence
b. 1926
Los Angeles, California
Contact:
Directors Guild of America
Los Angeles
(213) 656-1220

MARRIAGE OF A YOUNG STOCKBROKER
20th Century-Fox; 1971
SECOND THOUGHTS
Universal; 1982

Ullman, Liv
b. December 16, 1939
Tokyo, Japan
Agent:
Paul Kohner Agency
Los Angeles
(213) 550-1060

LOVE
co-director with Annette Cohen, Nancy Dowd & Mai Zetterling; Coup Films; 1981; Canadian

Ustinov, Peter
b. April 16, 1921
London, England
Contact:
Directors Guild of America
Los Angeles
(213) 656-1220

SCHOOL FOR SECRETS
General Film Distributors; 1946; British
VICE VERSA
General Film Distributors; 1948; British
PRIVATE ANGELO
co-director with Michael Anderson; Associated British Picture Corporation; 1949; British
ROMANOFF AND JULIET
Universal; 1961
BILLY BUDD
Allied Artists; 1962; British
LADY L
M-G-M; 1966; U.S.-Italian-French
HAMMERSMITH IS OUT
Cinerama Releasing Corporation; 1972

Uys, Jamie

DINGAKA
Embassy; 1965; South African
AFTER YOU, COMRADE
Continental; 1967; South African
LOST IN THE DESERT
Columbia; 1971; South African
BEAUTIFUL PEOPLE (Animals Are Beautiful People)
Warner Brothers; 1974; South African
THE GODS MUST BE CRAZY
Cat Films; 1980; South African

Vadim, Roger
(Roger Vadim Plemiannikov)
b. January 26, 1928
Paris, France

AND GOD CREATED WOMAN
Kingsley International; 1956; French
NO SUN IN VENICE
Kingsley International; 1957; French-Italian
THE NIGHT HEAVEN FELL
Kingsley International; 1957; French-Italian
LES LIAISONS DANGEREUSES
Astor; 1959; French-Italian
BLOOD AND ROSES
Paramount; 1960; Italian
PLEASE, NOT NOW!
20th Century-Fox; 1961; French
SEVEN CAPITAL SINS
co-director; Embassy; 1962; French-Italian
LOVE ON A PILLOW
Royal International; 1962; French-Italian
OF FLESH AND BLOOD (The Highways)
Times; 1963; French-Italian
VICE AND VIRTUE
M-G-M; 1963; French
NUTTY, NAUGHTY CHATEAU (Castle in Sweden)
Lopert; 1963; French-Italian
CIRCLE OF LOVE (La Ronde)
Reade-Sterling; 1964; French
THE GAME IS OVER
Royal International; 1966; French-Italian
SPIRITS OF THE DEAD
co-director with Federico Fellini & Louis Malle; American International; 1968; Italian-French

continued

Vadim, Roger
continued

BARBARELLA
Paramount; 1968; Italian-French
PRETTY MAIDS ALL IN A ROW
M-G-M; 1971
HELLE
1972; French
MS. DON JUAN
Scotia American; 1973; French
CHARLOTTE
Gamma III; 1974; French
UNE FEMME FIDELE
1976; French
NIGHT GAMES
Avco Embassy; 1980; French
THE HOT TOUCH
20th Century-Fox; 1981; Canadian

Valdez, Luis
Contact:
Directors Guild of America
Los Angeles
(213) 656-1220

ZOOT SUIT
Universal; 1981

Van Horn, Buddy
Home:
4409 Ponca Avenue
Toluca Lake, CA 91602
Messages:
(213) HO. 2-2301

ANY WHICH WAY YOU CAN
Warner Brothers; 1980

Van Peebles, Melvin
(Melvin Peebles)
b. 1932
Chicago, Illinois
Business:
Yeah Inc.
850 Seventh Avenue
New York, N.Y. 10019
(212) 489-6570

THE STORY OF A THREE-DAY PASS
Sigma III; 1968; French
WATERMELON MAN
Columbia; 1970
SWEET SWEETBACK'S BAADASSSSS SONG
Cinemation; 1971

Varda, Agnes
b. May 30, 1928
Brussels, Belgium
Home:
6 Eastwind
Venice, CA
(213) 392-7700

LA POINTE COURTE
1954; French
CLEO FROM 5 TO 7
Zenith; 1962; French
LE BONHEUR
Clover; 1965; French
LES CREATURES
New Yorker; 1966; French-Swedish
FAR FROM VIETNAM
co-director with Jean-Luc Godard, Claude Lelouch, Alain Resnais, William Klein & Joris Ivens; New Yorker; 1967; French
LIONS LOVE
Raab; 1969
NAUSICAA
1970; French; made for television
DAGUERREOTYPES
1975; French
ONE SINGS, THE OTHER DOESN'T
Cinema 5; 1977; French
MUR MURS
1981

Verhoeven, Paul
Contact:
RVD (GOVERNMENT INFORMATION SERVICE)
20 Binnenhof
The Hague, Netherlands
070-614181

WAT ZIEN IK (Strictly Business)
Rob Houwer Film; 1972; Dutch
TURKISH DELIGHT
Cinemation; 1974; Dutch
KEETJE TIPPEL
Cinema National; 1976; Dutch

continued

Verhoeven, Paul
continued

SOLDIER OF ORANGE
International Picture Show Company; 1979; Dutch
SPETTERS
Samuel Goldwyn Company; 1981; Dutch

Verneuil, Henri
(Achod Malakian)
b. October 15, 1920
Rodosto, Turkey
Contact:
French Film Office
745 Fifth Avenue
New York, N.Y. 10151
(212) 832-8860

THE VILLAGE FEUD
1951; French
BRELAN D'AS
1952; French
FORBIDDEN FRUIT
Films Around the World; 1952; French
THE BAKER OF VALORGUE
1953; French
CARNAVAL
1953; French
THE MOST WANTED MAN IN THE WORLD (Public Enemy No. 1)
Astor; 1953; French-Italian
THE SHEEP HAS FIVE LEGS
United Motion Picture Organization; 1954; French
LOVERS' NET
1955; French
DES GENS SANS IMPORTANCE
1955; French
PARIS-PALACE-HOTEL
1956; French
WHAT PRICE MURDER
United Motion Picture Organization; 1957; French
MAXIME
Interworld; 1958; French
THE BIG CHIEF
Continental; 1959; French-Italian
THE COW AND I
Zenith; 1959; French-West German
IT HAPPENED ALL NIGHT
1960; French
LOVE AND THE FRENCHMAN
co-director; 1960; French
LE PRESIDENT
1961; French-Italian
THE LIONS ARE LOOSE
Franco-London; 1961; French-Italian
A MONKEY IN WINTER
M-G-M; 1962; French
ANY NUMBER CAN WIN
M-G-M; 1963; French
GREED IN THE SUN
M-G-M; 1964; French
WEEKEND AT DUNKIRK
20th Century-Fox; 1965; French-Italian
THE 25TH HOUR
M-G-M; 1967; French-Italian-Yugoslavian
GUNS FOR SAN SEBASTIAN
M-G-M; 1968; French-Italian-Mexican
THE SICILIAN CLAN
20th Century-Fox; 1970; French
THE BURGLARS
Columbia; 1972; French-Italian
THE SERPENT (Night Flight to Moscow)
Avco Embassy; 1973; French-Italian-West German
THE NIGHT CALLER (Fear Over the City)
Columbia; 1975; French
LE CORPS DE MON ENNEMI
1976; French

Verona, Stephen F.
Agent:
William Morris Agency
Beverly Hills
(213) 274-7451

THE LORDS OF FLATBUSH
co-director with Martin Davidson; Columbia; 1974
PIPE DREAMS
Avco Embassy; 1976
BOARDWALK
Atlantic; 1979

Vogel, Virgil W.
Agent:
David Shapira & Assoc.
Beverly Hills
(213) 278-2742
Business Manager:
(213) 655-1190

THE MOLE PEOPLE
Universal; 1956
THE KETTLES ON OLD McDONALD'S FARM
Universal; 1957
THE LAND UNKNOWN
Universal; 1957
THE SWORD OF ALI BABA
Universal; 1965
THE RETURN OF JOE FORRESTER
Columbia TV; telefeature; 1975
THE DEPUTIES
telefeature; 1976
LAW OF THE LAND
QM Productions; telefeature; 1976
CENTENNIAL
co-director with Paul Krasny, Harry Falk & Bernard McEveety; Universal TV; television mini-series; 1978
POWER
co-director with Barry Shear; David Gerber Productions/Columbia TV; telefeature; 1980
PORTRAIT OF A REBEL: MARGARET SANGER
Marvin Minoff Productions/David Paradine TV; telefeature; 1980
BEULAH LAND
co-director with Harry Falk; David Gerber Productions/Columbia TV; television mini-series; 1980
TODAY'S FBI
David Gerber Productions; telefeature; 1981

Wadleigh, Michael
Contact:
Directors Guild of America
Los Angeles
(213) 656-1220

WOODSTOCK
Warner Brothers; 1970
WOLFEN
Orion Pictures/Warner Brothers; 1981

Wagner, Jane
Home:
(213) 275-5161
Agent:
William Morris Agency
Beverly Hills
(213) 274-7451

MOMENT BY MOMENT
Universal; 1978

Waite, Ralph

ON THE NICKEL
Rose's Park; 1980

Wajda, Andrzej
b. March 6, 1926
Suwalki, Poland

A GENERATION
W.F.F. Wroclaw; 1954; Polish
JE VAIS VERS LE SOLEIL
WFD Warsaw; 1955; Polish-French
KANAL
Frankel; 1957; Polish
ASHES AND DIAMONDS
Janus; 1958; Polish
LOTNA
KADR; 1959; Polish
INNOCENT SORCERERS
KADR; 1960; Polish
SAMSON
Droga-KADR; 1961; Polish
SIBERIAN LADY MACBETH
Avala Film; 1961; Polish
LOVE AT TWENTY
co-director; Embassy; 1962; French-Italian-Japanese-Polish-West German
ASHES
1965; Polish

continued

Wajda, Andrzej
continued

GATES TO PARADISE
1967; British
EVERYTHING FOR SALE
1968; Polish
HUNTING FLIES
1969; Polish
LANDSCAPE AFTER THE BATTLE
1970; Polish
THE BIRCH-WOOD
1971; Polish
PILATUS UND ANDERE
telefeature; 1972; West German
THE WEDDING
Film Polski; 1972; Polish
THE PROMISED LAND
Film Polski; 1974; Polish
SHADOW LINE
1976; Polish
MAN OF MARBLE
1977; Polish
WITHOUT ANESTHETIC
1979; Polish
THE GIRLS FROM WILKO
1979; Polish-French
THE CONDUCTOR
Film Polski; 1980; Polish
ROUGH TREATMENT
Film Polski; 1980; Polish
MAN OF IRON
1981; Polish

Walker, Nancy
Personal Manager:
Allan Carr
Hollywood
(213) 836-3000

CAN'T STOP THE MUSIC
AFD; 1980

Wallerstein, Herb
Agent:
Lew Sherrell Agency
Hollywood
(213) 461-9955

SNOWBEAST
Douglas Cramer Productions; telefeature; 1977

Walton, Fred
Contact:
Directors Guild of America
Los Angeles
(213) 656-1220

WHEN A STRANGER CALLS
Columbia; 1979

Wanamaker, Sam
b. June 14, 1919
Chicago, Illinois
Home:
The Surrey Dispensary
42 Trinity Street
London SE1 4J6, England
01-407-3712
Business:
S.W. Productions Ltd.
9100 Wilshire Blvd.
Beverly Hills, CA 90212
(213) 273-2782
Agent:
William Morris Agency
Beverly Hills
(213) 274-7451

THE FILE OF THE GOLDEN GOOSE
United Artists; 1969; British
THE EXECUTIONER
Columbia; 1970; British
CATLOW
M-G-M; 1971; U.S.-Spanish
SINBAD AND THE EYE OF THE TIGER
Columbia; 1977; British
MY KIDNAPPER, MY LOVE
Roger Gimbel Productions/EMI TV; telefeature; 1980
THE KILLING OF RANDY WEBSTER
Roger Gimbel Productions/EMI TV; telefeature; 1981

Ward, David S.
Contact:
Directors Guild of America
Los Angeles
(213) 656-1220

CANNERY ROW
M-G-M/United Artists; 1981

Ware, Clyde
Agent:
William Morris Agency
Beverly Hills
(213) 274-7451

NO DRUMS, NO BUGLES
Cinerama Releasing Corporation; 1971
THE STORY OF PRETTY BOY FLOYD
Universal TV; telefeature; 1974
THE HATFIELDS AND THE McCOYS
Charles Fries Productions; telefeature; 1975
THREE HUNDRED MILES FOR STEPHANIE
Edward S. Feldman Company/Yellow Ribbon Productions/PKO; telefeature; 1981

Warhol, Andy
(Andrew Warhola)
b. August 8, 1927
Cleveland, Ohio

KISS
Film-Makers; 1963
EAT
Film-Makers; 1963
SLEEP
Film-Makers; 1963
HAIRCUT
Film-Makers; 1963
TARZAN AND JANE REGAINED...SORT OF
co-director; Film-Makers; 1964
DANCE MOVIE
Film-Makers; 1964
BLOW JOB
Film-Makers; 1964
BATMAN DRACULA
Film-Makers; 1964
SALOME AND DELILAH
Film-Makers; 1964
SOAP OPERA
co-director; Film-Makers; 1964
COUCH
Film-Makers; 1964
13 MOST BEAUTIFUL WOMEN
Film-Makers; 1964
HARLOT
Film-Makers; 1964
THE LIFE OF JUANITA CASTRO
Film-Makers; 1965
EMPIRE
Film-Makers; 1965
POOR LITTLE RICH GIRL
Film-Makers; 1965
SCREEN TEST
Film-Makers; 1965
VINYL
Film-Makers; 1965
BEAUTY #2
Film-Makers; 1965
BITCH
Film-Makers; 1965
PRISON
Film-Makers; 1965
SPACE
Film-Makers; 1965
THE CLOSET
Film-Makers; 1965
HENRY GELDZAHLER
Film-Makers; 1965
TAYLOR MEAD'S ASS
Film-Makers; 1965
FACE
Film-Makers; 1965
MY HUSTLER
Film-Makers; 1965
CAMP
Film-Makers; 1965
SUICIDE
Film-Makers; 1965
DRUNK
Film-Makers; 1965
OUTER AND INNER SPACE
Film-Makers; 1966
HEDY (Hedy the Shoplifter)
Film-Makers; 1966

continued

Warhol, Andy
continued

PAUL SWAN
Film-Makers; 1966
MORE MILK, EVETTE (Lana Turner)
Film-Makers; 1965
THE VELVET UNDERGROUND AND NICO
Film-Makers; 1966
KITCHEN
Film-Makers; 1966
LUPE
Film-Makers; 1966
EATING TOO FAST
Film-Makers; 1966
THE CHELSEA GIRLS
Film-Makers; 1966
I, A MAN
Film-Makers; 1967
BIKE BOY
Film-Makers; 1967
NUDE RESTAURANT
Film-Makers; 1967
FOUR STARS (24-Hour Movie)
Film-Makers; 1967
IMITATION OF CHRIST
Film-Makers; 1967
THE LOVES OF ONDINE
Warhol; 1968
LONESOME COWBOYS
Sherpix; 1968
BLUE MOVIE (Fuck)
Factory; 1969
WOMEN IN REVOLT
Warhol; 1972
L'AMOUR
co-director with Paul Morrissey; Altura; 1973

Warren, Charles Marquis
b. 1912
Baltimore, Maryland
Home:
1130 Tower Road
Beverly Hills, CA 90210
Agent:
Creative Artists Agency
Los Angeles
(213) 277-4545

LITTLE BIG HORN
Lippert; 1951
HELLGATE
Lippert; 1952
ARROWHEAD
Paramount; 1953
FLIGHT TO TANGIER
Paramount; 1953
SEVEN ANGRY MEN
Allied Artists; 1955
TENSION AT TABLE ROCK
Universal; 1956
THE BLACK WHIP
20th Century-Fox; 1956
TROOPER HOOK
United Artists; 1957
BACK FROM THE DEAD
20th Century-Fox; 1957
THE UNKNOWN TERROR
20th Century-Fox; 1957
COPPER SKY
20th Century-Fox; 1957
RIDE A VIOLENT MILE
20th Century-Fox; 1957
DESERT HELL
20th Century-Fox; 1958
CATTLE EMPIRE
20th Century-Fox; 1958
BLOOD ARROW
20th Century-Fox; 1958
CHARRO!
National General; 1969

Warren, Mark
Agent:
I.C.M.
Hollywood
(213) 550-4000

COME BACK CHARLESTON BLUE
Warner Brothers; 1972
CRUNCH
Astral Bellevue; 1981; Canadian

Waters, John
b. Baltimore, Maryland

MONDO TRASHO
Film-Makers; 1970
PINK FLAMINGOS
Saliva Films; 1974
FEMALE TROUBLE
New Line Cinema; 1975
DESPERATE LIVING
New Line Cinema; 1977
POLYESTER
New Line Cinema; 1981

Watkins, Peter
b. October 29, 1935
Norbiton, England
Contact:
British Film Institute
127 Charing Cross Road
London W.C. 2
England
01-437-4355

CULLODEN
BBC-TV; telefeature; 1964; British
THE WAR GAME
Pathe Contemporary; 1966; British
PRIVILEGE
Universal; 1967; British
GLADIATORS
1969; Swedish
PUNISHMENT PARK
Sherpix; 1971; British
EDVARD MUNCH
New Yorker; 1976; Swedish-Norwegian
EVENING LAND
Panorama-ASA; 1977; Danish

Webb, Jack
b. April 2, 1920
Santa Monica, CA
Business:
Mark VII Ltd.
1041 N. Formosa Avenue
Hollywood, CA 90046
(213) 650-2492

DRAGNET
Warner Brothers; 1954
PETE KELLY'S BLUES
Warner Brothers; 1955
THE D.I.
Warner Brothers; 1957
-30-
Warner Brothers; 1959
THE LAST TIME I SAW ARCHIE
United Artists; 1961
DRAGNET 1969
Universal TV/Mark VII Ltd.; telefeature; 1969
O'HARA, U.S. TREASURY: OPERATION COBRA
Universal TV/Mark VII Ltd.; telefeature; 1971
EMERGENCY!
Universal TV/Mark VII Ltd.; telefeature; 1972
CHASE
Universal TV/Mark VII Ltd.; telefeature; 1973

Webster, Nicholas
Home:
4135 Fulton Avenue
Sherman Oaks, CA 91403
(213) 784-5690

GONE ARE THE DAYS! (Purlie Victorious)
Trans-Lux; 1963
SANTA CLAUS CONQUERS THE MARTIANS
Embassy; 1964
MISSION MARS
Allied Artists; 1968
NO LONGER ALONE
World Wide; 1978; British

Wechter, David
Agent:
Phil Gersh Agency
Beverly Hills
(213) 274-6611

MIDNIGHT MADNESS
co-director with Michael Nankin; Buena Vista; 1980

Weill, Claudia
b. 1947
New York, New York
Business:
Cyclops Films, Inc.
1697 Broadway
New York, N.Y. 10019
(212) 265-1375

THE OTHER HALF OF THE SKY: A CHINA MEMOIR
co-director with Shirley MacLaine; 1975
GIRLFRIENDS
Warner Brothers; 1978
IT'S MY TURN
Columbia; 1980

Weir, Peter
b. Australia
Contact:
Australian Film Commission
9229 Sunset Blvd.
Los Angeles, CA 90069
(213) 275-7074

THREE TO GO
co-director with Brian Hannant & Oliver Howes; Commonwealth Film Unit Production; 1971; Australian
THE CARS THAT EAT PEOPLE
New Line Cinema; 1974; Australian
PICNIC AT HANGING ROCK
Atlantic; 1975; Australian
THE PLUMBER
Barbary Coast; 1978; Australian; made for television
THE LAST WAVE
World Northal; 1978; Australian
GALLIPOLI
Paramount; 1981; Australian

Weis, Don
b. May 13, 1922
Milwaukee, Wisconsin
Agent:
Irving Salkow Agency
Beverly Hills
(213) 276-3141

BANNERLINE
M-G-M; 1951
IT'S A BIG COUNTRY
co-director with Charles Vidor, Richard Thorpe, John Sturges, Don Hartman, Clarence Brown & William Wellman; M-G-M; 1951
JUST THIS ONCE
M-G-M; 1952
YOU FOR ME
M-G-M; 1952
I LOVE MELVIN
M-G-M; 1953
REMAINS TO BE SEEN
M-G-M; 1953
A SLIGHT CASE OF LARCENY
M-G-M; 1953
THE AFFAIRS OF DOBIE GILLIS
M-G-M; 1953
HALF A HERO
M-G-M; 1953
THE ADVENTURES OF HAJJI BABA
20th Century-Fox; 1954
RIDE THE HIGH IRON
Columbia; 1957
MR. PHARAOH AND HIS CLEOPATRA
1959; unreleased
THE GENE KRUPA STORY
Columbia; 1960
CRITIC'S CHOICE
Warner Brothers; 1963
LOOKING FOR LOVE
M-G-M; 1964
PAJAMA PARTY
American International; 1964
BILLIE
United Artists; 1965
THE GHOST IN THE INVISIBLE BIKINI
American International; 1966
THE KING'S PIRATE
Universal; 1967
THE LONGEST 100 MILES
Universal TV; telefeature; 1967
NOW YOU SEE IT, NOW YOU DON'T
Universal; telefeature; 1968
DID YOU HEAR THE ONE ABOUT THE TRAVELING SALESLADY?
Universal; 1968
DEADLOCK
Universal TV; telefeature; 1969
THE MILLIONAIRE
Don Fedderson Productions; telefeature; 1978
ZERO TO SIXTY
First Artists; 1978
THE MUNSTERS' REVENGE
Universal TV; telefeature; 1981

Weis, Gary
Contact:
Directors Guild of America
Los Angeles
(213) 656-1220

ALL YOU NEED IS CASH
co-director with Eric Idle; NBC-TV; telefeature; 1978; British

continued

Weis, Gary
continued

WHOLLY MOSES
Columbia; 1980
YOUNG LUST
Paramount; 1982

Welles, Orson
(George Orson Welles)
b. May 6, 1916
Kenosha, Wisconsin

CITIZEN KANE
RKO Radio; 1941
THE MAGNIFICENT AMBERSONS
RKO Radio; 1942
THE STRANGER
RKO Radio; 1946
THE LADY FROM SHANGHAI
Columbia; 1948
MACBETH
Republic; 1948
OTHELLO
United Artists; 1952; U.S.-Italian
MR. ARKADIN
Warner Brothers; 1955; Spanish-Swiss
TOUCH OF EVIL
Universal; 1958
THE TRIAL
Astor; 1963; French-Italian-West German
CHIMES AT MIDNIGHT (Falstaff)
Peppercorn-Wormser; 1967; Spanish-Swiss
THE IMMORTAL STORY
Altura; 1969; French; made for television
F FOR FAKE
Specialty; 1977; French-Iranian-West German

Wenders, Wim
b. West Germany
Home:
8358 Sunset Blvd.
Los Angeles, CA 90068
(213) 654-2874
Business:
Zoetrope Studios
1040 N. Las Palmas Avenue
Hollywood, CA 90038
(213) 467-9253
Agent:
The Paul Kohner Agency
Los Angeles
(213) 550-1060

SUMMER IN THE CITY (Dedicated to The Kinks)
1970; West German
THE GOALIE'S ANXIETY AT THE PENALTY KICK
Bauer International; 1972; West German
THE SCARLET LETTER
A.J. Bauer; 1973; West German-Spanish
ALICE IN THE CITIES
New Yorker; 1974; West German
THE WRONG MOVE
New Yorker; 1975; West German
KINGS OF THE ROAD
A.J. Bauer; 1976; West German
THE AMERICAN FRIEND
New Yorker; 1977; West German-French
LIGHTNING OVER WATER (NICK'S MOVIE)
co-director with Nicholas Ray; Pari Films; 1980; West German-Swiss-U.S.
THE STATE OF THINGS
Filmverlag der Autoren; 1981; West German
HAMMETT
Orion Pictures/Warner Brothers; 1982

Wendkos, Paul
b. September 20, 1922
Philadelphia, Pennsylvania
Agent:
Creative Artists Agency
Los Angeles
(213) 277-4545

THE BURGLAR
Columbia; 1957
THE CASE AGAINST BROOKLYN
Columbia; 1958
TARAWA BEACHHEAD
Columbia; 1958
GIDGET
Columbia; 1959
FACE OF A FUGITIVE
Columbia; 1959
BATTLE OF THE CORAL SEA
Columbia; 1959
BECAUSE THEY'RE YOUNG
Columbia; 1960
GIDGET GOES HAWAIIAN
Columbia; 1961
ANGEL BABY
Allied Artists; 1961

continued

Wendkos, Paul
continued

TEMPLE OF THE SWINGING DOLL
20th Century-Fox; 1961
GIDGET GOES TO ROME
Columbia; 1963
RECOIL
Lion; 1963
JOHNNY TIGER
Universal; 1966
ATTACK ON THE IRON COAST
United Artists; 1968; U.S.-British
HAWAII FIVE-O
Leonard Freeman Productions; telefeature; 1968
GUNS OF THE MAGNIFICENT SEVEN
United Artists; 1969
FEAR NO EVIL
Universal TV; telefeature; 1969
CANNON FOR CORDOBA
United Artists; 1970
THE BROTHERHOOD OF THE BELL
Cinema Center; telefeature; 1970
THE MEPHISTO WALTZ
20th Century-Fox; 1971
TRAVIS LOGAN, D.A.
QM Productions; telefeature; 1971
A TATTERED WEB
Metromedia Productions; telefeature; 1971
A LITTLE GAME
Universal TV; telefeature; 1971
A DEATH OF INNOCENCE
Mark Carliner Productions; telefeature; 1971
THE DELPHI BUREAU
Warner Brothers TV; telefeature; 1972
THE FAMILY RICO
CBS, Inc.; telefeature; 1972
HAUNTS OF THE VERY RICH
ABC Circle Films; telefeature; 1972
FOOTSTEPS
Metromedia Productions; telefeature; 1972
THE STRANGERS IN 7A
Palomar Pictures International; telefeature; 1972
HONOR THY FATHER
Metromedia Productions; telefeature; 1973
TERROR ON THE BEACH
20th Century-Fox TV; telefeature; 1973
THE UNDERGROUND MAN
Paramount TV; telefeature; 1974
THE LEGEND OF LIZZIE BORDEN
Paramount TV; telefeature; 1975
DEATH AMONG FRIENDS
Douglas S. Cramer Productions/Warner Brothers TV; telefeature; 1975
SPECIAL DELIVERY
American International; 1976
THE DEATH OF RICHIE
Henry Jaffe Enterprises; telefeature; 1977
SECRETS
The Jozak Company; telefeature; 1977
GOOD AGAINST EVIL
Frankel-Bolen Productions/20th Century-Fox TV; telefeature; 1977
HAROLD ROBBINS' 79 PARK AVENUE
Universal TV; television mini-series; 1977
BETRAYAL
Roger Gimbel Productions/EMI TV; telefeature; 1978
A WOMAN CALLED MOSES
Henry Jaffe Enterprises; telefeature; 1978
THE ORDEAL OF PATTY HEARST
Finnegan Associates/David Paradine TV; telefeature; 1979
ACT OF VIOLENCE
Emmett G. Lavery, Jr. Productions/Paramount TV; telefeature; 1979
THE ORDEAL OF DR. MUDD
B.S.R. Productions/Marble Arch Productions; telefeature; 1980

continued

Wendkos, Paul
continued

A CRY FOR LOVE
Charles Fries Productions/Alan Sacks Productions; telefeature; 1980
THE FIVE OF ME
Jack Farren Productions/Factor-Newland Productions; telefeature; 1981
GOLDEN GATE
Lin Bolen Productions/Warner Brothers TV; telefeature; 1981

Werner, Jeff
Home:
206 S. Orange
Los Angeles, CA 90036
(213) 933-6531
Agent:
Creative Artists Agency
Los Angeles
(213) 277-4545

CHEERLEADERS' WILD WEEKEND
Dimension; 1979
DIE LAUGHING
Orion Pictures/Warner Brothers; 1980

Werner, Peter
Business:
A Joyful Noise Unlimited
520 Strand Avenue
Santa Monica, CA 90405
(213) 396-7143
Agent:
Creative Artists Agency
Los Angeles
(213) 277-4545

BATTERED
Henry Jaffe Enterprises; telefeature; 1978
AUNT MARY
Henry Jaffe Enterprises; telefeature; 1979
WILLIAM FAULKNER'S BARNBURNING
PBS-TV; telefeature; 1980
DON'T CRY, IT'S ONLY THUNDER
Sanrio; 1981; U.S.-Japanese

Wertmuller, Lina
(Arcangela Felice Assunta Wertmuller von Elgg)
b. August 14, 1928
Rome, Italy
Contact:
Minister of Tourism
Via Della Ferratella
No. 51
00184 Rome, Italy
06-7732

THE LIZARDS
1963; Italian
LET'S TALK ABOUT MEN
Allied Artists; 1965; Italian
RITA THE MOSQUITO
co-director; 1966; Italian
DON'T STING THE MOSQUITO
1967; Italian
THE SEDUCTION OF MIMI (Mimi the Metalworker, His Honor Betrayed)
New Line Cinema; 1972; Italian
LOVE AND ANARCHY
Peppercorn-Wormser; 1973; Italian
ALL SCREWED UP (All in Place, Nothing in Order)
New Line Cinema; 1974; Italian
SWEPT AWAY BY AN UNUSUAL DESTINY IN THE BLUE SEA OF AUGUST
Cinema 5; 1974; Italian
SEVEN BEAUTIES (Pasqualino Seven Beauties)
Cinema 5; 1976; Italian
THE END OF THE WORLD IN OUR USUAL BED IN A NIGHT FULL OF RAIN
Warner Brothers; 1978; Italian-U.S.
SHIMMY LAGANO TARANTELLE E VINO
1978; Italian
BLOOD FEUD
AFD; 1980; Italian

Wexler, Haskell
b. 1926
Chicago, Illinois
Business:
716 N. Alfred Street
Los Angeles, CA 90069
(213) 655-6800

MEDIUM COOL
Paramount; 1969
BRAZIL: A REPORT ON TORTURE
co-director with Saul Landau; 1971
INTRODUCTION TO THE ENEMY
co-director; 1974
UNDERGROUND
co-director with Emile De Antonio & Mary Lampson; New Yorker; 1976

Whatham, Claude
Contact:
British Film Institute
127 Charing Cross Road
London W.C. 2, England
01-437-4355

THAT'LL BE THE DAY
EMI; 1974; British
ALL CREATURES GREAT AND SMALL
Talent Associates/EMI TV; telefeature; 1975; British
SWALLOWS AND AMAZONS
LDS; 1977; British
SWEET WILLIAM
Kendon Films; 1980; British
HOODWINK
C.B. Films; 1981; Australian

Wiard, William
Agent:
Adams, Ray & Rosenberg
Los Angeles
(213) 278-3000

SCOTT FREE
Cherokee Productions/Universal TV; efeature; 1976
SKI LIFT TO DEATH
The Jozak Company/Paramount TV; telefeature; 1978
THE GIRL, THE GOLD WATCH AND EVERYTHING
Fellows-Keegan Company/Paramount TV; telefeature;1980
TOM HORN
Warner Brothers; 1980
THIS HOUSE POSSESSED
Mandy Productions; telefeature; 1981

Wickes, David
Contact:
British Film Institute
127 Charing Cross Road
London W.C. 2, England
01-437-4355

SWEENEY
EMI; 1977; British
SILVER DREAM RACER
EMI; 1980; British

Wicki, Bernhard
b. October 28, 1919
St. Polten, Austria
Home:
Weissgerberstrase 2
Munich 23, West Germany
348-998
Business:
263-745

WHY ARE YOU AGAINST US?
1958; West German
THE BRIDGE
Allied Artists; 1959; West German
THE MIRACLE OF MALACHIAS
1961; West German
THE LONGEST DAY
co-director with Ken Annakin & Andrew Marton; 20th Century-Fox; 1962
THE VISIT
20th Century-Fox; 1964; West German-Italian-French-U.S.
MORITURI (The Saboteur, Code Name "Morituri")
20th Century-Fox; 1965
DAS FALSCHE GEWICHT
1971; West German
DIE EROBERUNG DER ZITADELLE
1977; West German

Widerberg, Bo
b. June 8, 1930
Malmo, Sweden
Contact:
Swedish Film Institute
P.O. Box 27126
S-10252 Stockholm
Sweden
08-630510

THE BABY CARRIAGE
Europa Film; 1962; Swedish
RAVEN'S END
New Yorker; 1963; Swedish
LOVE 65
Europa Film; 1965; Swedish
THIRTY TIMES YOUR MONEY
Europa Film; 1966; Swedish
ELVIRA MADIGAN
Cinema 5; 1967; Swedish
THE WHITE GAME
co-director; 1968; Swedish
ADALEN '31
Paramount; 1971; Swedish-U.S.
STUBBY
1974; Swedish
MAN ON THE ROOF
Cinema 5; 1977; Swedish
VICTORIA
1979; Swedish-West German

Wiederhorn, Ken

SHOCK WAVES
Joseph Brenner Associates; 1977
EYES OF A STRANGER
Warner Brothers; 1981

Wilde, Cornel
b. October 13, 1915
New York, New York
Business:
Symbol Productions, Inc.
Sunset Gower Studios
Box 49
1438 N. Gower Street
Hollywood, CA 90028
(213) 466-3428
Agent:
William Morris Agency
Beverly Hills
(213) 274-7451

STORM FEAR
United Artists; 1956
THE DEVIL'S HAIRPIN
Paramount; 1957
MARACAIBO
Paramount; 1958
THE SWORD OF LANCELOT (Lancelot and Guinevere)
Universal; 1963; British
THE NAKED PREY
Paramount; 1966; U.S.-South African
BEACH RED
United Artists; 1967
NO BLADE OF GRASS
M-G-M; 1970; British
SHARK'S TREASURE
United Artists; 1975

Wilder, Billy
(Samuel Wilder)
b. June 22, 1906
Vienna, Austria
Business Manager:
Equitable Investment Corp.
Hollywood
(213) 469-2975

MAUVAISE GRAINE
co-director with Alexander Esway; 1933; French
THE MAJOR AND THE MINOR
Paramount; 1942
FIVE GRAVES TO CAIRO
Paramount; 1943
DOUBLE INDEMNITY
Paramount; 1944
THE LOST WEEKEND
Paramount; 1945
THE EMPEROR WALTZ
Paramount; 1948
A FOREIGN AFFAIR
Paramount; 1948
SUNSET BOULEVARD
Paramount; 1950
THE BIG CARNIVAL (Ace in the Hole)
Paramount; 1951
STALAG 17
Paramount; 1953
SABRINA
Paramount; 1954
THE SEVEN YEAR ITCH
20th Century-Fox; 1955
THE SPIRIT OF ST. LOUIS
Warner Brothers; 1957
LOVE IN THE AFTERNOON
Allied Artists; 1957
WITNESS FOR THE PROSECUTION
United Artists; 1958
SOME LIKE IT HOT
United Artists; 1959
THE APARTMENT
United Artists; 1960
ONE, TWO, THREE
United Artists; 1961
IRMA LA DOUCE
United Artists; 1963
KISS ME, STUPID
Lopert; 1964
THE FORTUNE COOKIE
United Artists; 1966
THE PRIVATE LIFE OF SHERLOCK HOLMES
United Artists; 1970; U.S.-British
AVANTI!
United Artists; 1972; U.S.-Italian
THE FRONT PAGE
Universal; 1974
FEDORA
United Artists; 1979; West German-French
BUDDY BUDDY
M-G-M/United Artists; 1981

Wilder, Gene
(Jerry Silberman)
b. June 11, 1935
Milwaukee, Wisconsin
Business:
9350 Wilshire Blvd.
Apartment 400
Beverly Hills, CA 90212
(213) 277-2211

THE ADVENTURE OF SHERLOCK HOLMES' SMARTER BROTHER
20th Century-Fox; 1975
THE WORLD'S GREATEST LOVER
20th Century-Fox; 1977
SUNDAY LOVERS
co-director with Bryan Forbes, Edouard Molinaro & Dino Risi; M-G-M/United Artists; 1981; U.S.-British-French-Italian

Wiles, Gordon
Home:
17123 Adlon Road
Encino, CA 91436
(213) 788-2536

GINGER IN THE MORNING
National Film; 1974

Williams, Oscar
Home:
856 S. St. Andrews Place
Los Angeles, CA 90005
(213) 387-6487

THE FINAL COMEDOWN
New World; 1972
FIVE ON THE BLACK HAND SIDE
United Artists; 1973
HOT POTATO
Warner Brothers; 1976

Williams, Paul
b. 1944
New York, New York
Agent:
William Morris Agency
Beverly Hills
(213) 274-7451

OUT OF IT
United Artists; 1969
THE REVOLUTIONARY
United Artists; 1970
DEALING: OR THE BERKELEY-TO-BOSTON FORTY-BRICK LOST-BAG BLUES
Warner Brothers; 1972
NUNZIO
Universal; 1978
MISS RIGHT
1981

Williams, Richard
b. 1933
Canada
Business:
Richard Williams Animation
3193 Cahuenga Blvd. West
Hollywood, CA 90068
(213) 851-8060

RAGGEDY ANN AND ANDY
20th Century-Fox; 1977

Williamson, Fred
b. March 5, 1938
Gary, Indiana

ADIOS AMIGO
Atlas; 1976
MEAN JOHNNY BARROWS
Atlas; 1976
DEATH JOURNEY
Atlas; 1976
NO WAY BACK
Atlas; 1976
MR. MEAN
Lone Star/Po' Boy; 1977; Italian-U.S.

Willis, Gordon
Business Manager:
Ron Taft
New York City
(212) 586-8844

WINDOWS
United Artists; 1979

Wilson, Richard
b. December 25, 1915
McKeesport, Pennsylvania
Home:
501 Ocean Front
Santa Monica, CA 90402
(213) 395-0012
Agent:
Eisenbach, Greene, Duchow
Los Angeles
(213) 659-3420

MAN WITH THE GUN
United Artists; 1955
THE BIG BOODLE
United Artists; 1957
RAW WIND IN EDEN
Universal; 1958
AL CAPONE
Allied Artists; 1959
PAY OR DIE
Allied Artists; 1960
WALL OF NOISE
Warner Brothers; 1963
INVITATION TO A GUNFIGHTER
United Artists; 1964
THREE IN THE ATTIC
American International; 1968

Winner, Michael
b. 1935
London, England
Business:
6-8 Sackville Street
London W1X 1DD, England
01-734-8385

CLIMB UP THE WALL
New Realm; 1960; British
SHOOT TO KILL
New Realm; 1960; British
OLD MAC
Carlyle; 1961; British
SOME LIKE IT COOL
Carlyle; 1961; British
OUT OF THE SHADOW
New Realm; 1961; British
PLAY IT COOL
Allied Artists; 1962; British
THE COOL MIKADO
United Artists; 1962; British
WEST 11
Warner-Pathe; 1963; British
THE GIRL GETTERS (The System)
American International; 1964; British
YOU MUST BE JOKING!
Columbia; 1965; British
THE JOKERS
Universal; 1967; British
I'LL NEVER FORGET WHAT'S 'IS NAME
Regional; 1968; British
HANNIBAL BROOKS
United Artists; 1969; British
THE GAMES
20th Century-Fox; 1970; British
LAWMAN
United Artists; 1971
CHATO'S LAND
United Artists; 1972
THE NIGHTCOMERS
Avco Embassy; 1972; British
THE MECHANIC
United Artists; 1972
SCORPIO
United Artists; 1973
THE STONE KILLER
Columbia; 1973
DEATH WISH
Paramount; 1974
WON TON TON, THE DOG WHO SAVED HOLLYWOOD
Paramount; 1976
THE SENTINEL
Universal; 1977
THE BIG SLEEP
United Artists; 1978; British
FIREPOWER
AFD; 1979; British
DEATH WISH II
Cannon; 1981

Winters, David
Business:
Harlequin Productions
6525 Sunset Blvd.
Hollywood, CA 90028
(213) 464-0461

RACQUET
Cal-Am Productions; 1979
JAYNE MANSFIELD - AN AMERICAN TRAGEDY
1981
THE LAST HORROR FILM
Neon Entertainment Company; 1982

Wise, Robert

b. September 10, 1914
Winchester, Indiana
Business:
Robert Wise Productions
Sunset Gower Studios
1438 N. Gower Street
Hollywood, CA 90028
(213) 461-3864
Agent:
Phil Gersh Agency
Beverly Hills
(213) 274-6611

THE CURSE OF THE CAT PEOPLE
co-director with Gunther von Fritsch; RKO Radio; 1944
MADEMOISELLE FIFI
RKO Radio; 1944
THE BODY SNATCHER
RKO Radio; 1945
A GAME OF DEATH
RKO Radio; 1945
CRIMINAL COURT
RKO Radio; 1946
BORN TO KILL
RKO Radio; 1947
MYSTERY IN MEXICO
RKO Radio; 1948
BLOOD ON THE MOON
RKO Radio; 1948
THE SET-UP
RKO Radio; 1949
TWO FLAGS WEST
20th Century-Fox; 1950
THREE SECRETS
Warner Brothers; 1950
THE HOUSE ON TELEGRAPH HILL
20th Century-Fox; 1951
THE DAY THE EARTH STOOD STILL
20th Century-Fox; 1951
THE CAPTIVE CITY
United Artists; 1952
SOMETHING FOR THE BIRDS
M-G-M; 1952
THE DESERT RATS
20th Century-Fox; 1953
DESTINATION GOBI
20th Century-Fox; 1953
SO BIG
Warner Brothers; 1953
EXECUTIVE SUITE
M-G-M; 1954
HELEN OF TROY
Warner Brothers; 1955; Italian-French
TRIBUTE TO A BAD MAN
M-G-M; 1956
SOMEBODY UP THERE LIKES ME
M-G-M; 1957
THIS COULD BE THE NIGHT
M-G-M; 1957
UNTIL THEY SAIL
M-G-M; 1957
RUN SILENT, RUN DEEP
United Artists; 1958
I WANT TO LIVE!
United Artists; 1958
ODDS AGAINST TOMORROW
United Artists; 1959
WEST SIDE STORY
co-director with Jerome Robbins; United Artists; 1961
TWO FOR THE SEESAW
United Artists; 1962
THE HAUNTING
M-G-M; 1963; British-U.S.
THE SOUND OF MUSIC
20th Century-Fox; 1965
THE SAND PEBBLES
20th Century-Fox; 1966
STAR!
20th Century-Fox; 1968
THE ANDROMEDA STRAIN
Universal; 1971
TWO PEOPLE
Universal; 1973
THE HINDENBURG
Universal; 1975
AUDREY ROSE
United Artists; 1977
STAR TREK - THE MOTION PICTURE
Paramount; 1979

Wohl, Ira

BEST BOY
IFEX Film; 1980

Wolman, Dan
b. October 28, 1941
Jerusalem, Israel
Contact:
The Israel Film Centre
30 Agron Street
P.O. Box 229
Jerusalem, Israel
02-227241

THE DREAMER
Cannon; 1970; Israeli
FLOCH
1972; Israeli
MY MICHAEL
Alfred Plaine; 1976; Israeli
HIDE AND SEEK
1980; Israeli

Wrede, Casper

ONE DAY IN THE LIFE OF IVAN DENISOVICH
Cinerama Releasing Corporation; 1971; British-Norwegian
THE TERRORISTS (Ransom)
20th Century-Fox; 1975; British

Wrye, Donald
Agent:
William Morris Agency
Beverly Hills
(213) 274-7451

THE MAN WHO COULD TALK TO KIDS
Tomorrow Entertainment; telefeature; 1973
BORN INNOCENT
Tomorrow Entertainment; telefeature; 1974
DEATH BE NOT PROUD
Good Housekeeping Presentations/Westfall Productions; telefeature; 1975
THE ENTERTAINER
RSO Films; telefeature; 1976
IT HAPPENED ONE CHRISTMAS
Universal TV; telefeature; 1977
ICE CASTLES
Columbia; 1979
HOUSE OF GOD
United Artists; 1981

Wynn, Tracy Keenan

HIT LADY
Spelling-Goldberg Productions; telefeature; 1974

Yates, Peter
b. July 24, 1929
Aldershot, England
Agent:
Chasin-Park-Citron
Los Angeles
(213) 273-7190

SUMMER HOLIDAY
American International; 1963; British
ONE WAY PENDULUM
Lopert; 1964; British
ROBBERY
Avco Embassy; 1967; British
BULLITT
Warner Brothers; 1968
JOHN AND MARY
20th Century-Fox; 1969
MURPHY'S WAR
Paramount; 1971; British
THE HOT ROCK
20th Century-Fox; 1972
THE FRIENDS OF EDDIE COYLE
Paramount; 1973
FOR PETE'S SAKE
Columbia; 1974
MOTHER, JUGS AND SPEED
20th Century-Fox; 1976
THE DEEP
Columbia; 1977
BREAKING AWAY
20th Century-Fox; 1979
EYEWITNESS
20th Century-Fox; 1981

Yellen, Linda
Agent:
Sy Fischer Company
Los Angeles
(213) 557-0388

COME OUT, COME OUT!
1969
LOOKING UP
Levitt-Pickman; 1977

Yorkin, Bud
(Alan David Yorkin)
b. February 22, 1926
Washington, Pennsylvania
Business:
Tandem Productions, Inc.
1901 Avenue of the Stars
Los Angeles, CA 90067
(213) 553-3600

COME BLOW YOUR HORN
Paramount; 1963
NEVER TOO LATE
Warner Brothers; 1965
DIVORCE AMERICAN STYLE
Columbia; 1967
INSPECTOR CLOUSEAU
United Artists; 1968; British
START THE REVOLUTION WITHOUT ME
Warner Brothers; 1970; British
THE THIEF WHO CAME TO DINNER
Warner Brothers; 1972

Young, Jeffrey
Contact:
Directors Guild of America
New York City
(212) 581-0370

BEEN DOWN SO LONG IT LOOKS LIKE UP TO ME
Paramount; 1971

Young, Robert M.
Contact:
Directors Guild of America
New York City
(212) 581-0370

ALAMBRISTA!
Bobwin/Film Haus; 1977
SHORT EYES
The Film League; 1978
RICH KIDS
United Artists; 1979
ONE-TRICK PONY
Warner Brothers; 1980

Young, Roger
Home:
(213) 506-6687
Agent:
Broder-Kurland Agency
Hollywood
(213) 274-8921

BITTER HARVEST
Charles Fries Productions; telefeature; 1981
AN INNOCENT LOVE
Steve Binder Productions; telefeature; 1981

Young, Terence
b. June 20, 1915
Shanghai, China
Agent:
Kurt Frings
Beverly Hills
(213) 274-8881

MEN OF ARNHEM
co-director with Brian Desmond Hurst; Army Film Unit; 1944; British
CORRIDOR OF MIRRORS
Universal; 1948; British
ONE NIGHT WITH YOU
Universal; 1948; British
WOMAN HATER
Universal; 1948; British
THEY WERE NOT DIVIDED
General Film Distributors; 1950; British
VALLEY OF THE EAGLES
Lippert; 1951; British
THE FRIGHTENED BRIDE (The Tall Headlines)
Beverly; 1952; British
PARATROOPER (The Red Beret)
Columbia; 1953; British
THAT LADY
20th Century-Fox; 1954; British
STORM OVER THE NILE
co-director with Zoltan Korda; Columbia; 1955; British
SAFARI
Columbia; 1956; British
ZARAK
Columbia; 1956; British
ACTION OF THE TIGER
M-G-M; 1957; British
TANK FORCE (No Time to Die)
Columbia; 1958; British
SERIOUS CHARGE
Eros; 1959; British

Young, Terence
continued

BLACK TIGHTS
Magna; 1960; French
PLAYGIRL AFTER DARK (Too Hot to Handle)
Topaz; 1960; British
DUEL OF CHAMPIONS
co-director with Ferdinando Baldi; Medallion; 1961; Italian-Spanish
DR. NO
United Artists; 1962; British
FROM RUSSIA WITH LOVE
United Artists; 1963; British
THE AMOROUS ADVENTURES OF MOLL FLANDERS
Paramount; 1965; British
THUNDERBALL
United Artists; 1965; British
THE DIRTY GAME
co-director with Christian-Jaque, Carlo Lizzani & Werner Klinger; American International; 1966; Italian-French-West German
TRIPLE CROSS
Warner Brothers; 1966; British-French
THE POPPY IS ALSO A FLOWER
Comet; 1966; European
WAIT UNTIL DARK
Warner Brothers; 1967
THE ROVER
1967; Italian
MAYERLING
M-G-M; 1969; British-French
THE CHRISTMAS TREE
Continental; 1969; French-Italian
COLD SWEAT
Emerson; 1970; French
RED SUN
National General; 1972; French-Italian-Spanish
THE VALACHI PAPERS
Columbia; 1972; Italian-French
WAR GODDESS
American International; 1973; Italian
THE KLANSMAN
Paramount; 1974
SIDNEY SHELDON'S BLOODLINE
Paramount; 1979
INCHON
One Way Productions; 1981; Japanese-South Korean

Yust, Larry
Agent:
I.C.M.
Hollywood
(213) 550-4000

TRICK BABY
Universal; 1973
HOMEBODIES
Avco Embassy; 1974
TESTIMONY OF TWO MEN
co-director with Leo Penn; Universal TV; telefeature; 1977

Zanussi, Krzysztof
b. July 17, 1939
Warsaw, Poland

THE STRUCTURE OF CRYSTALS
1969; Polish
FAMILY LIFE
1971; Polish
BEHIND THE WALL
1971; Polish
ILLUMINATION
1973; Polish
THE CATAMOUNT KILLING
1974
A WOMAN'S DECISION
1975; Polish
CAMOUFLAGE
1977; Polish
THE SPIRAL
1978; Polish
MAN FROM A FAR COUNTRY
Marble Arch Productions/RAI-TV; telefeature; 1981; British-Italian

Zappa, Frank

200 MOTELS
co-director with Tony Palmer; United Artists; 1971; British
BABY SNAKES
Intercontinental Absurdities; 1979

Zeffirelli, Franco
b. February 12, 1923
Florence, Italy
Contact:
Directors Guild of America
Los Angeles
(213) 656-1220

LA BOHEME
Warner Brothers; 1965; Swiss
FLORENCE - DAYS OF DESTRUCTION
1966; Italian
THE TAMING OF THE SHREW
Columbia; 1967; Italian-British
ROMEO AND JULIET
Paramount; 1968; Italian-British
BROTHER SUN SISTER MOON
Paramount; 1973; Italian-British
JESUS OF NAZARETH
Sir Lew Grade Productions/ITV; television mini-series; 1978; British-Italian
THE CHAMP
M-G-M/United Artists; 1979
ENDLESS LOVE
Universal; 1981

Zetterling, Mai
b. May 24, 1925
Vasteras, Sweden
Contact:
Swedish Film Institute
P.O. Box 27126
S-10252 Stockholm
Sweden
08-630510

LOVING COUPLES
Prominent; 1964; Swedish
NIGHT GAMES
Mondial; 1966; Swedish
DOCTOR GLAS
20th Century-Fox; 1968; Danish
THE GIRLS
New Line Cinema; 1969; Swedish
VINCENT THE DUTCHMAN
1972; Swedish
VISIONS OF EIGHT
co-director; Cinema 5; 1973
LOVE
co-director with Annette Cohen, Nancy Dowd & Liv Ullmann; Coup Films; 1981; Canadian

Zieff, Howard
Agent:
Creative Artists Agency
Los Angeles
(213) 277-4545

SLITHER
M-G-M; 1973
HEARTS OF THE WEST
M-G-M/United Artists; 1975
HOUSE CALLS
Universal; 1978
THE MAIN EVENT
Warner Brothers; 1979
PRIVATE BENJAMIN
Warner Brothers; 1980

Zemeckis, Robert
Contact:
Directors Guild of America
Los Angeles
(213) 656-1220

I WANNA HOLD YOUR HAND
Universal; 1977
USED CARS
Columbia; 1980

Zimmerman, Vernon
Agent:
Phil Gersh Agency
Beverly Hills
(213) 274-6611

DEADHEAD MILES
Paramount; 1971
UNHOLY ROLLERS
American International; 1972
FADE TO BLACK
American Cinema; 1980

Zinnemann, Fred
b. April 29, 1907
Vienna, Austria
Agent:
William Morris Agency
Beverly Hills
(213) 274-7451

THE WAVE
co-director with Emilio Gomez Muriel; Strand 1935; Mexican
KID GLOVE KILLER
M-G-M; 1942
EYES IN THE NIGHT
M-G-M; 1942
THE SEVENTH CROSS
M-G-M; 1944
LITTLE MR. JIM
M-G-M; 1946
MY BROTHER TALKS TO HORSES
M-G-M; 1947
THE SEARCH
M-G-M; 1948; U.S.-Swiss
ACT OF VIOLENCE
M-G-M; 1949
THE MEN
Columbia; 1950
TERESA
M-G-M; 1951
HIGH NOON
United Artists; 1952
THE MEMBER OF THE WEDDING
Columbia; 1953
FROM HERE TO ETERNITY
Columbia; 1953
OKLAHOMA!
Magna/20th Century-Fox; 1955
A HATFUL OF RAIN
20th Century-Fox; 1957
THE NUN'S STORY
Warner Brothers; 1959
THE SUNDOWNERS
Warner Brothers; 1960
BEHOLD A PALE HORSE
Columbia; 1964
A MAN FOR ALL SEASONS
Columbia; 1966; British
THE DAY OF THE JACKAL
Universal; 1973; British-French
JULIA
20th Century-Fox; 1977
MAIDEN MAIDEN
The Ladd Company/Warner Brothers; 1982; British

Zinner, Peter

THE SALAMANDER
ITC; 1981; British-Italian

Zucker, David
Contact:
Directors Guild of America
Los Angeles
(213) 656-1220

AIRPLANE!
co-director with Jim Abrahams & Jerry Zucker; Paramount; 1980

Zucker, Jerry
Contact:
Directors Guild of America
Los Angeles
(213) 656-1220

AIRPLANE!
co-director with Jim Abrahams & Jerry Zucker; Paramount; 1980

Index of Directors

A

B

Addendum

Index of Directors

Addendum

Due to the inherent nature of book publishing, there is a certain lapse of time between going-to-press and actual publication. In our efforts to make sure you have the most complete listings of directors' credits, we have included the following addendum.

Please note that only new credits are listed — not corrections of titles, distributors or release dates for films by directors already included in the book. An asterisk (*) in front of a director's name indicates a listing in the ADDENDUM only. A complete update will be available in the next edition of DIRECTORS: A Complete Guide.

IN MEMORIUM: Rainer Werner Fassbinder and Peter Carter

Argento, Dario

UNDER THE EYES OF THE ASSASSIN
Titanus; 1982; Italian

* **Arner, Gwen**
Agent:
Rifkin-David Agency
Los Angeles
(213) 550-0359

MOTHER'S DAY ON WALTON'S MOUNTAIN
Lorimar Productions/Amanda Productions; telefeature; 1982

Avedis, Howard

MORTUARY
Hickmar Productions; 1982

* **Avildsen, Tom**
Contact:
Directors Guild of America
Los Angeles
(213) 656-1220

THINGS ARE TOUGH ALL OVER
Columbia; 1982

Badham, John

BLUE THUNDER
Columbia; 1982

Badiyi, Reza

OF MICE AND MEN
Of Mice and Men Productions; telefeature; 1981

Baker, Roy W.

THE FLAME TREES OF THIKA
London Films Ltd./Consolidated Productions Ltd.; television mini-series; 1982; British

Baldwin, Peter

THE BRADY GIRLS GET MARRIED
Sherwood Schwartz Productions; telefeature:1981

Bartel, Paul

EATING RAOUL
International Classics/Quartet; 1982

* **Bearde, Chris**

HYSTERICAL
20th Century-Fox; 1982

Beaumont, Gabrielle

DEATH OF A CENTERFOLD: THE DOROTHY STRATTEN STORY
Wilcox Productions/MGM TV; telefeature; 1981

* **Beineix, Jean-Jacques**
Contact:
French Film Office
745 Fifth Avenue
New York, N.Y. 10151
(212) 832-8860

DIVA
United Artists Classics; 1982; French

Bergman, Ingmar

FANNY AND ALEXANDER
1982; Swedish-West German

Berry, John

SISTER, SISTER
20th Century-Fox TV; telefeature; 1982

Bill, Tony

SIX WEEKS
Universal; 1982

* **Birch, Patricia**
Contact:
Directors Guild of America
Los Angeles
(213) 656-1220

GREASE 2
Paramount; 1982

Black, Noel

THE OTHER VICTIM
Shpetner Company; telefeature; 1981
PRIME SUSPECT
Tisch-Avnet Television; telefeature; 1982

* **Blakemore, Michael**
Contact
Brit[illegible] Film Institute
12[illegible]aring Cross Road
[illegible]n W.C. 2, England
[illegible]57-4355

PRIVATES ON PARADE
HandMade Films; 1982; British

[illegible]uth, Don

THE SECRET OF NIMH
MGM/UA; 1982

* **Bole, Clifford**
Agent:
Shapiro-Lichtman Agency
Los Angeles
(213) 557-2244

T.J. HOOKER
Spelling-Goldberg Productions; telefeature;
1982

Bondarchuk, Sergei

INSURGENT MEXICO
Mosfilm; 1982; Soviet-Italian-Mexican
TEN DAYS THAT SHOOK THE WORLD
Mosfilm; 1983; Soviet-Italian

*** Bowen, Jenny**

STREET MUSIC
Specialty Films; 1982

*** Brickman, Marshall**
Contact:
Directors Guild of America
New York
(212) 581-0370

SIMON
Orion Pictures/Warner Brothers; 1980
LOVESICK
The Ladd Company/Warner Brothers; 1982

*** Bridges, Beau**
Contact:
Directors Guild of America
Los Angeles
(213) 656-1220

THE KID FROM NOWHERE
Cates-Bridges Company; telefeature; 1982

Bridges, James

MIKE'S MURDER
The Ladd Company/Warner Brothers; 1983

Brinckerhoff, Burt

BORN TO BE SOLD
Ron Samuels Productions; telefeature; 1981

*** Camfield, Douglas**

IVANHOE
Norman Rosemont Productions/Columbia TV; telefeature; 1982; U.S.-British

*** Castle, Nick**

TAG
New World; 1982

Chabrol, Claude

LES FANTOMES DU CHAPELIER
Gaumont; 1982; French

Chomsky, Marvin J.

MY BODY, MY CHILD
Titus Productions; telefeature; 1982
INSIDE THE THIRD REICH
ABC Circle Films; telefeature; 1982

*** Christian, Roger**

THE SENDER
Paramount; 1983

Clark, Bob

PORKY'S: THE NEXT DAY
20th Century-Fox; 1983; U.S.-Canadian

Clouse, Robert

THE RATS
Golden Harvest Productions/Toronto Filmtrusts Securities; 1982; Canadian

Coates, Lewis

HERCULES
Cannon; 1983; Italian

*** Cohen, Howard R.**

SATURDAY THE 14TH
New World; 1981

*** Cokliss, Harley**

BATTLETRUCK
New World; 1982; U.S.-New Zealand

Connor, Kevin

GOLIATH AWAITS
Larry White Productions/Hugh Benson Productions/Columbia TV; telefeature; 1981
THE HOUSE WHERE EVIL DWELLS
MGM/UA; 1982; U.S.-Japanese

Conway, James L.

THE BOOGENS
Jensen Farley Pictures; 1981

*** Cooper, Hal**
Home:
2651 Hutton Drive
Beverly Hills, CA 90210
(213) 271-8602
Agent:
Major Talent Agency
Los Angeles
(213) 820-5841

MILLION DOLLAR INFIELD
CBS Entertainment; telefeature; 1982

Coppola, Francis F.

THE OUTSIDERS
Warner Brothers; 1982

Coscarelli, Don

THE BEASTMASTER
Film Builders Corp.; 1982

Davidson, Boaz

PRIVATE POPSICLE (LEMON POPSICLE IV)
Noah Films; 1982; Israeli

Davidson, Martin

EDDIE AND THE CRUISERS
Aurora Productions; 1983

*** Davis, Barry**

OPPENHEIMER
BBC-TV/WGBH-TV; television mini-series; 1982; British-U.S.

Day, Robert

MARIAN ROSE WHITE
Gerald Abrams Productions/Cypress Point Productions; telefeature; 1982

Donner, Clive

OLIVER TWIST
Claridge Group Ltd./Grafton Films; telefeature; 1982; British

Donner, Richard

THE TOY
Columbia; 1983

*** Dornhelm, Robert**

THE CHILDREN OF THEATRE STREET
1977
SHE DANCES ALONE
Continental; 1982

Downey, Robert

MOONBEAM
Analysis; 1983

Dubin, Charles S.

MY PALIKARI
Center for TV in the Humanities; telefeature; 1982

Edwards, Blake

TRAIL OF THE PINK PANTHER
MGM/UA; 1982
CURSE OF THE PINK PANTHER
MGM/UA; 1983

Erman, John

THE LETTER
Hajeno Productions/Warner Brothers TV; telefeature; 1982
ELEANOR, FIRST LADY OF THE WORLD
Murbill Productions/Embassy TV; telefeature; 1982

*** Finkleman, Ken**
Contact:
Directors Guild of America
Los Angeles
(213) 656-1220

AIRPLANE II: THE SEQUEL
Paramount; 1983

*** Forsyth, Bill**

GREGORY'S GIRL
Samuel Goldwyn Company; 1982; British
LOCAL HERO
Warner Brothers; 1983; British

Fosse, Bob

STAR 80
The Ladd Company/Warner Brothers; 1983

Franklin, Richard

PSYCHO II
Universal; 1983

Freedman, Jerrold

THE VICTIMS
Hajeno Productions/Warner Brothers TV; telefeature; 1982

Friedenberg, Dick

FRONTIER FREMONT
Sunn Classic; 1976

Fruet, William

TRAPPED
Manson International; 1982; Canadian
BAKER COUNTY USA
Jensen Farley Pictures; 1982

Godard, Jean-Luc

PASSION
United Artists Classics; 1982; French-Swiss

Green, Guy

ISABEL'S CHOICE
Stuart Miller-Pantheon TV; telefeature; 1981

Greene, David

WORLD WAR III
Finnegan Associates/David Greene Productions; telefeature; 1982
REHEARSAL FOR MURDER
Levinson-Link Productions/Robert Papazian Productions; telefeature; 1982

Greenwald, Robert

FORTY DAYS FOR DANNY
Moonlight Productions/Filmways; telefeature; 1982
IN THE CUSTODY OF STRANGERS
Moonlight Productions/Filmways; telefeature; 1982

Haggard, Piers

MRS. REINHARDT
BBC-TV/WNET-13; telefeature; 1981; British-U.S.

*** Hall, Adrian**
Home:
176 Pleasant Street
Providence, RI 02906
(401) 421-4219
Personal Manager:
Marion Simon
Providence, RI
(401) 521-1100

THE HOUSE OF MIRTH
Cinelit Productions/WNET-13; telefeature; 1981

Hardy, Joseph

DREAM HOUSE
Hill-Mandelker Films/Time-Life Productions; telefeature; 1981

Hart, Harvey

THIS IS KATE BENNETT
Lorimar Productions; telefeature; 1982

Harvey, Anthony

THE PATRICIA NEAL STORY
co-director with Anthony Page; Lawrence Schiller Productions; telefeature; 1981

*** Heckerling, Amy**
Home:
1282 Devon
Los Angeles, CA 90024
(213) 271-9908
Agent:
Phil Gersh Agency
Los Angeles
(213) 274-6611

FAST TIMES AT RIDGEMONT HIGH
Universal; 1982

Hill, Walter

48 HOURS
Paramount; 1983

*** Holzman, Allan**

FORBIDDEN WORLD
New World; 1982

Hough, John

TRIUMPHS OF A MAN CALLED HORSE
Redwing Productions; 1983

Howard, Ron

THROUGH THE MAGIC PYRAMID
Major H Productions; telefeature; 1981
NIGHT SHIFT
The Ladd Company/Warner Brothers; 1982

*** Hughes, Terry**

MONTY PYTHON LIVE AT THE HOLLYWOOD BOWL
Columbia; 1982; British

Hussein, Waris

COMING OUT OF THE ICE
The Konigsberg Company; telefeature; 1982

Hutton, Brian G.

HIGH ROAD TO CHINA
20th Century-Fox; 1983

Hyams, Peter

STAR CHAMBER
20th Century-Fox; 1983

Ivory, James

HEAT AND DUST
Merchant-Ivory Productions; 1982

*** Jaffe, Stanley**
Contact:
Directors Guild of America
New York
(212) 581-0370

WITHOUT A TRACE
20th Century-Fox; 1983

Jameson, Jerry

KILLING AT HELL'S GATE
CBS Entertainment; telefeature; 1981

Jewison, Norman

BEST FRIENDS
Warner Brothers; 1982

Johnson, Ken

SENIOR TRIP
Kenneth Johnson Productions;telefeature;1981

Johnson, Lamont

DANGEROUS COMPANY
The Dangerous Company/Finnegan Associates; telefeature; 1982

*** Jones, David**
Contact:
British Film Institute
127 Charing Cross Road
London W.C. 2, England
01-437-4355

BETRAYAL
Horizon Pictures; 1982; British

Jordan, Glenn

LOIS GIBBS AND THE LOVE CANAL
Moonlight Productions/Filmways; telefeature; 1982

Kagan, Jeremy P.

THE NEXT STING
Universal; 1982

Kanew, Jeff

EDDIE MACON'S RUN
Universal; 1982

Kaplan, Jonathan

HEART LIKE A WHEEL
Aurora Productions; 1983

Katselas, Milton

THE RULES OF MARRIAGE
Entheos Unlimited Productions/Brownstone Productions/20th Century-Fox TV; telefeature; 1982

Katzin, Lee H.

THE NEIGHBORHOOD
David Gerber Company/Columbia TV; telefeature; 1982

Kaufman, Philip

THE RIGHT STUFF
The Ladd Company/Warner Brothers; 1983

* **Keeslar, Don**

THE CAPTURE OF GRIZZLY ADAMS
Sunn Classic; telefeature; 1982

* **Komack, James**
Agent:
William Morris Agency
Beverly Hills
(213) 274-7451

HI-JINX
Hi-Jinx Productions; 1982

Kotcheff, Ted

FIRST BLOOD
Anabasis Productions; 1982; Canadian

Kulik, Buzz

RAGE OF ANGELS
NBC Productions; telefeature; 1983

Landon, Michael

FATHER MURPHY
NBC Productions; telefeature; 1981

Lathan, Stan

DENMARK VESEY'S REBELLION
WPBT-Miami; telefeature; 1982

* **Layton, Joe**
Personal Manager:
Roy Gerber Associates
Los Angeles
(213) 550-0100

RICHARD PRYOR LIVE ON THE SUNSET STRIP
Columbia; 1982

*** Leach, Wilford**

THE WEDDING PARTY
co-director with Brian De Palma & Cynthia Munroe; Powell Productions Plus/Ondine; 1969
THE PIRATES OF PENZANCE
Universal; 1982

Lelouch, Claude

BOLERO (The Ins and Outs)
Double 13; 1982; French

Leone, Sergio

ONCE UPON A TIME IN AMERICA
The Ladd Company/Warner Brothers; 1983

Lester, Richard

SUPERMAN III
Warner Brothers; 1983; U.S.-British

Lewis, Jerry

SMORGASBORD
Warner Brothers; 1983

Lewis, Robert M.

CHILD BRIDE OF SHORT CREEK
Lawrence Schiller-Paul Monash Productions; telefeature; 1981
DESPERATE LIVES
Fellows-Keegan Company/Lorimar Productions; telefeature; 1982
BETWEEN TWO BROTHERS
Turman-Foster Company/Finnegan Associates; telefeature; 1982

Lieberman, Robert

TABLE FOR FIVE
CBS Theatrical Films; 1983

Lindsay-Hogg, Michael

BRIDESHEAD REVISITED
co-director with Charles Sturridge; Granada TV/WNET-13/NDR Hamburg; television mini-series; 1982; British

Lommel, Ulli

DOUBLE JEOPARDY
Ambassador Pictures; 1982
OLIVIA
New West Films; 1982
BRAINWAVES
Cinamerica Productions; 1982

*** Loncraine, Richard**
Contact:
British Film Institute
127 Charing Cross Road
London W.C. 2, England
01-437-4355

THE HAUNTING OF JULIA (Full Circle)
1977; British-Canadian
BRIMSTONE
Sherwood Productions; 1982; British
THE MISSIONARY
Columbia; 1982; British

London, Jerry

THE ORDEAL OF BILL CARNEY
Belle Company/Comworld Productions; telefeature; 1981
THE GIFT OF LIFE
CBS Entertainment; telefeature; 1982

Losey, Joseph

THE TROUT
Gaumont; 1982; French

Lowry, Dick

RASCALS AND ROBBERS: THE SECRET ADVENTURES OF TOM SAWYER AND HUCKLEBERRY FINN
CBS Entertainment; telefeature; 1982

Lumet, Sidney

THE VERDICT
20th Century-Fox; 1982

Lynch, Paul

CROSS-COUNTRY
MGM/UA; 1982; Canadian

* **Magyar, Dezso**
Home:
1539 Calmar Court
Los Angeles, CA 90024
(213) 277-0537
Agent:
William Morris Agency
Beverly Hills
(213) 274-7451

SUMMER
Cinelit Productions/WNET-13; telefeature; 1981

Mankiewicz, Francis

LES BEAUX SOUVENIRS
National Film Board of Canada; 1982; Canadian

Margolin, Stuart

BRET MAVERICK
Comanche Productions/Warner Brothers TV; telefeature; 1981
THE LONG SUMMER OF GEORGE ADAMS
Warner Brothers TV; telefeature; 1982

Markowitz, Robert

A LONG WAY HOME
Alan Landsburg Productions; telefeature; 1981
PRAY TV
ABC Circle Films; telefeature; 1982

Marquand, Richard

REVENGE OF THE JEDI
20th Century-Fox; 1983

* **Marshall, Garry**
Agent:
The Sy Fischer Company
Los Angeles
(213) 557-0388

YOUNG DOCTORS IN LOVE
20th Century-Fox; 1982

Martinson, Leslie H.

THE KID WITH THE BROKEN HALO
Satellite Productions; telefeature; 1982

Mastroianni, Armand

THE KILLING HOUR
Lansbury-Beruh Productions; 1982

* **Matalon, Vivian**

PRIVATE CONTENTMENT
WNET-13/South Carolina Educational TV; telefeature; 1982

Mayberry, Russ

THE FALL GUY
Glen A.Larson Productions/20th Century-Fox TV; telefeature; 1981
SIDE BY SIDE: THE TRUE STORY OF THE OSMOND FAMILY
Osmond Productions/Comworld Productions; telefeature; 1982

McEveety, Vincent

McCLAIN'S LAW
Eric Bercovici Productions/Epipsychidion Inc.; telefeature; 1982

Medford, Don

SIZZLE
Aaron Spelling Productions; telefeature; 1981

Metzger, Radley

THE TALE OF TIFFANY LUST
directed under pseudonym of Henry Paris; Entertainment Ventures; 1981

Michaels, Richard

THE CHILDREN NOBODY WANTED
Blatt-Singer Productions; telefeature; 1981
BLUE SKIES AGAIN
Warner Brothers; 1982

Mihalka, George

SCANDALE
Vivafilm/Cine 360; 1982; Canadian

Mizrahi, Moshe

LA VIE CONTINUE
Triumph Films/Columbia; 1982; French

Monicelli, Mario

THE MARQUIS OF GRILLO
1982; Italian

Mora, Philippe

THE RETURN OF CAPTAIN INVINCIBLE
Andrew Gaty-Seven Keys Productions; 1982; Australian

Morrissey, Paul

FORTY-DEUCE
Island Pictures; 1982

Mulligan, Robert

KISS ME GOODBYE
20th Century-Fox; 1983

Page, Anthony

THE PATRICIA NEAL STORY
co-director with Anthony Harvey; Lawrence Schiller Productions; telefeature; 1981
BILL
Alan Landsburg Productions; telefeature; 1981

Pakula, Alan J.

SOPHIE'S CHOICE
AFD/Universal; 1982

Palmer, Tony

WAGNER
London Trust Cultural Productions/RM Productions/Magyar TV; television mini-series; 1983; British-Hungarian

Paul, Steven
SLAPSTICK
Serendipity Productions; 1982

Peerce, Larry
LOVE CHILD
The Ladd Company/Warner Brothers; 1982

*** Petersen, Wolfgang**
THE CONSEQUENCE
West German
BLACK AND WHITE AS DAY AND NIGHT
New Yorker; West German
DAS BOOT (The Boat)
Triumph Films/Columbia; 1982; West German

*** Petit, Christopher**
Contact:
British Film Institute
127 Charing Cross Road
London W.C. 2, England
01-437-4355

RADIO ON
British Film Institute; 1979; British
AN UNSUITABLE JOB FOR A WOMAN
Boyd's Company; 1982; British

Petri, Elio
CHI ILLUMINA LA GRANDE NOTTE?
Iter Film/Gaumont; 1982; Italian-French

Petrie, Daniel
SIX PACK
20th Century-Fox; 1982

Philips, Lee
A WEDDING ON WALTON'S MOUNTAIN
Lorimar Productions/Amanda Productions; telefeature; 1982
MAE WEST
Hill-Mandelker Films; telefeature; 1982

Pollack, Sydney
TOOTSIE
Columbia; 1983

*** Rapoport, I.C.**
Agent:
I.C.M.
Los Angeles
(213) 550-4000

THOU SHALT NOT KILL
Edgar J. Scherick Associates/Warner Brothers TV; telefeature; 1982

Richards, Dick
MAN, WOMAN AND CHILD
Gaylord Productions; 1983

Roddam, Franc
THE LORDS OF DISCIPLINE
Paramount; 1983

Roeg, Nicolas
EUREKA
MGM/UA; 1982

Romero, George A.
CREEPSHOW
Warner Brothers; 1982

Rosenthal, Rick
BAD BOYS
AFD/Universal; 1983

Ross, Herbert
MAX DUGAN RETURNS
20th Century-Fox; 1982

Sargent, Joseph
TOMORROW'S CHILD
20th Century-Fox TV; telefeature; 1982

Saura, Carlos
SWEET HOURS
Elias Querejeta Productions; 1982; Spanish

Schaefer, George
A PIANO FOR MRS. CIMINO
Roger Gimbel Productions/EMI TV; telefeature; 1982

*** Schiller, Tom**
NOTHING LASTS FOREVER
MGM/UA; 1982

Schultz, Michael
BENNY'S PLACE
Titus Productions; telefeature; 1982

*** Schwartzman, Arnold**
GENOCIDE
Simon Wiesenthal Center; 1982

Scola, Ettore
LA NUIT DE VARENNES
Gaumont; 1982; French-Italian

*** Scott, Tony**
THE HUNGER
MGM/UA; 1982; British

*** Sharp, Ian**
Contact:
British Film Institute
127 Charing Cross Road
London W.C. 2, England
01-437-4355

WHO DARES WINS
Euan Lloyd Productions; 1982; British

Sherman, Gary
MYSTERIOUS TWO
Alan Landsburg Productions; telefeature; 1982

Skolimowski, Jerzy
MOONLIGHTING
Miracle Films; 1982; British

Stern, Sandor
MUGGABLE MARY: STREET COP
CBS Entertainment; telefeature; 1982

Stern, Steven H.
A SMALL KILLING
Orgolini-Nelson Productions/Motown Productions; telefeature; 1982
THE AMBUSH MURDERS
David Goldsmith Productions/Charles Fries Productions; telefeature; 1982
PORTRAIT OF A SHOWGIRL
Hamner Productions; telefeature; 1982

*** Streisand, Barbra**
Contact:
Directors Guild of America
Los Angeles
(213) 656-1220

YENTL
MGM/UA; 1983

*** Sturridge, Charles**
Contact:
British Film Institute
127 Charing Cross Road
London W.C. 2, England
01-437-4355

BRIDESHEAD REVISITED
co-director with Michael Lindsay-Hogg;Granada TV/WNET-13/NDR Hamburg;television mini-series; 1982; British

Swirnoff, Brad

AMERICAN RASPBERRY
Cannon; 1980

Syberberg, Hans-Jurgen

PARSIFAL
Zoetrope; 1982; French-West German

Tavernier, Bertrand

A WEEK'S VACATION (Une Semaine De Vacances)
Biograph; 1982; French

Taylor, Jud

MURDER AT CRESTRIDGE
Jaffe-Taylor Productions; telefeature; 1981
A QUESTION OF HONOR
Roger Gimbel Productions/EMI TV/Sonny Grosso Productions; telefeature; 1982

Teague, Lewis

FIGHTING BACK
Paramount; 1982

*** Tidyman, Ernest**

LAST PLANE OUT
Jack Cox Productions; 1983

Toback, James

EXPOSED
MGM/UA; 1982

Trikonis, Gus

DANCE OF THE DWARFS
Dove, Inc.; 1982

Tuchner, Michael

PAROLE
RSO Productions; telefeature; 1982
TRENCHCOAT
Buena Vista; 1982

Wajda, Andrzej

L'AFFAIRE DANTON
Triumph Films/Columbia; 1982; French

*** Wallace, Tommy L.**
Contact:
Directors Guild of America
Los Angeles
(213) 656-1220

HALLOWEEN III: SEASON OF THE WITCH
Universal; 1982

Weir, Peter

THE YEAR OF LIVING DANGEROUSLY
MGM/UA; 1982

Weis, Gary

MARLEY
Island Pictures; 1982

Whatham, Claude

MURDER IS EASY
David L. Wolper-Stan Margulies Productions/Warner Brothers TV; telefeature; 1982

Wiard, William

HELP WANTED: MALE
QM Productions/Brademan-Self Productions; telefeature; 1982
FANTASIES
Mandy Productions; telefeature; 1982

*** Wise, Herbert**
Home:
13 Despard Road
London N19, England 5NP
Personal Manager:
Fraser & Dunlop Ltd.
London
01-734-7311

SKOKIE
Titus Productions; telefeature; 1981

Wolman, Dan

NANA
Cannon; 1982; Italian-U.S.

Wrye, Donald

FIRE ON THE MOUNTAIN
Bonnard Productions; telefeature; 1982
DIVORCE WARS: A LOVE STORY
Wrye-Konigsberg Films/Warner Brothers TV; telefeature; 1982

Yates, Peter

KRULL
Columbia; 1983

Young, Roger

DREAMS DON'T DIE
Hill-Mandelker Productions; 1982

Young, Terence

THE JIGSAW MAN
MGM/UA; 1983; British

Zeffirelli, Franco

LA TRAVIATA
PSO; 1982; Italian

Zetterling, Mai

SCRUBBERS
HandMade Films; 1982; British

*** Zwick, Edward**
Home:
309 Sumac Lane
Santa Monica, CA 90402
(213) 459-5116
Agent:
The Artists Agency
Beverly Hills
(213) 277-7779

PAPER DOLLS
Leonard Goldberg Productions; telefeature; 1982

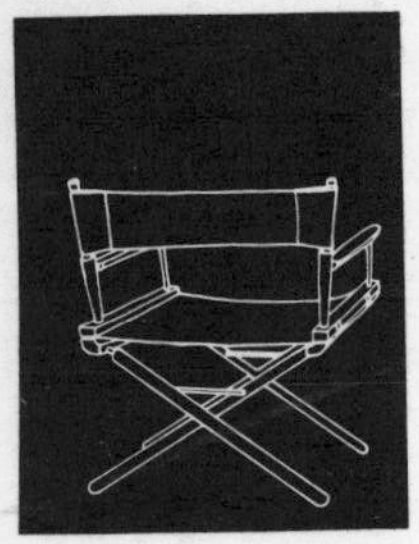

EDITOR/COMPILER

Michael Singer has worked as a motion picture producer's assistant, publicist, researcher and reader. He was born in New York City, and now lives in Los Angeles.